THE
ENLIGHTENMENT
IN AMERICA

Henry F. May

New York

OXFORD UNIVERSITY PRESS

1976

Copyright © 1976 by Henry F. May

Library of Congress Catalogue Card Number: 75-32349

Printed in the United States of America

To Bill and Beverly Bouwsma

Acknowledgments

I wish to thank the following libraries in Berkeley for helpful and tolerant assistance: The University of California library, especially the Newspaper and Microprint Room, the library of the Pacific School of Religion, the library of the Graduate Theological Union and those of its constituent institutions, especially the Starr King School for the Ministry. The staffs of the following other libraries all gave me generous help in locating material and permission to quote manuscripts in their possession: The American Philosophical Society, the Church History Society of the Episcopal Theological Seminary of the Southwest, the Diocesan Library of Maryland, the Doctor Williams Library in London, the Duke University Library, the Historical Society of Pennsylvania, the Houghton Library of Harvard University, the Library of Congress Manuscripts Division, the Library of the College of William and Mary in Virginia, the Maryland Historical Society, the Massachusetts Historical Society, the New-York Historical Society, the New York Public Library (Manuscripts and Archives Divisions; Astor, Lenox and Tilden Foundations), the South Carolina Historical Society, the University of North Carolina Library (Southern Historical Collection), the Princeton University Library, the Stadtbibliothek of Schaffhausen, Switzerland, the University of Virginia Library, and the Yale University Library. Mr. David Tennant Bryan of Richmond kindly gave me permission to quote the Bryan Family Papers at the University of Virginia Library. I should like to say a special word of thanks to the library staff and history faculty at the University of Virginia, who made me welcome during a prolonged stay in Charlottesville as an uninvited guest and shared with me their understanding of eighteenth-century Virginia. Dr.

John Boles, then a graduate student in Charlottesville, made available his knowledge of Southern manuscript collections. Mr. Duncan Forbes of Clare College, Cambridge, and Dr. Nicholas Phillipson of Edinburgh University helped me in my effort to understand the Scottish Enlightenment. I am most grateful for financial help from the American Council of Learned Societies, the Social Science Research Council, the Humanities Institute of the University of California, and the National Endowment for the Humanities, which enabled me to take time off from teaching at several crucial periods in my work. My manuscript was carefully and helpfully read by my friends William J. Bouwsma, Daniel W. Howe, Martin Malia, Robert Middlekauff, Nicholas Riasanovsky, and Henry Nash Smith. A succession of excellent research assistants included William Moore, Donald Critchlow, Carolyn Willson, Mark Summers, David Bailey, and Robert Holtermann. David Lundberg, also originally a research assistant, ended as a collaborator in a prolonged research project, related to this book but published elsewhere, concerning European books in American libraries. I should like to thank Grace O'Connell and Dorothy Shannon for excellent typing. Research assistance and typing have been provided by the Social Science Fund and the Margaret Byrne endowment of the University of California. Leona Capeless improved the manuscript by her excellent and rigorous editing. The generous and intelligent interest of Sheldon Meyer in all stages of this project went well beyond what one is entitled to expect from a publisher. In addition to these more or less tangible kinds of assistance, many students in classes and seminars have left their mark on this book and it depends throughout on the work of a great many lifelong students of the period it covers. I am grateful for so much generous help, and cheerfully assume full responsibility for all shortcomings.

Contents

Introduction

Since most of my work before this book has dealt with the intellectual history of nineteenth- and twentieth-century America, some of my friends have been surprised to learn that I have spent the last decade trying to understand the eighteenth-century Enlightenment. Since I share this surprise, I feel that a word of explanation should be attempted.

During most of the nineteenth and the early twentieth century, despite considerable conflict and one immensely violent civil war, the dominant American ideology seemed to most middle-class Americans to be something one could take for granted. This did not of course mean that they could expound it articulately, or that historians can do this for them. What people take for granted is usually more important than their pronouncements or manifestoes. The unexpressed and implied ideology of nineteenth-century America rested, I believe, on a series of tacit compromises. Of these the most basic was the compromise between a belief in moral certainties and a belief in the desirability of change and progress. This compromise was achieved and maintained not by intellectual argument, but by assertion and symbolization—almost without realization of its inherent fragility.

American nineteenth-century culture, with this compromise at its heart, took shape near the beginning of the century. Thus it must have drawn its ideas and assumptions from the previous period. My purpose, then, has been to find in the eighteenth century the roots of nineteenth-century American culture.

When one looks at the eighteenth century in America with this purpose, one finds two main clusters of ideas. One of these consists of the doctrines of Protestantism and particularly Calvinistic Protestantism, drawn from sixteenth- and seventeenth-century Europe but developed and institutionalized with great vigor in America, particularly in New England. The other cluster of ideas is drawn from the Enlightenment of seventeenth- and eighteenth-century Europe. The relation between these two major idea systems is basic to the understanding of eighteenth-century America, and indeed, I would say, the understanding of America in any period.

Here I have found what seems to me a surprising paradox of American historiography. First, most American historians of recent times are partisans of the Enlightenment: of liberalism, progress, and rationality. And yet there is no good book on the Enlightenment in America, indeed no general book at all.* There are excellent studies of many individuals and episodes, especially the major Enlightened political figures of the revolutionary age. But there is no serious attempt to define the Enlightenment in America, to say clearly where it came from, when it started and ended, or how far it spread; or to trace it through such fields as religion, science, politics, and social thought. The most nearly comprehensive book on the Enlightenment in America remains the one by Woodbridge Riley, published in 1907.

There is on the other hand a splendid and rapidly growing recent literature on the ideas of American Protestantism. One thinks immediately of the immense body of work on Puritanism, centering in the achievement of Perry Miller but including the work of many other first-rate historians. Nineteenth-century American Protestantism in its complexity has been explored with impressive results by many recent historians. The list of these should probably begin with the names of Sidney E. Mead and Sydney Ahlstrom.

Meanwhile, because of the lack of systematic treatment of the Enlightenment in America, people continue to make wild statements about it. Some say that the Enlightenment penetrated only to a small upper-class group, others that America is the country of the Enlightenment par excellence, where the program of enlightened Europeans was put into effect. Some quick summaries state with no apparent perplexity that most of the Founding Fathers were deists, but that American culture has always been deeply Calvinistic.

---

* Since this was written Donald H. Meyer has published a brief, able, and interesting treatment of the topic: *Democratic Enlightenment* (New York, 1976).

After thinking for some time about the lack of definitions and general histories of the Enlightenment, I can suggest two main reasons for this curious gap. One is the politicalization of intellectual history. I mean by this not just an overriding concern with political ideology, but also the tendency to force the entire history of ideas into political categories. This tendency makes it difficult, if not impossible, to use intellectual history seriously to illuminate political history, a very complex and very important task. Specifically, it seems to me to obscure the history of the Enlightenment if one assumes that Enlightenment means the same things as democracy, modernity, or secularism. The relation among all these is complex.

The second reason is the failure of European historians to provide us with a sufficiently broad, accurate, comprehensible, and usable definition of the Enlightenment. After 200 years of writing on the subject, much of it brilliant, historians have left us, as so often, very sophisticated and very confused. No definition of the Enlightenment fits all the men usually assumed to belong to it, or even those Europeans most directly influential in the United States, for instance Locke, Samuel Clarke, Montesquieu, Paine, and Thomas Reid—or, if one adds those who have been important as dangerous opponents and targets of polemic, Voltaire, Rousseau, and Hume. Any definition that includes optimism about human nature excludes Voltaire, Hume, and many French materialists. Any that centers on rationalism excludes Hume and Rousseau. A definition that emphasizes empiricism raises serious questions about Rousseau, Paine, and Condorcet.

My book, then, does not deal equally with the two main clusters of ideas influential in early America: the Enlightenment and Protestantism, but rather about the Enlightenment, with Protestantism always in the background as matrix, rival, ally, and enemy. It is not about the Enlightenment *and* religion, but rather about the Enlightenment *as* religion.

This is of course not the only legitimate way to treat the Enlightenment. It can be treated, and parts of it have been excellently treated, with an emphasis on science, epistemology, law, politics, and education. Certainly none of these fields can be entirely neglected in an effort at a general discussion. Politics especially was nearly always important to men of the Enlightenment. Yet I think we may be able to understand their political thought better if we start where they nearly always did, with religion. Men of the late eighteenth century, whether they were Calvinists or Arminians, deists or atheists, seldom thought about any branch of human affairs without referring consciously to some general beliefs about the nature of the universe and man's place in it, and about human nature itself. In this sense Jefferson and Paine were as religious as any New England Congregationalist. The denials and defiances of Enlightenment skeptics and materialists are denials and defiances of religious doctrine, usually religious in their own intent.

In an effort to be comprehensive I have found it necessary to strip my working definition of the Enlightenment as religion down to as simple and general a statement as possible, a statement which is almost implied by the word "Enlightenment" itself. Let us say that the Enlightenment consists of all those who believe two propositions: first, that the present age is more enlightened than the past; and second, that we understand nature and man best through the use of our natural faculties.

This is such a general statement, that it may at first glance seem to be too inclusive to define. And yet even these two propositions exclude some important eighteenth-century figures, among them Wesley, Blake, and (despite Perry Miller's arguments to the contrary) Jonathan Edwards. All are excluded, that is, who think that the surest guide for human beings is revelation, tradition, or illumination. Thus our simple definition excludes many, probably most, people who lived in America in the eighteenth and nineteenth centuries.

In the years when they were allies or rivals, neither the Enlightenment nor Protestantism was simple and undivided. Some enlightened individuals, in America as in Europe, believed that the fruitful processes of the mind were primarily deductive, others that they were primarily or entirely empirical, and still others consciously or unconsciously combined these beliefs. Many but not all believed that when men understand the universe they find it friendly to their aspirations. These concluded that men could use their reason to live more moral lives and build better societies. For some, these cheerful possibilities were open to all men; for many, only to an intelligent and well-educated minority. Men of the Enlightenment agreed that divine revelation could not establish truths which were contrary to reason. To some, revelation was a useful supplement to reason; to others a delusion or fraud.

In the Protestant camp, many believed that there were great possibilities for reason, even in a sinful and limited human nature. Many, especially in the eighteenth century, were sure that there was no ultimate conflict between the reason and revelation. In the process of argument, however, many were forced to the position that in the long run faith was the essential starting point, and that faith could never begin from argument. A great many people believed throughout the period that the religion of the Bible, understood best by simple people, was the safest foundation for all essential truths.

Many individuals, especially complex individuals, were partly in both camps. In the clearest cases, the difference is obvious; one does not have to read more than a few pages of Jefferson or Paine to be quite sure where they belong; the same is true of Samuel Hopkins or, I think, his master Jonathan Edwards. Others, James Madison or Benjamin Rush, are very difficult to allot to one camp or the other. Later, in the nineteenth century, one encounters figures like Emerson or Whitman or William James in whom the two sets of ideas seem to have fixed and fused past separation.

In my opinion the difference often can be seen best in the tricky realm of style and taste. A Presbyterian divine like John Witherspoon who likes everything simple and clear and hates mystery has one foot in the camp of the Enlightenment. A skeptical statesman like John Adams who believes that human beings are fundamentally impenetrable and contradictory has not altogether broken with his Protestant upbringing. Yet despite all nuances and divisions, in this conflict as in so many the time came when moderates and compromisers were finally forced to take a stand on one side or the other. When this happened, in about 1800, most Americans came out on the side of Protestant Christianity, in however battered or eroded a form. This is, I think, a major fact of American history, and not only of American intellectual history.

In the period when both the Enlightenment and Protestantism were full of diversity despite an essential unity, both demand classification and subdivision for the purpose of analysis. Historians of American Protestantism have accomplished this kind of dissection with great learning and skill. The Enlightenment, on the other hand, has been too often homogenized. This process was begun by the enemies of the Enlightenment in the 1790's, when the Reign of Terror was blamed at once on such sharply different thinkers as Voltaire, Hume, and Paine. Oddly, it has been carried on by leading contemporary historians who are devoted to the Enlightenment tradition and insist that Locke,

Hume, Voltaire, Rousseau, and Jefferson can be described and admired together. These men shared certain very generous loyalties whose nature I have just suggested, yet they differed very sharply on other important matters. The distinctions among them and their followers must be clearly made if one is to treat successfully the *history* of the Enlightenment: its spread, its victories, its defeats.

Since I could find no set of distinctions ready to hand, I have been forced to develop my own. For the purpose of discussing its impact in America, I have found it helpful to divide the Enlightenment in Europe into four categories. The first I am calling the Moderate (it might be called the Rational) Enlightenment. This preached balance, order and religious compromise, and was dominant in England from the time of Newton and Locke until about the middle of the eighteenth century.

The second category is the skeptical Enlightenment, which developed in Britain and especially in France about 1750. Its method was wit, its grand master Voltaire. Its dogmas were usually elliptically stated and often mere negations, but if it was pursued systematically it issued either in the systematic epistemological skepticism of Hume or the systematic materialism of Holbach.

The third category is the Revolutionary Enlightenment, the belief in the possibility of constructing a new heaven and earth out of the destruction of the old. It had its beginnings with Rousseau and its culmination in Paine and Godwin.

My final category I am calling the Didactic Enlightment, a variety of thought which was opposed both to skepticism and revolution, but tried to save from what it saw as the debacle of the Enlightenment the intelligible universe, clear and certain moral judgments, and progress. Its chief center was Scotland. It began before the middle of the eighteenth century, but its principal triumphs in America took place in the first quarter of the nineteenth.

Such categories are not, of course, immutable and final, they are organizing devices to be pragmatically tested. I am sure that other varieties of Enlightenment can be and will be suggested. I hope that these four may make it easier to think about a large and complex portion of American intellectual history. I hope, in fact, that these groupings, however tentative, may be one of the most useful contributions of this book, and therefore I have decided to organize it in terms of them. Though the four kinds of Enlightenment influenced America in roughly chronological order, I have usually subordinated both chronology and geography to these intellectual categories. To neglect entirely either chronology or geography would of course be disastrous.

For the sake of interpretive impact, I have cut my manuscript very sharply, eliminating many repetitive examples of each category. I have tried to give more attention to less well-known examples than to the most familiar, though no historian of this topic can leave out such figures as Jefferson, Franklin, or Adams. I have largely taken for granted such well-worn topics as the American Revolution, the formation of the Constitution, and the two Great Awakenings.

One thing that has been forced on university teachers by their students in recent years is that they abandon the comforting pose of academic impartiality and declare their allegiances, even—contrary to all their training—admit their emotions. I am glad to try to do this, but in relation to this topic I find it simply impossible to escape a congenital ambivalence. A. J. P. Taylor, in reviewing Peter Gay's study of the Enlightenment, said that the Enlightenment is still interesting only to those who are still worried about Christianity. I suspect he is right, but I think there are more such worriers than he assumes; I am certainly one of them.

I cannot, however, sympathize fully either with the firmest partisans of Christianity or its firmest opponents. My sympathies are with those who are not sure that they understand themselves and the universe rather than with those who make hard things easy. I do not think that either the formulae of any kind of Enlightenment or the creeds of traditional Christianity express the whole truth about human nature. This was the position also of those men of the eighteenth century whom I find most sympathetic.

It is impossible for most American historians not to point occasionally from the period they are studying to the conflicts and perplexities of the present, and I am sure that I am often "presentist" in this sense. I have tried hard, however, to immerse myself in the beliefs and assumptions of the period I am dealing with. My story ends with the defeat or perhaps the assimilation of the Enlightenment in the formative period of nineteenth-century culture. I take it for granted that this culture was full of shortcomings and failures, that it was a powerful and vital culture, and that it too has passed, or is on the point of passing. Perhaps this last assumption makes it easier than it has been to look clearly at the period when American culture and religion, as well as American nationality, were beginning to take their familiar shape.

In arguments among historians, intellectual history has been widely, severely, and sometimes justly criticized on two related grounds. It lacks quantification, and its findings exaggerate the role of the articulate elite. I consider both of these tendencies largely inevitable, and think that the best correction is to write other kinds of history using other kinds of sources. It is not true, as some proponents of democratic history rather surprisingly seem to imply, that ordinary people do not have general ideas. It is true, however, that it is hard for the historian to recover the general ideas of people who do not write them down. Moreover, I try to demonstrate that most forms of the Enlightenment developed among the middle and upper classes of European cities, spread mainly among similar groups in America, and failed to reach the agrarian majority. On the whole, various forms of Protestant Christianity served the emotional needs of most Americans better.

Yet for all that, it remains true that at some times and places some kinds of Enlightenment spread fairly widely in America, often inextricably mixed with Christian ideas. Obviously all Americans were influenced by the nature of their form of government, which in turn reflected several kinds of Enlightenment beginnings. In this book I have tried constantly to remember the existence of the inarticulate even though they are not my main subject and to consider carefully the question of the width and depth of the currents of thought with which I am dealing. I have tried elsewhere, with the collaboration of David Lundberg, to work out a very roughly quantitative treatment of certain important European books in American libraries and bookstores. When I make remarks about American reading tastes, these rest primarily on this inquiry, shortly to be published in the *American Quarterly*.

My main reliance for sources has been on printed pamphlets, sermons, and letters. In general I think that there is much to be said for the position of the late Perry Miller, who argued that the main concern of intellectual history is with the public record that people could read. However, when one deals with religion one cannot completely understand the public record without getting into private emotions, sometimes recorded in private sources. For this reason I have supplemented my work by reading manuscript letters in a number of the leading research libraries of various regions. This has been especially useful for the South, which was very important in this period and which published comparatively little. Since I am interested in anybody's opinion about anything which reflected his fundamental assumptions, this has been a fairly arduous and a somewhat random, trial-and-error process. Yet it has been very enjoyable, and sometimes, turning rapidly through a family correspondence dealing with farm prices, health and illness, and local politics, I have come across a sharp expression of feeling—sometimes in time of acute personal crisis—about death, human nature, or even cosmic anxiety. The passages that I have quoted represent a very small part of what I have learned from reading letters. The press, so richly quarried by early American historians, I have used only sparingly and for special topics. I have tried to acquaint myself with the European books most commonly read by Americans and also—almost as important—with some that Americans chose not to read.

I am a newcomer to the rich and very demanding field of early American history. It will be obvious to all expert readers that I depend completely and continually on the work of historians of this period both in America and Europe. To list even my principal debts of this kind would make the book too long; in my notes I refer only to authors to whom I am immediately indebted for particular facts or insights.

I

The Moderate Enlightenment,

1688-1787

One   *The Beauties of Balance*

In the middle of the eighteenth century most articulate Englishmen on either side of the Atlantic described their empire as "great, free, and happy." In sermons especially, prosperity was usually attributed first of all to one fact, that the British were a Protestant people. Often this fact in turn was related to the enlightenment of modern times. Far from being in contrast, Protestantism and enlightenment were almost two faces of the same happy history, whose great milestone was the rational and Protestant Revolution of 1688. After a somewhat precarious interlude, order and freedom had been made secure by the Hanoverian succession. Even David Hume, the most profound skeptic of the age and a historian not without sympathy for the defeated Stuarts, found that the advantages of Hanoverian rule far outweighed its inconveniences:

> Public liberty, with internal peace and order has flourished almost without interruption: Trade and manufactures, and agriculture, have increased: The arts, and sciences, and philosophy, have been cultivated. Even religious parties have been necessitated to lay aside their mutual rancour; and the glory of the nation has spread itself all over Europe; derived equally from our progress in the arts of peace, and from valour and success in war. So long and so glorious a period no nation almost can boast of: Nor is there another instance in the whole history of mankind, that so many millions of people have, during such a space of time, been held together, in a manner so free, so rational, and so suitable to the dignity of human nature.[1]

Reading Swift, looking at Hogarth, or studying social historians makes us realize that such words as order, freedom, and prosperity have to be understood in a special way. While the power of the great landed pro-

3

prietors and their close allies among the new men of finance steadily rose, most Englishmen lacked a secure subsistence. The misery of the English (let alone the Irish) poor, the ineffectual ferocity of the penal code, the horror of the slave trade, the prevalence of drunkenness and prostitution, even the frequency of riots and the lack of safety in the streets, all shocked sensitive consciences. Moralists and preachers constantly complained about the decline of morals, and many decent people concerned themselves about the condition of the lower classes. But improvement was best brought about mainly by simple goodness: by the example of a Squire Allworthy or the benefactions of a Sir Roger de Coverly, or at most by the founding of hospitals, orphanages, and charity schools.

Political economy taught that it was important that trade should flourish and landed property be secure, and both conditions obtained. The wealth of the old and new rich grew prodigiously. Magnificent country mansions, graceful and correct squares and crescents showed the confidence and taste of the rich. For systematic justification of the economic order there was little need; nobody had questioned it seriously since the forgotten levelers of the past. Laissez-faire theory was to develop later in the century along with evangelism, organized social reform, and the fear of revolution.

The political institutions so much admired by foreigners as well as Englishmen seemed to need little defense. Divine-right monarchy had long since been abandoned by all but a few eccentrics; republicanism or radical Whiggery was a stream running underground. It was easy to forget that English political institutions, like English world power, were new. By the middle 1720's, according to a modern historian, the mixed system, with monarchy, aristocracy, and democracy represented by the delicate balance between king, lords, and commons

> had begun to assume the air not only of stability, but also of historical inevitability; it had become a child of Time and of Providence, an object of veneration, the Burkeian fantasy, and a halo of glory was forming about those muddled, incoherent events of 1688, events that had so very nearly spelt anarchy and ruin to the English nation.[2]

The monarchy did not really need to be sacred or lovable; it was necessary. Admirers of the aristocracy emphasized its economic and political usefulness rather than its feudal grandeurs. The two institutions most universally admired were parliamentary supremacy and freedom of the press. Both were quite real, and nearly unique in the world. Few questioned the necessity of influence and patronage to make parliamentary government work. Few doubted that the freedom of the press should be denied to Jacobites, atheists, and other inveterate foes of good order, or that scurrility and sedition should be held on some sort of loose rein by the laws of libel.

Like English institutions of the mid-century, dominant English ideas about man and the universe tended to be compromises, growing out of the conflicts of the past but adapted to the needs of the present. Looking back to the brilliant and dangerous seventeenth century, when most of the extreme tendencies in Renaissance thought found their English spokesmen, most eighteenth-century Englishmen gave their allegiance neither to the harsh materialism of Hobbes nor to the soaring mysticism of Donne or Herbert. Rather, the eighteenth century rested its hopes for stability on the shoulders of the two late-seventeenth-century colossi, Newton and Locke.

The two giants had much in common. Both, like most really influential thinkers, were culminations as well as beginnings of long chapters in the history of thought. Both, seeming to solve the problems of their respective spheres, really left large areas wide open. Both sincerely tried to reconcile modern knowledge with traditional religion, and wrongly believed that they had succeeded. Yet there was also a major difference, which suggested two of the directions later to be taken by the English Enlightenment. Newton's great work, despite his insistence on experiment and caution against premature hypothesis, pointed toward the regularity and knowability of the universe. Locke constantly emphasized the limitations of the human instrument and the need to get along without certainty.

English scientists of Newton's great age came dangerously close to believing that the world was a machine, but they insisted that it was a good machine. Most were, like Democritus, Lucretius, or Leibniz, atomists. For most, matter consisted of irreducible particles in mathematical relation to each other. Yet almost all were sincerely, even fervently religious. By no means consciously forcing a pattern on nature, they were full of joy as their discoveries in physics, chemistry, and biology seemed to prove the immensity, variety, and goodness of God's order, and particularly its constant adaptation to the needs of man. One student of the history of science, describing the ideas held in common by Newton, Boyle the great and pious chemist, and John Ray the geologist, has stated the paradox succinctly. These men, he says,

> attempted to weld into a single philosophy of nature two not entirely compatible conceptions: one, the idea of nature as a law-bound system of matter and motion, and two, the idea of nature as a habitation created for the use and edification of intelligent beings by an omnipotent, omniscient, and benevolent God.[3]

Newton himself was even more pious than many of his less prodigious contemporaries. He was obsessed with the problem of elucidating Biblical prophecy. More important, all his work seemed to him an enquiry into the laws of God; the harmony of science and religion was assumed; its failure unimaginable. His nature philosophy needed God as creator and ruler. Absolute space and time, necessary to his metaphysical and even physical world, existed in the divine mind. And despite Leibniz's objections, Newton stuck to his belief that God's constant effort was needed to prevent irregularity and even disaster in the universe: to overcome the irregularities caused by comets and to keep the fixed stars from rushing together.

For most readers of Newton's popularizers, however (and this meant for educated Europeans, including Americans), it was the awesome regularities of his system, not its deficiencies, that proved the existence and beneficence of God. Not surprisingly, the belief in ultimate regularity was sometimes carried beyond astronomy and physics and beyond the data. In biology, God's greatness and goodwill seemed to show that he must have created all possible species from the amoeba to the angel in an orderly progression, and that no species could have been subtracted from the list or added to it since the beginning. Thus Cotton Mather eagerly reported to the Royal Society his sighting of a mermaid, filling the gap between man and fish; and a century later Thomas Jefferson reasoned that the mammoth must exist somewhere, since his bones had been found. Like the animals, man had his place in a hierarchical order; in the political world as in the cosmos whatever was unchanging, balanced, and orderly was preferable to whatever was extreme or innovative. In all degrees of crudity and sophistication, men reasoned in a circle: the discoveries of science proved the universe to be regular and beneficent; thus, if a given fact or theory led toward regularity and beneficence, it was more likely to be true. Mysterious fossils, evidence of past disasters, puzzling in the present state of knowledge, would prove later to fit the divine scheme.

For our knowledge of this universe, we depended, of course, on the reason God had given us. All agreed on this, but what reason was and how it worked was a subject on which no consensus existed. Building like Newton on vast structures of past thought, John Locke undertook nothing less than to set forth "the original, certainty and extent of *human knowledge*, together with the grounds and degrees of *belief, opinion*, and *assent*. . . ."4 He approached this task in a modest and conciliatory spirit. Disliking enthusiasm as did most of his English contemporaries, he also distrusted abstract rationalism and was suspicious of axioms and syllogisms. He was not, as the word is used today, a professional philosopher, but a psychologist, and he intended to be an empirical psychologist, studying his own mind and asking his readers to study theirs. Beyond this sort of inquiry, into the realms of metaphysics and religion, he really did not want to go: he is eloquent about the limits of human understanding and the need to stick to the knowable. His great *Essay concerning Human Understanding*, published in 1690, was resisted and attacked at first, but shortly became the common starting point of most of the eighteenth century's thinking about psychology, religion, morals, and aesthetics. But if Locke, like Newton, became an intellectual dictator his rule was far from iron. Whereas Newton's physical universe held together for more than a century, Locke's mental world started early to fall apart. There is scarcely a statement in his long, difficult, and ill-organized work that did not create more problems than it solved.

His central statements *seemed* clear and simple. First, he said, there were no such things as ideas innate in the mind, originally and perpetually present and unlearned. All our ideas arose either from sensation or reflection—from the impact of the external world or from the operations of the mind. And what were ideas? The subjects of our thoughts. Did they, then, have any clear relation to external reality, from which sensation must somehow arise in the first place? Once the question was asked, the century was never able to answer it.

In the second book of his *Essay*, Locke divided ideas into two categories, simple and complex. Of these the simple, arising from one sense directly, are the more reliable, and those which depend on combinations

or other mental operations less so. This division, which occupied philosophers, especially in America, for most of two centuries, proved impossible to sustain.

It is the fourth book of the *Essay* which occasioned most controversy
among religious and moral thinkers. We know one thing by intuition,
said Locke: our own existence. Thus sensations such as pain or cold have
a high order of reality (most of his readers probably nodded agreement).
Second, the existence of God is equally certain, and we know it by logical
demonstration. God, being demonstrated, is put on the shelf, to be
brought back from time to time to furnish additional certainty to
Locke's scheme. Beyond these two primal certainties, our perceptions
of identity and relation are reliable, but deal only with ideas in our
minds. Thus mathematical knowledge was certain, but moral knowledge
had to rest on probability, and physical science, for the present, was in
about the same position. Both natural and moral philosophy, Locke
hoped, would eventually attain mathematical certainty. For the present,
however, and for most of the subjects that concerned most people, thinkers had to rely on probability. They could move ahead from this precarious position only cautiously, relying on experience and on something like
common sense. The reason for this sobering conclusion is the gap which
Locke saw perfectly clearly in his own scheme: the ideas in our minds,
however they got there and whatever we did with them, simply could not
be proven to have any relation to things outside: to sustain this basic
correspondence even for simple ideas, Locke is driven to rely on experience and on the "Wisdom and Will of our Maker," who must have
made it so.[5]

Thus, the *Essay*, fertile in suggestions, flexible, various, immensely
penetrating, left almost all its main problems up in the air. The work
that provided the main basis for the Enlightenment's confidence in the
workings of the human mind proved in the not-very-long run to threaten
value, causation, and even (since we are our perceptions) identity. By
1750 Locke had become the acknowledged authority on the human mind
for most educated Europeans, and by then also his work had begun to
lead in a number of contradictory directions, especially toward idealism,
skepticism, materialism, and common-sense realism.

The first two, idealism and skepticism, are the most familiar to historians of philosophy, but the least important for our present purpose
(though each had its representatives in eighteenth-century America).

Bishop Berkeley demonstrated that Locke's distinction between primary and secondary qualities was untenable, and thus that the existence of matter independent of mind could not be demonstrated at all. Attacking much the same contradictions in Locke, David Hume, the cool and conservative Scotsman who became the century's most durable devil, brought out relentlessly the skeptical implications of the great *Essay*.

As clearly as it pointed toward skepticism, Locke's *Essay* raised the equally frightening specter of mechanistic materialism. His early clerical critics fastened on his offhand suggestion that the Creator might, if he chose, have endowed matter with the power to think, a suggestion which seemed to endanger the doctrine of an immaterial soul.[6] This curious idea of an immortal but material soul was to have an important career in America: Thomas Jefferson would pick it up from Joseph Priestley. More important, however, was the generally materialistic drift of a doctrine that often seemed to leave the mind largely passive, acted on from outside through the senses. Locke himself managed to avoid determinism. God, he said, had given the mind the power to suspend its operations, and thus to choose at its leisure from the various dictates of sensation.[7] This system of inner checks and balances was to prove pleasing to some Americans, including James Madison. To some of Locke's readers, however, Locke's answer to determinism seemed an evasion, and so did the halfway materialism of Englishmen such as Joseph Priestley and the Presbyterian David Hartley. In the stark stimulus-and-response version developed by Claude-Adrien Helvétius and other French philosophers, materialism was to present a challenge of which all sophisticated thinkers had to take some account.

Still other readers of Locke's *Essay* tried to escape from his fundamental dilemmas by an appeal to common sense. Hostile like his contemporaries to fanaticism and enthusiasm, Locke himself had insisted that God had given us sufficient faculties to deal with all our pressing problems, and that we need not wear ourselves out searching for ultimate solutions to questions that lay beyond these. Scottish thinkers, especially Thomas Reid, developed the implications of this modest assertion into a reassuring philosophical system. The resulting school of Common Sense philosophy was to have a big effect among Americans, who liked to think of America as a common-sense country opposed to useless speculation.

In the middle of the century Englishmen had only started in these directions. Locke seemed sufficient, Berkeley and Hume were largely ignored, Helvétius unknown, Reid not yet needed. The operations of the mind had been explained as clearly as the movement of matter. Both of these great achievements proved the genius of England and the enlightenment of the age.

Though at first many English divines were shocked by Locke's theories, especially his denial of all innate ideas, by midcentury the clergy had accepted his teachings as cordially as they had Newton's. They had little choice. Everybody agreed that society needed religion, and that religion, if it was to play its full part in men's lives, needed certainty. The traditional sources of certainty were badly impaired. The God-centered scholastic organization of all knowledge survived only feebly in such backwaters as the universities. The universal and authoritative church visible could hardly be separated from the Roman error, and the inner light had led to sectarian anarchy. Somewhat oddly, Roman infallibility and inner-light enthusiasm were often condemned together, and a modern, rational alternative to both was constantly demanded. Most could agree with the much-quoted statement of William Chillingworth that the Bible alone was the religion of Protestants. Yet it had long been clear that in practice, such agreement was not enough. Not everybody could read the sacred text, or apply its precepts, the same way.

For elucidating Biblical truth, as for all other purposes, man depended on reason, the faculty given him so that he might know his Maker. Already reason had explored the firmament on high, and made it show forth more clearly than ever the glory of God. Now Locke had shown how the judgment of the mind, about religious truth as about everything else, could be depended upon. Locke himself has been presented by historians as a Calvinist, a devout Anglican, a crypto-deist, and a trimmer. It seems reasonable that his frequent professions of Christianity were sincere enough, and unlikely that he was a man of profoundly religious temperament. What mattered most to churchmen of his day was that he, like Newton, made God a necessary and logical part of his scheme. He was certainly, in addition, an enemy of popery and enthusiasm.

The existence of God, the *Essay* said, was not indeed an idea innate in the mind, but it was as certain as if it had been. From our own existence, Locke like many earlier thinkers deduced the necessity of an eternal, all-wise, and all-powerful being. Regarding the Christian revelation his argument was somewhat newer. Whatever came directly from God must obviously be believed without question. But revelation coming from a human witness must be judged by reason. Its content might contain truths *beyond* reason; things might be revealed that the unaided mind could never have reached. But it was impossible that revelation could, as enthusiasts had suggested, run contrary to reason. Thus reason must judge revelation, first by the consistency and rationality of its content, and second, by applying to its witnesses the same tests that should be applied to any evidence.

To Locke's first readers, this approach seemed destructive. With obvious sincerity, Locke hastened to demonstrate that the whole of the Christian revelation passed his test. All that Jesus required his followers to believe, said Locke, could be summarized in one article: that Jesus was the Messiah. This was overwhelmingly proved by the fulfillment of Old Testament prophecies in his life, and by the miracles he performed.

For a great many Englishmen in the colonies and at home, Dr. Samuel Clarke, probably the most famous liberal Anglican divine, was an authority almost equal to Locke or Newton. In 1704 and 1705 Clarke delivered the Boyle Lectures, founded by the great scientist's will in order to defend the truths of Christianity.[8] Clarke, a rationalist rather than an empiricist, was far more systematic, less cautious, and less original than Locke. He sought to bring to theology the exactitude and certainty possessed by mathematics, and argued that any kind of truth so demonstrated was irresistible to the human reason.

In his first series of lectures Clarke proved the existence and traditional attributes of God much as Locke had, making use somewhat more fully both of the traditional ontological proof and the currently fashionable argument from the design of the universe. This accomplished, he set out in his second series to demonstrate the validity of morality and revelation. For Clarke, the correctness of such precepts as the Golden Rule was exactly as certain as the conclusions of geometry, and provable in the same way. Revelation, however, was needed to put morality on a basis which could be readily comprehended and obeyed by the ignorant and un-philosophical masses.[9] The doctrines of Jesus, though not all discoverable by the light of nature, proved, when once revealed to be exactly the sort one would expect from a divine being, and clearly conformable to the teachings of sound and unprejudiced reason. To make these teachings still more compelling, their divine origin had been verified by miracles and prophecies. This case formed "the most credible, certain and convincing Evidence, that was ever given to any matter of Fact," and the whole system of doctrines made up "an infinitely more consistent and rational scheme of belief, than any that the wisest of the ancient philosophers ever *did*, or the cunningest of modern unbelievers *can* invent or contrive."[10]

Putting together the Newtonian regularities, the Lockean psychology, and the rational theology of Clarke and many others, the clergy of the early eighteenth century believed that they had a system worthy of an enlightened age. Other paths to the sacred truth were difficult or dangerous; that of natural religion safe and easy. With many variations, the central doctrines set forth in book after book ran something like this: First, we can deduce the existence and nature of God by reason and by studying creation. Second, the maxims of morality can be found out in the same manner. Third, the Christian revelation teaches us some additional but not contrary things that we need to know, such as the rewards and punishments of the after life. Fourth, the validity of this revelation is proven by prophecy, by miracle, by the triumph of Christianity over all its foes, by the concurrence of great and good men from the Apostles onward, and by its own admirable and rational character.

To many, as to Clarke, this was a case that only the most stubborn and stupid could resist. Actually, insuperable difficulties developed almost immediately, and what had seemed to be a promising chapter in the history of Christianity came close to being disastrous.

The difficulties which beset the preachers of natural religion were of several kinds. Few, in this practical age, were troubled by the metaphysical problem of reconciling the Newtonian first cause with the Platonic supreme being. The question of freedom was more troublesome. Clarke and many others made the eternal relations of things, the character of the universe and the nature of right and wrong prior to the will of God himself.[11] Whether God merely acted in accordance with pre-existent moral verities or whether he to some degree determined these, he had to act justly. This came dangerously close to saying that everything had to be just as it was. This conclusion is what Basil Willey has called "Cosmic Toryism," a kind of determinism that is more depressing than Calvinist orthodoxy. For ordinary people faced with the tragedies of life, it may be possible to bow to the will of an inscrutable but personal God. To conclude rationally that everything must be just as it is, is emotionally unsatisfying: it is the conclusion against which *Candide* sensibly revolted.

Of course natural religion, in its many varieties, cannot be dismissed. Men of many periods, including Albert Einstein, have been moved to awe and reverence by contemplating the dimensions and complexity of physical reality. But in their overconfidence many eighteenth-century apologists went much farther: each new discovery had to confirm the beneficence of God and the moral teachings of revelation. On the simplest and most dangerous level, it was extremely difficult to see in the mighty abstraction of Newton, the logical necessity of Locke, or even the utterly rational deity of Clarke the same God who walked in the Garden, or confided his secrets only to the leaders of one nation (to many Englishmen, as to Hume, a remote and barbarous nation at that). Most terrifyingly of all, it was hard to imagine such a God condemning his own marvelous and flawless creation, and then sending his only Son to one insignificant planet to redeem some of its inhabitants.

None of these problems was new, but the new insistence on the primacy and sufficiency of reason presented them in acute form and barred some of the possible solutions. To make Christian doctrines symbolic of an inner truth, as many had done in the past, was out of accord with the plain and downright tastes of the age. To sever one kind of truth radically from another would throw away the great gains of the new knowledge, which seemed above all to offer harmony and continuity among all spheres of thought. To say simply that God's ways were beyond human understanding would be to resign from the task, accepted in vigorous good faith and confidence, of making them plain. All that remained was to fight it out on the one remaining ground: the reasonableness of Christianity. Having advanced to this front, the defenders found it untenable, and were forced little by little to give ground.

In this retreat, the signposts, starting from Calvinism, bore the successive labels of Arminianism, Arianism, Socinianism, latitudinarianism, and deism. This is a logical rather than a chronological order; few people moved through each stage successively. Working definitions are, however, necessary, since these theological terms furnished a vocabulary for religious, moral, and sometimes even political discussion, in America as in England, well into the nineteenth century.

In the sixteenth and the early seventeenth century, both establishment and budding Dissent had been Calvinist. The starting point had been the glory of God, and the key to God's purposes Scripture alone. Many had accepted the deductions of Calvin, systematized at Dort in Holland in 1619-20, the total depravity of man and his complete dependence on divine grace withheld or freely given by God according to irrevocable and unfathomable decisions made from the beginning of time. It was essentially this creed, adopted by the assembly of divines at Westminster in 1646, that came close to uniting British Christianity on a Calvinist basis. The Westminster Confession was adopted by the Church of Scotland in 1647, approved in part by the English Parliament in 1648, and incorporated in the authoritative pronouncements of all branches of English Dissent and American Puritanism. By the end of the century, however, Calvinism in general and the Westminster Confession in particular were associated in England with political revolution, and to insist on inscrutable decrees seemed out of keeping with the rational temper of the age.

Arminianism, which became a catchword for all kinds of departures from Calvinism, meant originally a denial that divine grace was irresistible, a belief that human action played some part in the drama of individual salvation. Preached at Leyden by Jacobus Arminius, condemned at Dort, Arminianism spread through Europe in the late sixteenth century. In England, it penetrated the established Church at the beginning of the seventeenth century and was vigorously and ruthlessly promoted by Charles I and Archbishop Laud. It was partly for this reason that an important fraction of the Calvinistic Protestants had found it necessary to leave for America in 1630.

Hated and feared in colonial New England, Arminianism has, more surprisingly, been treated somewhat contemptuously by modern American historians, following the lead of Perry Miller. It has often been made synonymous with a smooth and bland avoidance of difficult questions. Actually, like all major religious tendencies, it attracted many kinds of people. To a very large number of early modern thinkers, as to Samuel Clarke, God's justice was prior to his will; to say that omnipotent goodness cannot possibly condemn innocent infants to eternal suffering was not just lack of courage; but rather it was a metaphysical or semantic insistence that goodness cannot be bad. To others, moved less by logic than prudence, it was simply too dangerous to society to make behavior absolutely irrelevant to salvation. Where Calvinists called Arminians popish, Arminians called Calvinists antinomian, meaning that Calvinists believed the reign of grace had abolished law. Both epithets were deeply resented, partly because each had some truth in it: some Arminians longed for the reunion of Christendom and leaned toward Catholic doctrine, and some Calvinists had gone so far in preaching irresistible and unpredictable grace that they had opened the way to moral nihilism.

Arianism and Socinianism were both forms of heresy with regard to the doctrine of the Trinity. It was this doctrine above all others that proved difficult to defend by the only ways open in the eighteenth century. Yet to most Christians, whether or not they could unravel the Athanasian dispute or explain the Nicene Creed, the most central doctrines of their faith depended on the full divinity and sonship of Christ and the continuing inspiration of the Holy Spirit.

Though the Church of England made strenuous efforts to prohibit, and then simply to avoid, discussion of the Trinity, eager defenders rushed unwisely forward. Trying to defend the doctrine's complete rationality, they usually left it rigidified or confused.

Arianism was an ancient name for the belief that Christ, though divine, was different from the Father and lesser. Locke found it hard to deny that he tended in this direction. In 1712 Samuel Clarke characteristically tried to settle the matter once and for all by rigorously impartial examination of the Bible. He concluded, disastrously, that Scripture gave no support either for orthodox or Arian conclusions.

Socinianism was the sixteenth-century form of the more radical heresy that made Christ clearly a creature, without denying his divine mission. Spreading through central and eastern Europe, bitterly persecuted almost everywhere, it had found a few spokesmen in the Netherlands and in seventeenth-century England. In 1698 it had seemed enough of a menace to be excepted from the Act of Toleration. Yet the idea that Christ was a divinely ordained moral teacher was too congenial to eighteenth-century preferences to lack defenders, especially in private conversation among gentlemen.

Part of the reason for the loosening of doctrine was the vulnerability of English religious institutions. At the outset of the century, ecclesiastical questions as well as religious questions seemed to have been settled by reasonable compromise. Few doubted that religion was necessary for good order and sound morals. Many but not all believed that an established church was either a divine ordinance or at least a great convenience. On the other hand, toleration of Dissent was clearly both a practical necessity and a proof of enlightenment.

The faults of the Church of England in the eighteenth century have been made familiar by contemporary Calvinists, nineteenth-century evangelicals, and twentieth-century historians. It has been painted as worldly, ridden with place-hunting and partonage, dull in spirit and yet somewhat persecuting in practice. This picture is not without its truth. The fox-hunting parson and the political bishop are both real. In addition to these, the Church contained saintly and learned men, and many who tried without much soul-searching to do good in their stations.

The chief aim of the Church was to be comprehensive, and because of the controversies of the past this meant to be compromising. The reasons for compromise were many. They included fear of dissension, political and social conservatism, and sheer laziness. They also included the noble dream of catholicity and universality and the belief, inherited from poets and mystics of the past, that Christian truth can never be exhausted by formulations or defined by argument. Failing in the first half of the century to reconcile the Dissenters and include the Scottish Presbyterians, the Church and most of the people had learned to live with compromises. Bishops were sanctified by the apostolic succession, but appointed by the Crown. Dissenters were tolerated but excluded from the universities and political office. Thus history had produced ambiguity, and ambiguity produced continuous and bitter wrangling within the Church: over the limits of Church authority, the relative powers of king, ministers, Parliament, bishops, and Convocation; and the nature and meaning of the Church itself.

As the trinitarian argument developed, it too was carried on in terms of church government. Some, hoping to conciliate Arians, wanted to alter the trinitarian and strongly Calvinistic Thirty-Nine Articles, or to require clergy to subscribe to the Bible alone. Clarke, among others, suggested a reformed liturgy which would eliminate all clearly trinitarian emphasis. Such suggestions naturally produced fierce counterattack.

It is not surprising that a great many of the clergy, and particularly those who increasingly held the most powerful positions, made it their chief concern to keep controversy out of the pulpit, by simplifying theology and emphasizing simple morality. Latitudinarianism, originally a term of abuse, became accepted as a term for the tendency—lazy or charitable according to one's attitude—to cut Christianity to essentials. One of its earliest exponents was John Tillotson, who became Archbishop of Canterbury with the Glorious Revolution. Tillotson's sermons, undemanding in doctrine, edifying in morals, and admired by Addison for their limpid style, were enormously popular among Englishmen at home and in the colonies throughout the century.[12] Denouncing papists for their incomprehensible doctrine of transubstantiation, and enthusiasts for their unseemly asceticism, Tillotson insisted that the duties of a Christian were not too difficult. While God was sovereign and could have made any law he chose, He had generously "commanded us nothing in the gospel that is either unsuitable to our reason or prejudicial to our interest . . . nothing but what is easy to be understood, and as easy to be practiced by an honest and willing mind."[13]

Those who dealt with apologetics rather than morality were similarly likely, in the early eighteenth century, to emphasize what seemed easy and clear rather than what seemed complex and dangerous. Many set forth the religion of nature with only a brief appendix on its compatibility with revelation. William Wollaston, often mistakenly called a deist but actually a clergyman of the established Church, simply omitted revelation altogether in his widely read *Religion of Nature Delineated*. As an early editor explained, "he did not think it necessary to digress from his subject in order to insert his creed."[14]

The virtues of the Church were many, but its faults were obvious and its defenses weak. It is not surprising that its enemies found their best texts in the works of its apologists.

In the colonies, many Protestants looked toward the British Dissenters with special fraternal feelings and deep respect. Yet in the middle of the eighteenth century Dissent, like the Church, presented a disconcerting picture of disunity and doctrinal drift.

Dissenters, numbering about a quarter of a million in the English population of over five million, were mostly members of the middle class. Unpopular with the masses and looked at askance by high Tories, the Dissenters were devoted to the Hanoverian monarchy, which they saw as the protector of their liberties. While they were still barred from Parliament and the universities, and in theory from local office as well, their

periodical agitation for reform lacked militance. Remembering periods
of persecution under the early and later Stuarts and a revival of danger
under Queen Anne, most Dissenters, with different degrees of suppressed
resentment, accepted the existing compromise. As much as Churchmen,
though in somewhat different ways, they were affected by the ideas of
the Lockean age.

The principal group, the Presbyterians, had been forced to abandon
their once high hopes of becoming the national church in England as
well as Scotland, and forced to accept a position of tolerated dissent
along with the sectarians they had always disliked. Often wealthy and
well educated, shut out of the English universities, Presbyterians had
been exposed to all the currents of rationalist thought flowing through
the Dutch universities, where a number of them had studied. Their own
academies, at their best the most vigorous educational institutions in the
realm, were permeated by modern science and philosophy. As a Dissenting body, they had no authoritative means of defining doctrine. Tests
and subscriptions were associated with past oppression and impossible to
enforce, and no rich preferments existed to deter ministers from radical
paths. Thus the English Presbyterians, once the pillars of Calvinism,
drifted sedately through Arminianism to their own sober kinds of Arianism and Socinianism.

The Congregationalist independents, with their covenanted churches
and more deeply anti-establishment tradition, drifted less rapidly away
from Calvinism, while the small Baptist groups were divided, as they
long had been, between Calvinist and Arminian bodies. The Quakers,
sticking to their historic doctrine of the inner light though mitigating
the severity of some of their customs, were clearly out of the theological
mainstream, never being primarily dependent on the natural-religion
argument.

Like the Church, the Dissenting bodies were riddled with internal dis-
putes throughout the early eighteenth century, but unlike the Church,
they had no institutions capable of maintaining formal unity. Up to the
middle of the century, lacking both vigorous leadership and definite
identity, Dissent suffered continuing losses to the Church.

In this environment the most influential Dissenting individuals usually, like their Anglican contemporaries, tried to hold a middle theological ground. Philip Doddridge, the Presbyterian minister who with Tillotson and Clarke was one of the three divines most widely read in the

colonies, could not be called a latitudinarian, though several latitudinarian bishops were his friends and he had something in common with them. Not at all inclined to skepticism or moral laziness. Doddridge was a talented writer of hymns and homilies. Yet, since he ardently hoped for church union, he sought to reduce creeds and articles to a minimum and advocated leniency on such matters as baptism and predestination. A highly successful educator, he was humbly consulted by such leading American Protestants as President Aaron Burr of Princeton.[15]

Even in Scotland, where the 1690 settlement established the Presbyterian Church, and all ministers and professors had to subscribe to the Westminister Confession, the situation was not encouraging to religious conservatives. An effort to combine Presbyterian institutions with the English system of presentation to livings by landowners produced constant wrangling and sizable secessions. Within the church, there were two main doctrinal parties. The Moderates, who subscribed to the Westminster Confession in much the same spirit as English latitudinarians subscribed to the Thirty-Nine Articles, dominated the universities and played a leading role in the sober but vigorous social life of the Scottish towns. It was this group, officially led by the historian William Robertson as moderator and including Francis Hutcheson, Thomas Reid, and other Common-Sense philosophers, that was beginning to furnish ideas to many kinds of Americans. Its opponent, the Popular party, fought a strong rearguard action for Calvinism in theology and strictness in conduct, and against lay control. This faction was to furnish America with the most effective college president of the late eighteenth century, John Witherspoon of Princeton, and also with its most rigid anti-Jacobin, Charles Nisbet of the College of Carlisle, Pennsylvania.

Thus the differences between Churchmen and Dissenters, in the middle of the eighteenth century, were related more to class, geography, and style of life than to religious belief. Even the remaining political disabilities of Dissenters were an irritation rather than a revolutionary grievance, and most Dissenters were warm friends of the Hanoverian succession and the existing social order. Yet the embers of both religious and social discontent were still alive, and would blaze up before the end of the century. Dissenters were shortly to give effective backing to two major revolutions, invoking powerful republican and Puritan traditions.

In 1750, however, these traditions, embodied in the writers now called Commonwealthmen by historians, had painful connotations for most

Englishmen. Republicanism and puritanism were still associated, like Calvinism, with the exaltations and disasters, the revolution and tyranny, of the past century. Complacent yet timid, committed to rational argument, eager to avoid divisive definitions, the leading British defenders of Christianity—Churchmen and Dissenters alike—relied mainly on the plausible but dangerous simplicities of natural religion. They faced the aggressive deists with outward confidence but blunted weapons.

The challenge of the deists was especially dangerous because it proceeded from the reigning Newtonian and Lockean assumptions. The deists claimed many predecessors, often beginning with Cicero and Seneca, and disclaimed many others, usually including Spinoza and Hobbes. But most often, and with irritating unction, they gave their chief praise to Newton, Locke, Clarke, and especially Tillotson, who was according to one of them not only "the most Pious and Rational of all Priests" but the man "Whom all English Free-Thinkers own as their Head."[16]

Though their closeness to rationalist Christianity makes it difficult to establish a canonical list of deists, those usually listed by their English and American opponents were (in rough chronological order) John Toland, Matthew Tindal, Thomas Woolston, Anthony Collins, Thomas Chubb, Conyers Middleton, Thomas Morgan, Lord Bolingbroke, and Peter Annet. These all published works between 1696 (Toland) and 1761 (Annet). Lord Herbert of Cherbury and Charles Blount were clear forerunners in the seventeenth century. Other writers accused from time to time of being deists included such various figures as the aesthete and moralist Lord Shaftesbury, the skeptic Bernard Mandeville, the radical Whigs Gordon and Trenchard, and even the Catholic Alexander Pope.

Even among the central group of deists the variety was great. In social rank they ranged from Bolingbroke, the Jacobite foreign minister and later Tory statesman, through country gentlemen like Collins to the schoolteacher Morgan and the tallow-chandler Chubb. Though the arguments against the deists often began with an accusation of vulgarity and ignorance, their own general tone was more often than not patronizing toward the ignorant and credulous lower classes, and the scholarship of some (like Middleton) was fairly impressive. Most professed to be Christians purifying Christianity, and only a few had their tongues in their cheeks in such profession. (Annet, whose blasphemies made him a forerunner of Paine and earned him some time in the pillory, was untypical.)

The usual starting point of deism was the epistemology of Locke and the rational Christianity of Clarke. Like Clarke, Deists believed God bound by definition to act in an orderly, moral, and rational manner. His purpose was man's good. He had, all agreed, revealed both his own existence and nature and our moral duties in the book of nature, and had given us faculties which made us able to read this book. Therefore further revelation must be as rational and moral as natural religion. The only mistake of the great Mr. Locke had been to say that there could be truths beyond reason.

Mystery, said John Toland, could not possibly have a place in what was intended to disclose to men the most important truths. According to Tindal, faith contrary to reason was simply impossible, since "Men can no otherwise believe than as things appear to them."[17] Truth, said Tindal and Chubb, must have been made apparent by a beneficent deity to the ancient Greeks and Romans and must be available now to Chinese and Patagonians. Thus whatever was not rational, moral, and universally comprehensible, said Toland, "could only consist of Follies superadded, and in many Cases substituted to the most blessed, pure, and practicable Religion that Men could wish or enjoy."[18] The idea of a special revelation, different from the book of nature, had led to the impostures and persecutions of the Roman Church, incessantly catalogued and condemned by orthodox Anglicans themselves. It had led also to the barbarous and rigid laws of the Jews. Even in our own enlightened day, the same error had led to endless arguments over such meaningless questions as the nature of the Trinity.

The Bible, said orthodox Christian apologists, completed but did not supersede the book of nature, and its contents were both sublime and reasonable. Going only one step farther, the deists argued that whatever in the Bible was unreasonable and immoral could not come from God. With increasing glee, and not without a measure of the mild anti-Semitism widely prevalent in the Enlightenment, deists pounced on the immoral and cruel acts of David, or the impostures and complexities of Paul, the renegade Pharisee. Since most expressed respect for the pure doctrines of Jesus, their attack on the Gospels themselves was more selective. Sometimes these took the form of attacking the credentials of which apologists made so much, the fulfillment of prophecy and the authenticity of miracles. At their simplest, the deists nominated particular passages to be stricken out on moral or rational grounds. Jesus, in cursing

somebody else's fig tree for a purely demonstrative purpose, violated the
sanctity of private property. The evil spirits could not have been driven
into the bodies of the Gadarene swine, since it was well known that
Jews kept no pigs. Jesus could not really have seen, without the aid of
glasses, all the kingdoms of the world and their glory from any con-
ceivable mountain.[19]

If it is hard to imagine a great religion troubled by this sort of cavil-
ling, we must remember that any hostile examination of Scripture was
novel for most readers. Moreover, the more intelligent of the deists went
far deeper. It was unanswerably true that many of the most revered passages of Scripture went contrary to the precepts of natural religion, received morality, and even public order. Few enlightened Englishmen
could defend the unwise leniency shown the prodigal son, the imprudent
extravagance of Martha's sister Mary, or even the praise given improvi-
dence and ignorance in the Sermon on the Mount. And beyond the unjust condemnation of Adam, the undeserved trials of Job, loomed the gigantic injustice of the crucifixion; the punishment of a perfectly good
man for the sins of others.

It is usually maintained that the deists, none of them very penetrating
critics, lost their argument with the mighty army of learned Churchmen
and earnest Dissenters who rushed to the counterattack. Certainly, the
siege had long been lifted when Edmund Burke, in 1790, asked his famous question:

> Who, born within the last forty years, has read one word of Collins, and
> Toland, and Tindal, and Chubb, and Morgan, and that whole race who
> called themselves Free Thinkers? Who now reads Bolingbroke? Who
> ever read him through?[20]

Yet the historian's estimate of the outcome of the deist controversy
must be more cautious than Burke's. It was certainly not a victory for
the legions of Churchmen and Dissenters who rushed forward to prove
once more that Christianity was morally, rationally, and historically impeccable, or for what Dr. Johnson called "that Old Bailey theology in
which . . . the Apostles are being tried once a week for the capital
crime of forgery,"[21] and triumphantly acquitted. Benjamin Franklin was
not the only person converted to deism by reading anti-deist arguments.
In answering the deists on their own terms, the Christians had taken on
the job of proving their religion rational and moral in every detail. This

was a tactical mistake, and a gigantic failure of religious and historical imagination.

It is also clear that the high hopes of these early deists, to found a pure and rational religion, failed. Their doctrines, leading straight to the optimism of Dr. Pangloss, were as hard to believe and as paradoxical as Christianity when they were closely examined. They had no compelling symbols and excited little emotion. For its greatest triumphs, deism had to wait until the end of the century, when revolutionary enthusiasm could give it the passion it had always lacked.

The deists were defeated, and the defenders of rational Christianity—though they held the forts and the troops—fatally weakened. The real victory was to go to two other groups, opposite in conclusion but sometimes curiously similar in argument, the skeptics and those believers who concluded that religion must rest on faith.

In 1743 Henry Dodwell published a small book called *Christianity not Founded on Argument*. If, as has been suggested, Locke's title *The Reasonableness of Christianity* furnished "the solitary thesis of Christian theology in England for the great part of a century,"[22] Dodwell's far less familiar title pointed toward most of the paths that led from his day toward the nineteenth century, to the directions taken by Hume and Burke and Wesley and Edwards. Dodwell's suggestion that reason could not establish Christian truth was usually taken to be a sly attack on religion, and he was answered along with deists and skeptics. It is perhaps impossible now to determine Dodwell's intention, yet most of his book is devoted to the far from skeptical argument that salvation is by grace, and that faith must proceed and accompany rational assent to religious doctrine.

Joseph Butler, who ended his placid career as Bishop of Durham, was like most very popular thinkers a transitional figure. Like the legions of Christian apologists of his day, he accepted the premises of natural religion and tried to stick within the methods of rational proof. He laid great stress on the typically eighteenth-century argument that if we are not sure, it is safer to assume the reality of future rewards and punishments. Yet his reasoning led him to the conclusion that we cannot and need not understand God's entire plan to know our duty. In the long run Butler agreed with Dodwell, or for that matter with Hume, who admired him, that it is not reason but experience that is our instructor in religious matters. His principal contribution to apologetics, though by no means the whole of his argument, was what might be called the pessimistic variety of natural religion. Paradoxes, obscurities, and above all conditions contrary to human hopes were so plentiful in nature itself, that nobody should object to them in revelation. Natural religion and Christianity, Butler powerfully argued, must stand or fall together, not because both were clear, but because both were full of difficulty. Few doctrines could be less to the taste of adherents of the Moderate Enlightenment, and it was a long time before most Christians fully appreciated either the power or the dangers of this argument. Butler's *Analogy of Religion*, published in 1736, reached the peak of its influence early in the next century, and particularly in America. It was read there, however, before the Revolution, and one can guess that it owed some of its influence to its compatibility with Calvinist ideas.

In the second half of the century the most important paths taken by English thinkers were away from complacency and compromise, in both radical and conservative directions. From argumentative deism to the crusading deism of Paine, from the calm skepticism of Hume to the aggressive skepticism of Gibbon, from the moralistic dissent of Doddridge to the radical dissent of Priestley, from the rational and cheerful apologetic of Bishop Sherlock to the more convincing but less cheerful apologetic of Bishop Butler, all paths led away from the center, and we will eventually look down most of them. Probably more important than any religious or philosophic arguments was a change of intensity. Intense, undoctrinal religious emotion lay at the center of the most important religious movement of the day, the spreading Wesleyan revival. Passion ruled in the political world as well by the time of Burke and Paine. Blake and Wordsworth were the literary prophets, not Pope and Johnson. Sir Robert Walpole, the personification of early eighteenth-century compromise, had seen the beginning of the end of the age of moderation with dismay: "This nonsensical new light is extremely in fashion, and I shall not be surprised if we see a revival of all the folly and cant of the last age."[23]

Perhaps the only explanation of the change of mood is the one this comment suggests, that periods of consensus and compromise produce periods of intense controversy, and vice versa, in a cycle that reflects the basic ambivalence of human wishes. It is certainly true that Wesley and Rousseau and Blake and Burke were all consciously protesting against eighteenth-century complacency, just as Locke and Clarke and Tillotson had been reacting in horror to seventeenth-century enthusiasm.

Somewhat more concretely, it has been suggested that social change is at the bottom of the English change of mood. Compromise and complacency, political peace and religious moderation had fit the needs of a society peacefully accumulating capital through foreign trade. In the second half of the century the population was growing, technological invention was quickening, and agriculture was being revolutionized by improvement and enclosure. Though by our standards all these changes were proceeding with glacial slowness, all were unsettling to some groups in the English population—to displaced craftsmen and peasants, to factory workers, to all the poor and in another way to the new rich. In an age of change, people need to be sustained by deeper emotions than those aroused by calm appreciation of the beauties of balance.

In the second half of the century, while England itself was changing, the center of Enlightenment had moved from London to Paris. Both Voltaire and Franklin, it has been pointed out, were in London in 1726, and both were deeply influenced by Clarke and Wollaston and the deists. In France, an absolutist state linked to an authoritarian Church made the English compromise impossible. First skepticism, then revolutionary optimism were to be the characteristic forms taken by Enlightenment in France.

In the American colonies before the Revolution, however, French thought had only a limited effect. By and large, Englishmen in America read the same books Englishmen read at home, a little later and somewhat selectively. Thus the Moderate Enlightenment, the Enlightenment of Locke and Newton, of Tillotson and Doddridge, of Clarke and Wollaston, encountered in America another society—in some ways an archaic one. With its faults and virtues, its toleration, moderation, crassness, and complacency, the Moderate Enlightenment left its clearly visible traces on the shape of American culture.

Two *Progress and the Provinces*

Provincial societies are likely to be much more innovative in practice than in theory. If they inhabit a frontier they have to develop new working answers to new questions put by geography, climate, and a host of new conditions. Yet on the conscious and articulate level which is our main concern in this book, they are likely to be divided between jealousy of the metropolis and a desire to imitate. At one moment, they may protest that they are up with the last fashions from home, and at the next insist that life in their new country is better, purer, and healthier. Throughout American history, the West has been ambivalent toward the East in this manner. In the eighteenth century, with an ocean to separate metropolis from provinces, the ambivalence was deeper. Most of the inhabitants of British North America considered themselves Englishmen, yet they were increasingly conscious of differences between themselves and Englishmen at home. Trying to analyze these differences, modern historians find the colonies at once more modern and less so. Colonial society was less aristocratic and in many ways less traditional than English society. It was also less urban and more Protestant, and its Protestantism was not that of contemporary England. The older colonies had been founded a century earlier and had developed their own modifications of their seventeenth-century institutions. While their ambitions pushed colonists toward modernity, some of their deepest loyalties anchored them in the past. As in England, the ideas of the Moderate Enlightenment—the formulae of balance, order, and rationality—were especially attractive to the prosperous, the urban, the successful, the striving, the up-to-date. These ideas appealed far less to the bypassed, the resentful, the stymied, the unsuccessful—a loose grouping at once reactionary and potentially radical.

26

Intermittently and unevenly but also rapidly, the colonies had been growing, during the last two generations before the Revolution—growing in world trade, population, wealth, and cities. Especially in the last two decades of the colonial period, life in America had been growing—for some—more English. "English" connoted economic prosperity, elegant living, moderate religion, constitutional government, and above all a decent respect for gradations in rank.

It is always difficult to make generalizations about class divisions and relations between classes in America. For the eighteenth century, this is particularly difficult right now, because of the current explosion of social history. Problems of class, and of the degree of social discontent, fascinate the "new social historians" of eighteenth-century America.[1] Quite properly, most of these historians begin by minute examination of particular, often local, problems. As our knowledge of society grows richer, summary becomes more difficult.

One thing that is clear is that differences in rank were taken for granted by nearly all eighteenth-century Englishmen, including those living in America, to a degree which contemporary Americans find hard to imagine. William Livingston's *Independent Reflector*, the gadfly of privilege in New York, paused between attacks on corrupt local bigwigs to point out the importance of observing *just* distinctions. He appealed to the ideals of balance and order so much loved by the Moderate Enlightenment:

> . . . the great Variety of Powers, Characters and Conditions, so obvious in Human Life, is an illustrious Proof of the benignity and Wisdom of the Supreme Governor of the Universe. From this vast Diversity naturally result Superiority and Pre-eminence in some, and Dependence and subjection in others. To this *natural* Difference of Character, Society has introduced the additional Distinction of a political Disparity, by conferring on various of its Members, a Variety of Honours and Privileges in a gradual Subordination from the chief Magistrate, to the least dignified of his Subjects. Hence we owe a becoming Regard to those who are advanced by the Wisdom of the Common Wealth, in Proportion to their Elevation, unless they forfeit it by their Demerit.[2]

If this was the view of a colonial radical, it was still more the view of the rich and successful. In the decade before independence, the rich were growing richer, and their style of life more lavish. Real aristocrats were few; the most powerful leaders of colonial society were urban merchants and hard-working, slave-owning managers of estates. Only in New York was there a class of large landowners living on rents. The style of life of the top bourgeoisie was ample rather than magnificent. Copley's plain, sober, self-confident merchants, dressed according to Polonius's excellent advice, standing next to their competent and handsome spouses are a long way from the arrogant officers and languid ladies of Gainsborough. The commodious and elegant mansions of suburban Philadelphia or the generously proportioned but simply designed country houses of Virginia have little to do with the palaces of British grandees.

Yet in the middle of the century there were many recent signs that part of the top class of the colonies was trying to move a little away from its solid bourgeois origins, and as it moved, to close the doors behind it. Capital, credit, British connections, and political influence were becoming the keys to real success. In almost all colonies the rich dominated the upper houses of colonial legislatures and used their power without qualms to get land grants and other solid favors from the government. When they could, people of condition and family married each other, and in a few places—tidewater Virginia, southern Maryland, and of course rural New York—certain families had achieved a special exclusive position recognized by all.

Among the upper section of the upper class, imitation of aristocratic manners was increasing. A few scions of Carolina or Virginia families, a few sons of Boston and Philadelphia merchants, learned to gamble without flinching in London, to make a bow in Paris, even to buy paintings in Venice or Rome. At home, no amusements of gentlemen were lacking: theater, racing, or balls, pleasure gardens in the style of Vauxhall and Ranelagh. Provision was not omitted for the coarser pursuits of eighteenth-century Englishmen. In Boston in 1750 Captain Francis Goelet, "after having dined in a very elegant manner upon Turtle & Drank about three Toasts, and Sang a Number of Songs" and was "Exceeding Merry untill 3 a Clock in the Morning, from whence Went upon the Rake, coming home, still merry, at five."[3]

And yet, try as they would to imitate all the habits of well-born Englishmen, colonials were never entirely successful. Deference and gradation were nowhere as secure as they were in England. Nowhere was it true, as it still was and long would be in some parts of changing Britain, that the squire was in his hall, the parson in the church, the peasant at his plough, as it was in the beginning, is now, and ever shall be. In America deference to superiors, while often granted, was sporadic and unreliable: this was a constant complaint on the part of aspiring colonials as well as English visitors. No doors were securely shut: the new rich were trying to enter the ruling oligarchy, middle-class people were striving to be gentry; tradesmen, farmers, and artisans were insisting on taking part in politics, including church politics. Even those who had clearly made the grade could not always forget how recently they had made it: a Philadelphia merchant prince might well be the grandson of a humble Quaker artisan, the haughty Fitzhughs of Virginia were descended from an ancestor as ambiguous as an "armigerous maltster."[4]

However hard colonials tried to insist on their modernity, elegance, and taste, they seldom altogether succeeded in impressing English visitors. Some of these were indeed surprised by the neatness and comfort of colonial cities and still more by the polish of the best colonial society. Yet few visitors from the metropolis failed to rap the knuckles of the aspiring. Dr. Alexander Hamilton, a convivial Scotsman who in general enjoyed his tour of 1744, was annoyed by the New York "dons"

> who commonly held their heads higher than the rest of mankind and imagined few or none were their equals. But this I found always proceeded from their narrow notions, ignorance of the world, and low extraction, which indeed is the case with most of our aggrandized upstarts in these infant countrys of America who never had an opportunity to see, or if they had, the capacity to observe the different ranks of men in polite nations or to know what it is that really constitutes the difference of degrees.[5]

Below the ambitious and Anglophile upper crust came the large group of the solidly prosperous, and below these the "middling sort," including small merchants, successful artisans, and better-off farmers. This far down, society was more fluid than any in Europe. It was not uncommon for farmers, apprentices, and even indentured servants to rise rapidly to solid wealth. It is probably the rising middle class that formed the most perfect basis for the complacent opinions of the Moderate Enlightenment.

Yet the colonies were neither a paradise nor a democracy. Rising prosperity was not evenly distributed. Success, though possible, was chancy. There were many reasons, both economic and social, for insecurity. Studies of small towns have suggested that in the older areas of the colonies the supply of land per person was fast decreasing, some lands were becoming exhausted, while the frontier was neither near nor safe. In the cities new prosperity meant new specialization and for some, new relations of dependence. Foreign trade produced rapid ups and downs.

Bearing in mind all the changes going on, some of the new historians have suggested that late colonial society—or others would say, American society throughout the whole period covered by this book—was growing more discontented as it grew richer. Contentment is harder to measure even than riches, but it is clear enough that some people—even some white people—had neither. And the more some people prospered, the harder it was for those who did not, especially in a period which still had some traditions of fixed hierarchy and stability and had not fully developed a rationale for competitive struggle.

Aside from the tensions of uneven mobility, there were other sources of insecurity in this generally thriving society. Perhaps the most fundamental and most subtle was novelty itself. Colonists were aware that their society in some ways was breaking with precedent, and where there is conscious innovation there are both hopes and fears. Then as later one of the principal sources of American pride and insecurity was national and religious diversity. Though many observers reported that geographical and class differences of dialect were far less than in Britain, foreign languages were heard more. So generous a man as Franklin worried lest Pennsylvania become Germanized; travelers to Albany reported with irritation that one could not converse without knowing Dutch. Already stereotypes existed: Germans were dull-witted, the Dutch tight-fisted, the French frivolous, the Irish "teagues" hard-drinking and ignorant. Indians, on the frontiers a present danger, were everywhere a standing reminder of the failure of missionary work to spread Christian civilization and of the rapid abandonment of high intentions. Guilt about slavery and fear of blacks were more deeply buried. Yet Southern planters really knew that their imitation of the English country gentleman, the benevolent aristocrat surrounded by grateful and happy peasants, was false. In England, this image might require a certain degree of self-delusion; in Virginia, where the peasants were chattels, it amounted to farce. Sometimes, and not always in the South, guilt and fear broke through the surface in very ugly forms. New York in 1741 reacted with panic to an imaginary conspiracy; thirteen blacks were burned at the stake, eighteen hanged, and seventy transported.[6]

Religious diversity, the delight and astonishment of liberal visitors like St. Jean de Crèvecoeur, was seen by some colonials as the failure of high hopes for a city on a hill or a community of the pure. To others it suggested the loosening of a necessary social fabric. Boston and Philadelphia had lost their religious identity; New York had never had one; reports of travelers through the back country of the Carolinas suggested that the frontier was lapsing into sheer religious ignorance. It is not surprising that colonial society, with its unprecedented diversity and its feeble institutions, seemed to conservatives like Jonathan Boucher on the verge of falling apart:

> Though all nations no doubt are of one blood and kindred, and though therefore in the eye of reason and revelation every man is allied to every man as his neighbour and his brother, yet every observant man who has resided in America must have seen that men are less attached to each other, and the bond of social or political union is looser there than in almost every other country.[7]

Colonial population was increasing about twice as fast as English society, not only because of rapid immigration, but even more because of young marriages, higher birth-rates, and lower death-rates, especially of infants and children.[8] This kind of cheerful progress was much noted by colonials, and was the basis for many prophecies of future greatness. Yet the increase was not constant or even. It was checked regularly by epidemics, for which medicine had no real answers. New settlements suffered regularly from unexplained fevers; diphtheria raged among children; epidemics of smallpox, typhus, and yellow fever intermittently ravaged the towns. In the older sections, New England and Virginia, natural increase was slowing down. One historian goes so far as to say that "northern colonists had been too successful. Through their prosperity and their proliferation they had recreated the density of settlement and the intensity of disease they had left behind in Europe."[9]

One cannot read long in any collection of family letters without learning how frequent a visitor death was, or how ruthlessly and unexpectedly he swung his scythe. On colonial tombstones survivors are constantly urged to be always ready for the end. One of the highest forms of praise is the statement that the deceased "met the King of Terrors with fortitude." Thus despite comparative well-being no set of ideas that was too bland, none that failed to take account of sudden unpredictable disaster as well as progress and expansion, could fit the experience of all eighteenth-century Americans.

Fears and hopes, virtue, sin and guilt, were in this society, as in most, part of the province of religion. As we will see in detail shortly, colonial religion even more than any other aspect of colonial culture was a mixture of innovation and reaction. To religious conservatives, the ease and modernity in which some colonials rejoiced were a spiritual danger. Luxury and vice, which had destroyed Rome, seemed to be fast corrupting Britain and threatening her colonies. If American Protestants had not yet discovered that drinking was wicked, some of them were already alarmed by prostitution, which was becoming more open, and crime in the streets, which was growing. These and other evils were often linked in sermons with wealth, luxury, religious indifference, social pretentiousness, complacency, and the passing of the sound and simple manners of the past. All these, to some of the most fervently religious colonists, were signs of the times, indications that the retribution for apostasy and complacency were at hand. To others, these complaints were signs of ignorance and backwardness.

The self-conscious upper class was perhaps a phenomenon never quite reproduced in later America. For the rest, a large ill-defined middle class, confident and vigorous yet in some ways insecure, and below this people who had lost out in the struggle and resented those who had won—described in such general terms colonial society has much in common with American society later. Complacency, insecurity, ambition, jealousy, and reaction—there were reasons for all these in the social history of eighteenth-century America. All existed, and all affected the reception of current English books and ideas.

By mid-century the American provinces had a remarkably complete network of cultural institutions, and in all one could see much the same contrasting tendencies. On the one hand increasingly successful imitation of the metropolis, increasingly easy importation of its attitudes and customs, a striving for politeness and modernity. On the other, provincial biases, deeply bourgeois and, above all, invincibly Protestant.

In American society, as in most societies, it was assumed that the function of elementary and secondary education was mainly conservative.[10] For a long time, innovation in American schools was to be rare, and much of it was to originate with Europeans like Rousseau or Pestalozzi. It was, of course, rarest of all on the frontier.

From the very beginnings, the expressed purpose of colonial education had been to preserve society against barbarism, and, so far as possible, against sin. The inculcation of a saving truth was primarily the responsibility of the churches, but schools were necessary to protect the written word, the means of revelation. After the three R's came Latin and preferably a little Greek. This was equally taken for granted by town schools in Massachusetts, Quaker schools in Philadelphia, and private tutors in Virginia. The common languages of the learned were obviously necessary for those who would make the slightest pretensions to gentility. They were indispensable for the ministry, the law, or medicine. They were required for entrance to colleges; the effort of mastering them sharpened the faculties; classic texts, suitably selected, inculcated moral truth. By the middle of the eighteenth century critics, including Benjamin Rush and Benjamin Franklin, were suggesting that the ancient languages were not the most valuable equipment for an agricultural or commercial people, but they scored few successes.

The colonial colleges, founded like the lower schools to conserve tradition and transmit culture, had become mildly innovative in spite of themselves. The two English universities, Anglican, medieval in organization, and somnolent in spirit, offered few usable precedents. Colonial colleges consequently often looked for precedent and advice to the more lively Scottish universities and the far more innovative Dissenting academies of England.

Thus the curriculum was transitional. Latin and Greek were still the starting point, with a little Hebrew sometimes added. Logic and rhetoric were at once the means of cultivating a gentlemanly style and an avenue for the introduction of religious and political controversy. The New Learning of Newton and Locke, which had arrived with dramatic suddenness in the Dummer gift of books to Yale in 1714, had almost everywhere gained the victory over Protestant scholasticism by the middle of the century.[11] Natural philosophy, usually taught from the books of Newton's more pious popularizers, received some attention. For mental philosophy, students of course studied Locke's *Essay*. In the all-important field of moral philosophy, the Scottish writers were just beginning their long dominance.

Everywhere the method of instruction, recitations from memory on an assigned book, reflected the purpose of the colleges in the inculcation of strict principles, and everywhere strict rules showed an uneasy concern for the preservation of decorum and deference. Everywhere periodic student riots showed that these rules roused resentment. In their classes, their clubs, and their libraries, students encountered books and ideas that aroused more disturbing questions than their elders intended. The Founding Fathers were products of colleges which were conservative and didactic in intent but, fortunately, somewhat confused in practice.

Boards, presidents, and professors were the objects of recurrent outside attack—by conservative Calvinists who worried about Arminian gains at Harvard and even Yale, by revivalists who believed that conventional learning inhibited vital piety, by advocates of more utilitarian and less elegant objectives, by political and sectarian factions struggling for provincial power. The teapot tempests of these tiny colleges were, through the whole period of this book, among the most important registers of American ideological controversy. From the beginning, for better or worse, Americans took their colleges with intense seriousness, and not for granted. Nothing in the colonies remotely resembled the serene stagnation of Gibbon's Oxford.

Science, or "natural philosophy," an important secondary interest in the colleges, attracted still more attention outside them. Aside from the important dabblings of doctors, learned ministers, and private virtuosi, the colonies, in the period of rapid cultural advance immediately before the Revolution, could boast a sprinkling of full-time scientists. Useful inventions and interesting observations were regularly reported to the Royal Society by its American members and correspondents. Americans had formed one vigorous flourishing scientific society of their own and others were planned. In 1769 some of them had played a major part in a complex international enterprise, the observation of the transit of Venus.

In addition to the work of observing and classifying the flora and fauna of a new continent, some Americans had tried to join in the more general and theoretical work of understanding the universe. Sometimes, as in the case of Franklin, David Rittenhouse of Philadelphia, and John Winthrop IV of Harvard these efforts had resulted in serious contributions, perhaps a little too ecstatically assessed by their admirers. Mercy Warren, a close friend of Winthrop's wife, compared the Harvard scientist to the greatest astronomer of all:

> Tracing the depths of Nature's hidden Laws
> With Godlike Newton, mounts beyond the stars,
> And ranging o'er the vast ethereal plain
> Surveys each System of the wide domain.[12]

Already rash predictions were sometimes made about outstripping the Old World; already some were able to find an association between America, progress, and scientific achievement. If one forgets provincial hyperbole, the achievements of this scattered and busy people seem remarkable. It could well be argued that in the decades both before and after the Revolution American science was more impressive in relation to the means of the society than it was to be during most of the nineteenth century.

The literary culture of the colonies imitated that of England, with certain subtle and important differences. In England aristocratic patronage was still extremely important to men of letters, though a new middle-class public was growing fast.[13] This new public liked its literature to be didactic, exciting, and not too difficult; it enjoyed novels; it tolerated coarseness but not frivolity or cynicism.

John Adams once said that in New England an illiterate was as rare as a Jacobite or Roman Catholic, and he was right. The New England colonies, where education was basic to religion and provided by law, had reached almost universal male literacy. Through the colonies as a whole about two-thirds of the male population was literate, as against about 60 percent in England.[14]

In the colonies, no sinecures were offered to men of letters by great families, the government, or the church. Though coffee-houses and, despite religious opposition, theaters flourished increasingly in the cities, there was no great capital, no central gathering place for the witty and disaffected like London or Paris. Even more than in England, literature depended on the support of the rising middle class. Most well-to-do colonists welcomed, in ideas as in clothes or houses, whatever was useful, correct, and elegant; they rejected whatever was dubious, extravagant, or untried. Outside this group many Americans contented themselves with a Bible, a *Pilgrim's Progress*, a Foxe's *Book of Martyrs*, some almanacs, and a couple of manuals on medicine or farming.

Colonial publishing shows the immediate influence of two familiar and opposite kinds of people: the New England minister and the eclectic publisher-printer-bookseller whose most famous exemplar is Franklin. In the middle of the century an overwhelming but slowly decreasing majority of published items were sermons: formal utterances for funerals, ordinations, and elections, pieces of theological or moral exposition, and above all sectarian polemics. Provincial political controversy of all kinds produced a flow of pamphlets.

Newspapers, a major necessity for a dispersed provincial population in mid-century were still colonial in the most obvious manner. A large part of their content reported news from the courts of Europe, not only from London or Paris but from Berlin and Dresden, Naples, and even Constantinople. War in Europe or America was of course thoroughly reported, and sales, auctions, shipping news, and the official announcements of provincial authorities occupied much of the rest of the tiny sheets. For filler, colonial newspapers printed essays and poems sometimes imitated, but more often copied, from the *Gentlemen's* or *London Magazine*. So eagerly did provincial readers subscribe to these new repositories of middle-class metropolitan taste that efforts to found American magazines were short-lived and unsuccessful until well after the Revolution.

Already aspiring authors sounded complaints that were long to be familiar: of American concentration on material tasks, of lack of patronage and support. Polite Addisonian essayists expressed conventional hopes for the improvement of provincial taste, a few correct Augustan poets vainly implored the muse to wing her way to Schuylkill's groves or Hudson's noble stream.

Colonial demand for the latest English and Continental books was supplied by energetic printers and booksellers with surprising speed and completeness. Provincial preferences can be seen in lists of American editions of European authors, in catalogues of libraries and book sales, in the choice of books excerpted or serialized in the press, and in the references taken for granted in letters and speeches. All these show a remarkably catholic reception of European thought, with a certain time lag, and a clear preference for what was Protestant, Whiggish, moral, and moderate.

It was of course assumed that the Greek and Roman classics provided the basis of any gentleman's library. Even colonists who had forgotten their Latin and never learned Greek could read translations, and constantly encountered quotations and references. The lessons most often drawn from the ancients were those of Ciceronian virtue, Plutarchian heroism, the simple virtues extolled by Tacitus, political balance taught by Aristotle and Polybius. One cannot help guessing that the more sensitive readers must have found some of the ancients disturbing: Horace and Ovid were almost as widely read as Cicero, and a few colonists encountered even the sad and elegant materialism of Lucretius.

Of English authors, Shakespeare was taken for granted, despite the reservations of neoclassic critics. Milton, perhaps a little violent and extreme for modern taste, was less influential than he was to be in the nineteenth century. Of modern novelists, Smollett, Fielding, and especially Richardson were widely popular. An intriguing suggestion of Boston taste is given by Dr. Hamilton, who reports that the best sellers at an auction in the Puritan capital in 1744 were "Pamela, Anti-Pamela, The Fortunate Maid, Ovid's Art of Love, and the Marrow of Moderen [sic] Divinity."[15] Of all contemporary writers, however, the most praised and probably the most read were an odd pair: Alexander Pope and Joseph Addison.

Pope was the unquestioned arbiter of modern elegance. Frequently reprinted and constantly quoted, his most popular work was the *Essay on Man*. This magnificent compendium of Bolingbroke's somewhat stale deistic ideas, written by a Catholic, was praised even by orthodox ministers. It is hard to explain this fact except as a sheer triumph of style. Its combination of supreme complacency with cosmic doubt is not the sort of doctrine usually appreciated in America: Whatever is, is right, but the meaning of creation is clearly beyond human understanding and irrelevant to human aspirations.

Colonial worship of Addison is far more understandable. If the balanced and ordered splendor of the *Essay on Man* was occasionally attempted by colonials, the bland and sprightly prose of the *Spectator* was constantly imitated with fair success. A moderate in criticism as in everything, and a faithful Lockean, Addison allowed the unifying imagination a modest place among the faculties of the mind. Genius as well as taste had a place in poetry, just as a controlled wildness had its place in gardens. There is little to suggest that colonial taste went farther than this along the pre-romantic road.

A consistent enemy of upper-class vices, of gambling, obscenity, French foppery, and even décolletage, Addison praised cheerful, modest, natural manners. Neutral in politics, he was an orthodox Anglican in religion, equally opposed to infidelity and enthusiasm. His ultimate appeal to "our modern infidels" was hardly evangelical in tone:

I would therefore have them consider, that the wisest and best of men, in all ages of the world, have been those who lived up to the religion of their country, when they saw nothing in it opposite to morality, and to the best lights they had of the divine nature.[16]

Colonial readers of modern philosophy started with Locke's *Essay*, which they knew much better before the Revolution than his *Two Treatises on Government*. David Hume, who might have been supposed to epitomize as a Tory and a skeptic almost every idea to which colonials were hostile, was surprisingly widely known through both his history and his early essays, but had not yet reached the stature of a standing threat to religious and moral certainty. Perhaps this was part of the reason why the other Scottish thinkers, Hume's principal early opponents, were only beginning in the 1760's to become important. One must make an exception for Francis Hutcheson, whose moral sense theory influenced such opposite colonial thinkers as Jonathan Edwards and Charles Chauncy.

Most colonial libraries devoted a very high proportion of their shelves to divinity, and were surprisingly catholic in their choices. Calvin and other Calvinists were found in the libraries of Southern Anglicans, next to Jeremy Taylor's *Holy Living and Holy Dying*. Latitudinarian Anglicans were even more common in New England than Calvinists in the South. The three most read and quoted divines were the latitudinarian prelate John Tillotson, the cheerful and moderate Dissenter Philip Doddridge, and the Arian Samuel Clarke.

The deists, supposedly vanquished in argument yet still the subject of constant pulpit warnings, were more discussed than read. Deistic ideas were usually encountered in watered-down form, as in Pope. Wollaston's cautiously liberal *Natural Religion Delineated* was widely read, and found its way into even the orthodox libraries of two presidents of Princeton, Aaron Burr and John Witherspoon. Like Benjamin Franklin, many young men were probably converted to deism by reading works designed to counteract it, well-known books such as Charles Leslie's *Short and Easy Method*, John Leland's *View of the Principal Deistical Writers*, or Doddridge's *Three Discourses*.

Among political and historical writers, those most influential in the colonies were clearly those of Whiggish turn, and especially those radical and Dissenting Whigs who have drawn the attention of recent writers on the American Revolution. The most consistently popular of the seventeenth-century Commonwealth writers was probably Algernon Sidney, of the eighteenth-century radical revival Trenchard and Gordon, the authors of *Cato's Letters*.[17]

Some colonials read and even wrote French, a good many took lessons and used French phrases, and far more read French works in translation. In the imagination of the colonial Englishman, France played a complicated part: at once the dangerous enemy, the comic source of foppishness and frippery, and the grudgingly respected summit of refined taste. In their reading, colonials encountered at least three kinds of France: the neoclassical, the Protestant or Jansenist, and the Enlightened.

Probably little read, the French poets and critics of the seventeenth century were known through English commentators. By far the most popular of French traditions, however, ran through those who had been or were being defeated and suppressed. French Protestants had been influential since the days when Ramus's logic had dominated the founders of New England. Of Jansenists, Pascal was frequently quoted, and Franklin recommends the study of "Messrs of Port Royal." Fénelon was sufficiently suspect in France to be respected in America. The two most popular French authors (except Voltaire) were among the most popular and influential of all authors, the Protestant Paul (de Thoyras) Rapin and the Jansenist Charles Rollin.

Rapin, who followed William of Orange to England and fought against the Irish at the Boyne, was the author of an ultra-Whig history of England published in 1723. He attributed English liberty to the ancient Anglo-Saxon constitution, overthrown during the Middle Ages, revived through the efforts of the Puritans and Roundheads, and only fully restored in the Revolution of 1688. His history was gradually being displaced, to the regret of Thomas Jefferson and other Whigs, by Hume's new, delightful, but regrettably Tory *History of Great Britain*.

Rollin, who was deprived of his Paris rectorship for his Jansenist views in 1730, devoted his life to reconciling correct and classical learning with Christian morality. Both in his *Ancient History* and in his survey of *Belles Lettres*, Americans could follow the guidance of a Frenchman as impeccable in morals and religion as he was in taste and learning.

The most dangerous of all writers fairly widely read in the colonies was probably the French Protestant refugee Pierre Bayle. His *Dictionary*, bawdy and skirting the edge of atheism, seems now the obvious forerunner of Voltaire's *Philosophical Dictionary* and of the great *Encyclopédie*. (English colonists read the Voltaire *Dictionary* only rarely and hardly knew the *Encyclopédie* first-hand.) Actually Bayle's skepticism seems at times to run beyond that of either Voltaire or Diderot, and to point rather in the direction of Dodwell or even Hume. Destroying the rational arguments for religion, he destroys equally those of deist and Christian. He constantly insists, however, that he is doing this so that religious truth may rest on its true foundation, faith. Some modern critics take his fideism seriously and it must have helped make him acceptable to colonists, perhaps particularly to those inclined to radical Protestantism. Yet his tone is inescapably sardonic, and he insists on the necessity of faith far more than on its objects.

As for the French Enlightenment itself, as yet most literate colonists would probably have found the term startling and contradictory. *England* was the country of liberty and modernity. Yet two of the greatest spokesmen of Enlightened France were at least familiar names. American readers were barred by language from enjoying Voltaire's poetry, but his histories were widely read, and gave little offense. Americans reading the *Age of Louis XIV* can hardly have objected to Voltaire's condemning the persecution of French Protestants, and may not have noticed that he also condemned the Protestants themselves for foolish intransigence about unimportant matters. The *English Letters*, praising Locke and Newton, attacking France through its descriptions of British freedom, were naturally well received. Liberal Americans sometimes quoted Voltaire's dry comment on English religion, to the effect that one religion would have produced oppression, two would have set the English to cut each other's throats, but since there were so many, they lived together in peace and harmony. This comment on Dissent was apparently allowable to a learned and witty Frenchman, who was known to be still sharper in his comments on Catholicism. Only a few Americans seem before the Revolution to have read the unequivocally anti-Christian *Philosophical Dictionary*, which was published only in 1765. Sampled widely and talked about still more widely, Voltaire was known as the epitome of French polish and wit, not without a touch of French wickedness.

The most often praised and cited of the major French figures was the invincibly moderate and cautious Montesquieu. Like Locke, the author of the *Spirit of the Laws* was empirical, verbose, and inconsistent. Like Bayle, he was full of interesting tidbits of curious information. Perhaps a deist, he praised the Creator at the outset of his major work and after that treated religion in a relativist and utilitarian fashion not altogether unlike that of the English latitudinarians. Differing with Bayle, who respected an atheist more than a false believer, Montesquieu thought even a false religion desirable for the security of the state. His attitude toward the English government, however much based on misunderstanding, was flattering, and his generally relativist, pragmatic, and moderate tone exactly in line with the most advanced colonial preferences.

It is not surprising that the most challenging and radical writers of the Enlightenment were little known in America before the Revolution. The time lag in colonial reading was considerable, and the major radical works began to appear only in mid-century: the *Encyclopédie* from 1751, Hume's *Natural History of Religion* in 1755, Rousseau's *Émile* and *Social Contract* in 1762, Holbach's *Système de la Nature* in 1770. Of course, skepticism in religion, libertinism in morals, and materialism in philosophy had had their spokesmen since the Renaissance, or for that matter since the ancients. Yet only some, not all, kinds of European ideas had arrived with the settlers of America or been imported by their descendants. Authors like the atheist Hobbes or the antimoralist Mandeville, had little to say to the busy, serious Protestant inhabitants of British America, and such unsettling writers were in fact little read.

Benjamin Franklin, as always, embodied the preferences of many contemporaries when he urged that students of the new Philadelphia Academy should learn English grammar from "some of our best writers as Tillotson, Addison, Pope, Algernon Sidney, Cato's Letters, etc."[18] In literature as in life, most of the prosperous or rising Americans who bought modern books preferred whatever was solid, sensible, cheerful, and also, if possible, elegant. Only a few toyed, usually in private, with the more dangerous and skeptical varieties of modern thought. The writers of the Commonwealth tradition, we may guess, appealed to those who were for one reason or another discontented with modernity and prosperity. And of course surveys of library contents say very little about the preferences of the majority of Americans. Older loyalties, more desperate needs, and less elegant lives made many, in mid-century, seek assurances that could not be provided by Tillotson, Doddridge, or Addison or even, entirely by Locke, Rapin, or *Cato's Letters*.

Three *The Age of Reason and the Age of Enthusiasm*

Intellectual movements usually become self-conscious only when they have to defend themselves against attack. Until the middle of the eighteenth century, neither Enlightenment nor Protestantism was the slogan of a party in America; most Americans considered themselves enlightened British Protestants. In the 1740's and 1750's, partisans of order, balance, reason, and moderation were placed on the defensive by a revival of religious enthusiasm. Rather suddenly, and at about the same time, the doctrines and tastes of the Age of Reason were challenged by Wesleyans in England, by Jansenist convulsionaries in France (where the last remnants of militant apocalyptic Protestantism had just been suppressed by force), and by a host of Awakeners in America. Throughout the 1740's and into the 1750's, revival crackled, exploded, and burned out in one place after another throughout the colonies. Everywhere it aroused the opposition of partisans of the Moderate Enlightenment. Though the war between reason and emotion has never really ended either in American religion or American culture, this particular battle had died down by about 1760. In the struggle against revivalism and popular emotion, the Moderate Enlightenment was both defined and limited.

To believers in progress, rationality, balance, order, and moderation, outbursts of religious emotion were (and are) alarming, disgusting, and inexplicable. When the revivals began defenders of rationality feared a return of the dreamers and ranters of the seventeenth century. Contemporary critics could not understand why this outburst of enthusiasm took place in the middle of an enlightened age. Historians looking back, asking why the Great Awakening took place when it did, have also failed to find clear and definite reasons.

Many historians have looked hard for social explanations. It seems clear that in about 1750, in society as well as in religion, complacency seemed to be giving way to displacement, upheaval, and discontent. The major Awakeners were hardly social radicals: John Wesley was a political conservative and Jonathan Edwards was hardly concerned with politics at all. Yet it seems to be the case that the New Light of revival shone most brightly for those groups who were discontented or displaced, and not for the beneficiaries of the social order. In England, revivalism flourished mainly among the classes directly affected by the upheavals of the industrial revolution; in America, the Great Awakening started and spread mainly among the less prosperous farming regions. Landed aristocrats in England, planters or large merchants in America were only occasionally caught by the movement.[1]

Some historians associate the Awakening not only with social change but with change of style, and see in it something at least analogous to the move from neoclassic to romantic taste. Instead of correctness and balance in poetry, self-examination, inwardness, meditation on death, tears and transports fascinated young writers as well as young preachers. Methodists admired graveyard poets like Edward Young and James Thompson. Not only revivalists and poets, but also such various people as the gloomy Christian apologist Joseph Butler, the mystic William Law, even Edmund Burke, even Jean-Jacques Rousseau agreed in opposing complacent rationalism, though in nothing else.

For whatever reasons, the tidal variation between ages of complacency and ages of discontent, between satisfaction and longing, reason and (loosely speaking) romanticism, seems to run through all history.[2] Perhaps this is because human achievements all fail eventually to satisfy the human spirit. Perhaps what needs explaining is not the mid-century challenge to the doctrines of balance and order with their complacent corollaries, but rather the fact that these had held sway so long. Arguments demonstrating that whatever was, was right can never have satisfied people who knew that their lives were less than happy and their hopes unfulfilled. Even, or rather especially, when society seems reasonably stable and reasonably progressive, human beings long for fulfillment, reassurance, and certainty. It is these feelings that express themselves in revivals of religion. It does not make these deep emotions less genuine, nor does it assume any crude social interpretation of religion to point out, as the authors of the Gospels pointed out, that religious emotions seldom strike first or hardest among the rich.

Those who feel this sort of emotion and those who do not never understand each other. In the middle of the eighteenth century, partisans of the Moderate Enlightenment judged revivalists to be enthusiasts, madmen, dangerous levelers, crazy reactionaries; revivalists in turn thought those who opposed them to be hard-hearted, dull-souled, and headed for perdition. Somewhat similarly, in the middle of the twentieth century, ill-defined discontents and emotional needs were expressed in the revolt of youth. As in the eighteenth century, believers in progress and reason were outraged and hostile to movements that seemed anti-intellectual. As in the eighteenth century, their hostility and contempt were returned in kind by the partisans of peace and love.

In the Great Awakening of the mid-eighteenth century, the nature of the revival in each country was affected by the religious establishment against which it had to revolt. In England, John Wesley, trying to enliven but not to overturn the Church of England, was constantly placed on the defensive by accusations of enthusiasm, leveling, and (more oddly) popery. Thus it was necessary for him constantly to demonstrate his loyalty to Church and king, and to insist on his hostility both to sectarians and Catholics. To the common people, whom he reached as nobody else could with his simple message of comfort and inner change, he insisted that the constitution of Great Britain held all the freedom anybody could want. Through strict discipline, ingenious mechanisms of control like class-meetings and Sunday schools, and through emphasis on sober conduct, Wesley and his immediate successors managed to keep enthusiasm from taking off as it had in the seventeenth century on the road to wild antinomian radicalism. Somewhat earlier than America, England was to develop (in Methodism) a popular religion which would fit many of the needs of nineteenth-century British social order, combining an outlet for emotion and a vehicle for humanitarian reform with a new kind of respectability.

In America the dominant religion was Calvinism. This meant that both establishment and revolt had elements in them which were at once deeply conservative and potentially revolutionary. American Protestants did not believe that they were followers of a new variety of Christianity set forth in Calvin's *Institutes*, but rather that they clung to the unchanging truth. This truth, set forth in the Bible once and for all, explained and defended by fathers and councils in the first centuries of the Church, had been diabolically perverted during the dark ages of papal oppression. Then it had been gloriously rescued by the reformers, and in modern times the essentials had been authoritatively stated at Dort in 1632 and above all at Westminster in 1647. This central Calvinist formulary, reproduced countless times in American creedal statements, started from the existence and nature of God, "immutable, immense, eternal, incomprehensible, almighty, most wise, most holy, most free, most absolute," who had decreed all things from the beginning of time. To his creature, Man, God had given free will, and he had voluntarily made a covenant with Adam promising eternal life in return for complete obedience. Adam, however, had used his free will to break this contract, thus entailing eternal and merited punishment upon himself and his posterity forever. Out of his mercy, however, God had made a second covenant, the "Covenant of Grace," through which he freely offered men salvation through Jesus Christ, whom he had sent to undergo the punishment deserved by men. This sacrifice had made it possible for some men to believe, repent, and be saved. These elect had been known and chosen since before the beginning of time. Obviously, their salvation had nothing to do with their merits; indeed the works, however beneficial in themselves, of those who were not chosen were sinful and repugnant to God.

This creed, often referred to as "the Scheme of Grace" as against "the Scheme of Works" was to deists barbarous and grotesque, to liberal Christians immoral and embarrassing. To many, it was saving truth. To expect God to behave according to a human code of morality was in the first place blasphemous, in the second unimaginative. Moreover, it did not accord with the life experience of many people. The very grimness and arbitrariness of the ancient doctrines seemed to many to accord with their personal knowledge of life and death, in which it was obvious that reward was not according to merit. Both sides in the dispute sought for a kind of assurance. To deists and liberals, either the world was essentially moral, or all was chaos. To Calvinists, either God was sovereign, or all was confusion.

In America Congregationalists and Presbyterians, members of the German and Dutch Reformed churches, most Separatists and Baptists concurred on the Calvinist essentials. This does not mean of course that all

these people, in bustling and changing eighteenth-century America, devoted their lives to the contemplation of the Westminster articles. For
most inhabitants of the American colonies in the eighteenth century,
Calvinism was not quite in the position of scholasticism in the high
Middle Ages or Marxism-Leninism in the Soviet Union, since other
doctrines were heard. It was rather, perhaps, in the position of economic
laissez-faire in mid-nineteenth-century England or democracy in twentieth-century America: the normal doctrine received by good citizens
with different degrees of conviction, with a good deal of social pressure
and academic authority behind it. One can argue the meaning of such
a belief-system, and it can be stated in very many ways. One can pay it
lip-service and then ignore it. To rebel against it directly, however, takes
daring, and rebels themselves cannot escape the influence of beliefs and
emotions in which they have been brought up.

The Calvinist outlook entailed a view of history which put those who
held it in an odd relation, at once radical and reactionary, to the doctrines of the Moderate Enlightenment. On the one hand, God's inscrutable plan might well entail a continuation of the victories over his enemies which had so clearly begun in the Reformation, and the English
were especially charged with the burden and glory of the battle. To
Englishmen in America, the forces of darkness, represented by French
forts and French-led scalping parties, were especially concrete. In all
probability, the final victory not only against Catholic France but also
over the ultimate Enemy was close at hand. All intensely religious Americans longed for the millennium, for Christ's second coming and the
thousand-year reign of peace and justice. Thus Calvinism made people
look to the future more than the past. Yet history and prophecy both
suggested that God's victories would be won by many only through sacrifice and tribulation, all deserved by man's colossal failures. In comparison with the heroic days of the sixteenth and seventeenth centuries,
there seemed to many little doubt that the present was a time of degeneration, and one form of degeneration was religious lukewarmness. False
doctrine and dangerous luxury were spreading outward through the English world from the corrupt center. Thus the task of revival as the word
implies, was to recapture truths once firmly held and to defend them
against all forms of modern degeneracy.

American Christendom was full of paradoxes in form as well as doctrine. Starting with an ideal of purity and dedication, it had been forced

by circumstances to become plural, decentralized, and by contemporary standards tolerant. Toleration, by no means universal or complete, had come about through inescapable differences among the churches and within each, through the pressures of a politically Anglican but theologically indifferent central government, and through lack of means of control in a scattered, expanding, migrating society. Thus real prescription and enforcement were impossible, and yet orthodoxy remained an all-important ideal. Education, propaganda, and ostracism had all proved insufficient. Revivalism was the only remaining tactic.

During most of the eighteenth century, New England was the doctrinal center of American Calvinism. Despite much fragmentation and erosion, New England still possessed a historical theory, a social ideal, a set of institutions designed to make both concrete, and a close-knit, well-trained ministerial elite to preside over enforcement.

The mission of New England—an errand into the wilderness, a pattern, a refuge for the true church in evil days—had been often redefined. It was still stated in terms of its great antetype Israel: a nation chosen, watched over, specially favored and specially punished. The great essential for any society was pure religion. In New England Calvinist belief and history had combined to produce a concomitant social ideal, which combined frugality and essential equality with a due but subtle respect for family, station, and education. Above all, religious and social stability depended on order, and this in turn on the consensus of all decent people. Public opinion was the real means of enforcement of these values, and ministers still considered it their duty to educate public opinion. In theory and sometimes in practice, they could still reason with the backslider, try to reform the sinner, and expel the rebel.

This was the tradition, still powerful as an ideal despite the fact that the ideal had never been satisfactorily embodied in practice. By 1750 the mission was clouded and the institutions of church and state challenged. Migration and new immigration had threatened the old unities; new possibilities of wealth and power had led some to forget the old values; shortage of land had made it impossible for others to maintain a decent independence; contentiousness and competition had invaded church and town. And yet, all through the century, enough was left of the old ideal to be recognizable, much as the medieval pattern of village and strip farming is sometimes discernible from the air when one flies over modern Europe.

The New England religious establishment was by no means ranged unequivocally against all aspects of the Moderate Enlightenment. Both reason and science, properly defined, had always been welcomed by Puritans. For most purposes, the Newtonian universe and the Christian miracles could still be reconciled. Natural law was God's usual way of enforcing his will. Like the rest of his plans for us it was in the long run beneficial, and it could be set aside at his sovereign pleasure. Yet a constant harping on the glories and regularities of the physical universe had its dangers in New England as elsewhere. It could lead people to forget that for Christians God is ruler as well as creator, that what we see and reality are not the same thing, that the universe in the long run is mysterious.[3] It could lead, as in an unguarded moment it had led even Alexander Pope, to the crass conclusion that whatever is, is right.

Arminianism, Arianism, and deism, were the subject of occasional warnings rather than panic. With some difficulty and dubious success, ministers who openly renounced the Westminster doctrines could be eased out of their pulpits and then prevented by the state from exercising clerical functions (since a minister without a church, in Congregational tradition, was an impossibility). It was, however, impossible for the guardians of orthodoxy to do anything about those who subscribed formally to the traditional doctrines but preached natural religion or—still worse—mere morality.

Thus the position of the late colonial clergy was unenviable. Their authority was limited, their status insecure, their duties at once all-important but ill-defined. Where they were still centrally important, they were denounced and lampooned. Far worse, where the indifference of the age had spread most widely, they were beginning to be ignored.[4] Their most common complaint was not either heresy or apostasy, though both were serious, but rather the growing "neglect of the ordinances." Too many people were staying away from church, and above all too few were making the efforts demanded as the price of church membership. Where membership was made too difficult, people were discouraged; where too easy, they became indifferent. Everywhere there were complaints of false doctrine, greed, vice, even blasphemy, but the center of the problem lay in what would now be called secularism, and was then more likely to be referred to as Vanity, Worldliness, and Pride. This can also be referred to by a historian as the spirit of the age: a product of the mild breezes of English rationalism playing on the peculiar colonial landscape. The revivals were directed not so much against the Moderate Enlightenment, as against the whole social and emotional tendency of which it was an expression.

———————

The first and greatest figure of the Awakening, Jonathan Edwards, was also its least typical. Like most profound thinkers, he cannot be fitted into any category. Despite his eager appropriation of Locke and Newton and Hutcheson for his own purposes, he was not a man of the moderate, rational English Enlightenment of his day. Indeed he was the most powerful enemy of that way of thought. To Locke or Clarke, Tillotson or Tindal, greatly though they differed, the universe was orderly, intelligible, and moral; man was learning to understand it and could order his life accordingly. Edwards's universe was orderly and intelligible only on its surface. The operations of the mind, the relation of subject and object, the existence of personal identity were all, like the rotations of the planets, dependent on the exertion, from minute to minute, of God's inscrutable will. God himself was utterly unlike the prime mover of the deists or the benevolent contriver of natural religion, and not much more like the loving father of sentimental piety. Sometimes in Edwards's writings, he seemed a personification of ultimate reality, which must be accepted, worshipped, not fully understood, and never judged. "We cannot rationally doubt, but that things which are *divine,* that appertain to the Supreme Being, are vastly different from the things that are *human.*"[5] Human knowledge, much as Edwards delighted in it, was essentially worthless without divine illumination. The prudential Addisonian virtues were worse than useless; human virtue consisted only in selfless love of being in general, a quality unattainable by human effort alone. The Arminian, compromising, complacent spirit of the age was the worst enemy.

No more than he was a man of the Enlightenment was Edwards a founder of the American religious way of life. Busy, divided, generally optimistic but insecure, soon to be cut off still more sharply from its past, American society needed a religion which would control behavior as well as belief. Edwards's inscrutable God could not be drafted into the task of social control, and no society could have based its existence on his idealist metaphysics and absolutist ethics. The marvel is that he affected American culture as deeply as he did. His arsenal of arguments made it possible for any serious student to blow Arminianism out of the deep water. His works, for two generations, were quoted from Scotland to South Carolina, among Baptists and Methodists as well as Congregationalists and Presbyterians. His adherents dominated the Connecticut Valley for the next generation, and the most important New England seminaries for most of a century.

Yet Edwards's intellectual empire, like all empires, proved transitory. Edwards was not the forerunner of Jefferson and Jackson, as one student has curiously suggested,[6] nor would he have approved the giants of nineteenth-century popular Calvinism, Lyman Beecher and Charles Grandison Finney, who gave him nominal allegiance—still less their successors from Moody to Billy Graham. Edwards believed in recognizing and channeling human emotions, which were entirely necessary to the work of grace. He never approved, however, adapting what he saw as religious truth to accommodate human weakness. His vision of a community dedicated to the intellectual love of God, is hardly incarnate in the United States of America. It is rather, perhaps, the greatest of American lost causes, appealing powerfully to the numerous enemies of American optimism and materialism from Hawthorne and Melville to Perry Miller.

In his own day, though Edwards provided the most powerful defense of revivalism, the defense was a qualified and discriminating one. The New Light led its followers past him, first into simpler and easier ways and then into darker and wilder ones. Probably the most effective enemy of modern rationalism and decline, in New England as elsewhere, was, curiously, an Englishman and an Anglican, George Whitefield. A Calvinist who broke with his friend and ally John Wesley over the doctrine of predestination, Whitefield was nevertheless not one to insist on theological subtleties. Warm-hearted, simple, rather ignorant, combative, and generous, he knew when to conciliate his opponents and when to provoke a confrontation, when to comfort and when to shock. He could protest his loyalty to the Church and say that there was no more Christianity in Tillotson than in Mahomet, he could praise New England's institutions and bait her colleges. He had, that is, the gift for timing that is essential to all great actors and evangelists, and 1740 was his day.

By then the revival was general and had called forth a host of able,

pious, and often learned spokesmen. It had also produced its own caricature in James Davenport, who according to hostile observers made a
bonfire not only of the books of Tillotson and other liberal divines, but
threw in the silks and laces of his female admirers and finally even his
own plush breeches.[7] Far more important than Davenport, and in the
long run more destructive to the established New England religious system, were the courageous and simple Separatists and Baptists who in
town after town, against hostility and persecution, held out against uniformity.

By 1750 the Awakening had burned itself out in New England, leaving the "standing order" in disarray. In some towns two ministers struggled for legal recognition, in others separate churches, Baptist or ultra-
Calvinist, demanded that their members be exempted from church
taxes; everywhere controversy among ministers had increased the choices
and therefore the power of laymen.

Yet it is a mistake to think of the established New England clergy of
the second half of the eighteenth century as a negligible force. When
they spoke to popular emotions, as they sometimes still did, they could
exert formidable power. The new methods of revival, though dangerous,
were effective. Ministers were still paid from taxes. They still harangued
the faithful several times a week, and they had not given up the right
to rebuke individuals. On Election or Fast Days, the governor and General Court still assembled to hear how they had failed in their appointed
duties. The bands, the gold-headed canes and cocked hats, the red-painted
gates which John Adams remembered, could impress a village community
as deeply as priestly robes.

More importantly, the New England ministers were sustained by their
own character, ability, and learning. In many towns the minister was not
only the best-educated man but the one most in touch with the outside
world. Some kept up a busy correspondence with eminent Scottish and
English divines. And in time of common danger, they could call on new
allies a little to the south.

In the Middle colonies, the Great Awakening grew out of religious
chaos, and ended in relative order. In this region, Anglicans, Quakers,
and Calvinists speaking three languages were the principal groups;
smaller but important ones included Lutherans, Moravians, Schwenk-
felders, Dunkers, and several kinds of Baptists. All groups found it difficult, and most impossible, to provide ministers for their scattered congre-

gations and all reported heavy inroads of unbelief, blasphemy, and above all indifference. Yet unsatisfied seekings and longings were everywhere apparent, and they found their fulfillment. Revivalism, beginning among the German sects, next affected the Dutch Reformed in the Raritan Valley and then broke out powerfully among the Presbyterians.

Presbyterians were of two kinds, some stemming from New England and the rest Scotch-Irish newcomers. The latter, whose stern and somewhat literal faith had been forged in the tragic conflict with the Catholic Irish on the one hand and the English establishment on the other, believed above all in the necessity of preserving the Westminster articles and enforcing subscription to them. To the New Englanders, forced subscription was un-Protestant and destroyed genuine inward faith. Thus it was especially significant that the Presbyterian revival was led by a man from Ulster who had been much affected by a New England sojourn, William Tennent. William's son Gilbert Tennent became the principal exhorter of the fiery New Jersey revival.

To the conservative, mostly Scotch-Irish Synod of Philadelphia, the only acceptable ministers were those trained in Scotland or Ireland, and the revival seemed subversive both of faith and order. Using the ample powers afforded by Presbyterian organization, the Synod seemed about to squash the revival, when the Tennents and their friends were rescued by the arrival of Whitefield. Working closely with Presbyterian revivalists, the great Anglican maverick carried the fight into the enemy's country, drawing immense crowds and causing the building of a gigantic tabernacle in Philadelphia itself. Meanwhile the increasingly fiery attacks of Gilbert Tennent and others on the "dumb dogs," the learned, complacent, and rationalistic section of the Presbyterian clergy, brought about actual schism. From 1741 to 1748 American Presbyterianism was divided between Old Side and New (revivalist) Side. It was reunited almost entirely on New Side terms, and the victorious revivalists began to become moderate and conciliatory. The Presbyterian Church, well-organized, united, and truly national, became the most powerful American religious organization for the next generation and thus a major protagonist in our story.

In the South, the Church of England, established by law and somewhat sleepy, dominated tidewater Virginia and Maryland. Since about 1740 it had been gradually forced to concede toleration to the Presbyterians in the Shenandoah Valley. These orderly and mostly Scotch-Irish

Dissenters were led by the redoubtable Samuel Davies, a missionary from New Jersey. By 1750, when Davies left to become president of Princeton, Presbyterianism was strong in the piedmont and had penetrated the tidewater. Yet, partly because of the Presbyterian insistence on education and order, the Presbyterian Church could never dominate the unlettered and unorganized Southern frontier.

In 1755 Separate Baptists from Connecticut began a shouting, falling revival among the unchurched people of Sandy Creek, North Carolina. Never concealing their hate and fear of the Episcopal establishment, suffering mob violence and official imprisonment, the Separate Baptists spread through North Carolina and especially Virginia very rapidly, assimilating earlier established Baptist bodies and fighting for absolute equality. Meantime, by the early 1770's, the Methodists had arrived and were reaping harvests from the midst of the established Church.

Farther to the south, the piedmont of the Carolinas, according to Churchmen and Dissenters alike, was filled with blasphemers and gamblers, believers in everything and nothing, and was in danger of falling into barbarism. In Charleston, the highly civilized little capital of the wealthy Low Country, the Church of England uneasily shared power with equally well-organized Dissenters. Whitefield, traveling tirelessly up and down the South, was tolerantly received in Virginia, founded his orphanage in the new colony of Georgia where the Wesleys had prepared his way, and in Charleston berated the Anglican commissary to his face for tolerating assemblies and balls.

Thus Southern religion, a most important and neglected chapter of American history, barely began to take its characteristic shape. The shaken establishment still dominated tidewater Virginia and feebly claimed the whole region. In practice it shared power with Presbyterians and did its best to fight off Baptists. Baptists and emerging Methodists, still persecuted, retained their cutting edge. Both were still at war with planter society, denouncing it for deist tendencies, luxurious habits, and (as yet) the sin of slaveholding.

By 1750 the Great Awakening had both strengthened and weakened American Protestantism, divided it, and begun to define its complex relation to the Enlightenment. It had, first, given Calvinism a new vitality. All the principal pre-Revolutionary revivalists—Edwards, the Tennents and their friends, Whitefield, most Separatists and Baptists—saw themselves as reasserting the doctrines of divine sovereignty and human dependence, and thereby following not so much Calvin as Christ.

Yet it is almost always true that defenders of a great doctrine change it and make it their own, and the Calvinism of the Great Awakening was a new Calvinism. However much the revival preachers sought to convince their congregations of their desperate inability to save themselves, they also urged them to make the effort, to throw off their sloth, to cease their resistance. Calvinism on the attack, either rationalized or emotionalized, had come a long way from Geneva or Westminster.

Second, the Awakening increased the strong millennial tendency of American religion. Some of its preachers believed in the hopeful interpretation of prophecy, teaching that the thousand-year reign of Christ would precede, not follow, the fiery judgment. Many, like Edwards, wondered if the Awakening itself was not the beginning of that great good time, and looked for other certain signs: the downfall of the papal Antichrist, the conversion of the Jews and heathen. In these great events, the New World seemed destined to have a special role. The search for "Signs of the Times" thus pointed toward Manifest Destiny, and was soon to affect the way many people saw the French War, two revolutions, and the successive waves of Enlightened doctrine.

Third, and more immediately important for our story, the Awakening sharpened and dramatized the conflict between piety and the rationalism of the Moderate Enlightenment. Many Americans tried to keep a foot in each camp. The most fervent pietists and the most sincere rationalists, however, could not help making enemies of each other. Excited partisans of the Awakening, horrified by rationalist inroads, could not help calling the moderate clergy drunkards, adulterers, and fornicators. More cautious revivalists could be more irritating, praying that those who resisted them be forgiven their stubbornness and brought to see the light.

Often the subjectivity of the Awakeners sounded both anti-rational and anti-intellectual. Even Edwards, the greatest systematic thinker of the day, was sure that "The least beam of the light of the knowledge of the glory of God in the face of Jesus Christ is worth more than all the human knowledge that is taught in all the most famous colleges and universities in the world."[8] The New England Separatists in one of their early conventions confessed that some of their misguided members "were for destroying human Learning, and even human reason itself, as useless in Religion."[9]

The immediate effect of the revivals seemed often enough to lead people to a morbid concern with the details of conduct, a preoccupation with such matters as dancing and cards which was to disfigure American Christianity for a long time. Beneath this kind of censoriousness lay a fear of passion, especially sexual passion. At the other extreme, however, the certainty of assurance could produce a tendency to believe that a converted person could do no wrong. At the fringes of the Awakening, according to its concerned friends as well as its enemies, one could find "spiritual marriage" or free union, self-deification, even justified murder.[10]

In their determination to induce the feeling of hopelessness that was a necessary antecedent to the dawn of hope, even the more moderate revival preachers constantly harped on the terrors of eternal fire and the undying worm in physical terms, which repelled the fastidious. Finally, of course, there were endless instances, endlessly exaggerated, of falling, shouting, and speaking with tongues.

Thus the partisans of order, of intellect, of rationality—those to whom colonial life was steadily growing more civilized, more English, more pleasant, those who loved Addison and admired Pope—could not help taking alarm. Among the opponents of the Awakening were many utterly sincere Christians as well as many to whom religious feeling was a matter of hearsay. Not only were the revivalists destroying church order and social seemliness, they were making nonsense of the rational and moral teachings of modern Christianity. At their worst they were both superstitious and blasphemous, and in their facile separation between the saved and the lost, supremely arrogant. Not far beneath the counterattacks of Boston Arminians, Old Side Philadelphia Presbyterians, or Virginia Episcopalians were quite obvious feelings of class; the revivalists were stirring up the ignorant rabble, to the prejudice of social as well as moral order.

By 1750, opposition to the Awakeners had brought out in the open the latent Arminian rationalism of the clergy of eastern Massachusetts. These depended on Arminius far less even than the Calvinists on Calvin;

their European sources were the respectable mainstays of the Moderate Enlightenment: Locke, Clarke, Tillotson and those Dissenters who tended toward rationalism. Like English Churchmen and Dissenters fifty years earlier, they moved very gradually from one position to another, starting not with attack but with sincere defense of tradition as they understood it.[11] They and their opponents stuck to the rules. One published a sermon which moved from a text to its general consequences and particular applications, dealing scrupulously with all possible objections. It is of course not every form of religion that can be set forth in "Some Remarks on the Recent Sermon of the Reverend Mr. X., delivered in reply to the Animadversions of the Reverend Mr. Y." Polite sarcasm was allowable; textual sloppiness disastrous.

The essence of the Arminian attack on the ultra-Calvinist doctrines of the revivalists was that these were conducive to laziness and immorality. In 1749 Lemuel Briant of Braintree preached a sermon at the West Church, in Boston, called "The Absurdity and Blasphemy of Depretiating [*sic*] Moral Virtue." Meeting the ultra-Calvinists head-on, Briant chose one of their favorite texts, Isaiah's reference to the filthy rags of righteousness. The prophet referred, said Briant, only to a time of special wickedness among the Jewish people; those who misused this text misinterpreted "the pure and perfect religion of Jesus, which contains the most refined System of Morality the World was ever blessed with; which every where considers us as moral Agents, and suspends our whole Happiness upon our *personal* good Behaviour." They turn this admirable system into "a mysterious Faith, a senseless Superstition, and a groundless Recumbency; and, in short, every thing but what in Fact it is, viz. a Doctrine of Sobriety, Righteousness, and Piety."[12]

Charles Chauncy, the most effective because the most moderate of Edward's opponents, admitted that he found it hard to defend the doctrine of free will, and to reconcile it with God's sovereignty. He concluded that this problem was "too great and deep for us to fathom." Yet belief in human freedom, however difficult, was morally necessary, and without it the world "at once falls into desolation and utter ruin."[13] One is tempted to see in this strenuous and truly pragmatic argument the beginning of a current in New England intellectual history which led eventually all the way to William James's will to believe. Jonathan Mayhew, a younger, bolder, and less subtle man, said that all Christianity consisted of three simple, strenuous propositions:

I. THAT there is a natural difference between truth and falshood [*sic*], right and wrong.

II. THAT men are naturally endowed with faculties proper for the discerning of these differences.

III. THAT men are under obligation to exert these faculties; and to judge for themselves in things of a religious concern.[14]

To these Bostonians, effort and character, not passive conversion, were the foundations of morality.

Not only, the Arminians insisted, did Christianity offer a system of morality, it confirmed the moral truths which we could see by the light of reason. Until the time of Emerson, most New England Arminians and Unitarians, like English latitudinarians, found a useful function for the Biblical miracles as a quick teaching method for simple folk. Yet even Andrew Eliot, one of the more moderate of the Arminians, put rationality above not only Scripture but divine powers: "There is nothing in Christianity that is contrary to reason. God never did, He never can, authorize a religion opposite to it, because this would be to contradict himself." Christianity, to Eliot, was the religion of nature "with some wise and merciful additions."[15]

The religion of New England Arminians, as it had been worked out by 1750, was the moderate English rationalism adapted to a Calvinist audience. It was one version of the major religious task confidently undertaken by the Moderate Enlightenment, the effort to show that Christianity was everywhere both moral and intelligible. In 1750 most Arminians in New England continued to use the orthodox vocabulary in their arguments and remained within the established Congregational Church. Thirty years later, their rationalism was to lead them farther afield, to a denial of Hell and a tacit disbelief in the Trinity.

The rational God was also a benevolent one. Once one took it for granted, as the Arminians did, that his purpose was our happiness rather than his glory, Hell was doomed. Charles Chauncy, bellicose in argument but always somewhat timid in doctrine, suppressed for twenty years his conclusion that eternal punishment made no sense. As he published it, in 1784, his book on *The Salvation of All Men* does not seem very startling to a modern reader. Like all the Arminians, Chauncy strongly opposes deists and skeptics and deduces his conclusions from Scripture.

He insists that future punishment will be sufficiently prolonged and painful so that knowledge of it may still serve as an effective deterrent. Nonetheless, eventually, after we suffer enough to vindicate divine justice, it must be part of God's benevolent plan to reconcile us all to himself.

The doctrine of the Trinity was a more dangerous subject even than eternal punishment, and one which the liberals of New England tended to avoid. A satirical remark about its mysteries made by Mayhew in 1755 gave great offense.[16] Yet the moralistic and individualistic religion of the Arminians left little meaning for the Trinity and little function for its members. Unitarianism, in the late eighteenth century, remained latent much as Arminianism had been before 1750; a later phase of the battle with the Calvinists was to force it into the open.

To historians who look at them closely, as to many of their contemporaries, the liberal heroes of the Boston establishment are not altogether attractive people. Despite their courage and rationality, there is something both timid and nonrational in their frequent retreat from the deep waters of determinism and free will, or their avoidance of the problem of evil. They were likely to clinch their arguments by appealing to something like the common conclusions of all educated men, and in this appeal there was something unmistakably snobbish. Condemning revivalists for their rudeness, the Arminians were likely themselves to display a good deal of hostility and contempt:

> . . . tho' the unthinking Multitude may be best pleased with that they understand least, and be carried away into any Scheme, that generously allows them the Practice of their Vices, tho' every Article be a down right Affront to common Sense; yea, by a few rabble charming Sounds be converted into such fiery Bigots as to be ready to die in the Defense of Stupidity and Nonsense, as well as to kill (and that purely for the Glory of God) all that are so *heretical* and *graceless* as not to renounce their Reason in complaisance to their sovereign Dictates; notwithstanding all this, I say; There always was and always will be some in the World (alas that their Number is so few) that have Sense eno' and dare trust their own Faculties so far, as to *judge in themselves what is right*.[17]

These defenders of moderation were in their own eyes a saving remnant. Anathema to most American and even New England Protestants, they had by the time of the Revolution a solid base in Cambridge and Boston. By 1750, Boston religion was a post-Calvinist adaptation of the Moderate English Enlightenment. By 1850 it had changed very little in essential doctrine, and a whole culture, both moderate and enlightened, had grown around it.

Not daunted in the least by the Arminian challenge, the defenders of New England's Calvinist heritage rushed eagerly into battle. In their long polemic argument with the rationalists, most of the articulate defenders were forced to surrender some crucial territory.

The most eager fighters against the liberal menace were the immediate heirs of Edwards, who in their defense of the old doctrines created what was called the New Divinity, a codification of the teachings of their master Edwards. Long since almost forgotten, the champions of the New Divinity were great men in their day. The legends about them were largely true; their children and students were many; their dignity was great, their wit and gusto often appealing. Some of them really did wear holes in the floor with their chairlegs as they sat turning patiently through the Catholic and Protestant fathers in Latin, and at least as carefully through the works of the leading infidels: Hume, Voltaire, and Gibbon. Despite their belief that men's actions can never merit eternal reward, they fought evil vigorously where they saw it. Samuel Hopkins, the gentlest of them, attacked the slave trade in Newport, its profitable center.

The New Divinity men, devoted to the system of Dort and Westminster in the version of Edwards, seemed almost to delight in pushing to extremes the most repellent doctrines of Calvinism. Joseph Bellamy said flatly that the door to salvation was not a bit wider open than Christ intended it to be; Nathanael Emmons insisted on the duty of the saved, in heaven, to relish the smoke arising from Hell. None of the New Divinity men scrupled to preach a funeral sermon in which the bereaved were flatly told that a lost husband, wife, or child might well be damned.

Nonetheless, though they felt no need to make Calvinism palatable, they did in the late eighteenth century have to make it ultimately rational. Mysticism was to all except perhaps Hopkins as abhorrent as doubt. Edwards's idealist metaphysics, his skirting the edge of pantheism, above all, his fundamentally aesthetic definition of virtue, were not preachable. Exalting an absolute deity, they had also to explain and justify his every action.

In answer to the devastating question why it was necessary for an omnipotent God to pay the price of the death of Christ in order to save sinners, and the still more difficult one why, this price once paid, all were not saved, the New Divinity men refused to take refuge in the easiest answer: that the ways of God are beyond human understanding. Instead, they stoutly demonstrated that both the sufferings of Christ and those of the damned were necessary for the moral and orderly government of the universe.

Really uneasy with the statement in the catechism that God's purpose is his own glory, the heirs of Edwards insisted as firmly as any deist that his constant end was the happiness of humanity. Everything therefore necessarily was conducive to that end. In New Divinity arguments death, which had a dozen edifying and constructive uses, presented no great problem, but the existence of sin was more challenging. Both Joseph Bellamy and Samuel Hopkins accepted the challenge, and demonstrated to their own satisfaction that sin was a necessary means to a greater good, and that the world was thus better off with it than without it. As for damnation, Joseph Bellamy, reverting to arithmetic combined with the comforting doctrine of the approaching millennium, concluded that though the majority of those now alive would be damned, in the long run the ratio of saved to damned would be at least 17,000 to one.[18] Surely the eternal suffering of a small group was a modest price to pay for this great result. Each must be willing, Samuel Hopkins insisted, to be damned himself for the good of all and the fulfillment of the divine plan. Like his colleague Nathanael Emmons, Hopkins all his life remained unsure whether his own devoted life offered any assurance that he would avoid eternal misery.

Courageous to a fault, and given their premises rationalist to a fault also, the New Divinity men ranged themselves squarely against the easy doctrines of the Moderate Enlightenment. Those of the New England clergy who opposed both the liberal Arminians of the Boston region and the New Divinity men were called the Old Calvinists. These, moderate and practical in spirit, saw themselves as defenders of the reasonable and workable Calvinism of their ancestors against people who were pushing a good thing too far. We can legitimately see them as men who were trying to reconcile the doctrines of Calvinism with the spirit of the Moderate Enlightenment. Like the Arminian liberals, the Old Calvinists were disturbed by the moral and social consequences of predestination: surely sinners were right to make an effort to save themselves. Ezra Stiles, the most learned and catholic of the group, believed that one ought not to preach that God was the ultimate author of sin even if this was rationally provable.[19] Sometimes the Old Calvinists, ridiculing the New Divinity argument that sin was necessary to the ultimate good of man, sounded a little like Voltaire ridiculing the doctrine that all was for the best in the best of all possible worlds—a comparison that certainly would have shocked them.[20]

The question who won this three-cornered New England fight is difficult. Hopkins's works sold widely, Edwardsianism had a long future in the seminaries, and for some time the brightest of the young clergy in the Connecticut Valley were ardent New Divinity men. Like young intellectuals in many periods they were attracted by intensity, nobility, paradox, and for that matter despair.[21]

But an intellectual victory is not the same thing as a popular victory. According to the best available witnessses, New Divinity preachers grew from about four or five in midcentury to about forty-five by the Revolution, and over a hundred by 1796, when they were winning the pulpits and losing the people in some large districts of New England.[22] After the Awakening as well as before, many laymen were leaving altogether the established Calvinist churches of New England, joining the fervent and simple Baptists, moving in the other direction toward the liberal and tolerant Episcopalians, even toying with deism or neglecting religion altogether.

In Connecticut, where theology was a matter of political party, the seesaw battle between Old and New Lights was still going on when the Stamp Act controversy shoved it into the background. In the colleges the outcome was clearer. By the Revolution the Arminians had won a quiet victory at Harvard, and under Stiles the Old Calvinists uneasily dominated Yale. The center of controversy, and the defensive stronghold of American Calvinism, had shifted to Princeton, New Jersey.

The College of New Jersey was strategically situated, both theologically and geographically. It was a product of the Awakening, created by the revival and now the headquarters of the moderate revivalists who had won the battle for the Presbyterian Church. Though most of these men admired Edwards, they were sober and cautious. Often Scottish in origin, they tended to fear the divisions and vagaries of New England. Located halfway between the rising cities of New York and Philadelphia, the College was exposed to cosmopolitan influences yet somewhat insulated in its small town. From the beginning Princeton was influential among Presbyterians in Virginia and thus in the whole South. It became the parent of seminaries in Virginia and eventually in Kentucky and Tennessee.

With all its strengths, the young college had extraordinarily bad luck in its presidents. The first five, including the great Jonathan Edwards himself, all died after very brief terms in office. When President Samuel Finley died in 1766, Edwardsian theology and idealist philosophy were still powerful at Princeton. Since the conservative Presbyterians, defeated in the recent struggle, were struggling to regain a foothold, the trustees turned to Scotland for a neutral.

The man they invited, John Witherspoon, was a champion of the Popular (Calvinistic) against the aristocratic Moderate party in the Scottish Kirk. Young Benjamin Rush, who was studying medicine in Edinburgh, explained to Witherspoon that his staunch Calvinism, which in Scotland had made advancement impossible, was exactly what had now brought him the American invitation, and that Davies, as president, had been "from his Office as it were the Bishop of all our American Churches."[23]

From this distance it is not easy to understand how John Witherspoon became, as he certainly did become, the most admired and even loved of college presidents in the Revolutionary era. There is little in the eight volumes of his published works that is original or even controversial. He was not profound, and certainly not eloquent: even Rush admitted that his sermons had nothing but their good sense to recommend them. He was the sort of academic figure who wins student loyalty not by unbending but by rock-like dignity. His theology, philosophy, and politics were exactly appropriate to their time and place.

Greatly to the disappointment of the more fervent Calvinists among his supporters, Witherspoon turned out to be a moderate in theology and a determined, subtle opponent of the New Divinity. Much in the manner of the New England Old Calvinists, he combined orthodoxy with an insistence that religion teach morality. The start toward salvation was obedience to moral law and above all to conscience. For his definition of conscience and for defense of its central authority, Witherspoon relied on the new Common Sense philosophy of John Reid, to which he had been converted shortly before sailing. A powerful and discreet academic politician, Witherspoon within a year had gotten rid of the New Divinity tutors, and undergraduates who inclined to Edwardsian views were reduced to passing Bellamy's *True Religion Delineated* back and forth in secret.[24]

Witherspoon's greatest effect on his students came about through his delivery, year after year in unchanged form, of his lectures on moral philosophy. Well organized and not unduly demanding, they were taken down almost verbatim in student notebooks and eventually published after Witherspoon's death, though his successor admitted that "they were so hastily and imperfectly drawn up that he would never suffer them to be printed during his life."[25]

Assuming, but not arguing, the truth of basic Protestant doctrine, Witherspoon recommended to his students a catholic range of moralists, without much fear that these would be sought out and read. Most of these came from the canon of the moderate Enlightenment:

> Since the dispute arose in 16th and 17th Centuries, the most laudable Authors (mostly British) are:
>
> Leibnitz's Theodisays and Letters
> Hutchison's Inquiry into the ideas of Beauty & Nature
> Clark's Demonstrations, and his Letters
> Wollaston's Religion of nature delineated
> Collins' Human Liberty
> Nettleton on Virtue and Happiness
> Hume's Essay
> Kaim's Essay
> Smith's Theory of Moral Sentiments
> Reid's Inquiry.
>
> To these may be added all the Deistical writers, and the answers written to each of them in particular, a brief account of which may be seen in Leland's view of Deistical writers.

Having recommended Hume, Witherspoon dutifully warned his students against this author "who seems to have industriously endeavoured to shake the certainty of our belief upon cause and effect, upon personal identity and the idea of power; it is easy to raise metaphysical subtleties and confound the understanding on such subjects."[26]

Among metaphysical subtleties Witherspoon condemned such New Divinity ideas as the belief that virtue consists in the love of being, or that the difference between virtue and vice is based only on the will of God, a doctrine which would take away the moral character of God himself. Most vigorously of all Witherspoon denounced Berkeleyan and Edwardsian idealism:

> The truth is, the immaterial System, is an evil and ridiculous attempt to unsettle the principles of common sense, by metaphysical reasonings, which can hardly produce any thing but contempt in the generality of persons who hear it, and which I verily believe never produced conviction even in those who pretend to espouse it.[27]

Fortunately, skeptics and idealists had now been answered:

> In opposition to these, some late writers have asserted with great apparent reason, that their [*sic*] are certain first principles or dictates of common sense, which are either simple perceptions, or seen with intuitive evidence. These are the foundation of all reasoning, and without some such principles, to talk of reason, is to use words without any meaning. They can no more be proved than an axiom in mathematical science.
>
> Authors of Scotland have lately produced and supported this opinion, to resolve at once all the refinements and metaphysical objections of some infidel writers.[28]

Copying these words faithfully, the students ranged in front of "The Old Doctor" in Nassau Hall may not have realized that they were listening to the first promulgation of the principles that were to rule American college teaching for almost a century. As Charles Chauncy may have been said to have naturalized English rationalism, Witherspoon began the long American career of Scottish Common Sense, which eventually proved to fit still better the needs of a religiously disturbed and divided society. Witherspoon's teaching of the Scottish philosophical principles gained power from the fact that he coupled them with the equally simple and memorable maxims of the Whig political tradition, whose "chief writers" included Grotius, Pufendorf, Harrington, Locke, Sidney, Montesquieu, and Ferguson.

By the eve of the Revolution, the shape of nineteenth-century American Protestantism had begun to emerge. Despite schism and disorder and the birth of new sects, one can already discern two main camps: the camp of folk religion and that of intellectual Calvinism. The first of these consisted of the popular, fervent, relatively untheological religion of the simple Separatists, the scattered Baptists, and the recently arrived Methodists. In the democratic future, the victory was to go to this camp, which flourished in time of crisis and knew how to touch the hearts of the people.

This was, however, still the eighteenth century, and so far the dominant camp was the well-organized and highly educated camp of intellectual Calvinism, with its strongest organizations in Philadelphia and Princeton and its best brains in New England. Within this camp, power was gravitating away from extremes and toward a Calvinism heavily infiltrated by moralism, rationalism, and the Moderate Enlightenment. The New Divinity on the one hand, and Boston liberalism on the other, served to keep the powerful center properly in balance. Articulate and well organized, moderate Calvinism of one degree or another controlled Yale, Princeton, and the Virginia valley. For certain purposes, its leaders could muster much of American Protestantism. Moderate Calvinism was one of the main avenues to power of the Moderate Enlightenment, and a mainstay of the moderate Whig cause in the American Revolution. Yet its powerful forces could still be mobilized against any form of Enlightenment that seemed to its leaders to go too far, either in religion or politics.

Four *Slumbers and Dreams of the Church*

The Church of England, established in the South, the West Indies, and four counties of New York, a vigorous and growing minority in the Northern and Middle colonies, appealed especially to those Americans who considered themselves modern, rational, moderate, enlightened—in a word, English. The great Addison had stated as a maxim that "the greatest friend of morality, or natural religion, cannot possibly apprehend any danger from embracing Christianity, as it is preserved pure and uncorrupt in the doctrines of our national church."[1] In a very similar spirit the Reverend Thomas Cradock, preaching to a meeting of the Maryland clergy at Annapolis, characterized the national Church as "a religion, reformed & purged from those many errors, which for a long series of ages had obscured its beauties, & made now so nearly resembling that, which our blessed Lord himself taught, that the first-rate geniuses of our own Kingdom, *Bacon, Boyle, Locke, Newton, Addison,* have died in the profession of it, & men of genius of other nations, have by their writings approved & commended it."[2]

Almost united against the Great Awakening, the Church seemed to have surmounted and survived that threat. Whitefield, who denounced the vices of the Church while remaining within its fold, had presented a severe challenge. Almost all Anglicans had been alienated, and many infuriated, by his harsh denunciations of Church dignitaries. To many Anglicans, the frenzies, divisions, and hatreds brought about by Whitefield and the other Awakeners came to seem visitations of sheer madness, if not of diabolical possession. The extreme hopelessness preached by the New Divinity seemed to contradict flatly the "comfortable words," the message of joy in the New Testament: "Instead of instructing the people to 'serve the Lord with *gladness*' & to have 'joy in the Holy Ghost,' these miserable teachers advance a gloomy and dreadful religion which has thrown its followers into dereliction & despair & had made many of them fittter objects for a *Hospital* than a *Church*."[3] As the excitement waned, however, many Episcopalians could accept it as a blessing in disguise. In Virginia, Dissent seemed to be contained; in the North, nearly all Anglican missionaries saw the reaction to it as the greatest hope for the decorous, reliable Church of the English nation.

Holding their own amid hostile fervors, the Anglicans did not present an alternative of laxity or skepticism; one finds almost no American latitudinarians among the clergy. Nor does one find much mysticism or extreme sacramentalism; Protestant feelings were too strong. The note Anglican preaching tried hard to strike was one of rational piety, of a golden mean between Calvinism and Arminianism. God was sovereign, but could not violate his own goodness or forget his promises. Sudden and violent conversions were at most only one of many means to grace; others included prayer and—properly understood—the sacraments of the Church. Always emphasizing repentance and hope, discouraging too much speculation about predestination and eternal punishment, the Church sometimes seemed to hint that somehow everybody would eventually be saved. American Anglicanism tried to be at once fervent and comforting; at once missionary and comprehensive.

Many kinds of people in the colonies found something to respond to in the rather low-keyed Anglican appeal. Some were would-be aristocrats who admired the gentlemanly bearing and polished preaching style of the Church of England clergy. Natural conservatives approved the Church's unfailing support of the institutions of government. Some of these were well aware of the opportunities for advancement in a Church with powerful potential support, in London and in the provincial capitals.

The Church of England had more than her share of officials and rich merchants, yet one should remember that she also attracted, in considerable numbers, Connecticut and New Jersey farmers, and even Massachusetts fishermen.[4] A good many Virginians simply took the Church for granted as a familiar source of comfort and instruction, with words and actions appropriate to the daily rounds of life and also to its great emergencies.

In the South, where the Church was established, it was unaggressive;

Northern clergymen sometimes found their Southern brothers maddeningly contented. Especially in Virginia and Maryland, the only two provinces where the establishment was firm, the Church seemed satisfied to reflect, rather than to shape planter society.

That society seemed to visitors from the North remarkably easygoing and even frivolous. In Williamsburg and Annapolis, the two tiny capitals, cards, racing, and the theater were normal parts of the legislative season. Parsons seldom opposed these pursuits and sometimes took cordial part in them. In the correspondence of young men of the dominant class, a light tone was conventional, with much sighing over the cruelty of the fair Belinda or Phyllis and a complete absence of religious references. As the young men grow older, the lightness usually vanishes, giving place to irritable complaints about the unreliability of weather, prices, neighbors, and slaves, not without occasional reflections of the unsatisfactoriness of human nature itself. Good manners might require an appearance of ease and geniality, but what really counted were such virtues as prudence, caution, and hard work. Planters were seldom interested in theological dispute or mystical contemplation. What they wanted was a decent, orderly religion which would remind everybody of his position, his duties, and his limitations.[5]

Such a religion, to be effective, had to be broadly uniform, and to be uniform it had to be tolerant. Differences of opinion bothered nobody, especially if they were not insisted on aggressively. Those unable to conform to the Anglican liturgy should be tolerated, provided they stuck to their own licensed congregations. Proselytizing was a breach of an implied agreement, itineracy destroyed Church order, and enthusiasm was an affront to public decency. Thus imprisoning anabaptist fanatics was a civic, rather than a religious measure.

In Virginia the Church, like all other institutions, was completely under the control of the dominant class. In theory, authority was divided: clerical salaries were set by law; candidates for livings were presented by vestries to the governor, who was obliged then to induct them provided they had licenses from the Bishop of London to preach in the colonies; once inducted a rector could not be removed except for extreme malfeasance. In practice, the vestries, which had become self-perpetuating committees of local aristocracies, seldom presented clergymen for induction into livings. Instead, they selected likely candidates, sent them to England for ordination, and then made yearly contracts for their services. Only a minority of the clergy objected. Most, brought up in Virginia, took the system for granted almost as much as their parishioners and many were by no means eager for more supervision. Like slavery or the dominance of certain families, Virginia Church government was throughout the long uneventful history of the colony part of the unchanging nature of things. It was certainly not a part of the usual practice of the Church of England.

In Maryland an opposite, and in local terms less successful, answer had been worked out to the difficult problem of an episcopal Church without bishops to govern and protect it. Livings—the best in the colonies—were filled by the Lord Proprietor, acting through the governor; removal or discipline was almost impossible. The result was obvious: deep hostility between laity and clergy. In the 1760's there were two cases of armed resistance to the installation of clergymen appointed by the governor, and provincial politics was convulsed by efforts to cut clerical salaries and establish a means of discipline.

In Maryland especially, but also in Virginia from time to time, the clergy were denounced for laziness, neglect, drunkenness, and sexual immorality. The worst accusations naturally came from Dissenters, especially of course from persecuted Dissenters: a bitter Baptist said later of the Virginia clergy of this period that "Most of them were drunkards, whore-mongers &c. practising vice openly and boldly."[6] This was quite untrue; the evidence is strong that in both Virginia and Maryland the clergy were always literate, usually conscientious, and often pious. Yet the dissolute minority was real; there are too many complaints from inside the Church for us to dismiss them. It was possible, in Virginia, for a clergyman to settle indolently into gentlemanly looseness, if he could count on well-placed local friends. In Maryland he could do almost whatever he wanted. Thomas Cradock believed that some of his fellow clergymen were "vile wretches . . . of the most preposterous conduct . . . persons of no worth & no learning, no religion. . . ."[7]

Thomas B. Chandler, the fiery churchman from New Jersey, found a mixed picture on the Maryland Eastern Shore. The people, he reported to the Bishop of London, were "the most sober & orderly, the least vicious & the most religious, & at the same time the freest from enthusiasm of any people I have ever met with." There were no Roman Catholics, very few Dissenters; the livings were highly adequate. And yet this idyllic picture was marred: "The general character of the Clergy," he reported, was with some admirable exceptions "most wretchedly bad."[8] Both of these statements must be discounted somewhat since their authors were arguing the bad consequences of lack of supervision as part of the case for American bishops.

Even among the large majority of clergy who were not dissolute, some clearly failed to put first things first. Jonathan Boucher, the Maryland loyalist, remembered that as rector of Hanover in Virginia he had succeeded a well-known gambler, from whom he had once won a hundred pounds. Boucher got into trouble with powerful neighbors for disparaging his predecessor, not of course for gambling but for lack of literary ability. "It had been much safer for me to have called in question his orthodoxy, or perhaps even his moral honesty."[9]

The sermons of Southern Anglicans, within the pattern of rational piety, often strike a more complacent note than those of their Northern colleagues.[10] Sometimes they demonstrate, much in the English manner of a little earlier, that revelation rests on irrefutable evidence and confirms what we know from other sources. Sometimes there is an overtly conservative appeal impossible for Northern Episcopalians: one should not idly abandon doctrines and practices that have stood the test of time. A post-Revolutionary epitaph on an Eastern Shore magnate and his wife concludes with a summary of their (pre-Revolutionary) lives. This states the Chesapeake colonial ideal, one unimaginable in any other American community:

> In love and friendship all our years were spent
> In moderate wealth and free from want—content,
> Our pious souls with pious thoughts inspired
> To worship God and profit man desired:
> Religious laws and customs to pursue,
> Nor slighting old ones nor too fond of new;
> But choosing such, as since they first began
> Best served of praising God and common good of man.[11]

A religion which emphasizes the sober and traditional kind of virtues may regulate effectively the ordinary conduct of a society; one can hardly expect it to attack a deeply entrenched institution. The greatest moral failure of the colonial Church was its accommodation to slavery. Clergymen often enjoined masters to treat slaves kindly, doubtless with some effect. Bishops of London and their commissaries insisted repeatedly that Negroes must be given Christian education, but they proved un-

able to overcome local resistance. In vain they insisted that there were
no dangers in this plain duty, that Christian freedom was an entirely
spiritual matter, that religious instruction would render servants more
docile. It is a striking testimonial to the vitality of the Christian religion
that planters did not believe them; they could not get over the feeling
that spiritual equality might have dangerous consequences.[12]

The planters who controlled the Church in the South were suspicious
of Dissent and revivalism, partly because they correctly linked these to
anti-slavery. Whitefield, in his letter to the inhabitants of the Southern
provinces, went so far as to say that considering their treatment, he
wondered that the blacks had no "more frequently risen in arms against
their owners," and though he prayed God they might never get the
upper hand: "should such a thing be permitted by Providence, all good
men must acknowledge the judgment would be just."[13] Some Virginia
Baptists and, later, Methodists were ardently antislavery. In 1772 the
Episcopalian House of Burgesses, in an act defining the privileges of
Dissenters, provided stiff penalties for any "teacher or preacher, or pretended preacher or teacher" who should teach slaves not to obey their
masters' commands, teach them publicly or privately the "Unfitness or
Unlawfulness of Slavery," incite them to neglect their masters' service
under pretense of religious worship, or baptize them or admit them to
any religious society without the master's written permission.[14]

Deism hardly figures among the fears of Virginia or Maryland clergymen. Occasionally they preached against modern infidelity in general,
or lamented its growth along with more pressing evils like laxity or enthusiasm. The Reverend Thomas Bacon, in 1750, assured the Secretary
of the Society for the Propagation of the Gospel that deistic books, despite their prevalence, had not done nearly as much damage in Maryland as clerical laxity.[15]

Some Virginians, like some Englishmen, hoped the Church might
eventually abandon such trinitarian expressions as the Athanasian
creed.[16] Others abandoned doctrinal strictness in their own beliefs while
conforming in practice. The College of William and Mary, later to become the most effective academic base of American deism, was as yet
quiet and easygoing—so easygoing that Southern Presbyterians sent their
sons to the College of New Jersey. Its statutes recognized in 1727 that
the Aristotelian system had passed, provided that the president and faculty were to teach "what system of Logick, Physicks, Ethicks, and

Mathematicks they see fit" and that "the Studious Youth be exercised in Declamations and Themes on various Subjects, but not any taken out of the Bible. Those we leave to the Divinity School."[17]

George Washington, who was older than Madison or Jefferson, was more completely shaped by colonial Virginian culture. In religion as in style of life he was a man of the Moderate Enlightenment, a good deal like an English country gentleman of the early eighteenth century. A frequent but not a regular churchgoer, a vestryman and pewholder but apparently not a communicant, Washington was to sprinkle his official papers with references to "the great Disposer of events," "the father of Lights," etc. There is no reason whatever to question the genuineness either of his belief in an overruling providence or his nobly expressed belief in religious liberty (not, as he pointed out to the Jews of Newport, toleration). Only once was Washington to refer to "the divine Author of our Blessed Religion," though he frequently used the word "Christian" in a favorable sense.[18] Conservative by temperament, decorous, open-minded, with a strong sense of duty and little interest in theology, Washington throughout his life reflected the virtues, with few of the vices, of the Anglican past, thereby baffling the more strenuous pietists and skeptics of the future.

Informal but decorous, the Virginia Church was part of the familiar landscape. Few of the planter laymen who ran its affairs realized that it had failed to satisfy the spiritual needs of many whites, and therefore was already under mortal attack. With the Revolution and disestablishment, its weaknesses were exposed and it went into a period of almost fatal decline. It was at this point that a considerable part of the top class turned toward deism.

South of Virginia, Anglicanism had everywhere the status of a semi-established minority religion, dependent on support from England. North Carolinians wrangled over the terms of establishment right up to the Revolution. In Georgia, neither the colony's foundation by reformist and missionary Anglicans nor its important association with the Wesleys seemed to have left much effect by midcentury. The back country was still largely unchurched, the Savannah region closely attached to Charleston in culture and religion.

Seaboard South Carolina, with its Georgia extension, was the only Southern region culturally independent of Virginia. Instead of a fairly even scattering of large and small plantations and small towns, there was one dense, cosmopolitan and luxurious city, a vast, wild back country, and a coastal region consisting mainly of large, rich, isolated plantations. In the tiny chapels in the rice swamps, or even in the handsome churches of Beaufort or Georgetown, services were not usually held every week. In Charleston, two stately Episcopal churches competed with almost equally impressive rivals: one can still visit three colonial Presbyterian churches (one specifically Scottish), one Congregationalist, one early and handsome Baptist, one Roman Catholic, and one synagogue. Relations between the easygoing establishment and the powerful, familiar Dissenting bodies, once hostile, were on the whole cordial by midcentury. There were already wealthy Baptist as well as Presbyterian planters.

Within the establishment, there were fashionable conforming freethinkers of the English type, strictly observant Churchmen like Henry Laurens, and pious ladies like the diarist Eliza Pinckney. Though many read the more acceptable deists and quasi-deists, very few openly abandoned Christianity. Looking back, South Carolina's Revolutionary historian remembers that "Among the carolinians deism was never common. Its inhabitants at all times generally believed that a christian church was the best temple of reason."[19]

As in Virginia, Church authorities made an impressive effort to provide for the spiritual welfare of slaves. In a powerful pastoral letter, the Bishop of London had insisted that Christians must not "consider a Being that is endowed with Reason, upon a level with a Brute," and argued that religious training would make slaves more docile.[20] In South Carolina as elsewhere, Church missionaries reported that planter cooperation with this effort was sporadic at best.[21] A slave revolt produced, in 1740, a slave code which included provisions against cruel treatment and also tightened precautions against insubordination, prohibiting the teaching of slaves to write. Yet Alexander Garden, the Church Commissary, managed a few years later to found in Charleston a school in which slaves would teach other slaves to read, so that they might learn the Bible.[22] The paradoxes of slavery were more obvious in a society in which whites were far outnumbered by blacks, many of these fresh from Africa and of very dubious docility.

Fervent Protestants, from Whitefield on, often found the region lukewarm and apathetic in religion. In Savannah, the Independent Presbyterian John Joachim Zubly reported that for Dissenters apathy was far more of a problem than persecution: "What is more unfavourable to religious Liberty & the dissenting Cause, besides the low Estate of vital Religion every where, I take to be the dissenters Indifference to their own principles. Their too great conformity to the world prepares them for that Religion which is most fashionable & stands on rising ground."[23]

Yet within the fashionable religion, according to a young Episcopalian clergyman from Boston writing in 1786, seriousness was equally lacking in Charleston: "Nothing seems to be taught or done, with the rancour & feeling as pervades the opposite Clime. . . . Their religion is not affected but it is unmeaning."[24] More exasperated after a few months' longer stay, the same young man took an even harsher view of Savannah religion:

> There are various casts tints & hues to their religious appearances—yet scarcely an instance—nay I have not yet met with one, of rational, well informed, unmixed christian Principles. Some may be observed remarkably catholic—attending public worship at an Episcopal Chh in a morning and in a meetinghouse afternoon, professing an candid [sic] indifferency as to mode—an equal readiness to contribute to Support of both: —But giving away to his laziness, or Bottle & doing nothing the whole following week, for the real encouragement of either.[25]

It should in fairness be pointed out that this exasperated Yankee, after a return to New England, came back to the region that he had found so irritating: his son became Bishop of South Carolina.

The frivolity and laxity that startled some Northern visitors and enchanted others are undoubtedly part of the picture of colonial life in the Low Country. Yet there is another side. A recent and deeply informed analysis of pre-Revolutionary South Carolina finds the colony on the eve of the Revolution politically united in the "Country" ideology, a somewhat aristocratic version of radical Whiggery, with its roots in Shaftesbury, Bolingbroke, Locke, the Whig historians, and the revived "Commonwealth" pamphleteers. It is somewhat more surprising to find the same historian crediting this political consensus partly to the importance of Dissent and partly to the solidity of the aristocratic tradition. The main emphasis of the Country ideology was limitation of power, and this in turn, we are told, reflected a profound, general distrust of human nature and a fear of uncontrolled passions.[26] Such a frame of mind is often and correctly associated with Calvinism. It can also arise out of particular fears, and it is perfectly compatible with some kinds of eighteenth-century skepticism.[27]

For whatever reasons, with whatever doubts under the bland surface, the Church of England in the colonial South stood for moderation, comprehensiveness, liberality of doctrine, and stability of custom. It stood for, indeed it embodied, the old order. In the rest of the colonies the same Church, standing for the same ideals, was forced by circumstances to be an aggressive missionary body. Missionary clergy, reporting home from Connecticut or New Jersey or Pennsylvania, constantly reported that their churches were full of Dissenters. Some of these were converts, some, like Benjamin Franklin, were mere admirers of the liturgy. The most ardent Episcopalians in the decades before Independence were moved by a great hope—a hope very different from the New Jerusalem of the millennialists, but in its way as breathtaking—the vision of a great comprehensive Church of the English nation, neither Roman nor enthusiast but pious, rational, and orderly.

From the time of the Great Awakening on, and particularly with the great English triumph over the French and papist enemy in 1763, the Anglican dream glowed with increasing brightness. Why should not the Church of England extend its mild domain westward over a vast new empire, using perhaps some of the revenues which formerly supported papist clergy to Christianize the Indians?[28] As for the Dissenters, while coercion was not to be thought of and the utmost delicacy was necessary, were there not all sorts of encouraging signs?—Boston merchants of several Puritan generations transferring to King's Chapel, sons of Quaker families attending Christ Church in Philadelphia. With enough fervor and enough discretion, loyal Churchmen could hope for almost anything: a North America all English, all Protestant, united in the same broad and tolerant Church, with even the harshness of slavery mitigated by Christian instruction to both races, with a place for the lowliest and a glorious career for the most talented and devoted, with new worlds to conquer in Africa and India, in an empire united by secular and religious ties.[29]

If he allows himself a frivolous moment, the modern historian can try in his imagination to glance down this unfamiliar perspective. Had the Church prevailed in the colonies, would the empire indeed have held together, and would this have meant a different history for both England and America? Can we imagine the Methodists—as they almost were—contained, and the Presbyterians at least cordially allied? Would the combined weight of English and American evangelicals have transformed the establishment? Might slavery in the Southern and island provinces have been mitigated, then gradually abolished through the benign power of the united Church? Can we see a place for the talent of the American Revolutionary generation without a Revolution: Alexander Hamilton contending for the premiership with the younger Pitt; Washington and Jefferson taking the sacrament in order to sit for Virginia in an imperial Parliament; Franklin, president of the Royal Society, finally buried near Newton in the Abbey? Would the wars with Revolutionary France have been won earlier, and at less cost in reaction?

Such speculation brings out the pathos of the Anglican dream, but that is all: the hope of a comprehensive established Church was as illusory as the prophecies of the wildest millennial dreamer. The Church was by no means as militantly supported in London as its opponents feared; to the tolerant and practical government colonial revenue came a long way ahead of Church interests, and there was no point in offending the rich and influential English Dissenters.

In the colonies, wherever the Church took the offensive it drew militant opposition. To a large majority of eighteenth-century Americans, individualist, incipiently egalitarian, and Calvinist by tradition, all the virtues of the Church seemed vices: its comprehensiveness, looseness; its liberality, apostasy; its cheerfulness, overweening optimism; its decorum, vain ceremony; its loyalty, subservience. It was, moreover, fatally injured by its most ardent partisans, usually converts from Calvinist churches, who patronized and insulted their Calvinist countrymen, constantly appealed for more drastic assertion of the superiority of the king's Church, and proudly reiterated their own humble loyalty to English political, social, and ecclesiastical superiors. Some of these high-fliers were literally more Anglican than the Archbishop of Canterbury and more royalist than George III.

However illusory the dream of ultimate Anglican victory, Anglican expansion was in the middle of the century a fact, exciting to some and frightening to others. The practical burden of missionary work was borne by the Society for the Propagation of the Gospel in Foreign Parts. The S.P.G., chartered in 1701, was a part of the Anglican reform movement of its day, a reaction to laxity and irreligion. It was expected to concern itself with Christianizing the Indians and Negroes, and also with providing for the neglected spiritual wants of white colonists. As the latter of these objectives became dominant, the S.P.G. became the Anglican substitute for revivalism, the Anglican means of meeting the challenge of colonial ignorance and neglect of religion. It supported schools and provided libraries; it also provided modest subsidies for missionary clergy. At the inception of its work there were seven Church of England churches north of Virginia; by the time of the Revolution the Society was supporting seventy-seven missionaries, with perhaps twice as many church buildings.[30]

To many Congregationalists and Presbyterians, the purpose of the S.P.G. missionaries seemed primarily proselytizing among other and better Christians. In New England, support of the Church of England from the home islands revived frightening memories of earlier English efforts to subvert and destroy the New England establishment. To most colonial Episcopalians, on the other hand, it was absurd that Dissent should be established and the national Church only tolerated. The high-fliers were certain that His Majesty's religion was already constitutionally established in all His Majesty's dominions. This fundamental difference of opinion gave rise to all sorts of squabbles about taxes and schools. Matters of style and vocabulary were perhaps even more crucial: Churchmen resented being denounced as papists or Arians or opportunists; Congregationalists or Presbyterians equally resented references to their established clergy as schismatic teachers, their century-old churches as conventicles, or themselves as sectarians.

With boldness and considerable success, the Church carried its attack into the enemy stronghold, arch-Calvinist Connecticut. In 1722 the new rector of Yale, one of the tutors, and five other promising young Puritans announced that they had come, through their reading, to doubt the validity of Presbyterian orders and were going to apply to the Bishop of London for ordination. The effect in the colony was similar to that which might have been produced in 1925 if the Yale football team had suddenly joined the Communist Party. Provided with a fervent and able nucleus of young zealots, the Church in Connecticut profited further from the violent controversies and alternating persecutions of New and Old Lights during the Great Awakening and its aftermath. Anglican missionaries reported to the S.P.G. that the gloomy doctrines and sectarian excesses of the Dissenters were driving those who cherished hope and peace into the Church of England. Some Arminians and Old Lights agreed with them, blaming the dangerous growth of the Church of England on the extremism and cantankerousness of the ultra-Calvinists.[31]

The danger was exaggerated. Yet moderate overall growth and rapid increase in a few places were enough to cause alarm; churches in New Haven and Cambridge seemed to threaten the subversion of the young; conversion of ministers shocked public opinion from time to time; and above all the Church seemed, though it was not, on the point of receiving decisive support from the imperial government.

In the Middle colonies prospects for the Church seemed in some ways even better than in New England. Rather than persecution, the challenge especially in Pennsylvania and New Jersey was, for Churchmen and Dissenters alike, religious chaos and collapse. Old School Presbyterians, frustrated by the triumph of their adversaries, were promising allies and furnished some converts. Some Lutherans, accepting Church of England communion, offered the first real triumphs of comprehension. Among the Hudson landed gentry, or in the cases of rich converts like the Morrises of Morrisania, New York, there were close approximations of real Anglican aristocrats.

Certainly the reports of the Middle colony missionary clergy give no impression of opulence. Nearly always underpaid and often close to the edge of starvation, scrutinized suspiciously by Dissenters, struggling hard to discipline their motley flocks into something approaching Church correctness, the Society's correspondents were often close to despair. Yet they often report large numbers of baptisms, and also that friendly Dissenters attend the Church services in large numbers. With the frontier opening and the Indians quieter, it was possible to believe that the future of this complex and divided region lay with the national Church.

The center of Anglican hopes lay in the two cosmopolitan cities, New York and Philadelphia. Both were religiously divided, and in each the upper class was conservative and sometimes Anglophile. In both cities, moreover, the Church had promising leaders. New York's leading Churchman, Samuel Johnson, had begun as a bookish, earnest young Connecticut Puritan with a deep temperamental antipathy to turbulence and enthusiasm. When Johnson was eighteen, the New Learning had burst on him as a great light in the medium of the books recently given to Yale. Brought up on the dry meat of Puritan scholasticism he had discovered at once Shakespeare and Milton, Locke, Boyle, and Newton, and also the moderate, polished, learned Anglican divines like Tillotson and Sherlock. It is not surprising that Johnson joined the Episcopalian Yale secession of 1724.

In England for Episcopal ordination, the promising young convert was made much of by the eminent. Like many a later young American of his temperament he was bowled over by the stately glories of Canterbury and Oxford. He also caught up further with modern thought. Returning to take charge of the church at Stratford, Connecticut, he had read his way conscientiously through the Arian and deist controversies, emerging as a convinced and pious trinitarian Churchman. In 1728 he underwent one more conversion. Learning that the great idealist philosopher and then dean of Derry, George Berkeley, was living in Rhode Island, Johnson first wrote and then talked to him. Berkeleian idealism, of all options open to educated men in the eighteenth century, made the least impression on the American colonies. To Johnson, however, it apparently seemed the answer to the doubts left over from his Calvinist upbringing and his exposure to modern skepticism. Through the rest of his life, Johnson became an ardent proponent of idealism as well as Anglicanism. In the first cause, he achieved no success whatever, for the second he proved an inept though devoted leader.

Honest and without guile, Johnson made no secret of his view that the traditional institutions of church and state of his native province smacked of mobbish republicanism. The charters of Connecticut and Rhode Island should be recalled, all the colonies should become royal colonies somewhat on the model of Massachusetts, with a lord-lieutenant presiding over all. The most obvious of all necessities for the filling out of the decent and orderly English system was a colonial bishop. Johnson wrote tirelessly in this vein not only to his good friend Archbishop Secker but also to less committed acquaintances, including Benjamin Franklin.[32]

In 1753 Johnson was called to the presidency of the newly established King's College in New York. Long projected by Anglicans as a rival to Yale, the college had become the subject of fierce polemics between the province's powerful Presbyterian and Episcopalian forces. The result was a complex compromise, which provided for a mixed board and an Anglican president, and stipulated that the teaching should inculcate the general principles of Christianity and morality, and not the tenets of any sect.

Such liberalism, however tactical in origin, was new in its place and time. Shortly after the foundation of King's, another liberal and unsectarian college under Anglican leadership was established in Philadelphia.

Ardent Episcopalians could dream of a pincers movement against the college at Princeton, that chief nursery of Dissenters. When Johnson, beset by personal calamities, withdrew from the presidency of King's in 1763, the leadership of the colonial Church passed to his already prominent friend, Provost William Smith of the College of Philadelphia.

Philadelphia, the richest, fastest-growing, and most cultivated of American cities, had also become the most secular-minded. Its dominant bourgeois aristocracy was luxurious and sometimes arrogant; its literary culture was aspiring and imitative; its politics complicated and often bitter. Vigorous, tolerant, and humane, Philadelphia had forsworn Utopia. As one of its most perceptive historians has put it, the world did not, as the Quaker founders dreamed, become Philadelphia. Instead, Philadelphia became worldly.[33]

Right before the Revolution, a generation of fierce religious politics had produced a situation ripe for Episcopal leadership. The Quakers, suffering deeply from guilt over their own worldly tendencies and shaken by the struggle over Indian fighting in the Seven Years' War, had turned inward and abandoned political leadership. Old Light Presbyterians were still reacting to the Great Awakening. Thus the upper class was ready to draw together against the sometimes turbulent lower orders and especially the Scotch-Irish of the back country, perceived as bloody-minded ignorant fanatics. For upper-class leadership, the Church of England had many advantages. Ties with England meant not only patronage but sometimes breadth and scope. Anglicans had no ancestral opposition to theaters, music, or good living in general.

The last and most important leader of the Anglican forward movement, and one of the major figures of the Moderate Enlightenment, was the Reverend William Smith. Smith, an ambitious young Scot who originally sought his fortune in New York, published in 1753 a description of public education in the enlightened, mythical province of Mirania. The Miranians started with a clear division between those citizens destined for the liberal professions and all the rest, who were to be trained in the mechanic arts. The school for mechanics, conducted in English, taught the majority what they needed to know by the age of fifteen. The minority went first to a Latin school, after which their education was completed in a five-year college course emphasizing successively classics, mathematics, natural philosophy, rhetoric, and finally the lessons of agriculture, history, and politics. The gentlemanly graces, by no means to be neglected, were encouraged by voluntary extra lessons in modern languages, fencing, and dancing. Morality and religion were inculcated in all lessons, especially through the classics and natural philosophy. Finally, the college was to teach on Sunday evenings the simple doctrines of our common Christianity, but it was to play down sectarianism and theology. According to Smith, the Miranians "often had this sentence in their mouth, which I think, in other Words, I have read in TILLOTSON, That the knowledge of what tends neither directly nor indirectly to make better men, and better citizens, is but a knowledge of trifles."[34]

Benjamin Franklin, whose own proposals for an academy at Philadelphia had influenced the Miranian scheme, was impressed by its modernity, and at this stage of his career objected neither to its aristocratic character nor to the provision that the head of the college must be a member of the Miranian established Church. Largely through his influence, Smith was selected as the head of the Philadelphia Academy in 1753, and in 1755 became provost of the College of Philadelphia into which it developed.

Smith had so many enemies that it is difficult for the historian to treat him fairly. John Adams found him "Soft, polite, insinuating, adulating, sensible, learned, industrious, indefatigable. . . ."[35] Harsher critics called him sly, cynical, arrogant, slovenly, and drunken. All regarded him as ambitious, and few questioned his ability. More than a dabbler in science, Smith was an able minor poet and the master of a florid and effective prose, useful for preaching or argument. He had all the most important gifts of a successful college administrator, including a talent for raising money, an ability to compromise almost anything, and a love for public ceremonies. He had an excellent eye for talent, and incessantly encouraged and promoted a series of young protégés who gave him in return their loyalty and even affection. In his three trips to England, Smith played skillfully the eighteenth-century game of patronage. His many influential English friends, his honorary degrees from Oxford, Aberdeen, and Dublin, and above all his real intimacy with Archbishop Secker raised his stock immeasurably in his province.

Smith shared the Anglican imperial dream, and yet, unlike Johnson and the high-fliers, he fully realized that he lived in a plural society. Like many later Americans, he saw in war a chance to bring about domestic unity, and during the Seven Years' War his pulpit resounded with paeans to British liberty, its dangers and prospects. Fearful of German disloyalty, he promoted the cause of schools to teach Pennsylvania Germans the advantages of the English language, government, and Church. Cordial toward Lutherans, Smith despised the Quakers and German sectarians for their pacifism and developed an early alliance with Franklin. This broke down into fierce hostility when these two talented operators learned to understand each other's purposes, leaving as possible allies for Smith only the most conservative Quakers, the Old School Presbyterians, and the proprietors' machine.

It is difficult, and probably not very edifying, to discuss the actual religious opinions of a clerical politician like Smith. Charged with Arminianism by some fellow Churchmen and certainly hostile to Methodistical enthusiasm, he yet could abandon his usual smooth Augustan style for one of quasi-mystical religious emotion, a mode in which some of his young protégés were more at home. Despite his churchmanship, he was willing for the Church to receive Lutheran clergy as priests without reordination, and after the Revolution he was to side with those who wanted to remove the creeds from the Episcopal prayerbook. It is hard not to agree with Smith's critical contemporaries that he was the closest American equivalent to a latitudinarian bishop.

In presiding over his interdenominational college, Smith, who was also a trustee of the missionary S.P.G., was in an awkward position which he handled with great virtuosity. The college's history symbolized that of Philadelphia culture. Its first home was the "New Building" which had been built for Whitefield, and then used as Tennent's church under a charter which opened it only to Protestant ministers "sound in doctrine, acquainted with the religion of the heart."[36] The upper-class trustees Franklin collected for his academy promised, when they purchased the building, to maintain Calvinist teaching. Under Smith, however, the College not only forgot heart religion and Calvinism but steadily downgraded Franklinian utilitarianism, moving in an increasingly Anglican, classical, and aristocratic direction.

To Dissenting critics, Smith never tired of pointing out that the faculty was almost entirely made up of Dissenters, and he defended this liberal policy vigorously against ultra-Anglican protests. Yet in writing to the secretary of the S.P.G. he pointed to the largely Anglican board of trustees, the use of the Church liturgy and catechism, and the soundness of the students as evidence that "the Church, by soft and easy Means, daily gains Ground." The Presbyterians, increasingly unhappy, agreed with this estimate. In the future, Smith hoped, an increase of students from the Southern and island provinces would make the college an imperial and Anglican stronghold.[37]

The College's curriculum retained some echoes of both Mirania and Franklin. The English secondary school existed, but the Latin school received steadily more emphasis. In the College, the students studied the classics throughout their four years, with a very considerable supplement of natural philosophy, and the usual final hodgepodge of religious, moral, and political indoctrination. Authors prescribed included Bacon, Locke, Hutcheson, the Anglican Hooker, the Newtonian simplifier Ray, and even the republicans Sidney and Harrington.[38]

Above all, Smith, as a provincial patriot, believed in promoting the cause of polite literature against all gloomy Quaker or Puritan prejudices. On public occasions, the young gentlemen of the College were encouraged to present odes, music, and even suitably selected plays. In 1757-58 Smith published the *American Magazine*, which contained a mélange of patriotic political articles, scientific miscellany, and literary efforts. He was particularly proud of the poetry section, to which he and his young friends regularly contributed elegiac, religious, and epigrammatic pieces of competence and fluency.

One of the ablest of Smith's protégés was Jacob Duché, the assistant minister of Christ Church. Duché published a series of Addisonian essays in the form of letters from Philadelphia to a series of aristocratic English friends. Duché's tone is ecumenical; he has much to say in favor of Philadelphian toleration and diversity, finds the clergy of the various churches "generally moderate, quiet and charitable," and rejoices that even the Quakers are getting over their hostility to learning. Since, however, he dislikes all religious polemic, singularity, or arrogance he cannot praise the Methodists. "True politeness," he insists, "is the genuine offspring of true religion—a sullen severity of manners is nowhere inculcated in the gospel."[39]

Through Duché's two brothers-in-law, Dr. John Morgan and Francis Hopkinson, the Smith circle was significantly widened. Morgan, an able if choleric doctor, founded the College's medical school in imitation of Edinburgh, where he had completed his studies with distinction. An Anglican convert, and a member by marriage of the upper class, he was one of the city's leading collectors of paintings and, more or less inevitably, was first vestryman and then warden of Christ Church. Hopkinson, a talented writer of light verse, was the leading light of Smith's collegiate dramatic and musical circle.

Before 1775 nobody could have predicted that Morgan and Hopkinson, sharply breaking with Duché, would stake their careers on the Revolutionary side. Other talented young men discovered and promoted by Smith included Benjamin West, who left Philadelphia to become court painter and president of the Royal Academy, and the astronomer David Rittenhouse, whom Smith consistently and vigorously supported even though he remained a Presbyterian and inclined to the Quaker-Assembly rather than the proprietor-Church party.

In science as in literature Smith played his part in the eighteenth-century manner, never overlooking advantages to himself, the college, or the Church, but within these limits acting in a spirit both of generosity and patriotism. In the city's scientific organizations, as in the College, his influence seemed in the pre-Revolutionary decades to triumph over that of Philadelphia's greatest scientist. Franklin's first effort to organize scientific observation, his American Philosophic Society of 1744, proved premature but was revived in 1766 as the American Society for Promoting and Propagating Useful Knowledge, Held in Philadelphia. Practical, Whiggish, with its support largely drawn from the Quaker party, the American Society particularly emphasized invention and agricultural improvement. In 1769 Smith and others organized the rival American Philosophical Society, with a more aristocratic set of supporters and a greater interest in pure science, especially the great favorite of *virtuosi*, astronomy. This group had the good sense to put aside politics long enough to make Franklin its president, and in 1768 the two groups merged as the American Philosophical Society Held at Philadelphia for Promoting Useful Knowledge. This organization, the leading American scientific society both before and after the Revolution, played a major part in the empire-wide enterprise of 1769, the observation of the transit of Venus across the sun, through which it was hoped to determine the distance and size of both bodies. Much of the most effective work on the transit was done by Rittenhouse, but Smith furnished close and understanding cooperation, patronage, and highly successful publicity. Almost Smith's only failure as patron of science, and one which caused him much chagrin, was Witherspoon's capture, for the College of New Jersey, of Rittenhouse's famous orrery.

Smith's conception of progress, culture, and history can perhaps be best seen in his triumphant oration to the American Philosophical Society in 1773. It begins with a "sublime" passage celebrating the "rising Grandeur of America" and the "Progress of the Arts, like that of the Sun, from East to West." This is not to end, however, with the eclipse of the Old World. Smith's vision of manifest destiny is that of the whole empire. He looks forward to the day "when the Regions on this Side of the Atlantic, as well as those on the other, shall enjoy their *Day of Freedom, Light and polished Life*," together forming a vast free empire which will "give Law as well as Happiness to every other part of America." On this subject, Smith admits that he speaks with "fervor almost amounting to Enthusiasm." Smith's reference to the troubles already agitating this paradise is tactful and optimistic; he counts on societies like the A.P.S. "mixing men of different Parties and Persuasions," and thus reducing prejudices in a common search for the public good.

Appealing to a version of history his hearers took for granted, Smith points out that scientific societies had arisen a hundred years earlier, and that their first task had been to remove from true philosophy "that enormous Heap of Rubbish and Prejudice, which had been piled upon it, during the long long Night of Ignorance and Religious Usurpation." From that safe start, Smith pushes onto more controversial ground. The Royal Society was founded in the period of the Commonwealth,

> at a Time when the Constitution of their Country was overturned, and the Reins of Government seized by a Set of Men, who were elevated into Power by such Frenzies and Delusions among their Followers, as could not but be at enmity with all *sound* Philosophy and rational Enquiry; so that till the happy Aera, which saw Monarch and the Constitution restored, that Society received no public Sanction or countenance.[40]

This sad state is contrasted by Smith with that of the present society, encouraged by the governor and Assembly as well as the rich merchants of Philadelphia.

Two years after this celebration of progress, science, order, and empire the annual oration was given by Smith's former protégé David Rittenhouse, who linked progress and science rather, with religion, frugality, separation from Europe, and—by implication—republicanism. One year after that Philadelphia was under the control of a Revolutionary junta, Smith's friends were divided, and Smith himself proscribed. The radical triumph was not to be complete or lasting; conservatism was deeply rooted in Philadelphia and factional strife over the city's culture was to continue. Smith's cultural dictatorship, however, was ended, and the end may serve as a symbol of the downfall of the imperial and Anglican dream of ordered progress.

The conception held by Smith and his group about the general purpose of culture in America had a longer life ahead of it. It was one of the earliest forms of the Genteel Tradition. In all periods spokesmen of this critical viewpoint were to insist that the purpose of enlightenment and civilization was to make America a worthy part of the European tradition. In Smith's circle, this view was more taken for granted, and therefore its proponents were less defensive, than in later versions. There was not much need yet to argue the essential point; only a few people had yet proposed that American literary culture should be something new. It was in religion, so far, that spontaneity and native roughness had their defenders—in some circles, but not in upper-class Philadelphia.

In 1768 Smith was drawn into the Anglican drive for the appointment of American bishops. His correspondence makes it clear that he was less ardent and more realistic on this matter than Johnson, and despised the unsubtle tactics of the high-fliers. Though his enemies were sure he wanted to be Lord Bishop of Pennsylvania himself, he was actually willing to settle for a less official and obvious position as distributor of preferment. The bishop controversy wrecked his fragile empire, which was crumbling before the downfall of the larger empire on which its existence depended.

That controversy was no less bitter for being somewhat illusory. To serious Churchmen, the case for bishops was simple and obvious. As they tirelessly pointed out, without bishops it was impossible either to ordain clergy or confirm communicants. All that they were asking, moderate Churchmen insisted, was the completion of the Church's structure so that it could compete on an equal basis. To many heirs of seventeenth-century Puritanism, however, there was no such thing as a harmless bishop. These did not have to look very far in the indiscreet utterances of the high-fliers to find fuel for their fears that, once established, American bishops might be the spearhead of an ambitious campaign for eventual unity. Actually, both the hope and the danger were exaggerated. The king's ministers, anything but evangelical in temperament and sensitive to the pressures of English and colonial Dissent, repeatedly informed their lordships of London and Canterbury that the time was not ripe.[41]

The bitter polemic warfare of the 1750's and '60's, long given credit for helping to cause the Revolution, had several other consequences more directly a part of our story. It ended one form of the Moderate Enlightenment, the liberal Episcopalian dream of unity, toleration, and rational piety. Church liberalism, at its best graceful and generous, at its worst snobbish, manipulative, and bland, did not fit American society.

The bishop controversy split the religion of the Moderate Enlightenment in two. Many of the leading anti-bishop polemicists were themselves theological liberals: Old Lights like Stiles or Arminians like Mayhew. It was these liberals, not the extreme Calvinists, who were in direct competition with the Church of England. Though they could approve much of her doctrine, they feared her hierarchical structure. This conflict between two kinds of liberals and rationalists helped to sink the cause of religious liberalism, and thus to revive militant ultra-Protestantism.

The small argument about bishops foreshadowed the great argument over empire. The American Revolution itself may be seen as a decisive split in the Moderate Enlightenment, and the beginning of a new Enlightened radicalism.

Five   *The Moderate Revolution*

In the last quarter of the eighteenth century many Europeans and Americans turned their attention from religious and philosophical argument to political revolution. Though this book is mainly concerned with the former and not the latter, it is necessary to look briefly at the political meaning of moderation and Enlightenment (and later of enthusiasm). The great debate over liberty and order which took place in America from 1763 to 1789 was also a debate about the nature of man. It marked both the culmination and the end of the Moderate English Enlightenment in America.

Obviously, this is not the only way to look at the American Revolution. For two centuries, historians have been looking at it as a struggle over economic grievances or constitutional law or imperial institutions or internal class differences. Even if one turns one's attention strictly to ideology, moderate Whiggery is not the whole story.

On one side of the divided moderate camp, high-flying ultramarine Anglicans believed that loyalty to the Crown was a sacred obligation and extreme conservatives were sure that any concession to the mob would lead to leveling and anarchy. On the opposite side, from 1765 on, was a swelling tide of radicalism. Radicalism in this Revolution, as we will see later, had not yet developed a separate ideology but usually pushed the prevailing Whig views in subtly new directions. In the long run, however, the radical spirit of 1776 became associated with a new kind of Enlightenment as well as an old kind of religion, and eventually fused with the deeper worldwide radicalism of the 1790's. It was certainly strong enough from the beginning to frighten moderate Whigs as well as Tories.

For the present, our subject is the moderate Whig ideology of the divided center, a view shared by most of the articulate patriot leaders, many of the moderate loyalists, and most of the framers of the enduring American form of government. This ideology began with the deepest assumptions of the Moderate Enlightenment about man and the universe. Government must be framed to fit our mixed nature, in which reason and passion, public spirit and lust for power balance each other much as the orbits of the planets are controlled by the forces of mutual attraction and repulsion. Its primary purpose is to protect liberty, and liberty includes control of one's own property as well as one's person. Since men differ in ability, and thus property is and always will be unevenly distributed, the government must make sure that both rich and poor are able to enjoy in tranquility the rewards of their labors. To different degrees, men of the Moderate Enlightenment could be as callous to social suffering as they were sensitive to political oppression; in any case most of them assumed that the extremes of wealth and poverty were happily absent in British America.

Government must obviously be limited by its benign purposes, and when these are drastically overstepped, even the most moderate Whigs believed that resistance is justified, as it had been in 1688. The balance between authority and the right of revolution was usually stated in terms of the social contract, though few educated people believed that men had actually surrendered some rights and retained others at an actual time in the past. In forming particular frames of government, one must pay close attention to the special genius, traditions, and circumstances of a people, as Montesquieu (nearly always "the great" or "the celebrated") had pointed out. These basic truths, understood by all well-educated and enlightened persons, could be supported by a standard battery of citations from authority. Whig authorities included the most respectable of the ancients, Aristotle, Polybius and Cicero; and the best-known Continental writers on law and government, Pufendorf, Vattel, Grotius, and Burlamaqui.

In actual history, free and limited government was for Whigs embodied in the British constitution, the age-old repository of Saxon liberties, gloriously restored after Stuart tyranny in the Revolution of 1688, miraculously balancing a due proportion of monarchy, aristocracy, and democracy. The very large legalist and constitutionalist tendency of the English tradition was balanced in America by the wide acceptance of some parts of the Radical Whig tradition.[1]

This body of thought was especially strong among American radicals and ultra-Protestants, and its special meaning for them will be discussed later, but it was invoked by all Whig writers. Its varied canon included seventeenth-century republicans like Algernon Sidney and James Harrington, but most modern Radical Whigs fully accepted the settlement of 1688. They drew on historians of the decline of liberty like Rapin or Molesworth or Catharine Macaulay, on discontented Dissenters and liberal Anglicans and libertarian deists. Still more oddly, the Radical Whig tradition sometimes was stretched to find a place for the Jacobite free-thinking aristocrat Bolingbroke, and his spiritual descendants in the "Country" tradition, who believed in the virtues of the rural gentry as against the corruption of the capital and its parvenu placemen. Radical Whig tradition, that is, had a place for all those who suspected that English institutions had once more started on the course of decline *after* the Glorious Revolution, and despite their basic excellence needed reform and purification. In America, John Dickinson, the most conservative of conservative Whigs, invoked almost the whole list of Radical Whig authorities. The South Carolina Commons House of Assembly, dominated by wealthy slaveholding planters, insisted in 1769 on defying the royal governor by sending a gift of 1,500 pounds to the English radical John Wilkes.[2] Yet American spokesmen of moderate Whiggery balanced their militant defense of liberty with an insistence on the importance of order, moderation, and intelligent, well-educated leadership. Dickinson, one of the most important opponents of the Stamp Act and its successors, the Townshend Acts, is the best example of the moderate tone:

> The cause of *Liberty* is a cause of too much dignity to be sullied by turbulence and tumult. It ought to be maintained in a manner suitable to her nature. Those who engage in it, should breathe a sedate, yet fervent spirit, animating them to actions of prudence, justice, modesty, bravery, humanity and magnanimity.[3]

Revolutions force moderates to choose sides, and the process is always painful. As the argument over Parliamentary taxation or legislation was displaced by incidents of defiance and reprisal, it was not always clear who had first breached the social contract, or where the greatest dangers to moderate values lay. A number of men who had supported and even led the early protests finally refused to repudiate their allegiance to the

Crown. Depending on local circumstances, the options allowed these moderate Whigs, now in American terms moderate Tories, were sometimes more generous than those permitted in more recent revolutions. Some, like Daniel Dulany of Maryland, simply retired into non-cooperation with the new authorities; others like William Smith of New York, one of the editors of the *Independent Whig* which had fought for religious and civil freedom in that province before the Revolution, spent much of the war at home on parole and sailed for England only in 1783. Others, of course, had to hurry to the safety of British lines along with the more extreme loyalists. When the British ships sailed from Boston, then Philadelphia, and finally Charleston and New York, a portion of the Moderate Enlightenment sailed with them.

It is not always easy to explain why some enlightened moderates chose the Congress and some the Crown when decision was forced on them. Within the general school of thought it is hard to find clear ideological differences. It is also hard to distinguish clear differences of class between wealthy Tories and wealthy Whigs. Recently, it has been suggested that rapid economic development had left some men of ability stranded, without the possibility of social and political advancement. Some of these frustrated leaders found opportunity in the Revolutionary camp. On the other hand, it seems clear enough that some of the successful *arrivistes* who emerged in this struggle at the very top of colonial society stuck with the English Crown and the English pattern of life. It is also clear that some adherents of the Moderate Enlightenment who had personal experience of mob violence concluded, naturally enough, that British institutions offered the only hope for balance and order.[4]

In some places the choice was made by whole communities rather than individuals. In New England, for instance, towns and churches often moved together for independence. In Virginia, perhaps the most united province, the squirearchy with its dependents, including most of the Anglican clergy, stayed together, hung onto Whig leadership, and moved massively toward Revolution.

The relation of religion to political choices was, then as always, exceedingly complex. Most Quakers were either Tory or neutral. Deeply pacifist, and full of regrets about past political involvements, they could not follow the leadership of New England Calvinists and local Presbyterians whom they regarded as fanatics and persecutors. For the Northern Anglicans, mostly supported by the S.P.G. in England, the choice was agonizing. On the one hand, a clergyman in Connecticut in 1775 might choose to omit the prayer for the king and later take an oath to the Congress, thus keeping his church open but falsifying the oath he had taken at the time of his commissioning by the Society. His other choice was to shut his church, and thereby tie Anglicanism to a losing cause. Some brave and honorable men made one decision, some the other. For those who prided themselves especially on their support of ordered liberty the choice was especially hard. In Philadelphia, William Smith opposed the Stamp Act and denounced the theory of non-resistance, preached to the troops and the Congress, pleaded in his letters to England for moderation and understanding, and continued to predict the future greatness and enlightenment of America. His course, consistent with all he had stood for, is perhaps the most admirable part of his somewhat sinuous career. Unfortunately, he clung to a mediating position too long and wrecked, instead of saving, his prospects as provost of the university and potential bishop in the reconstituted Episcopal Church. As General Howe approached the city, Smith was arrested with other suspected Tory sympathizers. Paroled, he retired for the duration of the war and after its end struggled unsuccessfully to carve out a new position of leadership. Jacob Duché, his chief protégé, was so eloquent during the Stamp Act crisis that he was chosen chaplain of the Congress. In 1777, however, he wrote to George Washington urging him to use his influence to get the Declaration rescinded and negotiate for peace. His arguments for this course were not only that the military situation was hopeless but also that the members of Congress were a low set, and that the institution had lost all aristocratic tone. The letter was turned over to Congress, and Duché precipitately left for England, denounced by his Whig brother-in-law Francis Hopkinson.[5]

As the Tories continually complained, the most constant fomenters of resistance were the "black regiment" of Calvinist clergy. One possible way to explain this is that established clergy usually echo the political opinions that are dominant in their societies. Thus established Calvinists in New England, like established Anglicans in Virginia, usually went along with the patriot majority. Where Calvinists were outside the establishment and subject to its persecution, they sometimes sided against their Whig neighbors. Some sectarian Calvinists in New England, some Calvinist Baptists in the South, continued to hope until the eve of independence that the Crown would defend their rights to religious freedom against local oppressors. Almost all Calvinists, however, opted for the Whigs when the showdown came. Obviously, old traditions of resistance to authority, old suspicions of "mitre and sceptre" played a large part in uniting Calvinists.

Recently Alan Heimert has suggested a different sort of division, arguing with much learning and force that among the clergy it was the Awakeners, the evangelicals, particularly the New Divinity followers of Edwards, who were the fiery patriots, while Arminians like Mayhew, long regarded as leading proponents of revolution, were no more than lukewarm.[6] In this argument Heimert is consciously reversing an older assumption that religious and political "liberalism" are to be found on the same side.

In my opinion Heimert's theory is closer to reality than the conventional liberal view against which it is directed. It is true enough that fiery revivalists and ultra-Calvinists were almost always strong Whigs. Indeed, I will suggest when we look at the Revolutionary Enlightenment later that there is an antinomian, anti-rationalist, revivalist element in most American radicalism.

It is not true, however, that many Arminians, Old Lights, or Old Side Presbyterians were much inclined to loyalism. As we have seen, these feared the Church of England even more than their ultra-Calvinist neighbors, and they believed as deeply in the Whig sort of liberty. Moderate Calvinists and Arminians were, in reality, part of the moderate Whig consensus except for a very few, almost undistinguishable from their colleagues in religious opinion, who became moderate Tories.

As Heimert points out in his most penetrating passages, the most important and enduring difference between Old Lights and New Lights was one of style.[7] New Light Whigs thought and talked like radicals; Old Light Whigs were, above all, suspicious of popular emotion and of the anti-intellectual rhetoric in which it was sometimes expressed. In all revolutions, people who are temperamentally unable to share the millennial hopes and hatreds of their neighbors, who accept some revolutionary goals but few revolutionary slogans, find themselves in an uncomfortable position. In 1766 we find a correspondent of Ezra Stiles complaining about the position of moderates in Connecticut:

> The Stamp Act has drawn a gloom over every Face, and sowered the temper of not a few, and all that don't run the extravagant Length of a giddy and distracted Mob are looked upon as Enemies to their Countrey

and Betrayers of its Liberties. Among other fine Devices to set People together by the ears a Man's religious Principles are made the Test or shall I rather say badge of his political Creed. An Arminian, and a Favourer of the Stamp Act signify the same Man; think then in what a Situation some of your Friends are.[8]

Stiles himself was neither an Arminian nor a favorer of the Stamp Act, but a moderate Calvinist and a firm, consistent patriot. The principal Arminians of the Boston area, with a few exceptions like Ebenezer Gay of Hingham, also sided with the Revolution. However, liberty, to these Enlightened readers of Clarke and Tillotson, was associated above all with rationality. They were as suspicious of enthusiasm in politics as in religion, and they disliked mobs perhaps even more than other moderate Whigs. Thus it was natural enough for Mayhew to deplore the destruction of Governor Hutchinson's library, and not surprising that Andrew Eliot delayed his choice of independence until after the British occupation of Boston was under way.[9] But such men were no more Tories than the socially conservative, Arminian-inclined John Adams, or the conventionally Anglican George Washington.

South of New England the Calvinists, who had many enemies, were even more united. Former New Light Presbyterians were especially fiery in the cause of liberty, but Witherspoon's Princeton, no longer under New Light auspices, was a major cradle of revolutionaries. Even Francis Alison, vice-provost of the College of Philadelphia, long an enemy of revivalism, by 1769 had grave doubts about his tactical alliance with William Smith and was trying to cement relations with Princeton and New England.[10]

In some instances, it is impossible to explain the final decisions of moderates for or against independence by religion, status, interest, or ideology. One must resort to considerations of personal friendship or hostility, family tradition, ambition, experience of violence or insult from one side or the other, or finally the mysteries of individual temperament. Decision was hardest for moderate Whigs of the Middle colonies, where internal politics were turbulent and New England radicals deeply unpopular. (Middle colony moderates in 1775 looked at New England "fanatics" much as Middlewestern compromisers looked at New England abolitionists in 1860.) Joseph Galloway and John Dickinson were both lapsed Quakers and Philadelphia aristocrats.[11] Both disliked New England, opposed the Stamp Act, pled for moderation, and feared the results of independence. Yet these two statesmen made opposite choices. Galloway, after the failure of his Plan of Union in 1774, rapidly moved to overt Toryism. Dickinson supported a move to pay for the Boston tea in 1774 and voted against the Declaration of Independence in 1776 (along with such other Middle colony moderates as John Jay, Robert Livingston, and Robert Morris). Yet he never considered siding with the Crown against the colonies.

Once the choice was made and the moderate Tories disappeared, moderate Whigs found themselves in uneasy alliance with revolutionaries and democrats. Radical rhetoric disturbed them, and occasional brutality against Tory sympathizers, not unknown even in this most moderate of revolutions, disturbed them still more.

Victory over the greatest power in the world, the establishment of the first great republic of modern times, peace after a long struggle were of course occasions for general rejoicing, and utopian hopes abounded.[12] Yet most periods of exaltation are followed by disappointment, and for relatively conservative Americans hopes were always mixed with fears. In the 1780's these fears deepened and complaints increased. Historians differ on the actual dangers of the critical period, but there were enough signs of trouble to disturb partisans of balance and order.

In a few states, like Pennsylvania, new constitutions seemed to lack a proper balance between the few and the many; in Rhode Island inflation and in Massachusetts insurrection seemed to demonstrate that government would not work without an anchor in tradition. The rise of new men disturbed members of old families. Patterns of deference were ever more precarious. In some places, especially in the Middle states, schools, colleges and churches were struggling desperately to carry on, and everywhere the flow of books and ideas from England was interrupted. A contemporary sociologist, with scores of new nations to observe, has pointed to such common needs as legitimacy, unity, and neutrality.[13] Few of the new nations of the twentieth century are as fortunate as was the new United States, with its basic prosperity, its wide boundaries and sparse population, its relatively stable institutions. Yet in one way the United

States had a specially difficult situation; there were no precedents of successful political innovation; nobody had deliberately constructed a new government since the abortive English Commonwealth of the seventeenth century, and nobody had made a new nation for many centuries before that.

Conservatives had many qualms, but there was no Thermidor, still less an aristocratic and legitimist reaction like that of Europe in 1815. There had never been a base for real aristocracy. The colonial bourgeois elite was not destroyed, only divided and weakened.[14] Moreover, American conservatives were not romantic reactionaries, but Whigs and moderates.

After decades of controversy about the movement for the Constitution, it remains clear that it was in some sense a conservative movement.[15] Most of the members of the Federal Convention were quite conscious of this. Many predicted hostility from popular spokesmen, and they were not to be disappointed. The delegates to Philadelphia, while they did not represent only the rich, were members of the fairly large educated minority. In religion they were mostly either Anglicans or moderate Calvinists. There were no militant religious radicals, no New Divinity men, and Richard Bassett of Delaware was perhaps the only member who could be characterized as "a religious enthusiast" (he was a Methodist).[16]

Madison, the chief architect and chief defender of the Constitution, represented in himself, more than any of the other statesmen, the center of the American religious spectrum. Brought up in the undemanding Anglicanism of the Virginia establishment, he had early been repelled by persecution of the Baptists. He attended Princeton rather than Williamsburg, and came strongly under the influence of Witherspoon's didactic blend of moderate Calvinism with Scottish philosophy. As a young man, in Princeton and later during a period of ill health, he had undertaken a serious and concentrated study of religion, reading widely in standard Anglican and other divines and intensely in Scripture. He arrived at a consistent, lifelong defense of Christianity on the basis both of reason and intuition, shifting gradually like many contemporaries from the first to the second.[17]

Yet Madison, who like many Virginians always enjoyed slightly ribald conversation, was far from being a timid pietist. Always something of a Francophile, he read Voltaire early in life and with enjoyment, though he developed little sympathy for Rousseau. Madison drew some central insights of his political theory from Hume, without moving far in the direction of Hume's deep-going skepticism. A list of books he recommended for the use of Congress in 1783 included along with many standard religious works, books of Leibniz, Bayle, and even Diderot, still very little read in America.[18] Serious though not rigid in religious matters, Madison played his part in the struggle for religious liberty in Virginia in close agreement with the fiery Baptist John Leland. Like Jefferson, he stood not for the half-measure of toleration on which Virginia Anglicans and Presbyterians (but not Baptists and Methodists) could have agreed, but for complete separation of church and state. More than Jefferson, he stressed then and later the argument that such separation was necessary for vital religion.

Though he was no believer in enthusiasm, Madison was probably more seriously interested in religious questions than most of his Philadelphia colleagues. Perhaps because of the variety of religious opinions represented, the tone of the Convention was remarkably secular. At one point, when a deadlock developed, Franklin—of all people—suggested that it was necessary to invoke divine help. The Convention received this suggestion politely, as it received all the few statements of the aged philosopher. A motion for a fourth of July sermon and daily prayer was, however, quietly ignored.[19] Opponents of the Constitution, often closer than the delegates to the radical Whig ideology with its radical Protestant overtones, sometimes attacked it for lacking a religious test.[20]

The epistemology of the Moderate Enlightenment, a blend of rationalism and empiricism, pervaded the Convention, with empiricism furnishing the stronger element. Gouverneur Morris, one of the most articulate and also one of the most conservative delegates, argued "that we should be governed as much by our reason, and as little by our feelings as possible."[21] Madison, as a reader of Hume, did not underrate the power of passion, but regarded control of it as the central problem of politics. Ambition and avarice were the dominant motives of men, and neither virtue nor religion could be counted on to restrain them. (Indeed, religion might itself become "a motive to persecution and oppression," as Madison knew from his Virginia experience.) Thus institutions must be framed to protect the people not only from external oppression, but against their own impulses.[22] This was the attitude taken for granted by Madison and others in informal speeches to the Convention, well before it was given permanent expression in that complex masterpiece of balance, Federalist Paper Ten.

The already rather trite analogy between the Newtonian system and the political order was only occasionally invoked. Dickinson "compared the proposed National System to the Solar System, in which the States were the planets, and ought to be left to move freely in their proper orbits."[23] Delegates never expressed a romantic preference for ancient institutions as such, and seldom appealed even to the most orthodox political theorists. The political writer most often mentioned was not Locke but Montesquieu, the great patron of historical relativism. William Paterson of New Jersey argued that "The Plan must be accommodated to the public Mind—consult the Genius, the Temper, the Habits, the Prejudices of the People. . . . A little practicable Virtue to be preferred to Theory." Pierce Butler of South Carolina said much the same thing more succinctly: "We have no way of judging of mankind but by experience."[24]

The most important source of precedent and experience, delegates endlessly pointed out, was the British constitution. Dickinson, always conservative but also realistic, frankly believed that limited monarchy was the best form of government, but knew like John Adams that it was out of the question for the United States.[25]

Most of the delegates took it for granted that protection of property was the purpose of government, though James Wilson argued that it was rather cultivation and improvement of the human mind.[26] For either of these objectives, popular emotions had to be brought under control. The delegates believed that American institutions had swung too far in the direction of democracy. Even Elbridge Gerry, who later opposed the Constitution on democratic grounds, said that excess of democracy was the principal danger in Massachusetts. George Mason, another non-signer, hoped that the delegates, "soured and disgusted with the unexpected evils we had experienced from the democratic principles of our governments," would not "run into the opposite extreme."[27] On the whole they did not; again and again conservatives like Dickinson and Morris as well as relatively liberal delegates like James Wilson pointed out that so much democracy existed already in American governments that a strong democratic admixture in the frame of government was necessary if this was to be acceptable.[28]

The fact that the delegates agreed on essentials made possible the

Convention's familiar and extremely hard-won compromises, both on such institutional problems as the separation and division of powers and on equally difficult concrete questions like commercial regulations, taxation, and apportionment. Most of the opposition to the adoption of the completed plan reflected no fundamental difference of ideology. As predicted, some powerful politicians criticized the Convention as undemocratic. What they meant was that there was too much danger of an aristocratic preponderance in the Senate, or of executive tyranny. Their principal demands were for clearer guarantees of states rights, more rigid checks and balances to prevent one organ of government from prevailing over another, and more specific guarantees of the rights of the people against the government.[29] It did not occur to them to demand that the government be one that could be used by the people as an instrument of social change. It seems to me doubtful whether the Constitution could have been either framed or adopted if the Convention had been held only a few years later, when the Moderate Enlightenment had been challenged by a new kind of revolutionary ideology and most moderates had become reactionaries.

It is hard to exaggerate the greatness of the achievement or the creativity, boldness, and good sense of the Founders. The Constitution reflects all the virtues of the Moderate Enlightenment, and also one of its faults: the belief that *everything* can be settled by compromise. One of the Convention's sets of compromises turned out to be not only immoral but unworkable. Though the words slave or slavery were never used, the Constitution provided that in apportioning representatives and taxes, free persons should be counted and three-fifths of "all other persons" added. "Persons held to service or labour" who escaped from any state should be returned. And to get the adhesion of South Carolina and Georgia it was necessary to go even farther. "The migration or importation of such persons as any of the States now existing shall think proper to admit," that is, the slave trade, abhorred by all enlightened Europeans and Americans, could not be prohibited before 1808.

Enlightened Northern delegates and, still more, enlightened Virginians who detested slavery and longed for its end found these provisions, and especially the last one, hard to swallow. George Mason wrote bitterly to Jefferson that passage of the Constitution was finally obtained "by a Compromise between the Eastern & the two Southern States to permit the latter to continue the Importation of Slaves for twenty odd

Years; a more favourite Object with them, than the Liberty and Happiness of the People."[30] Madison at one point attacked slavery in terms that could hardly be stronger: "We have seen the mere distinction of colour made in the most enlightened period of time, a ground of the most oppressive dominion ever exercised by man over man."[31] Yet Madison also pointed out to Virginians that the fugitive slave clause would make slave property more secure. As for the slave trade clause, it did not make the situation worse than before, heavy taxes could be laid on the trade even before 1808, and finally, in words prophetic of the arguments made by moderates a generation later, "Great as the evil is, a dismemberment of the union would be worse."[32]

Samuel Hopkins, the most extreme of Edwards's disciples and a man far outside the Moderate Enlightenment, could not share the widespread pride in the new Constitution in 1788, and stated the dilemma more profoundly than Madison:

> How does it appear in the light of Heaven, and of all good men, well informed, that *those* States, who have been fighting for liberty, and consider themselves as the highest and most noble example of zeal for it, cannot agree in any political constitution, unless it indulge and authorize them to enslave their fellow men. I think if this constitution be not adopted, as it is, without any alteration, we shall have none, and shall be in a state of anarchy, and probably civil war: therefore, I wish to have it adopted: but still, as I said, I fear. And perhaps civil war will not be avoided, if it be adopted.[33]

The Constitution is perhaps the greatest monument of the Moderate Enlightenment in any country, and also the last. Well before 1789 the ideas of Locke and Newton were being radically reinterpreted, and the religious compromises of Tillotson and Clarke were fatally undermined. To some degree, the moderate conservatism of Dickinson and Morris and Madison depended on these fragile assumptions. In America, moreover, neither the religion nor the politics of the Moderate Enlightenment really fitted the needs of the changing society. Worship of a delicate balance between religion and science, reason and passion, aristocracy and democracy, freedom and order was in practice likely to be perverted into a reluctance to disturb the status quo, even though some men who believed in these values had led a revolution. Love of equilibrium could lead some, as it led Pope and Pangloss, to the conclusion that whatever is, is right. An expansive and rapidly changing society needed a more dynamic theory, even a more dynamic conservatism.

A number of Europeans and Americans were already asking skeptical questions that deeply undercut the philosophy of moderation. Soon the politics of balance were to be challenged by revolutionary prophets. The Moderate Enlightenment survived in America among judges and lawyers and other sober citizens, but it was placed on the defensive. When this happened, it was no longer moderate.

II

The Skeptical Enlightenment
1750-1789

One *Beyond Complacency*

In about 1750 both the character and the center of the European Enlightenment changed, and both changes made Enlightenment in general less acceptable for a while to the American provinces. The change in character is easier to state negatively than positively. The cheerful balances and compromises of the Moderate Enlightenment—between nature and revelation, reason and passion, liberty and order—the compromises proclaimed by Tillotson and Clarke and Pope's *Essay*, suddenly ceased to be satisfactory to sophisticated people even in England. Some reacted to their failure by invoking faith or aesthetic emotion, others moved beyond these criticisms to a deeper and far more destructive questioning of the bases of morality and knowledge as well as religion. Others simply gave up the search for certainty or consistency and devoted themselves to cultivating their minds or their gardens.

The center of culture, of innovation, and of literary fashion-making moved from London to Paris.[1] Voltaire, though he seldom lived in Paris, had helped to make it the intellectual capital of the world. He did this partly by importing ideas from England. His *English Letters*, read everywhere in Europe and also in the American colonies, were eloquent in praise of Bacon, Locke, and Newton, fervent in admiration for English liberty, and full of tongue-in-cheek admiration for the tolerance and diversity of English religion. Later, in his lifelong war with Christianity, he was to resurrect the English deists, quoting and misquoting Toland and Tindal and Bolingbroke for his own purposes.

By 1750 the vogue for England was well established. It continued through the Seven Years' War and reached its height after the English victory of 1763. In 1751, however, a whole new and specifically French stage of the Enlightenment began with the publication of the first volumes of the *Encyclopédie* and the emergence into the dangerous daylight of a new circle of *philosophes*, whose opinions, witticisms, and intellectual style were imitated from St. Petersburg to Lisbon, from Berlin to Naples.

The Moderate English Enlightenment, which had attracted many though not all Americans, had been formed in a society eager for compromise, worn out with political and religious controversy. The French Enlightenment was the product of a quite different past. Its thinkers, when they thought of the late seventeenth century, thought not of the Glorious Revolution, but of the Revocation of the Edict of Nantes, the end of French religious toleration. Yet few of them—least of all Voltaire —could help but admire the age of Louis XIV, with its triumphant absolutism, its orderly and disciplined Church, its rigid rules of manners and aesthetics, its centralized and flourishing culture: the world of Racine, of Boileau, even of Bossuet.

Officially the Catholic Church in France had triumphed over her enemies far more completely than had the Church of England: the Protestants in the mountains had been bloodily suppressed, the Jansenists and quietists had been forced to submit to authority. Yet the triumph of official Catholicism over so many ardent Christians had weakened the Church. In 1762 the Jesuits, who had led in the battle against Jansenism, were in turn expelled from France as a group too powerful for the safety of the state.

Thus the Enlightenment of the Encyclopedists and *philosophes* had to adapt itself to survival in a society that was nominally Catholic, officially both absolutist and intolerant, and also riddled with self-doubt. By the middle of the century many bishops and priests went a long way in all sincerity with some of the ideas of the *philosophes;* a few clerics admitted among friends to skepticism or atheism. Yet skeptics had to be cautious: the king's officials, who cared very little what anyone believed, cared a good deal about what was said in public on either political or religious subjects. In a way they were correct in their implied judgment: the regime they were defending was all of a piece: absolute monarchy could look the other way, but it could not compromise and survive.

The most dangerous kind of heresy was organized Protestantism, which of course attracted the *philosophes* as little as official Catholicism. Protestants in France, like Catholics in England, were suspected of being in league with the national enemy. In the 1750's participants in public Protestant worship were sometimes sent to the galleys. When Jean Calas was broken on the wheel in 1762 on charges of murder arising out of religious intolerance, Voltaire was able to tie the whole Church to the wheel that broke him; English anti-clericals had no remotely comparable atrocity to work with.

The *philosophes*, ranging from deists to skeptics and materialists, were obviously less dangerous to the unity of the state than Protestants or Jesuits, yet they were known Anglophiles and they constantly skirted the dangerous edge of blasphemy and lèse-majesté. Though the chief censor was the friend and patron of the *philosophes*, though princes of the blood read and praised their works, conservative forces did not surrender. Less and less supported by public opinion, the censors swooped when they felt able. In the fifties, the *Encyclopédie* was periodically suppressed, Diderot and Voltaire were jailed briefly, and dangerous books appeared at the authors' and publishers' peril. By the last decades before the Revolution, Voltaire was received on his rare visits to Paris with the ceremonious transports that the French reserve for ancient intellectuals. A vigorous network of smugglers and underground publishers hawked a large literature, running from pornographic libels on the queen and exposés of vice in convents to serious treatises by Holbach and Rousseau, which still could not be advertised and sold openly.[2]

The *philosophes* loved and hated the society that had rewarded and persecuted them; however they might praise the wise Chinese, the free English, or the virtuous Pennsylvanians, few could live long away from Paris except Rousseau, who baffled the others by his eccentric preference for the country, or Voltaire, who could make Parisians come to him. From Fontenelle in the previous century to Diderot, many of the *philosophes* addressed some of their best writing to brilliant women, assumed to be lacking in specialized knowledge and impatient of long-winded treatises. Much of their work was aphoristic and most of it was easily readable; they seldom exhausted a subject or an audience. Few of their ideas were new. They rephrased and brought up to date the skeptics and stoics of the ancient world, admired but did not follow the great systematizers of the previous century, Spinoza and Leibniz; deified but radically adapted Newton and Locke. Despite their allegiance to the new empiricism, they could not get out of their systems either their Jesuit education or the deductive method of Descartes.

Their early, decisive conquests were entirely among the upper classes, ranging from the higher bourgeoisie to the top aristocracy. Few of them, even in their most optimistic moments, saw their mission as the conversion of the masses to their ideas. The gap between their immensely cultivated audience and the peasants who still constituted the large majority of the population was too wide to cross. For the foreseeable future, mass education could not possibly go beyond bare literacy; for the people, Voltaire and Diderot agreed, the fables and rituals of Christianity were regrettably necessary. In the battle between the monarchical and feudal theories of the French state, and in the actual struggle between king and *parlements*, the characteristic position of the *philosophes* was —it could hardly not have been—on the side of monarchy, progress, and order and against reactionary aristocratic obstruction. Often sadly, and not without open quarrels and inner struggles, *philosophes* praised their own king and accepted employment and hospitality from Frederick of Prussia or even from that very dubious patron of enlightenment, the great Catherine.

Little in the theoretical allegiances of the *philosophes*, little in their political allegiances or social circumstances accustomed them to anything like the easy compromises of the Moderate Enlightenment. Their method in dealing with the censor was evasion and tongue-in-cheek irony; when they felt free they pushed all the ideas latent in the English Enlightenment to their varying extremes. Newtonian physics and Lockean psychology became the basis not of natural religion but of mechanism and behaviorism; the looseness of Gay or the amorality of Chesterfield became frank and systematic sensuality; even the skepticism of Hume, which could not be pushed any further, was welcomed with more delight. Of the major divisions into which British thought had already broken up, only the pious idealism of Berkeley and the moralistic common sense of Reid seem to have been uncongenial.

Partly because its characteristic modes of expression were encyclopedia articles, dialogues, and fables rather than systematic treatises, partly because of the fundamental contradictions in the ideas of the Age of Reason, the French Enlightenment was unabashedly paradoxical: its various members, and sometimes the same man, could be didactic and frivolous, primitive and progressive, reforming and determinist, coolly rational or, on principle, passionate. The group of *philosophes* agreed on what they were against—intolerance, ignorance, cruelty—but on little else. It has sometimes been suggested that the reason the French Enlightenment did not exert more influence in America is that its thinkers were too simple and optimistic about man and society to be attractive to a post-Calvinist society. The opposite is closer to the case: America could not follow the French thinkers because they were too divided and too complex: they pointed everywhere and nowhere.

The ideas of the *philosophes*, so often stated in plays and fables and epigrams, are hard to define. I am using the term "The skeptical Enlightenment" for all the kinds of thought that centered in Paris (with important contributions from Britain and elsewhere) between 1750 and the onset of the French Revolution. The term seems right for the aging Voltaire, who was hardly any longer a serious deist, for Hume, the most important visitor to Paris, and for the tone of the salons. It does not, of course, exhaust the possibilities for describing the thought of this brilliant and mercurial circle. It is worth considering, for a moment, a few other words which apply nearly, if not quite, as well. The thought of the Parisian Enlightenment tended to be scientific, pragmatic, skeptical, and materialist.

Science was the one common piety of the French skeptics. Though they praised Newton as the greatest genius in history, they abandoned in practice the easy profundities of the early Newtonian popularizers. Physical theory was seldom one of their major interests; the preference for pure as against applied science is a nineteenth- or a seventeenth-century phenomenon.[3] The Encyclopedists found the greatest excitement in the useful arts, engineering, agriculture, and technology. These pursuits were often contrasted with useless speculation in metaphysics and theology.

The term pragmatism, for the anti-metaphysical bent of the French *philosophes*, is anachronistic but not inaccurate.[4] I refer to their concentration on the immediate, the particular, the practical; their tendency to justify intellectual pursuits by their utility, or to appeal to the future for corroboration. This tendency, as it occurs in d'Alembert, Diderot, and their circle, might perhaps better be called particularism. From Montesquieu to Turgot, French thinkers tended to be interested in particular political institutions as well as particular scientific facts. The climate of decaying absolutism made proposals for improvement safer than general theories of the state, and an emphasis on the relativity of customs and institutions was a means of breaking with Catholic teaching about divine and natural law.

Pragmatism or particularism was probably the mainstream, but systematic materialism was a minor but growing tendency in the thought of the old-regime *philosophes*. One path in this direction ran through physical science.[5] The Newtonian system, carefully powered and tended by the deity, was reduced to a self-sufficient world machine of matter and motion, of which man and his mind were completely a part. The extreme point on this road was the mechanical man of Julien de la Mettrie, whose combination of determinism and eroticism strained the tolerance even of Holland and shocked most of the Paris *philosophes*. The other path was psychological. First Condillac abolished Locke's tenuous distinctions between primary and secondary qualities, sensation and reflection, to make all the operations of the mind directly dependent on the senses. Then Helvétius reduced all human motives to self-love, and this to physiological needs. By the 1780's Cabanis and others were working hard to establish by experiment that the faculties of the mind, so long described and classified by introspection, could be reduced to reactions of specific parts of the brain to external stimuli.

Oddly, people like Diderot who were determinists and materialists were also devoted to the moral and physical improvement of human nature. Acute thinkers could not help seeing the inconsistency between a taste for improvement and a belief in determinism. Where would the motive for improvement come from, or what would the criterion be, when mankind recovered from its superstitions? The characteristic response of the Parisian Enlightenment to this question was not to answer it at all. True skeptics, sometimes only tacitly, sometimes with brilliant and compelling arguments, rejected all conclusions including those of science. Voltaire, the greatest skeptic, publicly adhered all his life to his early deism, but was far more concerned to obliterate Christianity than to find, in the manner of some other deists, a set of doctrines to replace it. His strongest emotions were hatred of cruelty and dogmatism, and therefore of the religion which seemed to him the chief parent of both. Skeptics are of course free to have all the generous emotions they want, as long as they maintain no illusions about the relevance of these emotions to the constitution of the universe. Voltaire maintained few such illusions, nor did he consider it necessary to explain why, in the end, one should cultivate one's garden.

Even those *philosophes* who disagreed most sharply with Voltaire (always excepting Rousseau, who belongs in a quite different category) agreed with him in his hostility to Christianity, and most went beyond the easy and convenient deist compromises. In terms of the history of religion, at least, the word "skeptical" fits the whole group. If the word "agnostic" had been available in the eighteenth century, it would have fit many of them; among themselves some of them boldly used the word "atheist."

Skepticism was not the peculiar property of the French, and the greatest figure of the Skeptical Enlightenment, the chief skeptic of Europe, was a Scotsman. David Hume was in many ways a part of the Scottish group of thinkers who will be discussed in the last part of this book. He was a close friend of Adam Smith and a cousin of the moderate and tolerant Henry Home, Lord Kames, who had a wide influence in America. The greatest figures of the Scottish Enlightenment aside from Hume, Adam Ferguson and Adam Smith, were both bold and realistic thinkers, yet neither followed him into systematic skepticism. Hume himself, like some other great figures of the age, did not entirely belong to any country.

Despite many rejections and attacks, it was England that made Hume prosperous and famous. It says a lot for British tolerance that he achieved diplomatic and political office and was eventually granted a pension by the Crown. Yet Hume always felt like an outsider in London, and thought that England was deteriorating. As he wrote Gibbon, "Among many other marks of decline, the prevalence of superstition in England prognosticates the fall of philosophy and decay of taste. . . ."[6]

He wrote his first major work in the course of a happy sojourn in the French provinces, where he often considered living. When he was offered the post of secretary to the British ambassador after the peace of 1763, he hesitated only out of a sort of shyness, and finally accepted. His reception can be compared only to that of Franklin a decade later. The representative of a country associated with freedom, considered by many the leading philosopher of the world, Hume was all the more the rage because of his provincial Scottish manners. The Dauphin read his works (one assumes not the most demanding of them) in bed; the most brilliant of the great hostesses fell passionately in love with him; he was received as an intimate by the *philosophes*; in his extremely short, extremely reticent, and masterly autobiography he goes so far as to admit "a real satisfaction in living at Paris, from the great number of sensible, knowing, and polite company with which that city abounds above all places in the universe."[7]

Skeptics are seldom radicals, and Hume's political preferences were very close to those of the Moderate English Enlightenment of the preceding half-century—if anything, Hume's were more conservative. Both his *History* and his essays show a deep, consistent hatred of popular turbulence, especially when this was associated, as it had been in the seventeenth century, with religious fanaticism:

> Popular rage is dreadful, from whatever motive derived: But must be attended with the most pernicious consequences, when it arises from a principle, which disclaims all controul by human law, reason, or authority.[8]

In the perennial search for a proper balance between freedom and order, Hume, more frankly than most conservative theorists, said he would always give the benefit of the doubt to the forces of order.[9] A firm government was the prime necessity for the preservation of intellectual freedom, and the fostering of wise and moderate reform.

Yet Hume, who loved balance and order and moderation, devoted his life to the destruction of the religious and metaphysical compromises with which these social virtues had been associated by his English predecessors. Starting his career of good-tempered, serene destruction while the deist controversy was going on, he expected to end this by exploding the arguments of both sides. In his treatment of miracles he demonstrated that it is impossible to prove the reality of a miracle in the past, and that therefore belief in miracles must be a result of faith and not a justification of it. This nullified the favorite argument, always a weak one, of the eighteenth-century opponents of deism. He also demonstrated, however, that the deist belief that men everywhere had started with a simple, moral, monotheistic faith was simply mistaken. Primitive men began, Hume insisted, with polytheism based on fear. Finally, Hume discredited the argument from design, the chief reliance of British deism and British eighteenth-century Christianity alike; like Voltaire, he failed to find in human experience evidence of cosmic goodness and justice.

His horrified opponents could find in Hume no snap and crackle of infernal fire such as those they easily detected in Voltaire; he refused to give off an odor of brimstone, and insisted on being a kind, decent, genial good citizen. His relations with the moderate faction of the Scottish Church were excellent; at one point as assistant secretary of state he found himself disposing (conscientiously of course) of Church offices. He found Helvétius superficial, and objected to the atheistic dogmatism of the Baron d'Holbach and his circle. Faith in the long run was unarguable; though Hume himself got along without it, he by no means ruled out—even perhaps inclined slightly toward—its ultimate and simplest conclusions about the universe. All he insisted on, against Christians, deists, and dogmatic materialists, was that one could prove nothing about religious questions:

> The whole is a riddle, an aenigma, an inexplicable mystery. Doubt, uncertainty, suspense of judgment appear the only result of our most accurate scrutiny, concerning this subject.[10]

This pronouncement destroyed the religion of Tillotson and Clarke, both of whom were specific targets of Hume's criticism. This far many members of the learned world of Paris could accompany their favorite foreign philosopher. Not many read Hume's more systematic and less readable works which went farther, destroying causation as well as religion. Cause and effect, Hume argued, could be demonstrated only by experience, and experience was a most unsatisfactory guide for the intellect. Most completely of all, he shattered the dream of one major faction of the Moderate Enlightenment, the hope of founding an ethical system on reason. The will was ruled, Hume powerfully argued, not by the intellect but by passion and instinct. History and custom, not deliberate choice, were men's guide.

Hume, more than any other thinker of the Enlightenment, presents the main problem of intellectual history, that of influence. He knew and often said that he converted few to his system, or anti-system; the applause of the crowd was to him a sure sign of error. All the faiths he attacked, including orthodoxy, deism, and rationalist ethics, continued to flourish. Yet, as he tells us, answers to his arguments "by reverends and right reverends" caused his books to be esteemed in good company.[11] His major epistemological challenge, however little understood by his contemporaries, remained for all serious thinkers of any persuasion to deal with, and affected forever the manner, if not the conclusions, of philosophical argument.

The other major British figure associated with the Parisian Skeptical Enlightenment was Edward Gibbon. Gibbon admired Hume so much that he said with uncharacteristic humility that the ten years' work on the first volume of his *Decline and Fall* was overpaid by one cordial letter from the Scottish philosopher, written in 1776 while Hume was serenely facing the approach of death. Gibbon who, like Hume, had always felt at home on the Continent,[12] went to Paris after the peace of 1763, when "our opinions, our fashions, even our games were adopted in France; a ray of national glory illuminated each individual: and every Englishman was supposed to be born a patriot and a philosopher."[13] A less agreeable and modest person than Hume, Gibbon was a far less profound skeptic, yet he shared exactly the same criticism of the Parisian Enlightenment and judged the Holbach circle more harshly:

> . . . I was often disgusted with the capricious tyranny of Madame Geoffrin, nor could I approve the intolerant zeal of the philosophers and Encyclopedists, the friends of Holbach and Helvétius; they laughed at the skepticism of Hume, preached the tenets of atheism with the bigotry of dogmatists, and damned all believers with ridicule and contempt.[14]

Gibbon himself condemned Christianity more sharply than Hume and reprobated evangelical fervor as severely, partly because as he said his own temper was "not very susceptible of enthusiasm." His anti-Christian masterpiece, appearing in the same year as the *Wealth of Nations* and the Declaration of Independence, was received in London and Paris with more applause than either. Like Hume's, Gibbon's view of history rejected both primitivism and progress. Gibbon also detested enthusiasm: ignorant and credulous Christians are repeatedly contrasted with learned and tolerant pagan aristocrats. Civilization results from order and the useful arts: the eighteenth century looks back on the age of the Antonines from one height to another, across a deep valley of barbarism and Christianity.

The question of the relation between the French Enlightenment and the revolution of the eighteenth century is a difficult one. None of the tendencies I have discussed so far was revolutionary, though all were subversive of the *ancien régime*. The Encyclopedists' fascination with technology made artisans the superiors of noblemen; the sensationalist psychology of Helvétius made all men unfree and equal. Of course every idea that broke down official Christianity injured also the government and society to which the Church was riveted. Denis Diderot, in 1783, told the English reformer Romilly that submission to kings and belief in God would be at an end all over the world in a very few years.[15]

Diderot, more than any other one person, seems to sum up the tendencies of the Skeptical Enlightenment of the old regime and combine them with others, some of these quite new. He was at once a materialist and a romantic, a skeptic about human nature and a believer in its perfectibility, a determinist and a reformer, a wit and a didactic moralist. As Carl Becker has pointed out, he failed, and the French Enlightenment of the old regime failed in general, to solve the problem of basing confidence in the future on doubt about human goodness and wisdom.[16] That was why its Enlightenment had to remain skeptical.

The Skeptical Enlightenment in its pure Humean form has had a powerful effect among detached and academic thinkers up to our own day. Its sad wisdom has never persuaded a large number of people. Most human beings, whether in Greece, France, or America, need some way out of human perplexities and frustrations—whether by divine redemption, the creative imagination, or social revolution.

In its specifically Parisian form, the Skeptical Enlightenment could not survive the old regime, the milieu of corruption, good manners, tolerance, wit, and sadness. In the nineteenth century, especially in America, it became a favorite target for evangelists and romantic optimists. Then and later, it served as a refuge for many individuals who found democratic and optimistic culture hard to stomach. But on the level of accepted ideology, neither revolutions nor republics have much use for skeptics.

Two   *Doubters and Deists*

In September 1781 St. George Tucker, a young and ardent Virginian and a deist, wrote to his wife from camp outside Yorktown full of incredulous joy about the imminent and inevitable surrender of the British army. It is not surprising to find him praising Providence, Washington, and France with equal hyperbole.

> Let every aged parent, every tender mother, every helpless Orphan, every Blooming Virgin, and every infant tongue unite and with one voice cry out, God Save Louis the Sixteenth![1]

It is a little more startling to learn that the French and American armies, after the victory, attended a solemn High Mass.[2] By this time New England preachers were managing to praise Louis in the pulpit, and even to imply that anti-French prejudice had been forced on the colonies by British propaganda.[3]

The sudden and somewhat forced affection of America for France was fully reciprocated, not only by ardent young officers but by skeptical *philosophes*. The virtuous simplicity of American politics, the purity of American—especially Quaker—religion and mores, had long been mainstays of their propaganda against European tyranny and superstition. In 1776 a philosophical Italian abbé wrote to his favorite Paris hostess in bantering but semi-serious terms:

> The day is come of the complete downfall of Europe and the migration to America. Everything here is crumbling to dust: religion, laws, arts, sciences, and everything will be built anew in America. This is not a joke, nor is it an idea occasioned by English quarrels: I have been saying this, teaching it, preaching it for more than twenty years, and I have al-

ways seen my prophecies come true. Don't buy your house in the Chaussée d'Antin; buy it in Philadelphia! I will have my part too in this unhappiness, since there are no abbés in America.[4]

The love affair between the old regime and the young republic proved brief and superficial. Language was one barrier, though many well-educated Americans could read some French and quite a few merchants could use the language for correspondence. History was still more important: two centuries of fear and hate of French absolutism and Catholicism could not be wiped out easily, nor could the literary stereotype of the superficial and frivolous "Mounseer." Postwar reaction is not to be forgotten; America has always had a way of turning against its allies.

Parisian culture, which set the tone for polite circles in all the European capitals, could hardly be duplicated in Philadelphia or Boston. In these cities, alienated intellectuals were few and salons non-existent. Iconoclasts and scoffers had to contend with public opinion, not with inept royal censors. High culture depended for its support not on aristocrats but on wealthy merchants. These were glad to be informed about French science and letters, quite willing to have their children gain a smattering of French manners, and even occasionally to laugh at French wit. They had little taste, however, for ideas that were impractical and disturbing.

As we have seen, the modern French writers had long been read by educated Americans, but they had been and were still read selectively. Of the major currents of the Parisian Enlightenment, the pragmatic tendency was probably the most acceptable. Many Americans had long been concerned with inventions and improvement, and some welcomed the concern of the French philosophers with applied arts and sciences, with engineering, agriculture, and technology. Yet the strong and general technological bent in American culture was still to develop. The new republic did not for a long time develop a complete set of institutions for government promotion in the manner of the most advanced monarchies. Here the French, under the *ancien régime* and again, after a revolutionary interlude, under Napoleon, led the world, and some Americans tried to follow. In 1780 John Adams founded the American Academy of Arts and Sciences at Boston in imitation of the French Academy of Science, and d'Alembert was one of its original members. American members of the older American Philosophical Society of Philadelphia corresponded constantly with French colleagues. For whatever reasons, however—and expense and language may well have been quite as important as religious objections—the great *Encyclopédie* found its way to very few American readers, and its presiding genius, Diderot, was perhaps the least known of the major French writers.

The kind of experiment and reform which most absorbed American attention was the development of political institutions. Montesquieu, who best embodied the relativist, particularist wing of the French Enlightenment, was an early favorite. Beccaria, the Milanese reformer of criminal law and punishment, published his major work in 1764. It was reprinted in translation in America in 1777, 1778, and 1793 and read increasingly through the 1790's. Vattel and Burlamaqui, the Swiss theorists of natural law, were somewhat less popular; Turgot and the physiocrats were known and discussed, if not followed, by American theorists. In the glow of the new alliance, Quesnay de Beaurepaire, the grandson of the physiocrat Quesnay, planned a French academy of arts and sciences for America. This was to be located at Richmond, a center of pro-French feeling, with branches in other cities. Professors were to be selected by a committee in Paris. Money was raised in both countries, and the project had the backing of Jefferson, Franklin, Condorcet, and Lafayette among others. Unfortunately, the French Revolution prevented a test of its practicality.[5]

Those Americans who inclined toward any kind of materialism usually, like Jefferson, rejected anything approaching a completely mechanistic or behaviorist system, preferring something like the peculiar, protestant, moralistic materialism of Joseph Priestley. Helvétius seems to have been read very little before the 1790's. Holbach, genially militant against deism as well as Christianity, rejected the notions of a supreme being and immortality which were as important to Jefferson or Paine as to any Presbyterian. He and his aristocratic atheist circle, so influential in Paris society in the 1760's, were nearly unknown in America.

Skepticism of all kinds was unacceptable to most Americans, yet some skeptical authors wrote so well or so cautiously that their works were widely sold. As we have seen, Voltaire was much read in America before the Revolution and his popularity was to continue to increase. This is partly because much of his work either was inoffensive or pretended to be so. The first volume of Gibbon's iconoclastic masterpiece appeared in 1776, when the author's Toryism was a serious handicap.[6] Yet the *Decline* delighted some Americans immediately, and its popularity was to increase steadily and rapidly through the 1790's. Another skeptical author of a different sort, the Earl of Chesterfield, also reached America during the Revolution. Mercy Warren, the ardently Whiggish and severely moralistic New England historian, wrote her son not to take Lord Chesterfield too seriously. Despite the elegance of his style and his mastery of the graces he was admired mainly by "the race of fops and fribble," and "the celebrated Mr. Addison" was far to be preferred as a master of correct style.[7] Yet even in a Revolutionary age many Americans were apparently eager to be instructed in European elegance. Chesterfield's *Letters to His Son*, appearing in 1774, had been reprinted in America seven times by 1789; his *Principles of Politeness* (1775) nine times by the same date. Of course Chesterfield's cynicism was practical rather than theoretical; he rather ignored than attacked traditional morality.

The case of Hume, the profoundest skeptic, is the most complex. As he tells us in his autobiography, his ambitious early *Treatise of Human Nature* was little read anywhere. His posthumous *Dialogues Concerning Natural Religion*, in which the religion of the Moderate Enlightenment is devastatingly though delicately demolished, was known only to a select American public. He was chiefly known through his *History of England*, which broke sharply with almost every American historical preference. Hume was not actually a Tory and still less a Jacobite, though some contemporaries accused him of being both. He was a conservative Whig, whose Scottish emotions and historical imagination inclined him to a great deal of sympathy for the defeated partisans of the Old Cause. He wrote history partly with the purpose of answering America's favorite historian of the recent past, the ultra-Whig Rapin. Hume blamed the Civil War primarily on Puritan fanaticism, admired Charles I warmly and Cromwell grudgingly, and drew the moral that illegal violence always ends in despotism. English liberty, to him, had always depended on a strong monarchy in alliance with a strong gentry. It is not surprising that Thomas Jefferson, admitting Hume's brilliance, feared his effect on the young and suggested the publication of a revised American version of his *History*.[8] The suggestion was not taken. According to data from booksellers' lists, Hume's *History* was slightly less popular than Rapin's before the Revolution, rapidly passed it during the 1780's and 1790's, and was always well ahead of Catharine Macaulay's staunchly Whig work. In Harriet Beecher Stowe's novel of the post-Revolutionary period, drawn from authentic family tradition, Hume's *History* is one of Grandmother's three favorite books, in fascinating juxtaposition with Rollin's didactic *Ancient History* and Bellamy's ultra-Calvinist *True Religion Delineated*.[9] As a historian, Hume was like Gibbon and Voltaire so readable that his style made up for his principles.

Those Americans who went beyond the *History* seem often to have read Hume's *Essays,* or some of them. Because of the complicated problem of successive editions with differing contents it is hard to say exactly what this meant. After 1758, however, most editions of the *Essays* included the "Enquiry concerning Human Understanding," the essay "Of Miracles," and the "Natural History of Religion."[10] Thus the educated public in America probably had access to Hume's most heretical philosophical and religious ideas. It is hard to find any American who adopted these opinions.

The political and social views expressed in Hume's *Essays* did not rule out the possibility of influence in America. His opinions were those of an open-minded and benevolent conservative of eclectic tastes. There is no hint in his political essays of Burkean or romantic love of ancient institutions for their own sake, and there is a great deal of utilitarianism. His political economy is anti-mercantilist and very close to that of his intimate friend Adam Smith. Hume sympathized with the Americans in the early part of their struggle for constitutional freedom and was at his most liberal on the question of free speech. It may be as well for his American reputation that he died in 1776, since he had already said, and would doubtless have continued to maintain, that a people never had the right to overthrow their government. Indeed, Hume sharply differed with all the principal mainstays of Radical Whig theory; he no more believed in the social contract as the basis for liberty than he did in divine right, or the theory that the growth of wealth and civilization endangers liberty.[11]

Douglass Adair has shown that James Madison owed some of his most brilliant insights to suggestions in Hume's political essays concerning the dangers of faction, the means of overcoming these dangers, and the advantages of large republics.[12] Beyond these important particulars, Hume's general, deeply skeptical view that men are far more influenced by their passions—especially the passion for glory—than their reason played an important part in the political theory of Alexander Hamilton, the most skeptical and most European of American major statesmen.

Doubtless an acquaintance with Hume's political essays added a little skeptical bite to the belief of many Americans who, like Hume, believed in a balance between liberty and order and sought for means of containing popular passion.

This is a long way, however, from making Hume's thought in general a profound influence in America, or even on Madison. Madison, after all, had been educated by John Witherspoon, and Witherspoon, before he came to America, had written scathing satirical attacks not only on Hume, but even on his moderate cousin Henry Home, Lord Kames.[13] Hume's name, like that of Voltaire with which it was often coupled, was most often invoked as that of a great infidel. As for his most profound and original thought—his attack on the sufficiency of human reason in dealing with moral judgments or matters of cause and effect—it was, as Hume well knew, far too subtle to be a public danger.

Yet Hume's philosophy had one important consequence in America. It produced in Scotland a number of answers, including the serious and respectful refutation by Thomas Reid and the angry polemic of James Beattie. These answers, with their successors, constituted the Scottish philosophy of Common Sense, which was taught by Witherspoon, became the official philosophy of nineteenth-century America, and will be dealt with later in this book as the last major form of the Enlightenment in America. In summary, Hume in America was popular as a historian, selectively admired as a political and social theorist, feared as a critic of religion, and known as a philosopher or psychologist mainly through those who answered him.

It is an old and persistent legend that religious infidelity flooded into America with the French alliance. This theory was taken over by historians from orthodox preachers and pamphleteers of the 1790's and later, and it has endured into the twentieth century. It is really a scapegoat theory: by 1800 there were important challenges to American Protestantism: these had to be presented as the work of foreigners, bringing dangerous ideas to an innocent and religious people. It is in part a reading back into the Revolutionary and immediate post-Revolutionary period of the religious and political crisis of 1795-1800. This slight chronological difference is of great importance, since the militant, optimistic deism of the later period was quite different from the skepticism of the earlier time, and in America far more challenging. For the 1780's, there is no evidence of any massive turn against Christianity, or of any major effect of old-regime skepticism or materialism. There is evidence, however, that some of the orthodox were already worried about deism, infidelity, and general religious decline.

These fears were as yet well short of panic proportions. It should be remembered that some New England preachers had been worrying about decline since the mid-seventeenth century. On the whole, the Revolution seemed to them an immense victory over the forces of darkness. Yet these forces never slept, and there were always dangers in complacency. The New-Light Old-Light struggles of the past, the secession of Separates and Baptists, and above all the current lack of revivals and the turn of many people from religious to secular concerns were all disturbing. Not least of the puzzling and peculiar signs of the times was that the victory of God's most favored nation had been brought about in alliance with the old Catholic and absolutist enemy. More than one New England state in its new constitution restricted office-holding to Protestants, which suggests as much worry about papists as freethinkers.

When one looks closely at the instances of "French infidelity" in America presented by contemporary alarmists or, with different emotions, by later liberal historians, one finds some of the evidence melting away. Some alleged infidels are merely critics of the clergy, others Arminians or even liberal Calvinists. Beyond the realm of rumor and exaggeration some actual deists existed. These were unorganized and of several different varieties. Among these were a number of former New England Calvinists, who had been led by religious argument beyond the bounds of Christianity. Usually these were of rural origin, little attracted by the bland and cheerful Unitarianism of upper-class Boston or Cambridge. Calvinists who abandoned their Christianity seldom turned toward real skepticism. They were used to thinking of the universe as a system which, however depressing its tendency, ultimately made some sense since it was ruled by God. As deists, they continued to believe in a God who ruled through law, now seen as the inexorable and uniform law of nature. They were much more likely to turn for arguments to the English deists of a half-century earlier than to contemporary Frenchmen.

One example of a serious New England deist is William Plumer, later senator from New Hampshire, who in his youth was first converted from orthodox Congregationalism by a New Light Baptist in 1779. Despite a regime of strenuous fasting and praying, Plumer was tormented by doubts of his new as well as his old faith, and emerged a deist. He believed completely in the existence of a beneficent, rational God who ruled mankind entirely by the law of nature. Yet somehow this deity had failed to make his nature known to finite creatures with their inadequate faculties. It was yet demonstrable that all the instincts implanted by God in man were for a purpose: self-love for preservation, sexual love for procreation, anger for self-defense, etc.[14] Plumer found help in the writings of Addison, Bishop Sherlock, and Soames Jenyns, a former deist turned Christian apologist. His world was that of early eighteenth-century rationalism, cosmically benign. There is no evidence that he was aware that this world had already been ridiculed by Voltaire and logically exploded by Hume.

Plumer, though a lawyer and a strong Federalist until 1806, was a self-made man of farm origins. Some other serious New England deists were either uneducated or entirely self-educated, recognizable ancestors of the village iconoclast who was to become a familiar figure in nineteenth-century America. Of these Ethan Allen was the best-known example. Allen rose to fame as a leader of Vermont militia against the British and a consistent enemy, before and after the Revolution, of the New York landlords. His career is picturesque, but his deist manifesto, *Reason the Only Oracle of Man*, is dull. It is a long argument on familiar deist grounds that God, being by definition perfect, cannot deal illogically or unjustly with man, and that the simple original religion of mankind has been overlaid by priestly imposture. Such doctrine as the Trinity and Original Sin are proved false on moral and rational grounds, and the accuracy of the Bible attacked by familiar kinds of textual criticism.

Though his book is full of echoes of the early English deists, Allen insists in his introduction that he has made use in composing it only of a Bible and dictionary.[15] Scholars have pointed out that he was a friend of Thomas Young, a Connecticut doctor who was acquainted with Charles Blount and other deists, and some believe that Young is actually the main author of Allen's book. Allen, like many participants in the American Revolution, was a great admirer of America's ally, and wrote to his friend St. Jean de Crèvecœur asking to lay his book before the Academy of Arts and Sciences in Paris. The book had none of the qualities demanded for Parisian success, and indeed made little impact anywhere. It sold perhaps 200 copies, and the rest of the edition was burned in an attic fire.[16] The book's main immediate effect was to raise the temperatures of a few orthodox readers, most notably that of Timothy Dwight, later president of Yale and a leading enemy of the more militant infidelity of the nineties.

John Fitch, the inventor of the steamboat, was another independent and cross-grained Yankee. According to his autobiography Fitch, who was born in Windsor, Connecticut, in 1743, revolted early against his father, "a rigid Christian bigot," and against the clockmaker to whom he was apprenticed. This man was both an observant Christian and "a very small feeder." When he had finished eating he always "returned God thanks for what we had eaten; or, I believe I may say, because I had eaten no more." Fitch says he learned how to eat fast between prayers. He also picked up a lot of other useful knowledge and became both a very talented inventor and a daring speculator in religious matters. From his knowledge of mechanics Fitch inferred the existence of rigid natural laws in all spheres. He early rejected Christianity and became first a Socinian and then a deist. His long and unsuccessful struggle to get credit for his major invention took him to Philadelphia, where in 1791 he joined the deist circle of Elihu Palmer, another seceder from New England Calvinism, and a deist of the militant, post-French Revolution variety. Fitch always felt bitterly the limitations imposed not only by his lack of literary education but also by his undistinguished looks:

> My despicable appearance, my uncouth way of speaking and holding up extravagant ideas, and so bad in address, must ever make me unpopular; but was I a hansom man and a good Riter, I could do now more than Jesus Christ or George Fox did.[17]

A more convincing comparison is to Thomas Paine, who with *The Age of Reason* in 1795 was to become the greatest spokesman of popular deism. Between Allen and Fitch on the one hand and Paine on the other there are two main differences. First, Paine was a great master of popular prose. Second, like Elihu Palmer he drew from the French Revolution a militant vision of a world without kings or priests, injustice or fear. This kind of deism, a long way from village iconoclasm and still farther from salon skepticism, will be dealt with in a later chapter.

There were also, even in America, upper-class doubters who tended toward deism, sometimes concealing from themselves or others deeper social tendencies. Some well-read and well-to-do American doubters drew their ideas from the ancients, and others from Hobbes or Mandeville. There is no doubt that such people were cheered and fortified when they encountered, as they did, Voltaire.

It is not easy at this distance to detect this kind of quiet deist or near-skeptic, nor is it important to try to make a list. Some dabbled in doubt only briefly, like Chancellor James Kent of New York, who owned a complete Voltaire and belonged in the early nineties to a mildly free-thinking club in New York. Others, like the aristocratic Gouverneur Morris, never spoke much about religion, but *acted* somewhat in the Parisian manner. Morris detested Calvinism, demagogy, and cant; carried on frank amours in the French manner, enjoyed his sojourn in Paris, deplored the French Revolution, and rejoiced ecstatically in the Restoration of the Bourbons in 1815. In politics one might call Kent a standard American conservative and Morris an American ultra.[18]

The most spectacular American fall from grace was that of Aaron Burr, the grandson of Jonathan Edwards and the son of President Aaron Burr of Princeton. Burr was affected by a Princeton revival in 1772, but successfully "tranquillized" by President Witherspoon, who persuaded the young man that fanaticism, not true religion, had been upsetting him and his friends. Still not entirely able to lay the formidable ghost of his grandfather, Burr spent some time living and studying with Joseph Bellamy, the most rigid of Edwards's New Divinity heirs, reading divinity for long hours and disputing freely, in the New England manner, with his teacher. By 1774 Burr was ready to leave both Bellamy and Calvinism. Henceforth he avoided all arguments about religion and occasionally went, usually with a lady, to the Episcopal Church.

Burr's favorite authors in his early manhood are said to have been Chesterfield, Voltaire, and Rousseau. In his letters to his daughter, he urges her to study Chesterfield and Gibbon as well as the Greek and Latin poets. His tone in these letters is cosmopolitan, cultivated, and distinctly skeptical. When Burr became Vice-President he received a touching letter from the aged Samuel Hopkins. Hopkins referred politely to Burr's august Calvinist ancestry and hoped that he had not, as it was rumored, become an infidel. Hopkins was always a good personal exemplar of his favorite doctrine of disinterested benevolence, and here it is clear that he was concerned less about the Vice-President's influence than about the eternal prospects of Aaron Burr. His letter evidently had little effect, and Burr's downfall furnished a superb cautionary tale for orthodox polemicists. About Burr's character the New England clergy and Thomas Jefferson were in complete agreement.[19]

Benjamin Franklin was the only American truly at home in pre-Revolutionary Paris. His triumphs in the salons during his eleven-year embassy was even greater than that of Hume a decade earlier, and the salons he frequented were the same. Yet Franklin's quiet but profound religious skepticism cannot be put in any category and was not formed by any book: it was the result of a long lifetime's experience which included a sampling of all the main varieties of American religion.[20] Like many natives of Boston, Franklin early abandoned his ancestral Calvinism. In numerous parables and pamphlets, he hammered away at its most vulnerable points, particularly predestination and the uselessness of good works. In doing so, he was echoing the objections of Old Lights and Arminians, and in some of his early writing he sounds like these prophets of liberal uplift. Later, however, he moves from defiance to ribaldry and flippancy; his rejection of orthodoxy becomes so complete that he can treat it lightly. At twenty-two he wrote his parents:

> My Mother grieves that one of her sons is an Arian, another an Arminian. What an Arminian or an Arian is, I cannot say that I very well know; the Truth is, I make such Distinctions very little my Study; I think vital Religion has always suffer'd, when Orthodoxy is more regarded than Virtue. And the Scripture assures me, that at the last Day, we shall not be examin'd what we *thought*, but what we *did*; and our Recommendation will not be that we said *Lord, Lord*, but that we did GOOD to our Fellow Creatures. See Matth. 26.[21]

This is standard liberal-Christian stuff, except for its lighthearted treatment of theological terms. At fifty-two his tone is different. Many New England liberals attacked the Calvinists in long and serious sermons for preferring faith to works and thereby subverting morality. Franklin makes the same point with gleeful coarseness:

> A Man of Words and not of Deeds,
> Is like a Garden full of Weeds.

> 'Tis pity that Good Works among some sorts of People are so little Valued, and *Good Words* admired in their Stead; I mean seemingly *Pious Discourses* instead of *Humane Benevolent Actions*. These they almost put out of countenance, by calling Morality *rotten Morality*; Righteousness, ragged Righteousness and even *filthy Rags*; and when you mention

Virtue, they pucker up their Noses as if they smelt a Stink; at the same time that they eagerly snuff up an empty canting Harangue, as if it was a Posie of the Choicest Flowers. So they have inverted the good old Verse, and say now

A Man of Deeds and not of Words
Is like a Garden full of ———

I have forgot the Rhime, but remember 'tis something the very Reverse of a Perfume.[22]

In his long Philadelphia career as printer and publisher, Franklin was in the center of a unique free market in religions. He sampled its wares with keen and cool interest. The Great Awakening did not engage him on either side; he formed a permanent friendship with Whitefield, who failed completely to convert him. His observations of Quakers, Dunkards, Baptists, Jews, and Catholics are recorded in the tone of a friendly, but quite uninvolved, student of comparative religion or, less attractively, in that of a rising businessman and politician who sees no point in making enemies over unimportant matters.

The variety of Christianity which attracted Franklin most and longest was the Church of England. An early acquaintance of Samuel Johnson of New York and a longtime rival of William Smith of Philadelphia, he was perfectly willing to take the Church side in politics when it suited his purposes, and did not feel strongly on the question of bishops. Like other rising Philadelphians, he formed a connection with Christ Church, which he renewed in old age when he returned from France. He had a lifelong affection for the Book of Common Prayer, perhaps because of its profound ambiguities. Though he seldom attended church, he urged his daughter to

Go constantly to church, whoever preaches. The Acts of Devotion in the Common Prayer Book, is your principal business there, and if properly attended to, will do more towards amending the heart than sermons generally can do. For they were composed by men of much greater piety and wisdom, than our common composers of sermons can pretend to be.[23]

Yet even the prayer book was admirable rather than sacred. Like others in his day, he made efforts to simplify it; to abbreviate the creed and even to revise the Lord's Prayer.[24]

In his youth, Franklin made two brief but strenuous efforts to find a substitute for Christianity. One was a venture into secular pietism. With youthful didacticism and Puritan strenuousness, he tried to achieve moral perfection by checking off on a scoreboard his daily performance in a list of virtues. Perhaps this brief venture was Franklin's closest equivalent to a conversion; but there is little here of despair or exaltation: he tried, failed, and gave it up.

His other youthful excursion was in the direction of deism and dogmatic materialism. His famous youthful pamphlet, influenced by Wollaston, proceeded logically from the affirmation of God to the conclusion that everything is exactly as it must be, that the world is a machine, and that all actions proceeding from stimuli external to human beings are morally indifferent. If there is an afterlife, we will be without ideas, "And to cease to think is but very little different from ceasing to be."[25] This pamphlet was written on Franklin's first visit to England, where jejune iconoclasm of this kind was commoner than in America. His statement in his *Autobiography* about his abandonment of dogmatic deism says a great deal about the course and motives of his changing views:

> My arguments perverted some others . . . ; but each of them having afterwards wronged me greatly without the least compunction . . . I began to suspect that this doctrine, though it might be true, was not very useful . . . and I doubted whether some error had not insinuated itself unperceived into my argument, so as to infect all that followed, *as is common in metaphysical reasonings.*[26]

Abandoning the dogmas of deism, Franklin through his long life stuck to the simple and conventional deistic affirmations: belief in a supreme being, rewards and punishment, and a future state. He does not, however, state these beliefs, as Jefferson often does, as a credo which he passionately believes and needs; these are rather, salutary dogmas which may or may not be true but do no harm. Few other Americans of his time could have said, as he did in his famous later letter to Ezra Stiles, that the divinity of Christ was a matter not of belief or disbelief but of tolerant, benign indifference:

> It is a question I do not dogmatize upon, having never studied it, and think it needless to busy myself with it now, when I expect soon an opportunity of knowing the Truth with less Trouble. I see no harm, how-

ever, in its being believed, if that Belief has the good Consequence, as it probably has, of making his Doctrines more respected and better observed; especially as I do not perceive, that the Supreme takes it amiss, by distinguishing the Unbelievers in his Government of the World with any peculiar Marks of his Displeasure.[27]

Here there is a light trace of the view, widespread in the skeptical Enlightenment, that religion is necessary for the vulgar. Franklin expresses this view more overtly in a number of earlier utterances:

> You yourself may find it easy to live a virtuous Life without the Assistance afforded by Religion; you having a clear Perception of the Advantages of Virtue and the Disadvantages of Vice, and possessing a Strength of Resolution sufficient for you to resist common Temptations. But think how great a Proportion of Mankind consists of weak and ignorant Men and Women, and of inexperienc'd and inconsiderate Youth of both Sexes, who have need of the motives of Religion to restrain them from Vice, to support their Virtue, and retain them in the Practice of it till it became *habitual*, which is the great Point for its Security. . . . If men are so wicked as we now see them *with Religion* what would they be *without it?*[28]

Like some of his French contemporaries, Franklin at times can fairly be called pragmatic, and there is a lot in his early writings that can clearly be labeled utilitarian. Poor Richard's precepts are sometimes notoriously crass in their concern for worldly success. Yet it is well known that Poor Richard was not Franklin, but one of his many masks. In Franklin's own career both public spirit and sheer curiosity competed as motivations with the drive for riches and fame. His utilitarianism in theory was similarly sporadic, unlike that of Helvétius or later Bentham.

As a scientist Franklin was always empirical, but he was not only an obsessive inventor of useful gadgets. In the manner of his day he was equally interested in the nature of light or electricity and the cause and cure of smoky chimneys. Even at his most abstract, however, he abjures curiosity about ultimate causation or metaphysical meaning:

> Nor is it of much importance to us to know the manner in which nature executes her laws; it is enough if we know the laws themselves. It is of real use to know that china left in the air unsupported will fall and break; but *how* it comes to fall, and *why* it breaks, are matters of speculation. It is a pleasure indeed to know them, but we can preserve our china without it.[29]

At times, Franklin's skepticism goes beyond cheerful rejection of metaphysics. Perhaps his early Calvinist training left some doubts about the goodness of man and the morality of the universe. A late letter to Priestley sounds more like Swift than Mayhew or Jefferson:

> Men I find to be a Sort of beings very badly constructed, as they are generally more easily provok'd than reconcil'd, more disposed to do Mischief to each other than to make Reparation, much more easily deceived than undeceiv'd, and having more pride and even pleasure in killing than in begetting one another; for without a Blush they assemble in great armies at Noon Day to destroy, and when they have kill'd as many as they can, they exaggerate the Number to augment the fancied Glory; but they creep into Corners, or cover themselves with the Darkness of night, when they mean to beget, as being asham'd of a virtuous Action. A virtuous Action it would be, and a vicious one the killing of them, if the Species were really worth producing or preserving; but of this I begin to doubt. . . .[30]

This blackness of humor saves Franklin from blandness, and negates some of his conventional affirmations. It was, however, only sporadic. Franklin was not one of those human beings who are unable to enjoy a world they do not fully understand. Something in his physical or moral makeup made it possible to savor many kinds of physical and intellectual pleasure, to swim adroitly in the troubled waters of a revolutionary time, and yet to get along with very few illusions.

Perhaps because he was the ultimate provincial bourgeois and proud of it, Franklin thoroughly enjoyed his sojourns in aristocratic Europe, whose luxuries failed to arouse in him that mixture of guilt and fascination so common among American expatriates. On his first trip to England he fell so in love with the ease, polish, and learning of English society that he considered moving his residence. In the 1760's he was completely a member of the new London circle of rationalist, often radical, Dissenters—though his skepticism baffled and bothered the serious Unitarian, Joseph Priestley. Hume entertained and admired Franklin, while regretting his association with political factions.[31]

The most familiar image of Franklin is that of the simple philosophical "Quaker" at Versailles, a role which he played for high stakes with consummate and conscious art. In private, in Paris or Passy, he abandoned his public pose of rustic simplicity. His amorous friendships with brilliant women, carried on in his seventies, understandably shocked his colleague John Adams. Making crafty puns, sometimes in dubious French, he delicately proposed marriage to the widow of Helvétius and a liaison with the young Madame Brillon. In at least one of his baga-telles of this period, the fable of the *Ephemerae*, he expresses Voltairean sentiments in a style as light and elegant as that of La Fontaine. Men are compared to the mayflies in Madame Brillon's garden, who live but a day and speculate pompously about their destiny.

Inevitably, Franklin's legion of admirers forced a public meeting be-tween the patriarch of Ferney and the benevolent universal genius of the American woods. It is not the least of Franklin's diplomatic achieve-ments to have kept a straight face while Voltaire laid his hand on the head of his eighteen-year-old illegitimate grandson, pronouncing the words "Dieu, tolérance, liberté," while John Adams writhed with embarrassment.[32]

The similarities between Franklin and Voltaire are striking, but the differences are also important. Unlike Voltaire, Franklin in his youth had not had to fawn on the great, though he had certainly known how to make influential friends. Instead of pretending, like Voltaire, to aris-tocratic origins, Franklin was able to take the new and effective course of emphasizing his lowly origins. More in accord with his society, Frank-lin could serve his government and patronize its many religions; he did not need to hate or fear state or church. Like Voltaire, Franklin aban-doned his flippancy most completely when he was outraged by cruel bigotry, for instance in his denunciation of the massacre of peaceable and converted Conestoga Indians in 1764 by the "white savages" of Pennsylvania. In literary talent occasionally approaching Voltaire's level, in scientific achievement and political opportunity far greater, Franklin shares both the admirable and the unlovable traits of his fellow sage. Like the aged Voltaire, and unlike any other American I can call to mind, Franklin was relaxed in his skepticism—without the belligerence of the village infidel, the arrogance of the skeptical aristocrat, the self-torture of a Mark Twain, or the adolescent show-off manner of a Menc-ken. One of the great figures of the Skeptical Enlightenment in the world, he shared—but only occasionally showed—the sadness which per-vaded it.

Franklin's career in Paris is inevitably compared with that of his suc-cessor, Thomas Jefferson. Jefferson's ideas will be discussed in detail later, but one does not have to know him well to understand that skepticism is a tendency entirely missing from his makeup. Jefferson enjoyed the wine, music, and manners of France, but was repelled and saddened by the injustice, frivolity, and loose sexual morality of French society. Living among the Parisian philosophers, Jefferson was fascinated by French science, arguing heatedly with Buffon and Raynal about their theories that men and animals deteriorated in the New World environment. Jefferson was not shocked by materialism; he followed with interest the experiments in physiological psychology of Cabanis, and admired the systematic and naturalistic psychology of the young Destutt de Tracy. He had, however, no use either for Voltaire or Hume. His favorite companions among the philosophers were the liberal optimists of the very last phase of the French Enlightenment, Mably, Volney, and especially Condorcet, all of whom had broken with the past and saw visions of a virtuous and revolutionary future.

One can perhaps regret that there was so little place in America for the Skeptical Enlightenment. Though even the greatest of the eighteenth-century skeptics, Hume, Voltaire, and Franklin, seem so cool before the human enigmas they expose as to be a little inhuman, they are seldom inhumane. None expected to convert many followers to his own philosophical position. Hume and Voltaire had no confidence in the masses; Franklin was able to influence great events partly because he was a master of several quite different styles. In America the skeptical Parisian Enlightenment had a far less important influence than its moderate, rationalist, English predecessor. Neither could stand up against popular enthusiasm, religious and political. By the time Jefferson had succeeded Franklin in Paris, a new kind of Enlightenment was on hand, a kind that could rally enthusiasm and emotion to its support. Before we look at this, however, it is necessary to take account of the one important group of Americans who, for their own reasons, arrived at a special kind of skepticism of their own.

Three *The Stoical South*

In the top class of the South and especially in Virginia, in the period between the American and French Revolutions, the Skeptical Enlightenment was stronger than it ever was anywhere else in the United States.[1] Virginian skepticism was certainly not French, as some admirers of the Virginians used to say. The style and manners of the planter aristocrats, their books, and many of their ideas were those of the English aristocracy of fifty years earlier. Nor did their skeptical tendencies involve looseness or cynicism: their code of conduct was in some ways strict and their sense of duty strong. Only one fact linked the Virginians to the Parisian skeptics of the *ancien régime*: they lived with paradox. Like the *philosophes*, the planters lived in and from an organization of society which they could not approve or defend. Like the *philosophes*, they sometimes talked of social change, but saw little real prospect of it. Lightness and gaiety of manner are sometimes the surface product of such a situation. Close beneath it lies stoical resignation.

The paradoxes embodied in the existence of a slaveholding and libertarian aristocracy were sharpened by the American Revolution. Most planters supported the Revolution, denounced monarchical and aristocratic principles, and believed in republicanism, liberty, and the rights of man. Englishmen had always defined liberty in such a way as to exclude the propertyless and landless, and doubtless most Virginians could use these terms without conscious hypocrisy. Again and again slaveholding revolutionaries exulted in the end of chains and slavery, and almost in the next sentence denounced the British, especially Lord Dunmore, for trying to recruit the slaves to fight their masters, or for simply welcoming runaways to their lines.

Occasionally, white Virginians perceived these ironies clearly. Edmund Randolph, writing in the first decade of the nineteenth century, recalls the argument over the Virginia Bill of Rights in 1776 with penetrating frankness:

> The declaration in the first article of the bill of rights that all men are by nature equally free and independent was opposed by Robert Carter Nicholas, as being the forerunner or pretext of civil convulsion. It was answered, perhaps with too great an indifference to futurity, and not without inconsistency, that with arms in our hands, asserting the general rights of man, we ought not to be too nice and too much restricted in the delineation of them; but that slaves, not being constituent members of our society, could never pretend to any benefit from such a maxim.[2]

It is accepted by recent historians that Jefferson's noble effort to bring the laws and institutions of Virginia into harmony with his own under-standing of Enlightened principles did little if any damage to the power of the aristocracy.[3] Jefferson probably intended his Virginia revolution to end feudal cruelties and absurdities and create a society dominated by small landowning farmers, the best of whom would be liberally educated and would constitute an enlightened governing class. What this revolu-tion actually achieved was the perpetuation of a powerful oligarchy in uneasy power. The Virginia elite was protected by a moderate Whiggish constitution, weakened little if at all by the end of the English institu-tions of primogeniture and entail, threatened in the long run by the in-terests of the majority of small farmers, and made slightly uneasy by the prevalence of egalitarian rhetoric. Above all, its survival depended on adequate protection for slavery.

That slavery rested on force was always obvious. The kindest master did not hesitate to inflict severe punishment at the slightest sign of in-subordination. As yet Virginians seldom disguised from themselves the nature of the institution. As yet very few argued that blacks were bio-logically inferior to whites; nobody yet claimed that slavery was a delight to the slave. All these lines of defense were to be developed later, when they were more needed. As yet Virginia slaveholders were not much wor-ried either about slave revolt or abolitionist attack.

In their letters and even in some of their public statements and acts, there is plenty of evidence that many—not all—Virginian aristocrats de-tested the institution on which their style of life depended. A number of them discussed measures to bring the institution to a gradual end, and some of them took practical steps toward this goal. Manumission, especially deathbed manumission, was encouraged by law first in Virginia and then in all Southern states except South Carolina and Georgia.[4] Yet in the immediate future, few planters could easily imagine getting along without slaves and fewer still could imagine living as equals with former slaves. Few of his fellow Virginians agonized over the matter as deeply as Thomas Jefferson. Eventually, some of them hoped, the progress of enlightenment would bring slavery somehow to a humane and reasonable end. Meanwhile, these essentially realistic men knew both that slavery was wrong and that they were going to be living with it for quite a while. Thus in their daily lives and on a very deep level of conscience Virginians of this period had to find a place for contradictions.

Slavery was not the only aspect of postwar Virginian or Southern life that conflicted with post-Revolutionary euphoria. A recent Southern historian, who has collected the reports of fifty travelers in the post-Revolutionary South, is led to doubt the veracity of his sources because of the lack of Jeffersonian optimism:

These reports, far from conveying the feeling of a fluid new society taking a fresh start in a bustling, hopeful new land, seem to leave the opposite picture. Those writers who stayed any length of time portray a rather settled and elegant social life and an economy ridden by the problems of old communities. The South of the late eighteenth century was tardy in repairing the ravages of war. Its fields were invaded by imported and domestic pests and diseases; worn out and eroded, they were being abandoned. There were already signs of the depletion of the forests. The towns, although losing trade to more aggressive rivals, had problems of housing and sanitation. Almost the only college seemed to have lost hope as well as merit. Ripeness and decay show through the traveler's pages.[5]

Many Virginians seem to have prided themselves on two conflicting sets of characteristics: on the one hand honor, duty, devotion to the public good, republican virtue; on the other ease, generosity, hospitality, hatred of "Puritan" or "Oliverian" hypocrisy, and gentlemanly carelessness of expense. Sometimes these opposite parts of the same code, working together, combined with the actualities of slave labor and fluctuating prices, landed the Virginia aristocrats in an endless swamp of debt.

Travelers' reports make it clear that stately grandeur, real enough in a few of the richest houses, was usually mixed even there with a good deal of eighteenth-century casualness and even squalor, in the manner of Fielding's Squire Western. When Robert Hunter, an intelligent young Englishman, spent the winter of 1785-86 on some of the greatest Virginia estates, his diary lists any number of sumptuous dinners and balls. Yet these, together with innocent flirtations, heavy gambling, incessant juleps and grogs, hunting, and desultory reading, clearly failed to dispel ennui.

> I lament more and more every Sunday that we have no public place of worship to go to. There is a church to be sure, about three miles off, but unfortunately there happens to be no preacher. Being Christmas Day you miss it more than common, as so universal a day of worship in all parts of the civilized world. . . . I this day began to read Montesquieu's *Spirit of Laws*, which I mean to persue with great attention. I drank tea and spent the evening with Billy Ritchie. . . . Just as I was going to decamp about eleven o'clock, in came George McCall and kept us till one in the morning, when I absolutely insisted on leaving them. Ritchie and George had a frolic and kept it up till five in the morning. . . .
>
> We supped en famille, played some tricks at cards, gave the Negroes an electrical shock, and went to bed at eleven.[6]

It is a commonplace of early histories that deism and infidelity pervaded the Virginia aristocracy in this period. Some of the evidence for this generalization must be discounted, since it comes from pious works describing the great religious revivals of the end of the century. Partly in order to magnify the evangelical achievement, clerical biographies and sectarian histories begin with a description of the bad old days in Virginia. The planters were dissipated and blasphemous, the Episcopal clergy few and drunken, "French" infidelity rife.[7]

The memories of the pious are partly borne out by reports of travelers. John Davis, in Alexandria, saw a white man "in dalliance" with a "mulatto" girl of seventeen. Part of the repartee, from the girl, included the following mildly significant generalization:

> But, *Jemmy*, why don't you go to church? Ah! you need not smile! I know you are a *Deister*! People in your *spear* of life be all *Deisters*.[8]

The belief that deism and skepticism were common among postwar planters does not need to rest either on such scattered statements or on later pious exaggerations. In many letters exchanged by members of the top planter class, men who would have regarded it as both ungentlemanly and impolitic to discuss their religious opinions in public, expressed deist or skeptical opinions with wit and eloquence. Moreover, they clearly assumed that these views were both common and acceptable in their circles.

When it comes to accounting for the fact of Virginian skepticism, historians are likely to give the blame or credit to the French Revolution, Paine, and Jefferson. There was indeed in some Virginian quarters a brief and ardent flirtation with the revolutionary deism promulgated by Paine in 1795, and we will look at it later. But Southern skepticism began before the American Revolution and flourished, perhaps even reached its height, before the influence of Revolutionary France was felt. And the kind of deism prevalent before the French Revolution was not at all the same, in the South or elsewhere, as the kind that followed it. As for Jefferson, he very seldom discussed religion with his friends and relatives in Virginia, and when he did he was preaching deism to the converted.[9]

One unquestionably important fact was the collapse of the Episcopal Church in Virginia, after Jefferson, Madison, and their Dissenting allies succeeded in their struggle to disestablish it. Shorn of its special privileges, its legally determined salaries, its glebes and ceremonial recognition, the Church proved for some time unable to adapt to voluntarism. Its official historians, like contemporary travelers, paint a desolate picture of wrecked and empty churches. Devereux Jarratt, the Petersburg clergyman who had long been moving toward Methodism, reported that Episcopal congregations were "perhaps, in most places (I judge from report) not more than a dozen one Sunday with another; and sometimes about half that number."[10]

The College of William and Mary, before the Revolution a stronghold not only of the Church of England but of its high-flying, pro-bishop faction (small in Virginia), was especially hard hit by changing times. Of foreign visitors, Liancourt said that the only college in Virginia was "the most imperfect in point of instruction, and the worst managed of any in the union." Isaac Weld, an often hypercritical English visitor, gave a still more depressing picture of the college in 1797. Of half a dozen students dining at the president's table, the eldest was about twelve, and some "were without shoes or stockings, others without coats."[11] When Jedidiah Morse, the redoubtable defender of New England Protestantism, described Williamsburg he gave much offense:

> Everything in Williamsburg appears dull, forsaken, and melancholy—no trade—no amusements—but the infamous one of gaming—no industry, and very little appearance of religion.[12]

When St. George Tucker answered this canard in a pamphlet of 1795 his defense was revealing. The town, he pointed out, had never had more than two hundred families, the governor's palace and the College president's house had been burned by the British, and the town, like mighty Rome in its day, had suffered from the removal of the capital (to Richmond in 1780). The college

> though divested of three fourths of its revenues at the revolution, and wholly disorganized at that period, by the removal or resignation of most of the professors, has, since the peace, been successfully revived and generally the resort of from thirty to forty students, in philosophy, or in law.

As for religion, "A week rarely passes in which a number of the inhabitants do not assemble for the purpose of passing an hour or two at [Bruton] church."[13]

Tucker does not list divinity among the studies which have been revived at William and Mary, although this subject still claimed the best energies of most American colleges. Partly because the prewar divinity faculty had tended to Toryism, and partly because Jefferson and other members of the board thought such professorships incompatible with republican freedom, the chairs had been abolished, and the Episcopal Church in Virginia was to have no place to train her clergy until 1823. At the same time, knowledge of the classics was abolished as an entrance requirement, leaving few requirements either for matriculation or graduation.

Those of the Virginia gentry who still went to Williamsburg rather than heading north to college were more devoted than ever to its genial society and also to its kindly president, the Reverend James Madison, a cousin of the statesman. Madison, who did his best to hold the College together and revive its fortunes from his inauguration in 1777 until his death in 1812, was a patriot, a Jeffersonian, the first bishop of the Episcopal Church in Virginia, and above all a gentleman of the old Virginia school. He was certainly not an atheist, and not quite a deist, though he was often to be called both as the turn-of-the-century revivals progressed. The bishop's manners and tastes were those of his lay friends. In 1778 we find him writing to St. George Tucker in the sprightly vein which was common among his students. Tucker at the moment was courting Frances Randolph, a widow. This courtship, said Madison,

> is indeed a Path which has been trodden before, and your Fortitude, I think, should at least entitle you to the glory of exploring that Road which perhaps a less scientific Adventurer discovered before you. I admire however your Fortitude, I do not call it assurance, which even so buxom a Widow cannot subdue. But you like a good General, can vary your Mode of Attack into so many different Forms, that I hope if your Fortitude does not yet abandon you, you must at last find a Breach at which you may, Sword in hand, make a triumphal entry.[14]

Later, again teasing Tucker, Madison adopts a mock-religious style often affected by Virginians with humorous intent:

> I fear your Pennance [this apparently refers to his forthcoming marriage] has begun to work a strange Revolution, you seem to be so much in the religious state. Where in the World did you pick up so many pious Allusions?[15]

Like his banter, the bishop's literary tastes were those of his class: he read Voltaire and Gibbon as a matter of course and sampled Hume and Rousseau. Later, when he was attacked, reports differed as to whether he recommended skeptical authors to his students. General Winfield Scott, remembering much later what he calls "the spring tide of infidelity," says that the good bishop used to warn the boys of the seductive charms of "Hume, Voltaire, Godwin, Helvétius, etc. etc., then generally in the hands of seniors." Naturally, after this sort of warning, "each green youth became impatient to try his strength with so much fascination, to taste the forbidden fruit, and, if necessary, to buy knowledge at whatever cost."[16] William and Mary was to be one of the last strongholds of those who read and admired writers who were regarded as infidels by most Americans.

In Maryland after the Revolution the Episcopal Church was a little stronger than in Virginia, and one can find rectors denouncing Dissenters on the one hand and invoking standard Church of England defenses against deism on the other, just as though the Revolution had not happened. In the rest of the South, the Church suffered much the same fate as it had in Virginia. In Edenton, North Carolina, Robert Hunter reports a striking lament for this decline:

I cannot help recollecting some conversation I had with Mr. Ducket about religion yesterday. He was observing that they were almost all heathens in this country. To be sure, says he, they have a church at Edenton (but no parson now), and a sailor one day wrote upon the door:

A broken-windowed church,
An unfinished steeple,
A herring-catching parson,
And a damned set of people.[17]

Writing disconsolately from Tennessee, where fashionable preaching and other social graces were as yet largely lacking, young Theodorick Bland reports on an unusual experience.

I have been so often gorged with the hum-drum balderdash nonsense of Baptistical Preachers that I had resolved not to go to meeting today— but when I got in, to my most agreeable disappointment, I beheld in the Pulpit a tall genteel figure whose countinance [sic] bespoke Philanthropy & benevolence going on in quite an eloquent strain.

This exceptional figure turned out to be "a Mr. Coffin, from New England," and young Bland goes on to praise his kind of "Rational Religion" and to contrast it to the utterances of "Ranting tattering Puritannical Preachers."[18]

Somewhat similarly, James McHenry, a Marylander who was to become Adams's Secretary of War, writes to his wife from Sweet Springs, Virginia:

The care of souls is not neglected in this quarter. I attended a methodist sermon yesterday and heard card playing and dancing condemned as damnable sins. The sermon was scarcely ended when some of the gentlemen returned to the card-table, and others joined the ladies to receive their approbation for an assembly. . . .

In contrast, McHenry goes on to report that a sermon preached at the resort by Bishop Madison on the excellency of the Christian worship and the superiority of Christian morality was full of elegant figures, allusions, and similes, "most of them happily placed and some of the last perhaps new."[19]

Elegant or rational religion of the type approved by aristocrats was increasingly hard to find in the post-Revolutionary South. Bishop William Meade tells us that in 1811

I can truly say that then, and for some years after, in every educated
young man of Virginia whome I met, I expected to find a sceptic, if not
an avowed unbeliever.[20]

This is an exaggeration; there were believers among the Virginian aristocracy, and even beyond their circle many continued to attend church
occasionally and to sprinkle their discourse with conventional references
to Providence or the Creator. Others abandoned even these conventions.

Even the Baptists in Virginia were undergoing a brief period of decline, the Methodists had barely started their spectacular gains, and
the Presbyterians were resting on their achievements. In any case, many
Virginian aristocrats continued to be suspicious of new faiths. As Bishop
Meade later put it:

Although I am far from assenting to the conclusion that no gentlemen
are to be found in other denominations, or that there were none in Virginia at that time who had become alienated from the Episcopal and
attached to other churches, yet it cannot be denied that the more educated and refined were generally averse to any but the Episcopal
Church. . . .[21]

With their ancestral Church in ruins and its rivals socially unacceptable, there was something like a religious vacuum among the Virginia aristocrats. Such a vacuum is certain to be filled one way or another, and in nineteenth-century America it was certain to be filled by
revivalism. But that had to wait for the gradual decline of aristocratic
distaste.

Mixed with elegant indifference and cheerful satire, one can find in
the letters of Virginian deists and skeptics a tone of bleak stoical resignation. Both the light and dark manner are elegantly achieved in the
wide correspondence of St. George Tucker, the Williamsburg law professor, poet, and promoter of gradual abolition. Tucker came to Virginia from Bermuda and in 1778 married Frances Bland Randolph. This
made him a member of the top Virginia circle, and one of its favorite
intellectuals.

Some of our knowledge of Tucker's deism comes from later accounts
by his brilliant and eccentric stepson, John Randolph of Roanoke, who
after being a deist most of his life was converted to evangelical Christianity. Randolph by this time had developed a paranoiac hatred of his
stepfather, whom he accused of misuse of his mother's funds and many

other kinds of wrongdoing as well as of starting Randolph's own journey toward perdition. One of several versions of his angry letter to his stepfather asserts that:

> The germ of piety was sown in my opening heart by a mother's head—the sneer of scepticism the open daring habitual profanity of yourself and your companions some of them (Col Innes for instance) men of splendid genius could not kill the tender bud.

When the house was struck by lightning

> You taught me . . . to ascribe our salvation to principles of electricity. Franklin's name was honoured—not God's and we became little [illegible] philosophers.[22]

His stepfather's whole circle shares the blame in another letter about young Randolph's somewhat later development:

> For what cause I know not Mr. (Edmund) Randolph put into my hands, by way of preparation for the work of law, Hume's Metaphysical works. . . . The conduct and conversation of Mr. Tucker and his friends, as Col. Innes and Beverley Randolph (every other word an oath), had early in life led me to regard Religion as the imposture of priestcraft. I had become a deist and by consequence an atheist.[23]

Randolph's late memories of the Tucker circle are obviously suspect, but the religious vacuum in his upbringing is shown by a letter, genuine in feeling despite its conventional and stilted style, written to Tucker when Randolph was seventeen.

> I wish my dearest father, in your letters you would touch on a subject, with which, I am assured, it becomes every individual to be acquainted & of which I know nothing at all. I mean Religion. A man, I should think, derives more consolation from a firm belief in a rational Religion than from any other Source in life. But a man finding his Dissolution at hand, without knowing to what he is destined, must be in a situation too horrible for Description.[24]

I have not found a reply to this particular letter, but most of Tucker's letters to Randolph and his other sons and stepsons are prime examples of deist morality. The boys are urged to work hard, pay strict attention to their reputations, study the lives of such great men as Washington,

Franklin, and Rittenhouse, and strive to become adornments to their family and their nation.

In his correspondence outside the family, Tucker allowed his lighter vein to predominate. He and his friends sprinkled their letters with light verse, mock-sentimental essays in the manner of Sterne, mild ribaldry, off-hand philosophizing, and satirical imitations of revivalist piety.

At times of human tragedy, Tucker and his friends reverted to a tone of classical stoicism. A friend writes Tucker in 1779 announcing the death of a mutual acquaintance, who happened to be a Christian, and

> met death with the utmost serenity Confidence and Composure. His Exit has really give me a much better opinion of that Religion to which you know he was most enthusiastically attached than I have for some time past entertained.[25]

In 1787-88 Tucker's own deist religion had to meet a severe test in the death of his wife. Letters from his friends urge resignation, mostly in non-religious or deist terms. Tucker answers, expressing his deep affliction in similar terms. In a few years he returns to his usual alternation between lightness and stoicism. In 1791 he is translating amorous epigrams of Voltaire, and in 1806 we find him regretting, in time of further trouble, that he has never been able to accept the Christian faith to which by now many of his friends have turned.[26]

Only one Southern city was really independent of Virginian influence. Charleston, the rich and handsome subtropical capital of the rice planters probably had more commercial connections with Europe and the Northern cities than with the little towns on the Chesapeake. There were differences and also similarities: in Charleston some of the contradictory tendencies of Virginian culture were carried to a further extreme.[27]

Charleston was more Protestant than Virginia. The Church of England, weakened after the Revolution, had never controlled even the planting class, which included Presbyterians, Congregationalists, and even Baptists. The city was more churchgoing than postwar Virginia.

Perhaps even more than in Virginia, some families insisted on strict propriety of behavior, and particularly among the women sincere piety was common.

Charleston was also more oligarchical and pleasure-loving. Challenged by middle-class patriots during the war, the traditional rulers came back to power afterward. As the wealth of the state recovered, the rice planters resumed their stately seasonal round of plays, races, and balls. Houses and furniture, through the next few decades, grew ever more elegant and sumptuous.

Far more than in Virginia, mortal fear showed beneath the charming surface of Charleston life. Rice planters lived in the city in summer to escape malaria, but even there yellow fever and other diseases struck hard and often. In 1794 Edward Rutledge wrote to his daughter in London saying as a matter of course that

> The City has been most exceedingly sickly, thro' the whole Summer but none of your particular Friends have fallen a sacrifice; indeed the disorders have been fatal to new comers, in the general, & such as changed the air too late.[28]

As for slavery, where Virginians deplored it but took it for granted, South Carolinians feared the slaves and almost unanimously defended the institution. A very few men like Henry Laurens and David Ramsay expressed hopes for eventual abolition. In the Constitutional Convention the delegates from South Carolina fought the Virginians in defense of the slave trade. After a brief closure when funds were tight after the Revolution, the trade was reopened in 1803. Thus new Africans were still being added to the concentrated slave population. Slaves were sold even at the racecourse, and the necessity of maintaining order was constantly in people's minds.

In this environment of extremes both piety and skepticism were common among the upper class. Among those skeptically inclined, both light-heartedness and stoical resignation could be carried very far.

Francis Kinloch, the scion and heir of a leading Carolina family, was like many of his class sent to England for his schooling. After Eton he went to Geneva for further education. There he found a small group of young Charleston aristocrats. He also formed intense friendships with the deist philosopher Claude Bonnet and especially with his tutor, the historian Johannes von Müller. After leaving Geneva, Kinloch wrote frequent, affectionate, frank, and discursive letters to Müller all his life, and it is from these letters that we know most about his own views and tastes. Clever and cosmopolitan and something of a dilettante, Kinloch found himself in London during the early years of the Revolutionary War. Though he was heir to a substantial estate at home, he could get only limited funds from his London merchant, so he tried hard to get an appointment from Lord North. He moved in London partly in a society of American exiles and had connections on both sides of the struggle. He also enjoyed fully the gaieties of the city. "I have been rather unchaste since my arrival. I am however very prudent, & can I think ensure Noses to my posterity. . . ."[29]

Kinloch was far more devoted to literature than to amorous intrigue. He approved Wollaston and enjoyed Rousseau, whose *Nouvelle Héloïse* he considered "the book of books." His main admiration, however, was reserved for the two great British skeptics Hume and Gibbon. Reading Adam Smith's account of Hume's death, Kinloch is full of admiration:

> You see a great man meeting death with a serenity, which is far superior to the little pride of the Stoicks, who would wish to persuade us that they despise it—show me a Christian, who ever faced dissolution with so much Philosophy, or at least with more. . . .[30]

Kinloch not only accepts Hume's refutation of Christian arguments but uses the philosopher's method in his own literary experiments:

> I have got a little book by me upon the internal conviction of the Christian Religion exclusive of Miracles, prophecies &c: & amuse myself in Confuting the arguments upon Paper, by showing the little foundation they are built upon, or applying them to other Religions.—If I had your reading I would write a book upon this Subject.[31]

When Gibbon's first volume comes out, Kinloch is particularly delighted with the daring and witty chapter on Christianity, and compares the historian to Horace, Juvenal, Tacitus, and Hume.[32]

Sure at first that the rebellion will soon be put down, Kinloch gradually becomes doubtful, and impatient of ever receiving English preferment. With some chagrin he notices the rapid rise of some Americans. The new president of Georgia, he points out in August 1777,

> not many years ago sold garden stuff about the streets in Savannah—in Carolina 'tis the same, and men have become Admirals, Generals, and

Lords of Trade, whom nature designed for Overseers, Shomakers & Shopkeepers, & who, if they escape hanging, may yet fulfill his decrees.[33]

Saratoga convinces this essentially unpolitical young man that he has made a mistake and missed an opportunity for glory, and that he had better get home if he was to save his estate.[34]

Making his way to New York, Kinloch somehow gets through the British lines and back to South Carolina, and by 1783, when his interrupted correspondence with Müller is resumed, he has served both as an officer in the Revolutionary army and a member of the South Carolina delegation to Congress. His retrospective view of the Revolution in 1785, however, remains characteristically detached and skeptical:

> the disappointment of a few smugglers in New England worked upon by the ancient Oliverian spirit, that panted to suffer once more for the "good old cause," the idle opulence of the Southern provinces, where something was wanted to employ the heavy hours of life, the stupidity of two or three British Governors, & the cruel impolitic behavior of their government brought on & kept up the war, which was conducted on both sides, & terminated in a manner that has convinced me, that there are certain extensive operations determined upon by providence, which are not to be foreseen, aided, or obviated by human means.[35]

Finding his colleagues in Congress impossible to respect, Kinloch has little hope for the new government at first. The Federal Constitution reassures him somewhat, at least about the prospects for protecting property. In 1802 he writes that after his brief congressional service,

> I now retired altogether, lamenting the evils which had sprung from the folly of some, been promoted by the art of others, & assisted by the blind enthusiasm of the people. . . .[36]

During the rest of his life, Kinloch led the usual life of his class in Charleston and at his plantation in the High Hills of Santee, reading the classics, opposing the French and Jefferson (whom he suspected of anti-slavery feelings), and assisting in the effort to reinvigorate the Episcopal Church.[37]

Kinloch is a fine specimen of the light-hearted side of Southern skepticism. Thomas Tudor Tucker, a brother of St. George Tucker, who came from Bermuda to settle in Charleston, exemplifies the stoical and gloomy side. Like Franklin, Tucker was persuaded in his youth that since a beneficent being is in charge of the universe, whatever is must logically be right. Unlike Franklin, however, Tucker did not reject this conclusion on common sense grounds. All his life he struggled to persuade himself that the universe must make more sense than it seems to. Part of his unhappiness was a matter of temperament; he lacked either Franklin's gusto or the gaiety of spirit that sustained his brother St. George. His gloom was also deepened by the difficulty he found in getting a medical practice started in Charleston.

In the 1770's we find him expressing his cosmic anguish in a number of letters to his brother:

> I assure you that when I seriously reflect on what Terms we have our Existence, I can scarcely persuade myself that we are under any Obligation to the being that gave it. But when I consider what an insignificant part of the Creation our whole Globe constitutes, I no longer wonder that its groveling Inhabitants are destitute of Capacity to comprehend the Plan of the Deity, & to distinguish by what secret means every apparent Evil may be made in the End to contribute to their Happiness. I have scarcely seen a person who seemed to be happy, nor can I well conceive a possibility of Happiness in human Life with human Affections. Yet I have seen many who appear'd to deserve Happiness. If then the Deity is just, even without benevolence, he must in a future State make Compensation for all the Evils we undeservedly suffer'd in this present. . . .
>
> They tell us of future Punishments, but I am equally convinced that none of us will be as unhappy in a future life as in this. . . . I am a good deal of the Predestinarist too. . . . I consider every Being, so far as it falls short of Perfection, to be under similar Circumstances with a Madman, whom no one wou'd think of punishing, after he recovered his Senses, for the former Inconsistency of his Actions.[38]

Tucker's occasionally strenuous efforts at cosmic optimism were not very successful:

> Were it not incompatible with the Innate Persuasion (if I may so term it) of Divine Benevolence, I shou'd be apt to imagine that Man was created for the Sport of some Superior Being inconsiderate or merciless enough to torture him as children do Butterflies for their Amusement.[39]
>
> Often, But in vain do I endeavour to explore the deep Designs of Heaven, & to understand for what End Man was created. . . . Sometimes I am impatient to know what Compensation a future State of Existence may make us for what we suffer here. Sometimes again I almost

despair of ever being happier, & scarcely think Annihilation a Misfortune.[40]

In 1787 a third Tucker brother who had gone to London was converted, like quite a few inquiring spirits in the period, to the mystical doctrines of Baron Swedenborg. Dumbfounded and perplexed by this irrational behavior, Thomas Tucker writes St. George expressing his amazement and defending, more systematically than usual, his own labored deist conclusions.

> A general Propensity to Religion in Mankind, I have consider'd as Evidence of the Deity's Existence. The Tenets of all the different Sects appear to me to abound with Absurdities, as far as I have Knowledge of them. Not because I cannot explain every thing, but because many things seem to be contradictory to that Reason which has been given by God for our guide. He could not give us Reason & then take pains (if I may so express myself) to confound it's Operation.[41]

When St. George Tucker's wife died in 1788, Thomas Tucker, who had experienced similar losses himself, wrote his brother a letter full of affection and a desperate effort at religious consolation. A future life *must* exist, or else God is capricious and contradictory:

> I flatter myself (& think my Hope well warranted by a reasoning from the Nature of Things) that we shall in this way receive full Compensation for all our present Suffering. For, whence do we derive the Approbation of our own Consciences in a voluntary & virtuous Suffering, but from his Will who created us? . . . Could the Creator have given us Virtues which himself does not possess? Possessing them Himself, he could not have given them to be a Source of Misery to us. Reason rejects such an Idea as an evident Contradiction. . . .

One doubts whether Tucker found the answers to these questions as convincing as he would have liked. The whole tone of this letter and many others is really conveyed by its first sentence: "Almighty God, how bitter is the Cup of Human Life!"[42]

South Carolina was a politically divided state. While Kinloch's skepticism led him to Federalism, Tucker's led him with equal logic to a very special sort of Republicanism. A skeptic about the Federal Constitution as about most human phenomena, Tucker was a perfect specimen of what one historian has called the Antifederalists, "Men of Little Faith."

The apparent popularity of the Constitution caused him to suspect that it must be unsound.[43] Later, finding the Federalist rage for monarchy further evidence for his profound doubt of human reason, Tucker became a Jeffersonian member of Congress. He was rewarded in 1801 by Thomas Jefferson, who made him Treasurer of the United States.

Francis Kinloch and Thomas Tudor Tucker were both extraordinary individuals, and neither is representative of the South Carolina upper class as a whole. Yet both carried their skepticism farther than was usual even in Virginia, and it is impossible to imagine either in Boston or Philadelphia. Kinloch's skepticism was that of gilded youth; Tucker's that of a deeply unhappy man. Neither discusses slavery at any length in his letters, though both take its existence for granted. Yet I cannot help believing that the presence in their society of an irrational institution had something to do with their tendency to believe in an irrational universe. Other less speculative Southerners, especially in Virginia, simply gave up the effort to justify either the ways of God to man or those of men to other men.

Sometimes aristocratic and usually pessimistic in its tendencies, the Skeptical Enlightenment had little future in any part of the expansive republic. Yet for a while it seemed to fit the needs of some of the Southern upper class. Both it and they were part of an old-regime world, a world whose intellectual spokesmen indulged in few Utopian hopes for humanity but valued wit, courage, and intellectual honesty. At the end of the eighteenth century, what was left of the Skeptical Enlightenment, in the South as elsewhere, was overwhelmed by two successive tides of popular emotion, the first political and the second and more powerful religious. Southern aristocratic skepticism furnished exactly the right enemy for the triumphant popular revivalism that from 1800 swept and reshaped Southern culture.

III

The Revolutionary
Enlightenment,
1776-1800

One   *Secular Millennialism*

The Revolutionary Enlightenment began to take shape about 1760 in Europe and America, was stimulated and strengthened but not fully developed during the American Revolution, and became suddenly and fully manifest in Paris in 1793. Its teachings profoundly affected Europe, England, and America by the end of the century. Its adherents were sure that they lived in a new age. For them, Enlightenment was an unsparing sunrise, revealing the wickedness and folly of ancient ideas and institutions, illuminating also the fundamental goodness of man. For the first time in history, they believed, it was now possible once and for all to destroy irrational Gothic remnants, to plan and create a new society, and thus to achieve the happiness for which man was destined. Since the new order would be a natural order, there was usually some element of primitivism in adherents of the Revolutionary Enlightenment: the Enlightened future would reproduce some golden age of simple goodness. Since the approaching triumph would liberate mankind once and for all, believers in it were often ruthless: love of mankind made it a duty to crush those who blocked its advance.

The Revolutionary Enlightenment was not entirely unconnected with its predecessors, the Moderate Enlightenment and the Skeptical Enlightenment, but it was very different. Its adherents detested the compromise and complacency of Addison or Clarke and had little use for the skepticism of Voltaire or Hume. The later tendency to lump together all kinds of Enlightenment was partly the work of the most violent opponents of the Revolutionary Enlightenment. Some of these came to see all forms of Enlightenment as parts of the same gigantic conspiracy, a plot which began by questioning existing ideas and institutions with the purpose of destroying them eventually. Curiously, this homogenization has been continued by many historians who are partisans rather than enemies of Enlightenment in general.

Up to this point, all varieties of Enlightenment had been ranged in sharp opposition to popular enthusiasm and especially popular religion. The Revolutionary Enlightenment was itself enthusiastic and religious in spirit. Like Christians seeking revival, its spokesmen suffered because men were not good and free, and longed for some cataclysm in which they might become so. As a number of historians have suggested, there is much in common between millennial and sectarian movements and the new revolution of the late eighteenth century. The Revolutionary Enlightenment is linked to prophets and preachers of the past by its hatred of lukewarmness and cynicism, its demand for absolute commitment, its dedication and intolerance, its constant invocation of the instincts of the people against the sophistication of the learned.[1] The same traits link it to romantic and revolutionary seers of the future, and separate it sharply from the skeptics of the salons. In particular, certain kinds of Christian millennialists who flourished from the middle ages through the seventeenth century seem to resemble Jacobins and later revolutionaries in their fervent belief in a new day coming when injustice and oppression will cease, in their fear of conspiracies which stand in the way of this new day, and in their association of human brotherhood with necessary bloodshed.[2] It is possible, then, to look at men of the Revolutionary Enlightenment as one kind of sectarians or as one kind of revolutionaries.

It is also legitimate, however, to see them as spokesmen of one kind of Enlightenment. What they shared with men of the very different kinds of Enlightenment we have already looked at was their secularity and modernity. Their coming kingdom was of this world. Past culture, except for periods of rugged virtue like the Spartan or Roman republics, was not hallowed. Like Locke or Hume or Voltaire, Rousseau and Paine set themselves to take a new and clear look at matters once shrouded in sanctity. All these invoked knowledge and reason against superstition, though the last two differed sharply from the others as to what they meant by knowledge or reason, how these were to be achieved, and what truths they brought to light.

Replacing both English complacency and French skepticism, revolutionary zeal suddenly triumphed in France and much of Europe, shook

England, and threatened America. It is not part of the purpose of this book to answer the fascinating question of the origins of the revolution of the late eighteenth century, which were certainly social and political and even technological as well as psychological and ideological. In our own immediate perspective, the rise of radicalism can be seen as the other side of the decay of complacency. Thus the emotions aroused in England by Wesley and Wilkes as well as Rousseau and Paine were part of a reaction to midcentury equilibrium. One might almost suggest that the revolution of the late eighteenth century came about partly because the revolution of the seventeenth century was far enough in the past to be idealized rather than hated.

Whig radicalism was the principal antecedent of the Revolutionary Enlightenment and its revival in England marked the beginning of the revolutionary age. Even during the complacent heyday of the Moderate Enlightenment, this kind of radicalism had never entirely died out. It is true that Whig theory, with its emphasis on a social contract which legitimized government and its insistence on an exact balance among king, lords, and commons, could be a prescription for deadlock and a means of justifying the status quo. It had also, however, a radical potential.

The radical part of the Whig tradition, unlike the Revolutionary and Enlightened radicalism of the late eighteenth century, depended on a gloomy assessment of human nature. All Whigs believed that human nature was balanced between good and evil, and Radical Whigs believed this balance to be particularly precarious. Freedom was always in danger of corruption, and Radical Whigs believed that British freedom was in the process of decline. The chief evidence for this conclusion lay in the growth of wealth, luxury, and vice. Against decadence, Radical Whigs invoked the rugged virtues associated with the Roman Republic, the freedom-loving Germans, the sturdy Anglo-Saxons and the people in general. Public virtue, the mainstay in the battle against corruption and tyranny, depended above all on freedom of conscience. Free religion and free speech had always to be defended against all agents of corruption, including bureaucracy, standing armies, and established churches. Against

these powers, the right of revolution was in the long run the only safeguard. For revolution, English precedent lay in the Puritan revolution of
the seventeenth century.[3]

Whig Radicalism, and especially that part of it associated with the
Commonwealth, appealed powerfully to discontented Americans and
formed the major part of American Revolutionary theory. In this way it
entered into the whole revolution of the eighteenth century. It is difficult
to find much direct connection between Commonwealthmen and French
Jacobins; they are separated by religion, national tradition, and their
view of the nature of man. Nevertheless, Commonwealthman and Jacobin believed in common in the importance of republican virtue as
against aristocratic luxury and vice. In this they and the most radical
Americans linked together the radicalism of the whole century and connected it to the past. In our present terms, the Radical Whigs were not
a part of the Revolutionary Enlightenment, but they were a very important antecedent.

Those Radical Whigs who carried on the Commonwealth tradition
through the doldrums of the early eighteenth century and became heroes to discontented Englishmen and Americans were a very mixed group.
Some were genuine radicals who invoked Algernon Sidney, who had
died for his barely concealed republicanism in 1683, or repeated John
Milton's arguments for free speech. Others, more likely to cite Harrington or Locke, merely believed that the constitution needed to be shifted
back in a libertarian direction, or that the essential Protestantism of the
established Church needed to be reasserted. Benjamin Hoadly, the
Bishop of Bangor who argued against high-church sacramentalism, was
adopted into the Radical Whig canon. Beginning in 1720, the Commonwealth tradition was powerfully revived by those great colonial favorites,
John Trenchard and Thomas Gordon, authors of the *Independent Whig*
and *Cato's Letters*, who argued eloquently that Englishmen should
place their reliance in religious matters on reason and the Bible, and in
politics on constitutional liberty, freedom of speech, and the virtue of the
people.

Early in the century, English radicalism was a matter of invoking past
tradition to keep a tradition of resistance barely alive. In the 1760's John
Wilkes stirred the London mob to the brink of revolt with his denunciation of ministerial oppression and corruption, and his defense of parliamentary immunity. It is a measure of the complexity of the midcentury

changes in English society that Wilkes, despite his well-known libertinism and probable religious skepticism, was admired by English and
American Dissenters.

The radicalization of British Dissent is a neglected and important
stage in the growth of the revolutionary spirit in the eighteenth century.
Between about 1750 and 1770, the sober, theologically liberal, politically
complacent Dissenters of the Doddridge type gave place to several new
kinds of Dissenters, including on the one hand fervent Calvinistic revivalists but on the other radical rationalists, discontented with English
institutions, prepared to back revolutions first in America and then in
France, themselves halfway to belief in the ideas of the Revolutionary
Enlightenment.

In 1772 an American correspondent warned the secretary of the S.P.G.
of a formidable conspiracy in England "by which Deists, Arians, and all
non-conformists, except Quakers, act jointly to overturn the ecclesiastical establishment of the nation. . . . Probably this plan was first formed
by some of the Wilkes patriots, that the religious engine might be plied
in concert with the efforts of civil discord."[4] What he was referring to
was the dual effort, first to relieve Church of England clergy from the
necessity of subscribing to all the Thirty-Nine Articles, and second to relieve Dissenters from subscription to all but a few of these. This effort,
on the brink of success in 1772, failed in Parliament, most of whose
members whatever their private beliefs thought that some uniformity
was necessary, especially perhaps in troubled times. This rebuff, together
with rumors about colonial bishops and toleration of Catholics in Quebec, caused some English Dissenters to believe in a new conspiracy
against Protestant liberty.[5]

In 1763 Mrs. Catharine Macaulay began publishing her history of
England in the Stuart period, frankly dedicated to the defense of liberty
and virtue against corruption, tyranny, and their defenders, especially
David Hume. In 1771 James Burgh published his *Historical Essay on the
English Constitution*, telling the familiar story of decline from Saxon
liberty. In 1774, in his *Political Disquisitions*, he applied the same lessons to present dangers of corruption, militarism, and colonial oppression. Burgh supported universal male suffrage, and by the seventies the
most radical Dissenters were talking of natural rights rather than toleration, and demanding that English liberties be drastically broadened
rather than merely preserved.

Joseph Priestley and Richard Price, both fervent friends of the American Revolution and later of the French, represent a special kind of coming together of rationalist and radical Protestant ideas. Both were ministers, both were ardent Christians, and both were advanced theological liberals. Though both were immensely admired in America in 1776, both were more radical than most of their American admirers.

Priestley, who had been first a student and then a teacher at leading Dissenting academies, was a scientist of nearly the first importance despite some wrong conclusions. Completely lacking any shred of irony or skepticism, he moved all the way from Calvinism to Socinianism and a special kind of materialism while still fervently insisting he was a Christian. He believed in parliamentary reform, free speech, and the end of Dissenter disabilities. He welcomed the American Revolution, and saw it as a harbinger of the millennium.

Thoroughly opposed to some of the bland compromises of the Moderate Enlightenment, Priestley was uncomfortable with French skepticism. He disliked Voltaire, and remembered a visit to Paris without much pleasure:

> When I was dining at Paris fifteen years ago at Turgot's table, M. de Chatelleux [sic]—Author of *Travels through America*—in answer to an inquiry said that the two gentlemen opposite me were the Bishop of Aix and the Archbishop of Toulouse, but, said he, "they are no more believers than you or I." I assured him I was a believer; but he would not believe me; and Le Roi, the philosopher, told me that I was the only man of sense he knew that was a Christian.[6]

Richard Price, a close friend of Priestley, stopped short of his theological radicalism: he was an Arian rather than a Socinian and argued vigorously against Priestley's materialism in defense of free will and the immaterial soul. He was, in fact, a leading defender of the objectivity and rationality of moral judgments, which he applied unhesitatingly to history and politics. An admirer of the whole Commonwealth canon, he early convinced himself of the complete righteousness of the American cause, which like Priestley he tended to see in terms of millennial promise. In 1776 he contrasted colonial sobriety with British corruption:

> From one end of *North America* to the other, they are FASTING and PRAYING. But what are we doing?—Shocking thought! we are ridiculing them as *Fanatics*, and scoffing at religion.—We are running wild after

pleasure, and forgetting every thing serious and decent at *Masquerades*—
We are gambling in gaming houses; trafficking for Boroughs; perjuring
ourselves at Elections; and selling ourselves for places.—Which side then
is Providence likely to favour.[7]

Price, Priestley, Burgh, and other rationalist Dissenters encountered
the leading representative of colonial opinion in the advanced circles
presided over by Lord Shelburne, who employed Priestley as tutor, and
also in the coffee-houses and taverns frequented by scientists, Dissenters,
and partisans of America. Price and Priestley, Dissenters of the eighteenth and not nineteenth-century variety, could laugh over one of Franklin's smuttiest pieces, his "Letter to the Royal Society at Brussels," while
both labored to convert the colonial sage from his eclectic skepticism to
their own rationalist and radical kind of Christianity.[8]

Naturally, when American grievances accumulated and Americans
needed arguments against oppression, they turned to the Commonwealth and Radical Whig school, and particularly to the Dissenters
whom they had long admired.[9] Hoadly, Mrs. Macaulay, Trenchard and
Gordon, Priestley and Price were all quoted by Americans who were by
no means radical. Americans who chose the side of resistance could all
agree that the balance of the British constitution had been endangered
by corruption. As we have seen, many Americans who thought this remained fully within the tradition of the Moderate English Enlightenment, sure that reason must always rule against popular passion, and
that even in revolutionary times government must remain in the hands
of the wise and the good, which was very likely to mean the well educated and the well-to-do.

Popular passion is, however, necessary even to the most well-bred revolution, and enough of it was aroused to sustain a great deal of mob action and to keep alive a cause that often seemed desperate. Admitting
that American revolutionary radicalism existed, historians have found it
hard to describe. This is partly because they sometimes tend to see it in
the perspective created by the French Revolution and later revolutionary theory. It has proved hard to find a clear class basis for American
radicalism. Mechanics and farmers often turn into lawyers and merchants when they are looked at closely. It is hard to find a sustained and
unified set of social as opposed to political grievances. It is impossible to
find a separate radical ideology.

American radicals, like American moderates, drew on Whig and

Commonwealth ideas, but they cited the same sources with a different tone and emphasis. Radicals were likely to bear down hard on the large ascetic and even primitivist element in the Commonwealth tradition, the call for an end to luxury and a return to virtue and frugality. They were likely to use the words virtue and wisdom in a way that did not necessarily associate these qualities with educated restraint, but rather with popular instinct. In sounding these notes, radicals were forced to repudiate much of the Moderate Enlightenment, which had been ranged against the forces of popular instinct and emotion ever since the Great Awakening. Thus in American radicalism in this period as in many periods, there is a good deal of invocation of the purer and simpler past against modern complexity and decline.

The most important emotional reservoir for radicals was that provided by radical religion, and radical religion was as yet usually Calvinist.[10] Such expert propagandists as Samuel Adams understood their constituency, and played constantly on the fears aroused by rumors of a colonial bishop or the toleration of Catholicism in Quebec. Tories, for their part, knew well that the "black-coated regiment" of the Calvinist clergy, particularly in New England, was one of the most unified and effective supports of sedition.

That regiment was in fact more unified than it had been for some time. To some of the clergy, the Revolution was a heaven-sent opportunity to restore unity and arrest decline. Arminians, moderate Calvinists, and ultra-Calvinists could agree in hating bishops and demanding religious as well as civil liberty. But it was the Calvinists of various kinds who best manipulated the thunders of the jeremiad, who showed that America's trouble arose not only from British corruption but from New England's own sinful failure to carry out her divine assignment. It was Calvinists like Nathaniel Whitaker of Salem who most rigorously invoked the curse of Meroz on the lukewarm "because they came not to the help of the Lord against the mighty."[11] And above all it was Calvinists who most diligently searched Scripture for the hidden meaning of great events.

In the moderate Calvinist atmosphere of Witherspoon's Princeton, where sympathy with the colonial resistance was almost universal, two aspiring graduates, Hugh Henry Brackenridge and Philip Freneau wrote the class poem of 1771. First describing the westward migration of the arts, they confidently suggested a proper location for the millennium itself:

A new Jerusalem sent down from heav'n
Shall grace our happy earth, perhaps this land,
Whose virgin bosom shall then receive, tho' late,
Myriads of saints with their almighty king,
To live and reign on earth a thousand years
Thence call'd Millennium. Paradise anew
Shall flourish, by no second Adam lost.[12]

Mrs. Hannah Winthrop, the wife of the Harvard astronomer, during the Revolutionary years kept up her correspondence with Mrs. Mercy Warren, the historian and poet. Both these vigorous-minded women were liberal Calvinist in theology, interested in science, and deeply Puritan in culture. Their correspondence is an interesting mixture of science, literature, and patriotism. They have much to say about English decadence, insist on stern punishment for Tories, and see clearly a relation between the American Revolution and the Biblical millennium:

The grand Revolution of America may probably be big with consequences that will greatly effect [*sic*] the other hemisphere & make way for the accomplishment of those glorious Prophecies you mention. Some of these Prophecies lead us to expect a time when there shall be peace & love among all Mankind; but this can hardly be expected till the Gospel shall prevail universally.[13]

As the war dragged on, millennial sermons became ever more fervent and literal. For some, George III was the Great Beast himself, and America ever more clearly the theater of Armageddon. To some extent, millennial hope lessened the gloom of Calvinist radicalism and connected it to the secular optimism of the developing Revolutionary Enlightenment. Yet in the long run, after their moments of euphoria, radical Calvinists remembered that victory always carries with it dangers of pride and therefore of punishment. In America at least, the millennium which would arrive under direct divine supervision and only after severe trials was not yet entirely merged either with American destiny or world revolution.[14]

In the crisis of 1775-76 it was necessary to draw on all available feelings and ideas, and to bring together moderates and radicals, deists and

Arminians and Calvinists, to make the leap into the unknown, the exhilarating and frightening break away from monarchy, tradition, and Europe. Two men, Thomas Paine and Thomas Jefferson, wrote the two most influential pieces of patriot propaganda in this crisis. Both were to become major figures of the Revolutionary Enlightenment, but neither they nor this tradition was as yet fully formed.

Paine emerged from English poverty and English Quakerism of the time of reviving radicalism, and at least one historian has suggested that he is a part of the Dissenting tradition.[15] At least he had the same enemies as Burgh, Price, or Priestley, and talked some of the same language. In his early pieces in the *Pennsylvania Magazine* he appealed openly to Protestant feelings:

> Wherever the visible church has been oppressed, political Freedom has suffered with it. Read the history of Mary and the Stuarts. . . . Though I am unwilling to accuse the present government of popish principles, they cannot, I think, be clearly acquitted of popish practices.[16]

Common Sense is a radical masterpiece; it is full of the excitement of a moment when men have a chance to form their institutions anew; there is no Calvinistic concern that pride may lead them astray. Yet Americans steeped in Calvinism and the Commonwealth writers must have found some of it very congenial, particularly the statement that government was the badge of lost innocence, "A mode made necessary by the inability of moral virtue to govern the world." Some may have been reassured by the laborious use of the Old Testament. There was nothing to object to in the contrast between George the Third and the ultimate monarch: "But where, say some, is the King of America? I'll tell you, friend, he reigns above, and doth not make havoc of mankind like the Royal Brute of Great Britain."

It is not really surprising that *Common Sense* was read from Calvinist pulpits as well as in army camps. Its newness came not from innovating theory, but from its daring, its ardor, its timing, and also its universalism. Breaking sharply with Whig and even Commonwealth concentration on Anglo-Saxon liberties and the glories of the ancient constitution, Paine moved toward a new and profoundly important interpretation of the colonial struggle. "The cause of America is in a great measure the cause of all mankind." His exalted vision of the future, in places already proclaiming the Revolutionary Enlightenment, did not yet break completely with the vocabulary of Biblical millennialism. "We have it in our power to begin the world over again. A situation similar to the present has not happened since the days of Noah until now."[17] Many devoted Calvinists undoubtedly agreed. This explains why some of them were to be startled and horrified by Paine's later and fully secular works.

The Declaration of Independence, in religious terms, is more radical than *Common Sense:* not for what it says but for what it leaves out. Jefferson, whose religious views were still being formed and were still unexpressed, admired the Commonwealth writers and agreed with them completely in contrasting the ancient Anglo-Saxon frugality with modern British luxury and decadence. Yet he did not share with most dissenting radicalism its attachment to Protestant doctrine, especially the doctrine of original sin. In the Declaration there is none of Paine's laborious argument from Scripture; the principal truths about man and government are said to be self-evident. Not the restraint of evil or the restoration of virtue but the pursuit of happiness is the end of Government.

Most of the great Declaration is a summary of familiar and particular grievances. It does not, like *Common Sense*, denounce monarchy in general, nor does it imply any specific American mission to liberate mankind: these meanings were read into it later. Jefferson was determined, he said later, to introduce no divisive innovations in the document but to rest it on "the harmonizing sentiments of the day" and such well-known authorities as Aristotle, Cicero, Locke, and Sidney.[18] Yet in the exaltation of the moment, he stated the familiar theories of natural rights, the social contract, and the right of revolution in such ringing sentences and coupled with them such a fervent assertion of human equality that a few crucial sentences stand out. These sentences, read partly in the light of later events, have made the Declaration the mainstay of American radicals ever since.

Jefferson's colleagues on the drafting committee and then the Congress, made up of moderates and radicals, Episcopalians, Presbyterians, and covert deists, accepted the Declaration with only a few changes. Changes made by Congress included not only the deletion of the antislavery clause, but also the addition of "a firm reliance on the protection of divine providence." Probably most of the signers were men of the Moderate Enlightenment, believers in a mixed human nature offering both dangers and opportunities and the necessity of moderation and restraint. The document they signed in a moment of bold commitment moved them, and even their nation, some distance on the road from this kind of Enlightenment to another.

The most radical meaning of the American Revolution for the world in its day came not from its theory, but from the fact that it happened. There were no precedents: for the first time a continental nation with ample potential resources had a chance to establish natural institutions, to revive the virtue and greatness of republican Rome, even to bring forward the millennium.

Once this first modern revolution had taken place, all institutions everywhere lost some of their sanctity. Looking back from a little later, many Americans saw their Revolution in different terms from those which were usually used during its course.[19] As early as 1790 Caesar Rodney, a Delaware lawyer and war governor, wrote a letter to Jefferson clearly associating the American Revolution and a new kind of intellectual emancipation:

> The Revolution of America, by recognizing those rights which every Man is Entitled to by the laws of God and Nature, Seems to have broken off all those devious Tramels of Ignorance, prejudice, and Superstition which have long depressed the Human Mind. Every door is now Open to the Sons of genius and Science to enquire after Truth. Hence we may expect the darkening clouds of error will vanish fast before the light of reason; and that the period is fast arriving when the Truth will enlighten the whole world.[20]

One reason Rodney could say this was that by 1790 clear signs existed that revolution was spreading.

By the time the news of the American Revolution began to reach Paris, the French Enlightenment had spread widely among the French upper classes.[21] It was, however, increasingly fragmented. Enlightened people had long ceased to believe in Christianity, but by now they were finding it almost equally difficult to believe in human reason. Skepticism alone, or the grim and rigid materialism of Helvétius, were splendid weapons for the destruction of dogma, but provided no basis for positive commitment. A welter of ideas competed for the allegiance of intellectuals. Some, following Turgot, proclaimed universal progress; others, like Mably, insisted on the superiority of the simple child of nature. On the fringes of the Enlightened circle many plunged into faddish experiments: occultism, satanism, spiritualism, or mesmerism fascinated former skeptics.[22]

The government, struggling with financial and institutional crisis, could still show its teeth against open criticism. Theoretical radicals like Mably and Morellet dreamed of socialist Utopias in some vague future. Diderot, who combined in himself almost all the current tendencies, detested the regime more and more fiercely, but struggled without success against his belief that human affairs were determined by biology. In the last decades of the monarchy, most intellectual radicals were similarly paralyzed, hating the status quo, with no real confidence in reforming ministries, no trust in the masses and no knowledge of them, and no secure standard by which to judge and condemn society.[23] As in other periods of frustrated radicalism, opinion veered from one extreme to another.

Inevitably, the brave men who had early raised the standards of defiance were deified, particularly Voltaire and Rousseau, old enemies who both died in 1778. For many, the philosopher of Ferney was a great symbol of the past, and the Genevan prophet the greatest herald of the future. Despite his many contradictions and his political caution, Rousseau is the first great figure of the Revolutionary Enlightenment. Partly by ignoring contradictions, he was able to offer a standard for virtue, a focus for emotion, and belief in something like a Secular Millennium. Though man was everywhere in chains, he was born free and his freedom could be reconquered: the Fall was quite real but reversible.

Though Rousseau spoke for Enlightenment as against tradition, it is impossible to associate him except as a strategic ally with either the Moderate or the Skeptical Enlightenment. He did not range reason against passion or try to find truth by balancing extremes, and he had no confidence in inherited constitutions or representative institutions. Above all, he carried on a long polemic against the skepticism with which he was surrounded. Rousseau's dislike for the Parisian enlightenment went well beyond his personal quarrels with Voltaire, Diderot, and Hume. "Suspicion, shadows, fears, coldness, reserve, hatred, and treason always hide under this uniform and deceitful veil of politeness, under this boasted urbanity which we owe to the Enlightenment [*lumières*] of our century."[24] A deep and fundamental difference from his contemporaries was stated at the very beginning of his career, when he stated flatly that our souls are corrupted in proportion to the advance of arts and sciences.[25] This statement, often qualified and sometimes contradicted, was never withdrawn.

Like other figures of the Revolutionary Enlightenment, Rousseau had something in common with religious radicalism of the past. Like British and American Dissenters or Commonwealthmen, he inveighed against luxury and praised Spartan simplicity. Like revivalists, he invoked the wisdom of the simple against the folly of the learned.

Yet Rousseau's relation to his ancestral Protestantism is a complex and much-argued question. Though he knew the Bible well, he did not search its pages for the truth, which could be found only within the individual soul or in nature.[26] Rousseau's religion is that of a society which has rejected any literal kind of Christianity beyond possibility of return, and it was this fact more than any other that was to limit his influence in the new American republic. His Savoyard vicar is a sentimentalist, not unlike liberal Christians of much later periods who decide to forget doctrinal difficulties and believe what makes them feel good. A far harsher kind of religious utilitarianism is found in the famous pages in the *Social Contract* which deal with civic religion. Here, the religion of the Gospels is true and beautiful, but also incivic and debilitating. The central beliefs necessary to the state, including the existence of God and life after death, must be prescribed and enforced, with the penalty for non-belief, exile, and for backsliding, death.

This is only one extreme assertion of the mighty power of the General Will, the central doctrine not only of Rousseau, but of the revolutionary tradition he began. The General Will is not the sum of the wills of any actual individuals; it is neither additive nor utilitarian. It has about it something millennial and transforming, it operates through change and conversion. Against it, no rights may stand, because no real difference between it and the sovereign people is possible. The social contract provides that "anyone who refuses to obey the general will shall be forced to do so by the whole body; which means nothing more or less than that he will be forced to be free."[27] Rousseau was not, like some later revolutionaries, a believer in the creative power of violence. In *Emile* he tries to show how a child can be brought up in natural goodness by noncoercive manipulation. Nonetheless, in the fiery passages about the General Will many kinds of revolutionaries have found the best justification for a clean sweep, a break with the past, and a suppression of reaction.[28]

It is not surprising that the American Revolution was seen in Paris mainly in terms drawn from Rousseau. The virtuous Americans, free from prejudice and close to nature, had swept away the past and opened a new path for the whole world. During the last struggles to reform the French monarchy and the early days of the ensuing Revolution, some Frenchmen used the American example to attack those who wanted to remodel France in accordance with the English model, so much admired in the age of Condorcet. Turgot, Condorcet, and others of their generation were amazed and unhappy that the Americans themselves hung on to such relics of the English past as checks and balances and particularly a bicameral legislature. The mixture of balance-and-order moderation with archaic Commonwealth radicalism that had gone into American ideology had little meaning on the continent of Europe. Frenchmen of the early Revolution who admired America were the first of a long line of European radicals who were to love an ideal America and misunderstand the real one.

In nineteenth-century America it was customary to talk about the coming of the French Revolution in terms of fiery dawns or baleful comets. These figures, implying sudden cataclysms, make it hard to understand both the Great Revolution and its impact on other countries, particularly the United States. Its contemporary meaning becomes clearer if we divide it into three periods: 1789-92 the period of easy triumphs and Utopian hopes; 1793-95 the period of Jacobin glory, virtue, and terror; and 1795-99 the period of reaction and corruption in Paris, but victory abroad.

In the first period, the French seemed to be giving the world a complete lesson in the possibilities of peaceful revolution. With much euphoria and comparatively little bloodshed, the Estates turned themselves into a National Assembly, the aristocracy surrendered its privileges, the Church was subjected to state control, and the king accepted the constitution. In this period, more than either before or after, the ideas of the Revolutionary Enlightenment were stated in benign and Utopian form. Its typical spokesmen were often aristocratic in origin, without the resentments that come from a past of deprivation or suppression, and without a belief in the necessity of revolutionary coercion. Less contradictory and less inward than Rousseau, they were more radical in their immediate program but less in their long-run potential.

Count Constantin de Volney, who had contemplated the ruins of empires in the Near East, blamed the decline of earlier civilizations in somewhat Gibbonian manner on the corruptions of kings and priests, and the depressing doctrines of gloomy religions. In 1791 this theory led Volney, as it had not led Gibbon, to a glowing vision of the future, starting with the Revolution already under way in France. In his widely read *Ruins*, Volney foresees a vast meeting, at which the people are taught that all religions originate only in the sensations and wants of men. Converted, they decide to dispense with monarchy and the Church and make an entirely new start.

In his eulogy of Franklin delivered before the National Assembly, the Marquis de Condorcet compared the bloody Revolution of the English Puritans to the peaceable and constitutional one then going on in France in the spirit of Newton and Boyle.[29] A little later, in immediate danger of the guillotine, Condorcet wrote the most glowing of all projections of human progress. Enlightenment and revolution were part of the same story. The triumph of man had begun with the overcoming of superstition and the glories of the new science; it was furthered by the American Revolution despite its disfiguring taste for checks and balances and far more by the Revolution in France. In the universal reign of reason, toleration, and humanity, at last disease, overpopulation, language divisions, and—in large part at least—death itself would be overcome. Condorcet was able to accept with genuine nobility the likelihood—his most accurate prophecy—of personal disaster. In one way at least his optimism was justified: his version of the past and future had a long life ahead of it in America and Europe. One can find it almost intact, for instance, in the New History of H. G. Wells or J. H. Robinson in the early twentieth century.

In the second period of the Revolution, Condorcet was proscribed and died in flight. Volney, with other Enlightened aristocrats, fled to Philadelphia. Events succeeded each other with terrifying speed: the proclamation of the Republic, the execution of the king, the outbreak of international ideological war, the mounting fear (some of it justified) of internal and external enemies, the executions of deviants, the lukewarm, and the suspect, and finally the brief reign of terror and virtue presided over by Robespierre, "Democrat, prophet, and puritan."[30] It is this stage of the Revolution, as Hannah Arendt has pointed out, which displaced all others in the world's imagination, and has shaped world history ever since.

Not only the end of official Christianity but the break with tradition of all kinds was symbolized in every possible way. The new Republican calendar began time itself with the first year of the Republic. The Academy of Sciences, a symbol of royal patronage and also of elitism, was abolished in 1792. Some historians of science have seen the emergence of a new "Jacobin science," replacing Newtonian determinism by a dynamic and organic synthesis.[31]

In its break with the past, the Jacobin Revolution broke specifically with past forms of Enlightenment. In the earlier period, Voltaire had been seen as a hero of liberty, and in 1791 his body was reburied in the Pantheon with official honors. As the Revolution progressed, however, his skepticism and pessimism as well as his monarchism made him increasingly suspect. Later, the bust of Helvétius like that of Mirabeau was removed from the Jacobin Club. At the climax of his power, Robespierre bitterly denounced the Encylopedists for their compromises with the monarchical regime, their propagation of materialism, and their cynicism. The great advances of the eighteenth century, in which France had played the major role, had left the globe half Enlightened, and half in darkness.

> The peoples of Europe made astonishing progress in what are called the arts and sciences, and they seem still to be ignorant of the first notions of public morality. They know everything, except their rights and their duties.[32]

Much the same things were soon to be said, with opposite connotations, by American opponents of both Enlightenment and Revolution, and this particular speech of Robespierre can be seen either as the culmination of the Revolutionary Enlightenment or as its end. Condorcet was even more a target of passionate denunciation than his skeptical predecessors. Of the sages of the past, only Rousseau remained beyond criticism, elevated into the status of a seer and prophet, in some extreme quarters into that of a new Christ, preaching a revolutionary redemption.

In June 1794, Robespierre, partly out of concern about the extremes of Revolutionary cults but mostly from a sincere belief in the necessity of religion for the Republic, proclaimed a whole series of new festivals (of Truth, of Justice, of Modesty, to Glory and Immortality, etc.) and himself presided over the celebration of the first of them, the Festival of the Supreme Being. Less than a month later, having lost touch with all but a small faction of followers, he was himself guillotined.

In Paris, for the time, the Revolutionary Enlightenment had come to an end. Robert Palmer has reminded us, however, that in the ensuing period of the Directorate, the period of corruption, of plot and counter-plot, of bourgeois moderation, the Revolutionary armies carried the slogans of Enlightenment and Revolution through most of Western Europe.[33] It is in this last period that the decisive intellectual and political battle took place in the United States.

Ironically, American opinion of the Revolutionary Enlightenment was shaped in large part by English reflections of the events in France. More than ever Americans were influenced by the opinion of those Englishmen, especially Dissenters, who had supported their own struggle. Some Dissenters had moved far beyond their earlier kinds of discontent, and were now fervent friends of the Revolution in France. They saw France, of course, through their own very British and Protestant glasses.

The triumph of their friends in America had made radical Dissenters in England more confident. Some of them had become more interested in antislavery, reform of penal institutions, and radical expansion of the suffrage. Their new drive to remove the archaic and insulting restrictions embodied in the Test and Corporation Acts had been joined by secular liberals and Foxite Whigs. In 1787, alarmed conservatives in the House of Commons again beat a motion for repeal of these acts.

Coming right after this smarting setback, the French events of 1789 had special meaning for Dissenters. Now for the first time religious freedom was wider in France than in England; the National Assembly gave French Protestants complete equality in holding office, a privilege still denied English Dissenters—let alone Catholics. This made it possible to link the new revolution with the tradition of 1688 or even the 1640's. In the network of reform societies, where Franklin had once met British radicals, Dissenters rubbed shoulders with deists, romantic poets, discontented Irishmen, and visiting French republicans. The tone of Dissenter demands increasingly became more radical and secular. In demanding equality, said one of them, it was not "as Dissenters we wish to enter the lists; we wish to bury every name of distinction in the common appellation of Citizen. We wish not the name of Dissenter to be pronounced, except in our theological researches and religious assemblies."[34] Benjamin Vaughan, a leading British propagandist for the American Revolution and a member of advanced dissenting circles, wrote his brother in New York that American statesmen now seemed out of date. Only Madison and one or two more seemed familiar with recent writings in Europe "where the new doctrines make most rapid strides. We all consider America as of the old school, and no pattern."[35] Among radical Dissenters, advanced rationalism mixed oddly with millennial prophecy. Like many American Protestants, some British Dissenters could understand the events in France only as the dawn of the long-awaited age of peace, justice, and brotherhood.

Rationalism and millennialism were mixed in both the two leading figures of Dissenting radicalism, who had also been the two best known Dissenting friends of the American Revolution: Richard Price and Joseph Priestley. In 1789, at the meeting of the Revolution Society, named in honor of the Glorious Revolution a century earlier, Price preached a sermon calling on Britain to complete the task which the men of 1688 had left partly undone. The true meaning of the Glorious Revolution, he insisted, included not only religious liberty but the right of resistance and the right to choose and dismiss one's governors:

> Be encouraged all ye friends of freedom, and writers in its defence! . . . Behold, the light you have struck out, after setting AMERICA free, reflected to FRANCE, and there kindled into a blaze that lays despotism in ashes, and warms and illuminates EUROPE![36]

Priestley, more hostile than Price to French skepticism and more dubious about France in general, was also more of a student of Biblical prophecy. Something of a pre-millenarian, he expected the new day to break with apocalyptic violence, and could thus rejoice in the French Revolution even while disapproving its excesses. Brave and incautious, he gave many opportunities for his enemies to quote fiery passages, and the enemies of radical Dissenters were rapidly increasing.

As stress increased with the threat of war, some Dissenters changed their minds, some were silent, and a number including Priestley moved to America. Some of the leadership of British radicalism passed from Dissenters to secular radicals. Yet the break is seldom a sharp one; Price and Priestley on the one hand, and Godwin and Paine on the other, there are both similarities and differences.

William Godwin, the most radical theorist of the day, was the son of a Dissenting minister, and had been taught by a clergyman who was at once an extreme Calvinist and a Wilkite radical. He had read Edwards in his youth, and after attending a Dissenting academy became a minister himself. In the eighties, however, he had been powerfully attracted by the materialism of Holbach, and after a brief stop with Priestley's Unitarianism, became a non-believer and a professional hack writer. In London radical circles he encountered Price, Paine, the Vaughans, and also Joel Barlow of Connecticut. The French Revolution stirred him, and like Burke, he connected it with the writings of Rousseau and Helvétius.[37] In 1793 he published *Political Justice*.

In this work Godwin starts from the principles of Locke and arrives at an extreme and optimistic rationalism. We draw our ideas from sensation, yet the mind is so constituted that the truth, properly presented, must always win the day. Thus it is safe to question all institutions, judging them for their rationality and utility. Most existing institutions failed this test: Godwin condemns monarchy, aristocracy, such monarchical survivals as the United States presidency, corporations, contracts, punishment of criminals, and coercive education of children.

An extreme though entirely pacific spokesman of the Revolutionary Enlightenment, Godwin has no use for custom or tradition in any sphere, and differs from Rousseau in placing the state of nature more definitely at the end rather than the beginning of human development. At least equaling the optimism of Condorcet, Godwin believed that finally, with the systematic inculcation in the young of "a stricter sense of justice, and a purer theory of happiness,"[38] men would cease to find their gratification in wealth and show, and the rich would share what they had with their neighbors. Machines would end manual labor; marriage would become free, dissolvable at will, and unexclusive; population surplus would be held in check; and, since mind modifies body, disease and death would be in a large measure overcome.

In 1797 Godwin, somewhat contradicting his principles, married Mary Wollstonecraft, who in 1792 had applied revolutionary principles to perhaps the most dangerous cause of all, the rights of women. Taking off from Rousseau, whom she vigorously condemned, this vigorous and handsome woman struck boldly at the tradition of bringing up women for the sexual enjoyment of men, denouncing prudery, separate education, and frivolity. Before marrying Godwin, she lived openly with another man. Her day was not yet, though as we will see later her work, like Godwin's, was well known in America at the height of the Revolutionary Enlightenment.

The most important link between Anglo-American Dissenting radicalism and the French Revolution, indeed the most important link among revolutionaries of three countries, and by a long way the most effective prophet of the Revolutionary Enlightenment in the United States, was Thomas Paine. In *Common Sense* and his other American writings, Paine's full radical development had been inhibited by circumstance and perhaps by immaturity; it is only in the period of the French Revolution that one can see the whole man. Somewhat simplistic and always humane, Paine was less complicated than Rousseau, less dreamy than Condorcet, and far less ruthless than Robespierre. Never original in doctrine, he owed his effectiveness to two things. One was his bold, simple, sometimes epigrammatic style: the style of a great preacher. The other—not apparent in his early career—was his bringing together of political and religious radicalism, often separate in other major figures of the Enlightenment. Paine simply assumed that both deism and democracy were the primary beliefs of all rational men, a view that spread so widely that we can hardly understand its impact.

Paine's *Rights of Man* (1791), his first major pronouncement on the French Revolution, belongs with the writings of Condorcet and Volney as a part of the first Revolutionary period. It was intended as an answer to Burke, whose great polemic against Price and Priestley had contrasted the French Revolution to the traditions of 1688. That British event, said Paine, had been eclipsed by the "luminous" revolutions in America and France; mixed government by "this, that, and t'other." Paine rejoiced that the Revolution in France had been less arduous and bloody than that in America. The French king, who was far more well meaning than most of his kind, should be pensioned off. America, France, and a reformed Britain should make an alliance and end war, which finds no friends among republics. The new order in Britain will include freedom of commerce, the end of the degrading poor rates, payments for marriage and children, support of the sick and old as a matter of right, common workshops for the unemployed, and—his most radical sugges-tion in the England of his day—progressive taxation. This program was far more consistent and practical than anything enacted or even pro-posed by the French Jacobins in their brief time of power.

Paine, who was a friend of many of the radical Dissenters, had prob-ably abandoned his Quaker upbringing long since, but he still did not find it necessary to raise religious issues at length. *Common Sense* had been entirely acceptable to most American Protestants, and the religious implications of the *Rights of Man* were still unalarming. Its attacks on priesthoods or establishments could be read by British Dissenters or American Protestants as anti-Roman or anti-Anglican. Its political pro-gram, like that of Condorcet, made short work of existing American institutions, yet Paine managed to praise the American Constitution.

Prosecuted for sedition in England, Paine proceeded naturally to his third country, where the National Assembly made him a citizen along with Priestley, Bentham, Washington, Hamilton, Madison, Joel Barlow, and other virtuous foreigners. Elected a deputy, Paine vigorously op-posed the execution of the king, and with the arrest of the Girondins found himself in prison. Not without fears that "the just and humane principles of the Revolution, which philosophy had first diffused, had been departed from," he wrote his last major work in order to defend rational religion against atheism, "lest in the general wreck of supersti-tion, of false systems of government, and false theology, we lost sight of morality, of humanity, and of the theology that is true."[39] The *Age of Reason* (1794-6), which fascinated and shocked Americans more than any work of Voltaire, was written by a man who believed passionately in God and hoped for a future life.

There is absolutely nothing new in the book. Most of it is an attack on all revelation, and especially the Old and the New Testament, in the manner once made familiar by the English deists. He attacks the Bible as a forgery, points out its internal contradictions, contrasts its teachings to the findings of science, and above all constantly drums on its im-morality: "It is a book of lies, wickedness, and blasphemy for what can be more blasphemous than to ascribe the wickedness of man to the or-ders of the Almighty?"[40]

Paine, in religion as in politics, has no taste whatever for paradox and no appreciation of complexity: he finds the ethics of loving one's enemy unrealistic, and disposes of the prophets by calling them poets. He abominates mystery, gloom, obscurity, and cruelty. His criterion of truth is a simple one: ". . . any system of religion that has anything in it that shocks the mind of a child, cannot be a true system. . . ."[41]

Never smooth or insinuating, Paine makes deliberate use of the technique of shock. Christianity is compared unfavorably with paganism and Mohammedanism.

> What is it the Bible teaches us?—rapine, cruelty, and murder. What is it the Testament teaches us?—to believe that the Almighty committed debauchery with a woman engaged to be married, and the belief of this debauchery is called faith.[42]

Faith can seldom be fought by argument; what gives Paine his power is his own faith in his own religion. He did not read much, and insists in the *Age of Reason* that the most important ideas come spontaneously to the mind, and not from books.[43] Thus he would still insist, like the latitudinarian and deist writers of the past generation, that the physical world is clearly designed to teach us religious and moral truth. Neither Butler nor Hume nor the Voltaire of *Candide* made any difference to his acceptance of this comforting article of faith. The part of the Bible he liked best was the nineteenth Psalm. In prison he quotes it from memory in Addison's translation: the stars sing in comforting and metrical unison that the hand that made them is divine.[44] Paine is as sure as Godwin that truth will prevail, that American religious institutions will be transformed like American government, and that the world will follow American and French examples in both fields. In a moment of rapt prophecy he boasts:

> I have now gone through the Bible [here he means the Old Testament, but he goes on to the New and would say the same of it] as a man would go through a wood with an axe on his shoulder, and fell trees. Here they lie; and the priests, if they can, may replant them. They may, perhaps, stick them in the ground, but they will never make them grow.[45]

In a way he was right. As simple and unsophisticated as the arguments of any backwoods Methodist, his attack like that of the early deists was easy to answer but hard to forget. Like them he was endlessly answered, but most of the answers are forgotten while the *Age of Reason*, with all its crudities, survives. What Paine destroyed was not Christianity but the complacent insistence of the early eighteenth century and the Moderate Enlightenment that Christianity, properly understood, is rational, cheerful, and moral. It is not, and where it survived and flourished in the generation after 1800 it did not pretend to be. Paine, unlike Toland or Tindal, Voltaire or Diderot, got his message to the masses. After the *Rights of Man* and the *Age of Reason,* religious and political institutions had to be defended in a different way from before.

Simple, encouraging, and fervent, the Revolutionary Enlightenment in Paine's version and some others flourished for a while in the new American Republic. Unlike other forms of Enlightenment, this one aroused militant enemies. Ultimately, it was defeated in its pure form. Transformed and watered down, it left major effects on the culture, including the religious culture, of nineteenth-century America.

Two *New England and the New Nation*

In the last stage of the *ancien régime*, it was natural that frustrated Frenchmen should place their hopes in the new Enlightened nation across the sea, a nation without old traditions or institutions, able to start from scratch in an atmosphere of untutored and unspoiled virtue. In America religion especially was henceforth to be concerned only with morality; priests, mysteries, and dogmas would cease to exist and all men would come to resemble the virtuous Quakers, who were really deists of some sort. All that was necessary, according to some of the last generation of *philosophes*—Mably, Turgot, Raynal, and others—was for America to eschew luxury and commerce, remove from her constitutions the archaic remnants of English checks and balances, and maintain the innocence and virtue associated with the early Roman republic and best exemplified by the venerable Franklin.

In the 1780's, though Americans were trying hard to be grateful to their ally, only a few managed fully to return in kind the affections of the current generation of Enlightened Frenchmen. The *philosophes* of the Revolutionary Enlightenment were only beginning to be read: their major impact on American opinion had to wait until the 1790's. Preoccupied with their own Revolution, most Americans (unlike their ambassador Thomas Jefferson) knew little about the ferment of revolutionary opinion in Paris. Some, though not nearly as many as in the 1790's, were intrigued by the lively, encyclopedic, and unreliable *History of the Two Indies* by the Abbé Raynal, which attacked both slavery and Protestantism as well as Catholicism. Gabriel Bonnet de Mably, one of the most doctrinaire of French critics of American political institutions, irritated both Thomas Jefferson and John Adams and was actually hanged in effigy in some American cities.[1] Volney, later important in America, was only beginning to be read. Condorcet's major work was not published until 1795, after his death and the death of his stage of the Revolution. He was, however, one of ten Parisians well known enough to be given the freedom of the city of New Haven in 1785.[2]

As for the greatest early figure of the Revolutionary Enlightenment, the question of Rousseau in America is almost as difficult as the question of Rousseau in general. The major works were known in America in the 1780's and some of them, especially *Emile*, were fairly widely read. (All were to become popular in the 1790's.) Yet, like Voltaire, Rousseau seems to have been read far more often than he was approved. As yet, in America, virtuous emotion, exaltations of the popular will, and hostility to decadent skepticism were still acceptable mainly in specifically Christian forms. Ardent Christians, whether politically radical or not, were offended by Rousseau's deism. On the other hand, most enlightened Americans were still partisans of moderation, and inveterate enemies of mass emotion. People who had long feared religious enthusiasm could hardly welcome it when it appeared in semi-secular disguise. People trying to perfect and adjust complex institutions could make little use of the prophet of the clean sweep, the believer in direct democracy.

In the long run, Rousseau affected European culture so profoundly that he inevitably affected American culture as well, but much of his message was to arrive in America indirectly. Majoritarian democrats preferred the simpler Paine; later on transcendentalists and liberal Christians got their ideas from more respectable German sources. Perhaps in the long run Rousseau's direct effects on Americans are the hardest to document. A young woman weeping over *Héloïse* or a young man reading the *Confessions* with a thrill of self-recognition may not have been conscious themselves of the full effect of a new literary and intellectual style.

The problem that faced the early proponents of the Revolutionary Enlightenment in America was that America was not, and could not turn herself into, a really new country, free to choose her traditions where these would be most helpful. Nor were the Americans, like some later colonial rebels, trying to throw off the rule of an alien conqueror and seeking to revive a native culture. Most, and especially most of the Revolutionary leaders, were English by descent. All were accustomed to English institutions and had been taught to be proud of them.

To make a new political start, abandoning such universal European norms as monarchy, aristocracy, and religion was at once invigorating and frightening. Mixed with the exultation of independence were plenty of worries. One could choose one's worries according to one's temperament and position: some worried most about inflation, extravagance, and luxury; others about egalitarianism leading to anarchy. The events of the eighties, the failures and successes of the Confederation, the economic dislocation and renewal, the unsolved problems of foreign relations, the rebellion in Massachusetts and the unrest in some other states, the adoption of the Federal Constitution and the struggle to put the new government into effective operation, all offered fuel both to hopes and fears. At the center of both lay the problem of creating a national identity.

For the building of such an identity there were and are two possibilities, innovation or adaptation. The American choice in the first years of the new nation was a mixture of these, leaning heavily toward the latter.

Historians have been arguing for several generations about the amount of social change that came with the Revolution.[3] It was more than a colonial revolution, but far less than a complete social upheaval. The number of Tories who left or were driven out was, in proportion to population, almost five times as great as the number of royalist refugees from the French Revolution, and many belonged to the top class of colonial society.[4] But on the whole these émigrés were not replaced by the rise to power of another class; their places were taken by patriots of views and habits similar to their own. Some old scores were paid off; some able parvenus made it to the top. Increased social mobility doubtless had a democratizing effect: old habits of deference and with them ideologies of social balance and hierarchy were weakened. But mobility works as much against revolutionary feeling as for it in all periods: while displaced and frustrated people certainly feel resentment, the holders of new wealth and prestige quickly learn to believe that class divisions are right and necessary.

Though many Americans called for a purification of society, and some for a drastic overhaul of institutions, the reforms that were carried out were piecemeal. Slavery was abolished in the Northern states, where no really large vested interests supported it, and the institution was kept out of the new Northwest. Religion was disestablished where, as in Virginia, the establishment was weak or unpopular. Suffrage was widened in six states, and in one, Pennsylvania, a radically democratic constitution was adopted. Criminal law was made more humane in some states, but nowhere was the legal system completely made over.

Most of the energies of the new nation, struggling for identity, centered on arguments about its most important institutions. Aside from the governments these were the schools and the churches. The paradox faced by those who want to remodel a culture through education has become a familiar one. To remodel, whether one is a Whig, a Jacobin, or a Bolshevik, means discipline; and discipline usually carries with it tradition. Thomas Jefferson's famous proposal for finding and training the natural aristocrats and rendering the rest of the citizens safe repositories for political power was hardly a complete departure from prevailing modes. Jefferson's friend Benjamin Rush insisted that the schools must inculcate the truths of the Christian religion and also love of country.[5] Everybody who discussed education believed that the schools must inculcate *something*, and this usually meant some version of both morality and patriotism. Where education ceases to be traditional and taken for granted, and especially where its task is centered on moral indoctrination, it becomes a focus of controversy. Colonial schools and colleges had already been expected to do a lot. The Revolution increased their assignment while cutting away some of the remaining traditional props. Now, most Americans agreed, the schools were to teach morality, sound religion, and love of freedom. This program was not one likely to give rise to widespread innovation in specific content or in teaching method.

For many Americans the churches remained the most important institutions the country possessed. They were still at once conservative and innovating forces. In the post-Revolutionary decade, each denomination made its own adjustment to new conditions. In general, the Calvinists held precariously to their traditional prestige, the shattered Episcopalians tried to regroup, while Baptist and Methodist revivals flickered sporadically, suggesting where future strength would lie. This process is so central to our story that we will look at it in detail in several times and places.

Thus the Revolutionary Enlightenment dawned only gradually on the first revolutionary nation of modern times, and when it came it was welcomed by some but resisted by others. The 1780's in America can be seen as a time of uneasy equilibrium, of innovation and conservative adaptation everywhere mixed, of enthusiasm and fear both muted by the necessities of compromise. In terms of this book, this is a period of competition between the familiar Moderate Enlightenment and the slowly dawning Revolutionary Enlightenment, and of both with inherited Protestant culture. Then in the 1790's, events at home and abroad brought this conflict to a brief climax.

After the Revolution as before, the influence of various kinds of Enlightenment must be discussed mainly in terms of the several different societies that inhabited different parts of the new Republic. In the South, little seemed to have changed on the surface of society in the eighties, and yet the Revolutionary Enlightenment was to achieve a brief success. In the Middle states, and especially in the capital, Philadelphia, where the Revolution had been most fiercely fought and conservatives and radicals were most equally balanced, the Revolutionary Enlightenment was to battle the Moderate Enlightenment on equal terms. The problem of innovation and revolution was especially complicated in New England, at once the section most closely identified with the Revolution and the section most devoted to traditional institutions.

In New England in the 1780's, Enlightenment, Protestantism, and patriotism still seemed almost interchangeable terms, and New England seemed unquestionably the natural home of all three. Nobody described the standard New England self-image better than the Reverend Jedidiah Morse of Charlestown, Massachusetts, who was America's leading geographer:

> In the Eastern states, property is more equally distributed than in any other civilized country. Religion, here, also, except in Rhode Island, is, and always has been, supported by law. At present, not far from 2,000 clergymen, generally well informed and orthodox, and all chosen by the people themselves, are weekly and daily employed in enlightening and reforming their congregations. Schools are established within every little distance, and a grown person, a native of these states, can scarcely be found, who has not some acquaintance with reading, writing, and arithmetic. The inhabitants universally live in villages or towns of a moderate size, and have no overgrown capital, in which to learn profligacy of manners. The great body of them are farmers. These circumstances have given these states very much the manners and morals of Scotland.[6]

This tradition of austere and frugal republicanism, with equality subtly combined with respect for one's betters and underpinned by universal education and sound religion, was taken for granted not only by New Englanders but surprisingly often accepted by outsiders. During and right after the Revolution, which New Englanders considered largely their own achievement, New England got a better press nationally than ever before—perhaps better than at any time since. And yet all was not well in this rocky and virtuous land. Even more than any other part of the United States, postwar New England combined uneasiness with complacency.

During the Revolution itself the frequent warnings of possible decline can perhaps be seen as part of an old tradition, the propitiatory tradition of the jeremiad, in which God's people are warned of their special responsibilities and dangers. In the eighties, those who warned of decline had plenty of evidence to point to. New England's wealth and population were slowly declining in relation to New York and Pennsylvania, with their flourishing commercial cities and rich Western lands. More and more, traditions of frugality and equality were contradicted by growing wealth on the one hand and poverty on the other. Those who adapted quickly to postwar patterns of trade—speculators in land and public securities, and in general the richer inhabitants of the seaboard towns—flourished while many farmers were struggling with debt. Daniel Shays's agrarian uprising in western Massachusetts was put down without bloodshed, yet the fact that such a thing could happen at all in Massachusetts was a harsh blow to New England self-esteem. Both the Shays affair and the Rhode Island inflation were often blamed on a decline in morals and religion. Emigration, contentiousness, Sabbath-breaking, crime, and vice all seemed to threaten inherited order and republican freedom. As one sensitive historian puts it, by the 1790's, New England authorities of church and state had undertaken "a somewhat nervous patrolling of the boundaries of the Federalist social order."[7]

To many New Englanders, and certainly to themselves, the clergy were the center of that order long before it was called Federalist. The tradition of the Revolution, in which New and Old Lights, Arminians and orthodox, had stood together for Protestant freedom, had left them exultant. They could count on the cordial support of the powerful Presbyterians of the Middle states. To many of them, the future seemed to promise further progress toward the millennium. Nathanael Emmons, perhaps the most rigid of Edwards's ultra-Calvinist heirs, could argue in 1786 that *for most purposes* the future was one of increasing light.

> One generation has been improving upon another from age to age. And the improvements and discoveries of the last and present century are truly surprising. . . .
>
> The only bounds that can be set to their [men's] improvements, must be such as have respect to the kinds—and not the degrees of their knowledge. There are, indeed, certain kinds of knowledge, which men are totally incapable of understanding; but these are only such kinds of knowledge, as require more than created faculties to understand. . . .
>
> Again, we live under that form of government, that has always been the friend and nurse of the arts.

Yielding to none in his admiration of Benjamin Franklin, who had given a library to Emmons's town of Franklin, Massachusetts, Emmons urged his congregation to emulate the great man's life, with no suggestion that their benefactor had any dubious religious views.[8]

One of the facts that sustained men like Emmons was that the establishments of Massachusetts and Connecticut were supported by the new governments, with suitable provisions for exemption from church taxes for duly recognized Dissenters. With much grumbling and with determined opposition by Baptists and Separates, New Englanders still continued to pay taxes for the support of religion. Each year in each New England state the governor and legislature assembled to hear an election sermon, and in time of crisis governors still designated days of thanksgiving or fast, when every clergyman was expected to remind the people of their public and private duties. Religion was still important in politics: in some parts of New England an accusation of unorthodoxy was almost as damaging to a politician as an accusation of immorality or Toryism.

Yet it comes as no surprise to learn that the established clergy felt themselves, now as in the past, surrounded by a host of enemies and perils. Congregationalism was in fact losing ground to its rivals. One old enemy seemed at first to be much weaker. The Revolution had ended the aggressive, proselytizing days of Anglicanism in New England, and the high-flying loyalist clergy had disappeared. Yet by the middle of the 1780's the reorganized Protestant Episcopal Church was making enough progress, particularly in Connecticut, to cause some concern among its enemies in the Standing Order. Here and there, Universalists outraged their neighbors by suggesting that it was God's intention to save everybody. Methodists were only beginning to spread their fiery and optimistic message in New England, but some Calvinists correctly saw them as a future menace. The chief present danger arose from the growth of the Baptists, who were not at all satisfied with the halfway toleration accorded by the new arrangement. To later historians, the Baptists are heroes of religious freedom. To many dissatisfied New Englanders, they were a refuge from the rigidities of the establishment and the superior airs of its college-trained clergy. To ministers of the Standing Order, the Baptists were disruptive sectarians who threatened New England traditions of order and learning. William Bentley, the famous Salem liberal minister, complains testily in his diary of "The Anabaptists upon the river in Beverley immersing their disciples in water and ignorance."[9]

Within the establishment itself the chief complaints were also old ones: cantankerousness and its apparent opposite, indifference. Though the breaches made by the Great Awakening had partly closed during the Revolution, New Divinity men continued to imply that moderate Calvinists were lukewarm and worldly. Moderates retorted that New Divinity men were cranky and censorious extremists. Both increasingly distrusted the Arminians of the Boston area. This group, the chief surviving center of the Moderate Enlightenment of the early eighteenth century, will be dealt with later at some length.

Ever since the early part of the century, New England divines had occasionally blasted deism, and by now Rousseau, Voltaire, and sometimes Ethan Allen were added to the familiar list beginning with Tindal and Toland. Later, New England historians and writers of memoirs were likely to blame the beginning of the fearful deist danger on the influence of French troops during the Revolution. It is not easy, however, to find contemporary evidence that the soldiers of Louis XVI spread the ideas of Rousseau or even Voltaire. Young Simeon Baldwin at Yale in 1780 was given the negative side of a college debate on the question "Whether the Alliance with France will be beneficial to the Inhabitants of America." Not deism or atheism but popery, luxury, and debauchery were the horrors Baldwin dutifully summoned up, and it is not known whether he won the debate.[10] The great fear of deism arose in the mid-1790's and centered on the *Age of Reason*. Then, but not before, deism or infidelity became the main surrogate for every sort of clerical fear.

As yet, the enemies of true religion, while real enough, were only vaguely linked together. Among them were civil strife, luxury, indifference, immorality, deism, factionalism inside the Standing Order and sectarian attack from outside. Not least of the symptoms of decline was the lack of respect and support for ministers. None of these complaints conflicted with the republican and patriotic pride taken for granted by most ministers. The many dangers to the New England social and religious system were important precisely because this system was and always had been the best and most advanced in the world.

With Boston in the grip of luxury and Arminianism, Connecticut furnished the purest pattern of what New England ought to be. Provincial, without great cities, Connecticut was known to its inhabitants as the Land of Steady Habits. Yet even here, faction threatened to tear society apart. During the Revolution, hatred of Tories and Anglicans had been especially fierce. In the state's postwar politics, a handful of leading families together with the established clergy clung to their position of special influence. Social, political, and religious factionalism was reflected in the struggles over Yale College, in this period far the largest of American colleges,[11] and the intellectual capital of Calvinist New England.

From 1777 until 1795 the College was presided over by Ezra Stiles, the most Enlightened of New England Calvinists, and the best specimen of the special New England compromise between Protestantism and Enlightenment in the period just before this compromise broke down. Stiles was a learned, speculative, somewhat pedantic man who enjoyed statistics, college ceremonies, and occasionally compared the Hindu Vedas and the Koran to the Pentateuch. Like most New England ministers, he had been an ardent and jubilant partisan of the Revolution. Unlike many, he carried his Commonwealth beliefs to the point of believing in the spread of democracy, and actually used this word with a favorable meaning. He deeply admired Franklin and tried with dubious success to prove to himself that both Franklin and Washington were really friends of revelation. He was a regular correspondent of Jefferson, who received an honorary degree from Yale in 1786. Stiles's wide reading included Rousseau, Voltaire, and even Mary Wollstonecraft.[12] He was an ardent supporter of the French Revolution from its outbreak until his death in 1795.

Stiles was, however, a firm Old Light Calvinist. He had, like Franklin, had an encounter with deism in his youth, but unlike Franklin had returned to Christianity. He was a firm defender of the necessity and truth of revelation. Though he admired Joseph Priestley's science he sorrowed over his *The Corruptions of Christianity*, which Jefferson admired.[13] Throughout his mature life, in fact, Stiles disliked deists almost as much as he did Episcopalians, whom he considered schemers, and New Divinity Calvinists, whom he thought fanatics and obscurantists.

During the reign of Stiles's formidable successor, Timothy Dwight, and among Dwight's friends and students the legend was created that Yale under Stiles was a hotbed of deism and infidelity, narrowly rescued by Dwight. It has been clearly demonstrated that this picture is untrue, though some Yale undergraduates dabbled in dangerous thoughts and others affected fine clothes and foppish manners.[14] Students were required to read Locke, and in 1789 Stiles added Montesquieu. Some students were assigned Rousseau's *Emile* and some certainly read Voltaire on their own. The rest of their reading was a standard blend of the English and Continental authors popular before the Revolution. Calvinist divinity retained a major place in the curriculum. Topics for discussion, meticulously listed in Stiles's diary, ran the gamut of the most controversial questions of philosophy, theology, and politics, including "Whether Liberty for all Religions, Pagan Mahom. as well as Xtian ought to be allowed in the United States," "Whether Human depravity total," and "Whether Deists ought to be admitted into magistracy."[15]

Contemporary Yale reminiscences convey an atmosphere of religiosity, republican patriotism, belief in progress, and concern for the future of American letters, with only a slight admixture of fashionable tastes and ideas. This difficult combination, and many of the deeper tensions of New England culture, is reflected in the work of the group of Yale graduates and tutors who made up America's first important literary coterie, the Connecticut Wits. The Wits were all associated with Yale, nearly all came from substantial Connecticut families, and a number were leading doctors, lawyers, or politicians. Clubby and mildly convivial in their own tastes, they wanted to encourage, of course within decorous bounds, the more modern and cheerful tendencies of Stiles's Yale. Their major purpose, however, was to provide America and New England with a national literature, and in doing so to show the world that republicans were capable of wielding a correct and elevated style.[16]

Compared by some of their contemporaries to Swift and Pope, these men were most successful when they imitated Samuel Butler and the minor Augustan poets. Both in their ideas and in their style, the Wits were a survival in an odd environment of the early eighteenth century. Indeed, the Moderate Enlightenment tradition of balance and order fit very well the New England self-image of moderate prosperity:

> For here exists, once more, th'Arcadian scene
> Those simple manners, and that golden mean:
> Here holds society its middle stage,
> Between too rude and too refin'd an age . . .[17]

From the Scottish philosophers, especially Lord Kames, the Wits had learned the Common-Sense opinions about art that were later to become the official aesthetic of conservative America. Anti-metaphysical, they were by consequence anti-speculative and by taste anti-romantic. "A just taste in the fine arts," one of them said, "by sweetening and harmonizing the temper, is a strong antidote to the turbulence of passion and violence of pursuit."[18]

This gentlemanly dislike of extremism led the Wits, while remaining within the orthodox Congregational fold, to oppose New Light and particularly New Divinity extravagances. Most of them believed that too much hair-splitting religious argument was not only ungentlemanly, but likely to be unsettling and to play into the hands of deists and free thinkers. Some of them skirted the edge of danger by ridiculing old-fashioned Calvinist piety. Dr. Lemuel Hopkins described a hypocrite:

> *Good works* he careth nought about,
> But *faith* alone will seek,
> While Sunday's pieties blot out
> The knaveries of the week.[19]

Just before the Revolution, John Trumbull, one of the more talented Wits, had thoroughly tested the permissible limits of anti-clericalism.

The first part of his satirical poem *The Progress of Dulness* was a slashing and effective attack on the superficiality of Yale education and the pompous ignorance of the ministers it produced.

Not surprisingly, this was too much for Connecticut. In the preface to the second part of his poem, Trumbull angrily denounced intolerant and malicious attacks on his poem, but also insisted on his great respect for college and clergy. For the second part of his satire he chose a safer target. His new subject was Dick Brainless, a foppish and luxury-loving Yale student, who indulged in French manners and novel-reading, ran up debts, and dabbled in fashionable irreligion:

> Then lest Religion he should need,
> Of pious *Hume* he'll learn his creed,
> By strongest demonstration shown,
> Evince that nothing can be known;
> Take arguments, unvex'd by doubt,
> On *Voltaire's* trust, or go without. . . .
> Alike his poignant wit displays
> The darkness of the former days,
> When men the paths of duty sought,
> And owned what revelation taught;
> E'er human reason grew so bright,
> Men could see all things by its light,
> And summon'd Scripture to appear,
> And stand before its bar severe,
> To clear its page from charge of fiction,
> And answer pleas of contradiction . . .[20]

Trumbull's position here is exactly that of a moderate and polished defender of decent and gentlemanly religion in the England of about 1740—a position which had little future in Connecticut.

In dealing with politics, the early work of the Wits was full of jubilation about the American and republican future, often identifying it with the dawn of the Christian millennium. Their denunciations of extravagance, clod-hopping egalitarianism, and paper money, like their early attacks on deism, were uttered in a tone of confident contempt which made something like Augustan satire possible. This is the tone, for instance, of *M'Fingal*, Trumbull's popular Revolutionary mock epic satirizing the Tories, in which the Tory squire before he is tarred and feathered gets off some effective jabs against mob rule, unworkable constitutions, and worthless currency. (These were made good use of later by

Federalists.) Trumbull, in fact, offers the perfect example of the knife-edge along which the Connecticut Wits were compelled to walk. Apparently the struggle exhausted him; after *M'Fingal* his considerable talent seems to have largely dried up.

For present readers, the Wits are most enjoyable in their lighter and shorter efforts. Their own dearest hope, however, was to provide the republic with poetry in the grand style. Somehow the heroic couplet and the sweeping invocation did not fit the praise of the sober New England virtues:

> Hail favour'd State! CONNECTICUT! thy name
> Uncouth in song, too long concealed from fame;
> If yet thy filial bards the gloom can pierce,
> Shall rise and flourish in immortal verse.
> Inventive genius, imitative pow'rs,
> And still more precious, common-sense, is ours;
> While Knowledge useful, more than science grand,
> In rivulets still o'erspreads the smiling land.[21]

It was no use: neither the style nor the ideas of the early eighteenth century fit the post-Revolutionary scene. To be an Augustan wit and a Calvinist was hard enough: to be an advocate of republican frugality as well made the combination impossible. Most of the Wits by the middle or late 1780's had given up their deepest ambitions and confined themselves to occasional patriotic odes and heavy, scolding satires against debtors, vulgar democrats, or deists.

The two best-known figures of the group, Timothy Dwight and Joel Barlow, were also the two most tireless contenders for the status of major poet. Their lives illustrate the precarious unity of post-Revolutionary New England and its breakdown in the 1790's.

Because of his central place in the anti-Jeffersonian hysteria of 1798 to 1800, and sometimes also because he was Jonathan Edwards's grandson, Dwight is often treated as a monster of Calvinist obscurantism and reaction. Actually he was a moderate theologian—whose moralistic and utilitarian bent took him a long way from Edwards—and a sympathetic, affectionate pastor and teacher. From his early post-Revolutionary sermons until his "Greenfield Hill" of 1788 he frequently expressed his exalted hopes for his nation. America was the future site of the Christian millennium, and in the meantime the home of pure religion, free government, progress, reason, and—the phrase still seemed perfectly inno-

cent—the "rights of man."[22] In America, some day, literature would
flourish without its old-world licentiousness:

> Another Pope inchanting themes rehearse,
> Nor the meek virgin blush to hear the verse;
> Improv'd, and clouded with no courtly stain
> A whiter page than Addison's remain.[23]

Above all, Dwight turned out hundreds of couplets in praise of Connecticut, doing his best to achieve sublimity in his descriptions of "Longa's
bays" and "Connecta's waves," and tirelessly contrasting "sweet Competence" with the crimes and extravagances of Europe. In his anti-
European patriotism, as in his agrarianism, Dwight agreed entirely with
his later enemy, Thomas Jefferson.

His fears were, however, different, and Dwight had a large tendency
toward gloom and fear latent in his personality. In 1788 he published the
first major American anti-deist work, "The Triumph of Infidelity." This
poem, though ill-tempered and so censorious that many of Dwight's
contemporaries condemned it, still does not mark any rising panic, either
in Dwight or in Connecticut. Satan, the spokesman, gloats over a list of
disciples that is anything but new, consisting mainly of the English
deists of the early part of the century, Hume, and Voltaire. Priestley is
the only European contemporary who achieves a mention. A major
drubbing is given Charles Chauncy, Edwards's opponent who had just
died, and some sly digs are reserved for several unidentifiable liberal
clergymen. In the end Satan leaves the New World, discouraged by his
lack of success.

In the same year as "The Triumph of Infidelity," Dwight published
his "Greenfield Hill," an almost entirely positive description of Connecticut virtues, managing to pack into its seven books a full-length sermon
in verse, advice about farming and instilling correct habits in children,
and one of his most ambitious paeans to American progress. It was only
in about 1795 that Dwight's fears for New England began seriously to
obsess him and displace his hopes. It was also in that year that he succeeded, as president of Yale, his old and bitter enemy Ezra Stiles. One
of his early actions was to remove the portrait of his former fellow-Wit,
Joel Barlow, who was not only a far more admired poet than Dwight
himself but by now a frank advocate of international revolution.

Barlow's earliest works were patriotic Revolutionary poems much like

Dwight's, and equally full of visions of the Christian millennium in America:

> Then LOVE shall rule, and Innocence adore,
> Discord shall cease, and Tyrants be no more; . . .
> The Church elect, from smouldering ruins, rise,
> And sail triumphant thro' the yielding skies . . .[24]

Barlow versified psalms in the manner of Watts, wrote hymns and meditations on death, and even was ordained minister in order to serve as Revolutionary chaplain.

From the beginning, however, it seems likely that his heart was not in his orthodoxy. By temperament he was as ambitious as Dwight and far more flexible. Not austere, wanting both to excel and make money, Barlow tried the law, diplomacy, and speculation as well as preaching and writing. From the mid-eighties on, there are hints in his writing of speculations that take him beyond the Connecticut norm and also beyond the Moderate Enlightenment. In an unpublished dissertation on the law, Barlow denies the favorite Moderate Enlightenment axiom that human nature is unchanging, and suggests that it can be molded by society.[25] In 1787, in an address to the Connecticut Society of the Cincinnati, he sounds a secular and optimistic note, not yet clearly unorthodox but startling in its vocabulary: "The present is an age of philosophy; and America, the empire of reason. Here, neither the pageantry of courts nor the glooms of superstition have dazzled or beclouded the mind."[26] (At the same time, Dwight was *contrasting* sound "reason" with vain "philosophy," a word he already used to mean dangerous speculation.)

In 1787 Barlow published the first full version of his epic *Vision of Columbus*, and there was little in it to affront Connecticut subscribers. This poem, the most ambitious, best-received, and worst production of the Connecticut Wits, is dedicated to that great friend of freedom Louis the Sixteenth, who obligingly subscribed for twenty-five copies. Addressing the monarch, Barlow notes "That change in the political face of Europe, that liberality of sentiment, that enlargement of commercial, military and philosophical knowledge, which contrast the present with the fifteenth century,"[27] and clearly result from the discovery of America. Columbus, disconsolate in prison, is visited by an Angel. Perhaps more wordy and repetitive than any other such supernatural consoler in epic literature, the Angel takes Columbus on a tour of the universe, dwelling on American prehistory and twice going through the history of Europe from a strikingly Protestant point of view. Sketching the great results of Columbus's discovery which have become manifest in North America, she points to Washington, Franklin, Rittenhouse, Benjamin West, and not least Barlow's Connecticut colleagues:

> For daring Dwight the Epic Muse sublime
> Hails her new empire on the western clime.
> Fired with the themes by seers seraphic sung,
> Heaven in his eye, and rapture on his tongue . . .[28]

Columbus, however, still unsatisfied after eight books of progressive prophecy, asks the Angel why human progress is so difficult and intermittent, and why God did not reveal everything man needs to know at once.

Her answer is not much more successful than most answers to this difficult question, and she relies at first on standard doctrine of the early eighteenth century. Man must learn his limitations, must abjure passions, which lead to the damaging extremes of skepticism and zeal. He must rely on revelation to supplement reason. And finally, he must have confidence in the coming of the millennium, foretold by the prophets and made manifest by the whole tendency of history. In the final book, after first coyly refusing, the Angel consents to give Columbus a glimpse of this great event, when war will end and mankind will have not only one religion but one language. In an explanatory footnote, Barlow cites Richard Price to support his own view of human destiny:

> It has long been the opinion of the Author, that such a state of peace and happiness as is foretold in scripture and commonly called the millennial period, may be rationally expected to be introduced without a miracle.[29]

This was Barlow's last attempt to reconcile his Connecticut heritage with his optimistic temperament. In 1788 he left for France as an agent of a land company. Almost immediately he was caught up by the excitement and newness of the Revolutionary Enlightenment. Within a few years Barlow was to become an honorary citizen and passionate advocate of the French Republic, an atheist, and a bad word in Connecticut.

Noah Webster, the author of the famous speller, grammar, reader, and dictionary was not quite a member of the Wits' inner circle, though he was a friend of Barlow and several other members of the group. A farmer's son as well as a Yale graduate, Webster never commanded the aristocratic wit of Hopkins or Trumbull, nor did he speak in his early work for balance and moderation in the early eighteenth-century manner. He disliked liberal upper-class Bostonians, who in turn made fun of the earnestness, innovative spelling, rural accent, and self-promotion of "No-ur Webster eskwier junier."[30] Better perhaps than any other man, Webster epitomized the peculiar New England combination of Commonwealth radicalism, religion, frugality, and egalitarianism. Like Dwight he hoped that America would remain isolated from European culture and literature, and, going farther, that it would develop its separate language.

In the post-Revolutionary years Webster was an advanced defender of democracy, which in his view depended above all on popular education. Utilitarian and somewhat austere, Webster's educational proposals were far more democratic than Jefferson's.[31] In the early 1780's he opposed the least hint of religious establishment, and in 1788 he strongly denounced Dwight's "The Triumph of Infidelity" for its uncharitable lumping together of deists and liberals.[32] (He did not know that Dwight was the author of the poem, and had elsewhere compared him to Homer and Virgil.) The young Webster read and approved Rousseau, Raynal, and Priestley and, like Barlow, was much influenced in his view of the enlightened American future by Richard Price. In the preface to his *Spelling Book* (1783) he sounded the familiar Commonwealth warnings against decadence and corruption in radical tones:

> Europe is grown old in folly, corruption and tyranny—in that country laws are perverted, manners are licentious, literature is declining and human nature debased. For America in her infancy to adopt the present maxims of the Old World, would be to stamp the wrinkles of decrepit age upon the bloom of youth and to plant the seeds of decay in a vigorous constitution.[33]

By the late 1780's Webster, like many other New Englanders, was being pushed by various fears for the New England social order toward a more conservative position, but Webster as yet remained, in a special New England way, a democrat. Like most of his New England contemporaries, he greeted the French Revolution with nothing but enthusiasm.

New England, quite as generally as any other section of the United States, welcomed the new order in France with civic feasts, processions, and fraternal orations.[34] There was, from New England's point of view, every reason to rejoice in the downfall of an ancient enemy, the Catholic and absolute monarchy of France, and to hope for better things from a republic. Still looking back with nostalgia to the English revolution of the seventeenth century as well as the American Revolution of the eighteenth, New England commentators were surprisingly little troubled by the execution of the king or even the reign of terror. Even the cult of the Goddess of Reason, even the abolition of the Sabbath, disturbing as these developments seemed, could be explained as part of the necessary cost of getting rid of a bad government and a worse church. With the outbreak of war in 1793 almost all New England opinion still sided, not altogether uncritically, with France against England, the corrupt enemy of republics. Samuel Otis, one of the strongly Republican and Commonwealth-minded Warren family connection, expressed a typical hope in 1794: ". . . may they go on conquering and after all conquer themselves."[35]

The New England clergy had a special way of looking hopefully at events in Europe. Many of them had long suspected that the millennium would be ushered in by a series of cataclysmic events, including the overthrow of kingdoms and especially the humiliation of the papacy.[36] David Tappan, of Newbury (later Harvard professor of divinity) pointed to the glorious prospect in a Fast Day sermon of 1793:

> Cast your eyes, my hearers, on the old world, which a few years hence appeared generally sunk in torpid ignorance, superstition, and bondage. What a glorious revolution suddenly bursts upon our sight! what freedom of thought! What justness, energy, and grandeur of sentiment! What enlightened and ardent philanthropy! What a rapid progression of knowledge! See tyranny both in Church and State tottering to its foundations! See Popery fast sinking into contempt and ruin, deserted and trampled under foot by millions of her late bigotted admirers! See a mighty combination of events, manifestly tending to one great issue, the renovation of the face of the world by the introduction and universal triumph of knowledge and freedom, of virtue and peace.

This glorious vision was, to be sure, clouded by the tendencies toward "anarchy and ferocity" shown by our French allies. Yet the cause of the

French nation was still "the cause of truth and reason, comprising the sacred rights and most valuable interests of human nature."[37]

In the middle of the nineties New England clergymen, struggling bravely with various and mounting fears and doubts, were still reluctant to deny their traditions by putting New England Protestantism into the anti-Revolutionary camp.[38] Jedidiah Morse, the Charlestown clergyman-geographer, was later to be the principal mobilizer of anti-Jacobin hysteria. In 1794 he wrote his constant correspondent, Professor C. D. Ebeling of Hamburg, that he was still praying for peace and even hoping for French victory.[39]

Another of Morse's frequent correspondents, the Reverend Henry Channing of New London, commented on a Morse sermon in tones which were still mainly optimistic:

> You say that you approve the cause of the French but not the measures. If by the measures, you mean the drownings at Nantes, and the numerous executions after a *mock trial*, under the administration of Robespierre, I reply, no man, possessing only the reliques of humanity, can approve of these measures. But I believe the execution of Louis and *his wife*, was a just reward of perfidy; and in *the latter case*, a small reward; as it is well known that this ci-devant Queen, was the head of the combination and the main-spring in the corrupt politics of the court. But— Laus Deo! France triumphs—and Holland is delivered. The present day is so loaded with momentous events, that my heart exults in having a portion of time at the close of the 18th century.[40]

Samuel Stillman, a moderate Boston Baptist, in a Thanksgiving sermon of 1794, criticized those Americans who emphasized the "cruelty, irreligion and instability" of the French, "and on account of these condemn the whole." "This conduct," Stillman went on,

> is very unreasonable, and creates a suspicion, that they are in heart unfriendly to the liberties of mankind. . . . For many ages, Protestants have been praying for the downfall of Popery. JEHOVAH is now accomplishing that great event, but with circumstances that wound our feelings.[41]

Beyond the circles of the clergy, Noah Webster in 1794 published a long essay on the revolution in France, blaming it on the faults of French religion, alternately praising and condemning the philosophers who had liberated the nation from superstition only to plunge it into atheism, denouncing Jacobin excesses but praising the French cause as "the noblest ever undertaken by men," and wishing that the Revolution had stopped short of its latest phase.[42] From this obviously unstable position Webster was to move, like all his literary friends except Barlow, toward an increasingly conservative position. By 1798 he had drawn closer to Dwight, sharply repudiated Barlow, specifically abjured some of his own earlier democratic opinions, and denounced many thinkers he had earlier admired, including Rousseau and (with special virulence) Priestley.

Up to 1795, Protestantism, republicanism, and Enlightenment seemed to most New Englanders to belong together. To separate these and range Protestantism and (American) republicanism *against* Enlightenment amounted to a profound and momentous upheaval. In this upheaval European revolution and European revolutionary spokesmen played a part. But events got most of their meaning for New England from their relation to a long accumulation of New England doubts and fears.

Three *Philadelphia and the World*

To move from crabbed Connecticut, or even from Federalist and Unitarian Boston, to post-Revolutionary Philadelphia is to move from the theater of a vigorous but declining provincial culture into a major center of modernity. Philadelphia, especially in the 1790's, was the capital not only of the American Enlightenment, but also of American culture. For a decade America had a capital which fulfilled, on a small scale, some of the functions of London and Paris.

There was no other city much like Philadelphia. The closest was New York, also a cosmopolitan commercial city but one with a weaker cultural tradition in a province whose politics were complicated by family cliques and aristocratic quarrels.[1] Philadelphia, aside from being the national capital during the early Revolution and again from 1790 to 1800, was the largest and most rapidly growing American city (about 44,000 in 1790); the principal center of the American press and bar; the leader in American science and medicine; the capital of American deism, Presbyterianism, Northern Episcopalianism, and Lutheranism; the urban center for much of the upper South, the city which had long had the most cosmopolitan population, and the center of attention for foreign visitors.

As in Paris or London, the prevailing variety of Enlightenment depended a good deal on an elite, but here the elite was responsive to pressures from below. The elite of post-Revolutionary Philadelphia was a very special kind of elite: a republican and bourgeois aristocracy, diverse and tolerant in religion, in politics republican and progressive but also anti-radical and property-conscious, not intensely intellectual but fond of supporting humane and scientific institutions, in short, Enlightened in

197

a thoroughly eighteenth-century manner. In books and ideas, its tastes looked back to the Moderate Enlightenment in which its members had been brought up, and also forward to republican innovation along the same lines. Moreover, this upper class had experienced the threat of social revolution from below, and was warned and chastened by this experience. In postwar Philadelphia, history had produced a delicate balance between the Moderate and the Revolutionary forms of Enlightenment.

The ruling class of colonial Philadelphia had been drastically damaged first by Quaker withdrawal from public affairs and then by the dawn of revolution. In early 1776, however, the province was still politically dominated by conservatives and moderates, ranging from reluctant Tories like Joseph Galloway to reluctant Whigs like John Dickinson, who drove through Philadelphia behind four white horses and entertained right-thinking Continental Congress delegates at his handsome country estate. Against Tories and moderate Whigs, Episcopalians and Quakers, and rich Philadelphians in general, the fiery Presbyterians of the West nourished old and real grievances, in which they were joined by a sizable, also mostly Presbyterian, and largely disfranchised lower-class faction in the capital. Outside the province and in the Congress, supporters of independence were deeply concerned about the foot-dragging of the Philadelphia provincial regime, which continued to hope for reconciliation long after the fighting had started. In particular the Pennsylvania Assembly, once more dominated by conservatives after a new election in May of 1776, clung to the old provincial charter and refused to repeal its anti-independence instructions to the Pennsylvania delegates. Ironically, it was John Adams who introduced in the Congress a resolution calling on each colony to adopt a new government "where no government sufficient to the exigencies of their affairs hath been hitherto established."[2] This resolution was seized on by Pennsylvania radicals, with some justice, as ample warrant for a local revolution. It was this revolution which established the famous radical constitution of Pennsylvania, admired by French *philosophes* and denounced by Adams in his major political work.

Supported by revolutionary committees of civilians and soldiers, an extralegal provincial conference called for the election of a new constitutional convention and proceeded to enfranchise its friends and disfranchise its enemies. All males who paid any taxes were allowed to vote, provided they subscribed to a stringent set of oaths, not only abjuring the British Crown, but also swearing to support a provincial government based only on the people. Anybody who had ever been "published by any committee of inspection, or the committee of safety, in this province, as an enemy to the liberties of America" was forbidden to vote. So far, the procedure sounds familiar enough to students of more modern revolutions, but the conference went on to require that delegates to the constitutional convention must declare their faith in the Trinity and the divine inspiration of the Scriptures.[3]

The new Constitution produced by this convention was the principal official American embodiment of revolutionary radicalism. Its political provisions were for the period ultra-democratic: a unicameral legislature, a plural executive, annual elections, easy naturalization, popular election of militia officers and justices of the peace, and a curious Council of Censors to watch over the representatives of the people and call a new convention if necessary. The Constitution provided for little economic reform. Debtors who surrendered their property were to be released from prison, but proposals to condemn or discourage large accumulations of property were defeated.[4]

The religious provisions of the document were among its most striking. Providing for freedom of worship, the Constitution nonetheless demanded that legislators declare their belief in "one God, the Creator and Governour of the universe, the rewarder of the good and punisher of the wicked," and that they "acknowledge the Scriptures of the Old and New Testament to be given by Divine Inspiration." This oath, regretted by Franklin and Benjamin Rush and some other supporters of the new order as unduly repressive, was attacked at least as often by those who regretted that the provincial conference version had been watered down, and that Jews and deists were enfranchised by it. It probably escaped few that Quakers, opposed to all oaths, were thus excluded from the legislature.

Furious conservatives and moderates denounced the oath and the fact that the Constitution was not submitted to the people. To all adherents of the political precepts of the Moderate Enlightenment, the weakness of the executive and especially the absence of checks and balances flew in the face of Montesquieu and Polybius, and the Pennsylvania Constitution became a focus of argument between Adams and the French *philosophes*. Above all, Philadelphia conservatives harped on the accusation that the new government was dominated by ignorant nobodies.

This was not strictly true. Undoubtedly unlettered frontiersmen took some seats and attracted much attention, but the radical party was supported by David Rittenhouse and the artist Charles Willson Peale. Thomas Paine had played a background role. The principal radical leaders were indeed new men, but by no means hayseeds. They included George Bryan, a judge and leading Presbyterian layman; Timothy Matlack, a convivial ex-Quaker colonel; and James Cannon, an Episcopalian professor of mathematics at William Smith's College who had become secretary of the private soldiers' committee. Cannon, despite or perhaps because of his background, is said to have denounced all learning "as an artificial constraint on the human understanding," advised the people to choose no lawyers or other professional men to lead them but rather men with "unsophisticated understandings," and even insisted that he himself "should be glad to forget the trumpery which had occupied so much of his life."[5]

In their egalitarian and ascetic sentiments and in their bourgeois origins, these American radicals resembled the Jacobins of two decades later. They were, however, only halfway members of the Revolutionary Enlightenment; like other American radicals they looked back with enthusiasm to the Puritan Commonwealth. When the new government got around to it, in 1779, it destroyed Smith's College as a hotbed of Episcopalianism as well as Toryism, establishing a new State University under largely Presbyterian auspices. In 1786 it abolished the Philadelphia theater.

Conservative Whigs, supported by Tories as the lesser evil, refused allegiance to the 1776 Constitution, and the war effort of Pennsylvania was gravely hampered by the intensity with which the two sides feared and distrusted each other. Efforts to forge a compromise were aborted by the British occupation of Philadelphia from September to May, 1777-78. Though eighteenth-century wars, even revolutionary and civil wars, did not yet approach the ferocity we take for granted today, feelings were intense as rebels were punished and expropriated. Spartan-minded radicals deeply resented the true stories of Philadelphia ladies, of Whig as well as Tory families, dancing with British officers at lavish balls while Washington's army was near starvation. When the American forces re-entered the city, they found much destruction. Significantly, Presbyterian, Methodist, and Lutheran churches had been used for stables and barracks.[6]

In their turn, the returning revolutionaries arrested a long list of Tories and neutrals, including the unfortunate William Smith, who had dominated pre-revolutionary Philadelphia high culture and struggled hard to preserve a neutral position in the crisis. Loyalty to the new government was assured by tighter oaths, and failure to support the Revolution after 1776 was defined as treason. Over the protest of moderate Whigs, two men were executed for collaborating with the enemy—not members of the Tory aristocracy but Quaker artisans who had apparently assisted both sides. For a while, not only Tories but Quakers and moderates went in fear. The height of revolutionary violence was reached in October 1779, when a mob attacked the house of James Wilson, leader of the Anti-Constitutionalist (conservative) Party. This mob was repelled by gunfire in a battle which left six killed and twenty wounded.[7] It is worth being precise about the casualties of this minor Bastille-day-in-reverse because they were so few. The episode ended with a general pardon, and civil violence in Philadelphia largely ended with it.

Through the decade of the 1780's, patiently and cautiously, the conservatives regained first their morale and then political control. They were careful to disassociate themselves from Toryism, and to attack the radicals where it hurt by demanding a popular reconsideration of the Constitution. The fight centered on such diverse issues as the proscription of Tories, incorporation of the Bank of Pennsylvania, and how strictly to deal with army mutinies. By the middle of the decade conservatives had the upper hand. Two-to-one ratification of the Federal Constitution was interpreted by both sides as a defeat for local radicals. In 1788 the theater was restored, the next year all loyalty oaths were abolished, and local government incorporated. At the same time the old College charter was restored and the undaunted William Smith brought back from Maryland exile to head it. Finally, in 1790, the detested radical Constitution of 1776 was replaced.

The striking fact is that the Philadelphia moderates and conservatives, restored to power, unlike almost all restored conservatives, acted with intelligence and moderation. In the 1790 state constitutional convention both sides were represented, and in the new charter there were indeed two houses, but to the chagrin of the ultras both were popularly elected.

One may try to account for this by pointing out that the radicals were defeated only with difficulty and not overwhelmed. Yet in other revolutionary periods elsewhere, it is precisely the difficult victories that give rise to the panics and proscriptions. The important fact that there was no "White Terror" in Philadelphia, as there had been no real "Red Terror" either, must be laid to the fact that this was still the eighteenth century, and that *both* sides saw themselves as partisans of enlightenment and progress, members of the only modern government in existence. In the monster parade with which Philadelphia celebrated the Federal Constitution of July 4th, not only the elite but the sailors and apprentices marched in order, as did representatives of all religions, including the Jews. The final toast at the ensuing banquet was to "the Whole Family of Mankind."[8]

To Philadelphia moderates in 1790 the future looked bright. All could join in another great procession for the funeral of Franklin, whose support had been claimed by the left but never forsworn by the right. The federal government, returning to the city, was headed by Washington, a lofty figure above all politics, and included the patriotic Adams, the gifted Hamilton, and the generous Jefferson. Not least important, the principal ally of the United States had just established religious toleration and a constitutional monarchy, establishing its new regime in enlightened fashion with only a minimum of bloodshed. So confident, in fact, were the restored leaders of Philadelphia society in the future and in their own good sense and moderation, that they tended to ignore the social resentments which, in the West and also within the city, had lasted through all political ups and downs and were to surface again before the end of the 1790's.

Philadelphia in the 1780's and '90's, even before the floodtide of refugees from the French Revolution and the subsequent slave revolt in Santo Domingo, had a more French flavor than any other American city. From the alliance of 1778 onward, society women did their best to copy even the most preposterous Parisian headdresses, and sober merchants found it to their interest to learn the language of the world's second most important commercial nation. The diplomats of Louis XVI helped to introduce French music and manners, and at least one of them married a Philadelphia girl. The birth of the Dauphin was celebrated not only with one of the customary parades but by a mass, tolerantly attended by the Congress. Among the more distinguished of the many curious visitors were the Marquis de Chastellux, a member of Washington's staff; Brissot de Warville (shortly to give his name to the moderate faction of Paris revolutionaries), and the Duc de Rochefoucauld-Liancourt, who unlike some of his fellows charmed aristocratic Philadelphians by his democratic manners.

These visitors, full of the generous emotions of the dawning stage of the Revolutionary Enlightenment, were almost always impressed by Philadelphia's regular and harmonious street patterns, by her religious diversity and tolerance, and by Quaker humane institutions. They also admired the simple but dignified and lofty manners of Washington, the head of the first modern republican government and the nearest modern equivalent to an antique hero. Sometimes these favorable impressions made up for the social life, which Frenchmen usually found dull, and for the climate and food, which they always found atrocious. Sometimes these liberal aristocrats were shocked by the presence in the republican capital of such luxuries as coaches and carpets, or by the survival of such old-fashioned customs as bowing and curtsying.[9]

At least two wartime immigrants from France remained to play a major role in the city's life. Peter Du Ponceau, who brought with him an unusual taste for English literature and Protestant religion, played an important part in the Philadelphia legal profession from 1785 and later became an authority on Indian languages. Stephen Girard, who was astute enough to build a fortune out of a quarter-century of international trading in time of revolution and war, was by no means an aristocratic charmer but a tough and sometimes brutal self-made man. Nonetheless, he was to name ships *Liberty*, *Voltaire*, *Rousseau*, *Helvétius*, and *Montesquieu*, and eventually to emerge as a common-sense hero of the 1793 yellow fever epidemic.[10]

The gaiety and extravagance of Philadelphia society hardly reached Parisian levels, but nevertheless shocked those natives and visitors who clung to the Spartan principles of the Commonwealth ideology.[11] As in modern instances, the influx of government employees and visitors to the capital sent up prices and rents and increased the pace of social competition. According to tax records, the city had 84 carriages in 1772 and 847 in 1794. Exclusiveness varied: the subscription ball specifically excluded the wives and daughters of tradesmen. When this gave offense another more democratic series of assemblies was started, and Washington tactfully attended both.[12] As in later capitals, members of government complained of the exhausting rounds of visits, and rival social leaders set different styles. Robert Morris, probably the richest Philadelphian until he succumbed to speculation and went to debtor's prison, entertained in the handsome but unostentatious profusion of a provincial magnate. Mrs. William Bingham, on the other hand, did her best to raise local mores to European levels. In the Binghams' grand new mansion, servants bawled out the names and (when possible) titles of guests as they ascended the marble staircase. It is not surprising to learn either that the Binghams left for England and Bermuda at the end of the 1790's, or that the hall of their Philadelphia mansion contained busts of Voltaire, Rousseau, and Franklin.[13]

In the nineties, Tories could make a comeback if they had not been too conspicuous. Dr. William Smith, however, who was not a Tory but had tried to be a neutral, was too closely associated with past hopes and styles. In 1779 the College had been restored to its old trustees and Smith, unchastened, had victoriously assumed his old place as Provost. For a while the old College and the new State University existed as rivals. In 1791 they were amalgamated under the provostship of John Ewing, a moderate and mildly rationalist Presbyterian in religion and a former defender of the radical Constitution.[14] In 1794 Dr. Smith, still fighting, was forced to retire with a cash settlement.

The Episcopal Church in Philadelphia, part of which had been involved in prewar Anglican dreams of control, was reconstituted. Only two of the clergy actually left for England, during or after the war, and one of these, the unfortunate Jacob Duché, was permitted to come back, chastened and enfeebled, in 1792.[15] For the new post of Bishop of Pennsylvania, Smith was passed over in favor of William White, one of the few Episcopal clergy who had been strongly in favor of the Revolution.

One other defeat of William Smith marks the end in America of latitudinarianism, one of the oldest forms of the Moderate Enlightenment. In the struggle over revision of the prayerbook for independent America, Smith had joined the effort to omit the Nicene and Athanasian creeds.[16] This effort was closely related to the earlier British struggle to change the Thirty-Nine Articles or at least abolish the obligation to sub-scribe to them. As in England, the move for liberalization was defeated; only King's Chapel, in Boston, moved into the Unitarian camp. No longer either imperial or latitudinarian, the Protestant Episcopal Church moved for a while toward the mainstream of American Protestantism. In Philadelphia, a battered and conciliatory Episcopal Church shared the allegiance of the upper class with the moderate Presbyterians and the Quakers.

The pattern for catholicity, enlightenment, and sheer brilliance was set by Washington's government, which after 1790 drew to the capital a set of philosopher-statesmen with few equals in the Enlightened world. Certainly the presence at one time of Washington, Adams, Jefferson, Madison, and others greatly affected the culture of the capital, but none of these had helped to form it, and Philadelphia in turn affected some of them. In the early 1790's, national and local political leaders mixed freely, and the gradual growth of political parties did not at first affect social and intellectual discourse.[17]

Philadelphia politicians were mostly lawyers, and Philadelphia law-yers tended to be conservative in their views. In the struggles of the 1770's and 1780's, many of them thought they had seen law itself men-aced by revolutionary violence and egalitarianism. The tone was set by conservative Whigs like Thomas McKean or Francis Hopkinson, but among leading lawyers and judges of the 1790's one finds a surprising number of wartime neutrals like Benjamin Chew, William Tilghman, or John Ross, and even some professed Tories like Edward Shippen.[18] Of lawyer-politicians the most important at the beginning of the nineties was James Wilson, the embodiment of Enlightened and moderate con-servatism.

Wilson was a Scottish immigrant, and, despite his education at St. Andrews, a self-made man. Arriving in Pennsylvania right at the begin-ning of the Revolutionary struggle in 1763, he had become a pupil of John Dickinson, who grounded him not only in the law but in all the principles of the Moderate Enlightenment. As a rising young lawyer in Carlisle, he had early become a member of the revolutionary provincial convention and a much stronger opponent of Parliamentary legislation than his mentor. Nevertheless, as a delegate to the First and Second Continental Congresses he moved only slowly toward independence. From the beginning, Wilson was the ablest and most effective (because the least hysterical) opponent of Pennsylvania's radical Constitution, writing under the prestigious pen name of "Addison" against the still more illustrious "Common Sense" (Paine). This stance, together with Wilson's haughty bearing, made him especially hated by Pennsylvania radicals. Curiously, he seems to have been educated rather than embittered by the attack on his house in 1779.

In the Federal Constitutional Convention, to the dismay of Dickinson and his other conservative friends, Wilson turned out to be the chief advocate of advanced democracy. What annoyed them was that he quoted all the most respectable authorities of the Moderate Enlightenment, from Grotius to Montesquieu, but argued on behalf of easy naturalization, equality of new states, and particularly popular election of *both* houses of the legislative branch. In the Pennsylvania ratifying convention he defended the Constitution not as a means of curbing the people but as providing a frame of government which depended entirely on them. In his peroration this Philadelphia conservative sounded like Jefferson, or even Condorcet, rather than like Dickinson or the Morris brothers:

> on the success of the struggle America has made for freedom, will depend the exertions of the brave and enlightened of other nations . . . [the new government] will draw from Europe, many worthy characters, who pant for the enjoyment of freedom. It will induce princes, in order to preserve their subjects, to restore to them a portion of that liberty of which they have for so many ages been deprived. It will be subservient to the great designs of providence, with regard to this globe; the multiplication of mankind, their improvement in knowledge, and their advancement to happiness.[19]

Finally, in the convention that finally destroyed the Pennsylvania Constitution of 1776, Wilson, again breaking with some of his conservative friends, held out for conciliation and moderate liberalism. He agreed with the conservatives that the new frame should have a two-house legislature, but sided with his old enemies from the west in insisting that both houses should be popularly elected.

It was thus as a symbol of reconciliation and unity, and not just of conservative triumph, that in 1789 Wilson was selected to give a series of lectures on the law at the restored College of Pennsylvania before an audience including Washington, other officials of the federal government, state dignitaries, and Philadelphia moguls with their wives. Wilson accepted this assignment with obvious pride and deep seriousness. In typical Enlightened style, he covered not only systems of law from divine to municipal, comparative constitutions, jurisprudence, and government, but also and centrally the nature of man, his knowledge, and his duties. Wilson's purpose was clearly to link venerable British tradition with the American and republican, even democratic, future. No doubt startling his audience, he challenged not only Blackstone but also Locke.[20] The error of Blackstone lay in his insistence that law implied the existence of superiors and inferiors. Locke's teachings had led in two regrettable directions, one to the destructive idealism of Berkeley and the dangerous skepticism of Hume, and the other to the materialism of Hartley and Priestley. Such principles, like Hobbesian skepticism of human nature, were dangerous to republics. What the United States needed, to sustain that moral responsibility necessary to liberty, had fortunately been provided by Thomas Reid in the new philosophy of Common Sense.

In reaching this particular conclusion Wilson, a Scot like John Witherspoon, was a little in advance of his time in America. The overwhelming importance of Common Sense philosophy for American thinkers was not generally apparent until the French Revolution had made other forms of Enlightenment suspect.[21] Otherwise Wilson, in these lectures as in his whole life, represented accurately a special and fleeting stage of Enlightenment in America and Philadelphia, a time when it seemed that the wisdom and moderation of the English tradition could in America be infused with a hopeful democratic and even revolutionary spirit.

Some irreverent outsiders have suggested that Philadelphia owed her leadership in medicine to her many epidemics, which gave doctors lots of practice. Health care in the city certainly owed something to excellent Quaker traditions and foundations. In the period right before and after the Revolution, Philadelphia medicine like Philadelphia culture in general was solidly imperial. A steady stream of young Philadelphians flowed to the great medical school of Edinburgh and the hospitals and dissecting rooms of London.[22] Some returning students, like Dr. John Morgan, were determined to make Philadelphia the Edinburgh of America. Morgan succeeded in organizing the medical school of William Smith's College with a faculty entirely consisting of men trained overseas. Despite Morgan's own loss of influence in bitter wartime controversies, Edinburgh men continued to dominate the new postwar university and also the restored College, though the stiff colonial standards for degrees were lowered.

Young Philadelphians who studied in Britain brought back not only the best available training but also some European airs and graces, and a passionate involvement in current arguments about the principles of medicine and of science in general. The great Doctor William Cullen at Edinburgh and some of his colleagues were part of an intense reaction in medical thought against "mere empirics," an effort to classify diseases as Linnaeus had classified plants and even to find, in the manner of Newton, the laws that underlay all disease. Following both his teachers and his temperament, Benjamin Rush was sure that the great break-through was at hand—the discovery of the single cause of all disease.[23] Thus Rush, an attractive, learned, brave, and generous man and a major figure in the Philadelphia Enlightenment, serves as the best possible warning of the dangers of Enlightenment without the slightest mixture of skepticism.

He also illustrates, perhaps better than anybody else, the deep religious and philosophical paradoxes that characterize the Enlightenment in America. Full of confidence, hope, and ardor; given also to gloom and resentment; violently intolerant of opposition, Rush was convinced that all important ideas must necessarily be simple: "Truth is simple upon all subjects, but upon those which are essential to the general happiness of mankind, it is obvious to the meanest capacities. . . ." To suppose the contrary "is to call in question the goodness of the Supreme Being, and to believe that he acts without unity and system in all his works."[24] So far, Rush is in the world of Rousseau, Condorcet, and (despite his very different temperament) Jefferson.

Yet this Enlightened believer in goodness and progress was also, from childhood on, a fervent evangelical Christian. Rush's religious origins were Pennsylvanian, which means eclectic. His ancestors were Quaker, Baptist, Presbyterian, and Episcopalian, and he was baptized in the Episcopal Church. He was, however, permanently and deeply affected by the Great Awakening. Under its auspices he became a Presbyterian and, more permanently, a Calvinist. He went to school under one Calvinist Awakener, Samuel Finley, and to college (at Princeton) under another, Samuel Davies. Rush fervently admired both teachers and said later that after Finley's teaching he never doubted the inspiration of the Bible.[25] Studying medicine in Edinburgh he disliked, even more than

Hume's teaching, the compromising, watered-down Calvinism of most of the Common Sense philosophers.

By 1782 Rush had modified his Calvinism in one respect only: he had become a universalist, firmly persuaded that it was part of God's ultimate purpose to save all men.[26] In 1787, partly for political reasons, he left the Presbyterian Church and became an Episcopalian, siding against the proposed liberalization of the Calvinistic Thirty-Nine articles. During the rest of his life he shuttled back and forth between the Presbyterians and Episcopalians, but he never doubted that the triumph of reason and republicanism was indissolubly connected to the salvation of all men by Christ. Gradually, he was sure, these forces together would bring on the millennium, and with it the end of strife, disease, and pain.[27]

In philosophy, as in religion, Rush combined opposite elements in an individual manner, arriving at a mixture of apparently incompatible doctrines. Though he could not approve the moderate anti-Calvinist liberalism of most of the Scottish philosophers, he fervently admired the most conservative of them, James Beattie, and specifically approved Beattie's crude attack on Hume.[28] From Beattie he learned—as he could have learned from any of Beattie's more liberal colleagues—a firm belief in the moral faculty, innate, instinctive, and certain in judgment. Like Jefferson and many other contemporaries, he combined this reassuring certainty with considerable dabbling in environmentalism and even materialism. Here he followed David Hartley, partly because Hartley was a good Presbyterian. Like Hartley, Rush was certain that all mental activity consisted of vibrations, and that the manipulation of these vibrations and of the associations set up by them was God's way of governing the universe. Insisting that there was no possibility of life even continuing without the constant exertion of this mighty power, Rush could sound as determinist as Edwards. The "Being that created our world never takes his hand, nor his eye, for a single moment, from any part of it."[29] Like many of his predecessors and contemporaries, he concluded with satisfaction that God preferred to work through second causes.[30]

In his politics, Rush had originally the feelings of a New Side Presbyterian and a lower-middle-class Philadelphian, which meant that he hated the Quaker elite and was an early and fervent supporter of the Revolution. In Britain he knew and liked James Burgh and Catharine Macaulay, and his early view of public affairs was deeply influenced by

Commonwealth radicalism of a very Protestant kind.[31] He hailed the dawn of American independence as an event comparable to the birth of Christ. Rush signed the Declaration of Independence and sacrificed himself endlessly in an effort to improve army medicine. He also quarreled bitterly with Dr. William Shippen, a Philadelphian who headed the army's medical division, and denounced Washington's military leadership as a danger to the cause.

At first a supporter of Pennsylvania's radical Constitution, Rush quickly turned against it, and was promptly ejected from his seat in the Continental Congress. Soon, siding completely with old enemies like James Wilson and John Dickinson, he became convinced that one-chamber legislatures and loyalty oaths amounted to despotism worse than Turkey's, and to "mobocracy."[32] By the mid-eighties Rush was cheered by the gains for wisdom, virtue, and property in the politics of Pennsylvania, and he was moved by ecstasy by the ratification of the Federal Constitution. Unfortunately, by 1789-90, when his new conservative friends fully triumphed in Pennsylvania, Rush had made so many enemies of so many kinds that he felt isolated and abused, and withdrew from active participation in politics and public life.

As a social reformer Rush was again eclectic. He was a fervent opponent of slavery (though he long kept a slave himself), a fighter for prison reform, the end of capital punishment, and more humane treatment of the insane. All these are familiar Enlightenment causes, but Rush also called for the end of fairs, horseracing, cockfighting, clubs, and Sunday amusements.[33] Here he sounds like a nineteenth-century evangelist, but at his best he went beyond both the eighteenth and nineteenth centuries, insisting, for instance, that the poor must be given medical care in such a way as not to damage their dignity. His greatest efforts went to the enlightened and evangelical cause of education. He hoped for the development of a state system, in which children would be trained not in Latin and Greek but according to a modern system emphasizing governmental science and aimed at producing "republican machines." Eventually all officeholders must be trained at one national university, where they would be well grounded in "federal and republican ideas." So far, Rush clearly resembles Rousseau. He also insisted, however, that the Bible must be at the center of education, and thought it best that schools should be divided among the various sects, with each fully free to inculcate all its own tenets.[34]

Rush's deep confidence in the simplicity of all important ideas led him to some lucky guesses in medicine, and also to some disastrous mistakes. Both his greatness and his limitations emerge from the story of his heroic service in the devastating yellow fever epidemic of 1793.[35] While the rich left town and many deserted their sick in terror, Rush tended the sick and especially the poor night and day, doing his best even to ignore his own symptoms. His method was derived from his theory that all fever, even all disease, originated in a disorder of the blood vessels. As he bled people for mental disorders, consumption, measles, so he bled them copiously for yellow fever, adding to his heroic treatment colossal purges—sufficient, his enemies said, for treating horses. If a patient did not respond to this treatment, he was given more of it. All opposition to these heroic measures was condemned as deliberate obstruction and obscurantism. Rush's many opponents, some of whom like Stephen Girard were French, had no rival panacea but were convinced by experience that more cautious treatments killed fewer people. Trying to prevent people from abandoning their sick, Rush insisted that the disease was not transmitted from person to person, but that it was somehow connected with Philadelphia's gutters and marshes. He blamed the disease on effluvia rather than mosquitoes, but there is no doubt that the city would have been better off if it had followed his advice and drained its standing water.

In many ways Rush was a leading American specimen of the radical temperament. In his republican fervor, his belief in the simplicity and certainty of all problems—moral, political and scientific—in his generous ardors and his intolerance of opposition, he had something in common with Rousseau and even with the Jacobins. Yet he was also a lifelong believer in original sin, divine grace, and the Christian millennium. The result was a zigzag course in his political and religious loyalties and eventually, when party politics and the French Revolution forced people to choose sides, withdrawal into neutrality.

Rush and other doctors were among the mainstays of Philadelphia science, and science was to Philadelphia what literature and theology were to New England. It was the principal expression of civic pride and enlightenment. Flourishing before the Revolution with considerable support from London, scientific enterprise had naturally languished when Philadelphia scientists, Rush and Rittenhouse among them, turned their talents to immediate wartime necessities like military medicine and munitions. After the war, scientific recovery was impeded by the loss of some important cognoscenti through emigration, wartime destruction and erosion of colleges and other institutions, and particularly by the weakening of ties to Europe. Yet in science as elsewhere, Americans were confident that the great republic was destined quickly to equal and surpass the decadent monarchies of Europe.

Historians of science agree that the great hopes of American science went unrealized in the postwar decades and for long afterwards. Republican and nationalist ardor cannot take the place of libraries, laboratories, leisure, specialization, wealthy patronage, and above all government support. Neither the republic nor its capital nor its constituent states for long supported American science as American statesmen and others hoped.[36] Sadly enough, great ages of science seem to be associated not with frugal and Spartan republics but with centralized and even warlike national or imperial states: Stuart England, monarchical and Napoleonic France, Wilhelmine Germany, perhaps mid-twentieth-century America. Post-Revolutionary American science hardly produced a Franklin or perhaps even a Rittenhouse. Its most illustrious figures, starting with Jefferson, were those most deeply conversant with Europe. In Europe, the confident generalizers of the post-Newtonian age were giving way to the more specialized experimenters. This was the time of Lavoisier, Lamarck, Cuvier, Priestley, and others who carried their researches well beyond the level that could be achieved in America.

Despite all their handicaps, including the excesses of patriotic enthusiasm, American scientists managed to perform solid and valuable work. The most important American scientific organization was the American Philosophical Society. The APS, with its impressive roster of members from many states and countries, had some hopes of becoming the center of a nationwide scientific federation. Yet it was always in large part a Philadelphia organization. In addition to scientists and doctors, it included among its members the city's leading clergy and principal politicians. Inevitably, the Society's history reflected the seesaw and sometimes violent politics of Pennsylvania and Philadelphia. In doing this, however, the leaders of the Society made a remarkably successful effort, typical of the practice of the Philadelphia elite, to preserve conciliation and catholicity.[37]

Shortly after David Rittenhouse, in the oration for 1776, had linked republicanism and science for the first time in the Society's history, wartime conditions forced the organization to suspend its functions. It was revived in 1779, and for some years its officers (aside from its august and absent president, Franklin) belonged mainly to the radical Constitutionalist faction. Yet, even in this period Francis Hopkinson, a conservative Whig but a close friend of Rittenhouse, remained treasurer. Rittenhouse helped prevent the radical legislature from limiting the amount of property the Society could hold and requiring that only citizens of Pennsylvania could be members. The first annual orations under the new order, by the patriotic radicals Timothy Matlack and Owen Biddle, were paeans of praise for agriculture and invention, democratic in spirit but not very controversial.[38]

By the mid-eighties, the Society like the city was moving back in a conservative direction. When Franklin died in 1790, William Smith and David Rittenhouse received equal votes for the honor of giving the official eulogy. After some discussion Smith gave it, getting help on scientific matters from Rittenhouse. In the oration, which presented Franklin as a friend of revelation, Smith must have had his tongue even farther in his cheek than usual. According to family tradition, his daughter believed that he didn't believe more than a tenth of what he said about "Old Ben Lightning Rod."[39]

In 1791 Rittenhouse succeeded Franklin as president. This clearly moved the Society once more toward the radical side. In a masterpiece of Philadelphia compromise, however, the three vice-presidents chosen to serve with Rittenhouse were the still uncowed William Smith, his old rival and enemy the Constitutionalist and Presbyterian John Ewing, and an outsider, Thomas Jefferson of Virginia, the Secretary of State. When Rittenhouse died Jefferson, who was now Vice-President of the United States as well, succeeded him as president, a post he held from 1797 until 1814. In the turbulent years at the very end of the century, the Society inclined somewhat to the politics of its president. Two leading members, Rittenhouse and Charles Willson Peale, served as presidents of the Democratic Society. Yet Robert Morris, James Wilson, and other conservatives and Federalists were also members. Among the foreign members elected during this period were both Condorcet and the bland

and reassuring Scottish philosopher, Dugald Stewart. The official rule of the Society in the nineties was that it did not take any position as a body even on scientific matters, a rule which must have helped avoid involvement in Philadelphia's fierce medical fights as well as her politics.[40]

The range of the APS in religion ran from Rush, a very special kind of devout Calvinist, through Rittenhouse, a lifelong Presbyterian who talked much of God and not at all of the Christian redemption, ultra-cautious deists like Peale and cautious ones like Jefferson, but not further. Paine, though resident in or near Philadelphia, active in its politics until 1787, and much more concerned with scientific invention than many members, was never elected, and John Fitch found the society hostile.[41]

Perhaps the leading symbol and chief maintainer of catholicity and moderation in the Society was John Vaughan, its treasurer and its most active functionary from 1791 until well into the nineteenth century.[42] Vaughan was the son of Samuel Vaughan, a wealthy British merchant, and the brother of Benjamin Vaughan, a member of Lord Shelburne's Radical Whig circle who sympathized so vocally with both the American and the French Revolutions that he had to emigrate during Pitt's counter-revolutionary persecutions. Vaughan himself, no radical, had come to America with Franklin's recommendation and become a leading member of Philadelphia society. A Federalist and (rare in Philadelphia) a Unitarian, he was known both for his snobbery and his elegant manners. Yet Vaughan maintained good relations with Joseph Priestley, a family friend, and wrote (in French) to such *philosophes* as Pierre S. DuPont de Nemours. In the politically critical year of 1800 we find him asking Adet, the minister of the French Republic, to check deficiencies in the Society's set of the *Encyclopédie*.[43]

Both the Philadelphia Enlightenment and the APS found a place for Samuel Stanhope Smith. Smith was John Witherspoon's son-in-law, and a Presbyterian clergyman orthodox enough to succeed Witherspoon as president of Princeton. An elegant Latinist, a lover and occasional writer of Augustan poetry, a man famous for his stately bearing, Smith was so urbane that the Reverend Archibald Alexander, seeing him at a General Assembly in Philadelphia in 1781, never dreamed he was a clergyman but "supposed him to be some gentleman of Philadelphia, who had dropped in to hear the debate." Smith's brother, a less friendly observer, is said to have told him, "Brother Sam, you don't preach Jesus Christ and Him Crucified, but Sam Smith and him dignified."[44]

Smith in this period indulged secretly in writing innocently gallant letters to a female cousin in the fashionable sentimental style derived from Sterne. He also dabbled, in his correspondence with his close friend Benjamin Rush, in what was advanced liberalism for a Princeton Presbyterian. In 1790, for instance, he suggested that there might be "no need of any other millennium than the general progress of science, & Civilization." In saying this, Smith was of course merely suggesting that God might choose to use secondary causes in improving human nature. He knew, however, that he had gone pretty far, and that if the letter "should fall into the hands of some pious champions of orthodoxy, they will swear it was written with a design to bring in *universal redemption*."[45] Smith, elected to the APS when he assumed Princeton office in 1786, delivered the Society's annual oration the next year. This was his well-known *Essay on the Causes of the Variety of . . . the Human Species*, in which he argued that Negroes were not innately inferior to whites and were, in fact, becoming whiter under the influence of climate—a position taken with liberal intentions if somewhat contradictory assumptions. A decade later, Smith was to be turned in a conservative direction by student turbulence, and by the end of the decade he was an extreme and violent opponent of Jacobinism and "French" philosophy.

Despite their large range, from Smith and Vaughan to Jefferson and Rittenhouse, the active members of the Philosophical Society shared a common view of nature and science. This scientific ideology reflected the common position of the Philadelphia elite of this period, balanced between the left of the Moderate Enlightenment and the right of the Revolutionary Enlightenment. One and all, the liberal Christians and moderate deists who controlled the APS saw nature as designed by a wise creator for the use and edification of man. This view was more important to the deists, whose God depended solely on the evidence of nature, than it was to the liberal Christians, for whom nature merely corroborated revelation. As for the Bible, those more inclined to deism left it alone in their scientific utterances, while those more specifically Christian, from Rittenhouse to Samuel Smith, insisted that true science and Scripture could never be in disagreement.

The most famous example of the teleological view of nature comes from Jefferson, who insisted in discussing mastodon bones that the mastodon must exist somewhere, because for a form of life to disappear would serve no purpose in the economy of nature. Like Jefferson, Samuel Stanhope Smith was certain that man must have been created as he is now, endowed with reason. Like Rush, Benjamin Smith Barton, the nephew of Rittenhouse, was convinced that in all regions of the earth the Creator had placed natural remedies for the most prevalent diseases.[46]

Barton was perhaps the most skeptical and secular-minded of leading members of the APS. His famous essay on the rattlesnake, an excellent piece of observation and argument like much of his work, is largely devoted to patient debunking of the widely held view that this creature has the power to fascinate its prey. In places the essay sounds almost Voltairean:

> It is obvious, from contemplating the manners and the history of nations, that a part of their religions, and a large part of the fabrick of their superstitious notions, have arisen out of fear. . . .
>   . . . to the cultivators of science, the discovery of truth must, at all times, be a source of pleasure. This pleasure will even rise to something like happiness, when, in addition to the discovery of truth, we are enabled to draw aside the veil, which, for ages, has curtained superstition and cruelty.

Yet part of Barton's argument is that the rattlesnake has not been given the power in question because he does not need it. Discussing the defense of their young by birds he sees such faithful attachments as demonstrating "in language most emphatick, the existence, the superintendance, the benevolence, of a first great cause" and he declares himself "always happy" in the study of natural history, "to discover new instances of the wisdom of providence. . . ."[47]

Without conscious contradiction, some members of the Society combined with their creationism and teleology a tendency toward environmentalism, even materialism of the Priestleyan variety. Jefferson and, as we have seen, Rush agreed with Priestley that God could endow matter with the power of thought. Smith agreed with Rush that environment was gradually whitening the Negro, and also observed that in general "the exercise of the human faculties is greatly aided & retarded by the external circumstances in which men are placed. . . . The progress of science & perhaps of virtue, is found to keep pace with the progress of society."[48]

A second major point in the common APS ideology was a utilitarian conception of science. This followed obviously from the belief in a beneficent creator: it is the object of scientific research to understand the human benefits for which creation was intended. "For what use," asks Peale, "would the sun display its beams? For what use would this spacious world be furnished by the great and bountiful Author of Nature were there no rational beings capable of admiring them and turning them to their advantage?"[49] In this period "useful science" was less often contrasted with "mere theory" than in later American periods, though such crude distinctions can be found. More generally, it was assumed that any discovery of the workings of nature, even any particular fact, from a new plant to mastodon bones or Indian customs, was bound to prove useful to man—that was how all nature had been framed. The Society itself urged its members to look keenly for prehistoric remains. It also offered prizes for a system of "liberal education and literary institutions" and for improvements in ship-pumps, stoves, vegetable dyes, lamps, and methods for dealing with the diseases of peach trees.[50]

Finally, the leading members of the APS, moderate or radical Whigs, shared a fervent but enlightened nationalism. Romantic love for wild or shaggy American nature was rare, though appreciation for the continent's boundless opportunities, closely related, was very common. America's destiny was not to preserve wildness, but to combine increasing enlightenment with republican simplicity and thus surpass Europe in European achievements. "Useful" science meant useful to mankind, but especially to the republic. In an essay of 1789 published as an introduction to the Society's *Transactions* for 1793, the rector of the Swedish church in Philadelphia argues for concentration on what is most important to the new nation: medicine, agriculture, machines for abating human labor, and discoveries of useful plants.[51] Peale similarly insisted that "Natural history is not only interesting to the individual, it ought to become a NATIONAL CONCERN, since it is a NATIONAL GOOD."[52]

National glory as well as national use concerned these Enlightened savants. Timothy Matlack, in his Society oration of 1780, compared America to Russia, as a nation recently rising to glory, partly through her patronage of men of science. The honor and fame of America, her reputation in Europe, he insisted in the midst of armed revolution "rests on a broader base than that of Arms alone."[53] This was exactly the motive for which the writers of Connecticut, in their very different mode, were determined to equal and excel the poets of Europe. In science, even more obviously than in literature, this effort was self-defeating: the more America cut herself off from the Old World, the more she lost the necessary means of scientific progress. Nobody knew this better, and nobody was more deeply divided in his feelings toward Europe, than that great nationalist, the president of the American Philosophical Society and of the United States.

The American Philosophical Society, like the Philadelphia culture on which it rested, looked back to the colonial and cosmopolitan past for its loyalties and ideas as well as forward to the new revolutionary age. Its members constituted a conscious elite, some of whom believed in democracy, and all of whom believed in rigorous education. Some, like Rush, questioned the importance of the classics; probably most, like Jefferson, did not. Their pursuit of science, unspecialized, taxonomic, and somewhat utilitarian yet resting on taken-for-granted moral and metaphysical assumptions, was not that which was to make the advances of the nineteenth century. The religious and moral principles that members of the Society constantly invoked rested on compromises which were wearing thin: divine beneficence, all-sufficient and unchanging creation, the influence of the environment on all of life. Jefferson, for one, sensed the precariousness of these compromises. Perhaps there is a certain timidity implied in the Society's insistence on sticking to immediate and practical tasks: its most eulogistic historian has suggested this.[54] Like the makers of the Federal Constitution, the leaders of the APS were men of great energy, public spirit, and political skill. Like them, they used this skill with remarkable success to avoid the extremes of ideological conflict. Suddenly in the middle of the 1790's, this became impossible.

In 1793-94 the intellectual life of Philadelphia was enriched by the arrival of several new waves of French refugees, from the Jacobin terror in Paris and also the black revolution in Santo Domingo.[55] All sorts of French politics were discussed in the refugee newspapers and boarding-houses. The most distinguished group of new arrivals consisted of idealistic noblemen who had played a part in the first stages of the Revolution and represented the beginning or middle stages of the Revolutionary Enlightenment. Some of them had well-known names: Constantin de Volney, the optimistic prophet of universal religion; C. M. de Talleyrand-Périgord, for once in his long career unable to climb on the leading bandwagon; Moreau de St. Méry, who as governor of Paris had received the keys of the Bastille from the mob in 1789 and now kept the leading French bookstore in the city. As British sympathizers with the French Revolution also found it necessary to emigrate, the city drew Matthew Carey, with an important future in the American press and in economic argument; Alexander Wilson, the Scottish botanist; and Thomas Cooper, the Unitarian radical. Moreau, Volney, Talleyrand, Wilson, and Cooper all became members of the APS, added to its distinction, and inevitably pushed its political center a little to the left.

Far the most important refugee to arrive was Cooper's friend Joseph Priestley. There was no question that Priestley, the discoverer of oxygen, was a major scientific figure, despite his stubborn adherence to the increasingly dubious existence of phlogiston, the principle of combustibility. He was also a Unitarian, in his own opinion a devout Christian, and a determined enemy of religious skepticism. Indeed, skepticism of any kind was remote from Priestley's nature. A hopeful, honest, and generous man, he was also sometimes credulous, a little self-important, and in controversy inclined to be heavy-handed and moralistic: the sort of man who unwittingly attracts both affection and dislike.[56]

Priestley had been a leading defender in England of the American Revolution, and a member of the Radical Whig circle which included Paine and Franklin. Like many English Dissenters and American Protestants, he was a keen student of Biblical prophecy and thought he saw in the French Revolution the advent of pure government and religion, and indeed the harbinger of the millennium. At some points he debated with himself whether it was not his duty to go to Paris and do his best to set the Revolution on a liberal-Christian rather than an atheistic track. Attacked by Burke along with Paine and Richard Price, Priestley replied in kind. His pro-French and republican statements exaggerated by the Tory press, he became an object of official suspicion. In July of 1791 his Birmingham house was destroyed by a "Church and King" mob, not without suspicions of official connivance. Priestley, like other radical Englishmen, decided to emigrate to America.

He came with high hopes. Landing in New York, where he was greeted by Governor Clinton and delegations of distinguished citizens, he was thrilled to find himself breathing republican air, and wrote home to his close friend Theophilus Lindsey:

> I feel as if I were in another world. I never before could conceive how satisfactory it is to have the feelings I now have from a sense of perfect security and liberty, all men having equal rights and privileges, and speaking and acting as if they were sensible of it.[57]

Proceeding to Philadelphia, Priestley was again warmly welcomed, especially by the American Philosophical Society, whose President Rittenhouse praised him as an illustrious fellow member and an enlightened republican. In his reply Priestley assured the APS that "a Society of Philosophers, who will have no objection to a person on account of his political or religious sentiments, will be as grateful, as it will be new to me." He went on to express the high hopes for American science he shared with many Philadelphians:

> I am confident . . . that it will soon appear that Republican governments, in which every obstruction is removed to the exertion of all kinds of talent, will be far more favourable to science, and the arts, than any monarchical government has ever been.[58]

Priestley was made especially welcome by his old friends John Vaughan, a supporter of the government, and Thomas Jefferson, Secretary of State and leader of the developing opposition. He wrote Vaughan's radical brother that he intended to stay out of political trouble.

> I take no part in the politics of the country, and consort chiefly with your brother and his friends, who are warm friends of government, as the phrase would be in England. I perceive, however, that the opposition is very considerable, and I am persuaded does not consist, as your brother will have it, of ill intentioned men.[59]

As is so often the case with all sorts of expatriates, for Priestley the glow of the new country soon wore off. He had hoped, with Vaughan, to help turn Philadelphia Christianity in a rational Unitarian direction, and was hurt that Philadelphia clergymen seldom invited him to preach from their pulpits. Withdrawing from the city to Northumberland on the Susquehanna, he tried hard to settle down in this quiet retreat and devote himself to science and—far more important in his eyes—theology. Apparatus, books, and stimulus were lacking, it was hard to get servants, the climate and food were trying. More serious, Priestley found himself once more, in what he had hoped would be a republican haven, the object of fierce political attack.

The praise lavished on Priestley by civic and learned bodies in America, and his enthusiastically republican replies, had aroused the fierce resentment of William Cobbett, a recent immigrant from England with deeply conservative sympathies and a talent for polemic. Mixing a few quotations with a great deal of exaggeration and falsehood, Cobbett depicted Priestley as a dangerous malcontent, who had got only what he deserved from a long-suffering English government and people, a preacher of sedition and irreligion, the enemy of sound institutions everywhere, and an apologist for everything that had happened in France: "The French revolution is his system, and sooner than not see it established, I much question if he would not with pleasure see the massacre of the human race."[60]

This attack, which outraged the Doctor's friends and rallied the members of the APS to his defense, was the beginning of several miserable years for the aging philosopher, who rushed bravely to his own defense and lived to see the triumph of his friend Jefferson. Aside from embittering Priestley's exile, the episode had much broader significance. It signaled the end of a period in which rising political storms had been kept outside the charmed circle of the Philadelphia savants.

In the political crisis at the end of the century, the APS did its best to stick to its political neutrality, honoring Jefferson, defending Priestley, but never proscribing Federalists. Yet its great days were over for many reasons, including the passing of its social and ideological base in the peculiar Philadelphia Enlightenment of the post-Revolutionary years. Since the early 1780's, Philadelphia politics, despite the sharp divisions which had never been forgotten, had been conducted with reasonable amenity. In about 1792 or 1793, however (earlier than in most of the country), foreign and domestic policy led to increasingly bitter divisions. As national parties formed, the capital was the inevitable center of organization and of an increasingly polemical party press. It was in Philadelphia that the egregious Citizen Genet, minister of the French Republic, overstepped the bounds of diplomatic practice in his attempts to rally popular support. The griefs and hatreds of the refugees, reading each week of the guillotinings of friends, made the news from Paris more real and concrete. Even the yellow fever exacerbated political feelings, as it was blamed by different sufferers on God's anger with irreligion, contagions brought by the French, neglect of urban conditions by the rich, or the mistakes of Enlightened doctors. Always ethnically and socially divided, Philadelphians found new vocabularies for old resentments only recently suppressed.

Cobbett's attack on Priestley, one of the opening guns in the fierce American struggle over the French Revolution, had special significance also in the history of the Enlightenment in America. The pamphlet repeatedly referred to Priestley as a "philosopher" and "a doctor with half a dozen initials to his name." "Philosophy" and "Enlightenment," moreover, were linked to the French Revolution. This event, said Cobbett, however dreadful, might prove to be a necessary example for mankind. "Indeed some such example was necessary to cure the world of the infidel philosophy of Voltaire, Rousseau, Gibbon, Priestley, and the rest of that enlightened tribe."[61] More than ever before, Enlightenment had suddenly become controversial: in the next few years Americans were asked to accept or reject it as a whole, complete with its new religious and political connotations.

Four *American Radicals*

The Revolutionary Enlightenment, with its sweeping prophecies of a Secular Millennium, affected some Americans deeply in the years following 1793. New visions of the triumph of republicanism combined with old hatred of tyranny and corruption, and American politics were transformed. Nevertheless, the Revolutionary Enlightenment in its full European form, combining a new religion with a new politics, prophesying a new man in a new society, failed to set down deep roots in America. By the end of the century, even as Americans were electing their most enlightened president, this form of Enlightenment was already being rejected by an overwhelming majority. The brief but fervent admiration of the Revolutionary Enlightenment among some Americans, and its angry rejection by others, had much to do with the American fate of all varieties of Enlightenment.

The excitement caused in America by the establishment of a second great republic is a familiar story. The events that took place in Paris, despite language and distance, had a massive effect in the United States. Their impact was felt in three ways: through the press, through the works of European revolutionary writers, and through the increasing stream of exiles.

In 1790 the nation had about ninety newspapers, all small, most of them struggling to keep alive, and only eight appearing daily. Ten years later the number had almost doubled.[1] After 1793, the leading party papers of Philadelphia, Boston, and New York carried on a violent argument over French events, and their polemical essays were widely copied. Many papers, however, continued to report French events with what objectivity they could muster. News came six to eight weeks late, and information sometimes rested on the report of a single traveler or on a hostile British source. Yet Americans throughout the straggling nation were remarkably well informed about the general course of events.

Though nearly everybody in America approved the first outbreaks in 1789, and Congress decorously praised its favorite king for accepting the Constitution of 1791, the first great wave of American emotion arose only with the end of the monarchy in 1792. History was following America: another great nation was now a republic. Emotions rose to a still higher pitch at the outbreak of war between France and England in 1793. The familiar enemy, George III, was seen as trying again to suppress republican freedom, and the survival of America seemed to many to depend on his defeat. Already, however, this strong emotional current failed to affect a skeptical minority, which saw freedom in terms of British law and institutions.

While Americans condemned as treason Louis XVI's desperate flight to Varennes, his execution divided American opinion. The division continued through the arrest and imprisonment of the Girondin deputies in July 1793. If they chose among French factions, pro-French Americans were usually Girondins like Edmond Genet, the ambassador whose arrival in April 1793 was feasted and toasted from Charleston to Boston. As Genet was dismissed and Paine imprisoned, as reports multiplied of mass executions in Paris and the provinces, as Americans read about the cult of Reason and the dictatorship of Robespierre, the numbers of anti-French Americans and the boldness of their criticism increased. Most pro-French Americans, and in 1794 that probably meant most Americans, apologized with more or less difficulty for French excesses. Some blamed them on the reaction to centuries of oppression, others on the anti-French conspiracy of kings, and still others insisted that reports of atrocities were British fabrications.

Nevertheless, the fall of Robespierre in July 1794 was greeted by nearly unanimous relief; the "sea-green incorruptible" had only a tiny personal following in America.[2] Some Americans, like their ardently pro-French minister to Paris James Monroe, found much to praise in the unexciting but apparently less bloodthirsty Directorate, and believed that France was at last following America toward stable republican government. Many rejoiced in the early victories of Bonaparte and found it hard to believe in the possibility of his becoming dictator. Nevertheless, it was in the period 1795-1800, the period of the Directorate and Consulate, and not during the Reign of Terror, that the anti-French party reached the peak of its power in the United States.

In the 1790's, during the period of intense emotional debate about the French Revolution, the intellectual representatives of the Revolutionary Enlightenment reached impressive heights of popularity in America. Rousseau, long familiar, was read as never before, and all his major works were republished in America. Raynal and Volney were circulated widely and so to a lesser extent was Condorcet. British defenders of the French new order spoke still more powerfully to Americans. William Godwin's combination of boundless optimism, anarchism, and non-violence moved some Americans who could not completely come to terms with the Reign of Terror. Americans seem to have been still more impressed by Godwin's wife. Mary Wollstonecraft's *Vindication of the Rights of Women* sold widely and was reprinted four times in America. Writing from Tennessee, a young Virginian recommended the *Vindication* to his sister: "I do sincerely wish women enjoyed all their Rights according to Mrs. Woolstoncraft's idea of them, a wife would then be indeed a Treasure of inestimable value."[3]

At Harvard in 1796, a poem "Women," delivered at a public exhibition in the chapel, after listing the famous women of antiquity, daringly added to his list not only the popular Commonwealth historian Catharine Macaulay, but also the radical champion of women's rights:

> Illustrious *Wollstonecraft*, desert shall twine
> Thy honor'd temples with the living vine;
> Applauding ages to thy name shall raise
> The lasting monument of grateful praise. . . .
>
> Curs'd be the thought, that man unkind could prove,
> A proud oppressor to his fondest love. . . .[4]

William Ellery Channing, at this period a young Federalist visiting Jeffersonian Virginia and as always the epitome of New England seriousness, found himself irresistibly charmed and moved by the writings of Rousseau, Godwin, and especially Mary Wollstonecraft. He confided his inner struggles to a friend:

> It seems that you cannot love Mrs. Wolstonecraft. I do not mean to fight with you about her. Her principles respecting marriage would prove fatal to society, if they were reduced to practice. These I cannot recom-

mend. But on other subjects her sentiments are noble, generous, and sublime . . . what a melancholy reflection it is that the writers I have now mentioned were all deists![5]

Godwin was so influential that he shortly became a major target of leading anti-Jacobin polemicists like Timothy Dwight and Nathanael Emmons.

For Americans, however, the most powerful radical writer was Thomas Paine. In 1791, when Paine answered Burke's attack on the French Revolution with the *Rights of Man*, Jefferson's endorsement created a furor and touched off his first serious quarrel with John Adams.[6] Most Americans clearly sided with Paine and Jefferson against Burke, though Paine's agrarian doctrines were seldom literally endorsed.

It was only with *The Age of Reason* that Paine became the most controversial of all writers. The book stirred the tiny minority of militant deists, deeply troubled a great many friends of France, and gave anti-French conservatives their favorite target. Reprinted in America twenty-one times within the decade, the *Age of Reason* received thirty-five replies, mostly polemical. The furor probably surprised the author. Like many European and some American deists of his warm-hearted type, Paine assumed that America, having led the way to political freedom, would soon discard her obsolete religious prejudices.

Apparently one kind of anti-Christian criticism sometimes opened the way for another. Such non-revolutionary and skeptical works as Hume's *Dialogues*, Gibbon's *Decline*, Voltaire's *Philosophical Dictionary*, and Helvétius's *Treatise on Man* were more widely circulated than at any earlier or later time. Quite mistakenly, alarmed conservatives concluded that skepticism and revolution were the same thing.

European exiles in America helped to spread and make real the debate over European destiny. French royalists, Girondins, and miscellaneous refugees from the Terror in France and the racial upheaval in Santo Domingo thronged the streets of American cities. Philadelphia, New York, and Boston had French bookstores, and seven French newspapers of differing views were published in America. At French coffee-houses, exiles met to argue fiercely over news from home.

Yet again, English exiles were better able, by reason both of language and religion, to influence American opinion. After the outbreak of war between England and France in 1793, as pro-French opinion became unsafe in England, many English supporters of both the American and

French Revolutions decided that the best hope for liberty lay in the New World. Most of these were religious Dissenters, and many represented the old rationalist and radical Dissent of Priestley and Price, now menaced on the one side by "Church and King" mobs and on the other by Methodist revival.

Probably the best-known of the English refugees were Priestley and his friend and fellow-scientist Thomas Cooper. Others included James Ogilvie, the leading Virginia pedagogue, an ardent Godwinian and a friend and frequent correspondent of Jefferson; Joseph Gales, a Unitarian radical who became a leading Jeffersonian journalist in North Carolina; and Harry Toulmin, who in 1794 became president of Transylvania Seminary, later Transylvania University, in Kentucky. William Duane, the passionately republican editor of the *Aurora*, and James Callender, the most scurrilous of republican pamphleteers, both arrived from Britain in the nineties. Less well-known newcomers included John Stewart, the eccentric deist, and John Cheetham, who had been tried for Jacobin sympathies in England but in America became the bitterly hostile biographer of Paine. The voluminous correspondence of Jedidiah Morse, the Congregationalist minister who was shortly to organize American anti-Jacobinism, contains several letters of the mid-nineties from Dissenting British clergymen who were dismayed by British reaction, eager to inquire about the possibility of American pulpits, and wrote to Morse because they had read his geographies. One of these, William Wells of Worcester, writes that he would like to join in the celebration of the French Revolution but is afraid to, and shows his sympathy for America by warmly praising the work of Paine and Joel Barlow. Wells was successful in his search for an American pulpit and immigration had the effect on his radicalism which it has had on many immigrants in many periods. In 1799 he wrote to Morse again, this time from Brattleboro, Vermont, to thank him for his violently anti-French Thanksgiving sermon and to express his wholehearted agreement with its message.[7]

Most English radicals, however, seem to have remained radicals in America. Not only the presence of these immigrants, but also their boldness and talent helped to polarize American opinion.

The extremism, the vituperativeness, the broken friendships and bitter hatreds, above all the pervasive fears of both sides in the political debate of the 1790's are part of a familiar story. The relative unity of the period right after the adoption of the Constitution was succeeded by a revival of the passionate politics of the Revolutionary period. Scurrilous lampoons, burnings in effigy, stonings, and Congressional fistfights became common enough. For a brief period, ardent republicans in America expressed their feelings in the new symbols: with liberty caps, tricolor cockades, and civic feasts. Some learned to struggle through the "Marseillaise" and "Ça Ira." A surprising number, for a short period, dated their letters Ventôse or Brumaire, instead of March or October, in the first or second year of freedom instead of 1794 or 1795 A.D., and addressed each other as "citizen" and "citizeness" instead of "Mr." or "Mrs." To alarmed conservatives it seemed as though pikes and torches were close at hand, and the guillotine on the way.

Actually, the violence of American politics in this period had far more native than foreign roots. First came divisions over the nature of the American republic, expressed now in terms of the Constitution, the bank, funding and assumption, and reflecting old arguments about the nature of the American Revolution. Behind even this lay the Commonwealth tradition. Brutus and Sidney, Wilkes and Franklin, remained common pen-names of radical writers, and were never displaced by Danton or Marat, or even Rousseau.

The fact that American radicalism had long been nourished from Commonwealth rather than from French revolutionary sources made one major difference: in America a larger element of apocalyptic fear was linked with the period's millennial hopes. Americans had been taught to fear the frailty of republics, which rested on the frailty of human nature. Corruption, the nemesis of republican government, was the chief menace arising from the Hamiltonian system, or even from the new commercial wealth which it fostered. Thus the inherited American set of hopes and fears had in it much that was agrarian and, at least in origin, Puritan. These feelings produced, according to one acute historian, "a peculiarly volatile and crisis-ridden ideology, one with little resilience, little margin for error, little tradition of success behind it, and one that was vulnerable both psychologically and historically."[8]

Most American republicans, even the most radical, were deeply separated from French revolutionaries by experience as well as theory. Few of them could imagine the life of a Parisian sans-culotte, or, for that matter, of a peasant in the more backward parts of France. Differences in ideology and experience produced at least one major divergence in practice. Among American republicans the French revolutionary mania for centralization was almost entirely lacking. In Jacobin France "federalism," the defense of local interests, was a major counter-revolutionary crime, the crime of Lyons or Brittany. In America, on the other hand, republicans feared the bank or the tariff or assumption as tools of consolidation and thus of tyranny. Thus the constitutions of the several states, and also the Federal Constitution as understood by republicans, became the bulwarks of republican piety to be defended against the omnipresent threat of anti-republican perversion.[9] This was suddenly the view of some republicans who had earlier heartily opposed the Constitution of 1787, and among some who had condemned the constitutions of their states. Neither ideology, nor the history that lay behind it, left much room for great new departures in the 1790's. Americans had already made, two decades earlier, all the new departures that most of them could bear.

The network of Democratic Clubs that sprang up from 1793 to 1795 was closer to the spirit of the Revolutionary Enlightenment than most other organizations or leaders of the growing Republican Party.[10] In part, these clubs were immediate results of Genet's tour, and some of them consciously imitated the clubs of Paris. They were also a response to the necessities of politics, designed to thwart the plots of the Federalists and to further the careers of their principal members. Less precisely, the Democratic Clubs were part of a current vogue for organized discussion. Ever since Franklin created his famous junto in 1727, the doctrines of all kinds of Enlightenment had been spread by small groups of earnest men, usually young and aspiring, formed to improve, through study and discussion, the virtue, wisdom, and well-being of their members and of society in general.

Aside from their universal and fervent support of the French Republic and their equally intense hostility to the programs of Alexander Hamilton, the Democratic Clubs differed considerably among themselves. Some but not all used the millennial rhetoric of the Radical Enlightenment. Some supported such causes as women's rights, penal reform, popular education, and occasionally anti-slavery. All were socially egalitarian in theory, though their egalitarianism was sometimes tempered in practice by the aspirations of the lawyers, doctors, printers, and merchants who led them. All, like the Jacobins themselves, were devoted to the institution of private property.

Even these relatively radical political organizations stopped short of advocating any sweeping changes in existing institutions of the American Republic. The Democratic Clubs were not, as their opponents charged, secret, nor did they, like their opponents or like the French Jacobins, advocate forcible suppression of counter-revolutionary opposition. They were leery of organized resistance to government. When the clubs were attacked by the Federalists for their alleged support of the Whiskey Rebellion in western Pennsylvania, most of them denied the charge (some had protested the excessive use of repressive force). Sometimes proclaiming a new dawn for mankind, the clubs insisted as often on the special importance of defending the existing American republican order against its enemies. The opening manifesto of the Philadelphia club, widely distributed all over the country, began by rejoicing that modern men had learned "to erect the temple of LIBERTY on the ruins of *palaces* and *thrones.*" Reflecting an older kind of radicalism, however, it went on to urge patriots

> to preserve and perpetuate the blessings which Providence hath bestowed upon our country; for, in reviewing the history of nations, we find occasion to lament, that the vigilance of the people has been too easily absorbed in victory; and that the prize which has been achieved by the wisdom and valor of one generation, has too often been lost by the ignorance and supineness of another.[11]

There is little in this last statement that would not have seemed appropriate in a New England election sermon of 1776 or even 1763.

The most divisive and complex problem, in the Democratic Clubs as elsewhere among organizations and individuals inclined toward the Revolutionary Enlightenment, was the relation between radical religion and radical politics. In America, the two were sometimes separate and sometimes linked, but only occasionally welded together into the new vision of the Secular Millennium, the view of man and society changed utterly, the theory that formed the heart of the Revolutionary Enlightenment. Among the Democratic Clubs, the leaders were often deists, but some of the most radical members were at once pious Protestants and ardent supporters of the French Republic. Some clubs attacked superstition and clericalism and seemed to verge on deism in their official statements while others, like those in Vermont and New York, made it their practice to attend church in a body and hear a patriotic sermon on the Fourth of July.[12]

As we have seen earlier, deism in America as elsewhere was of many kinds. Some deists were earnest and serious religious seekers, others urbane aristocrats tending toward skepticism. One can also find, easily enough, examples of the new revolutionary deism in its full vigor, evangelical and millennial, democratic and secular.[13] The archetype of this kind of deism was the blind preacher Elihu Palmer. Palmer, originally a Connecticut minister, gradually rejected all the tenets of Calvinism, starting with original sin. Moving to tolerant Philadelphia, he stretched its tolerance too far by advertising in the press that he would deliver a discourse against the divinity of Christ. A mob prevented him from entering the Universalist church, and according to an early biographer he was "induced to quit the city, somewhat in the stile of the ancient apostles upon similar occasions."[14]

Abandoning preaching, Palmer was admitted to the Philadelphia bar. This profession in turn became impossible to him when he lost his sight in the yellow fever epidemic (some Christians were unkind enough to speak of a judgment). After this Palmer became a full-time deist orator, speaking eloquently and indefatigably wherever he could find an audience from Baltimore to Georgia, but especially in New York. There he attracted a handful of steady followers, and until his death in 1806 he continued to proclaim the approaching triumph of the new religion.

The deist tradition invoked by Palmer and his few rivals often included Tindal, Toland, and other English deists of the early eighteenth century, usually added Rousseau, and among moderns included Volney, Condorcet, Paine, Godwin, and sometimes Joel Barlow. The central tenet of this kind of deism was the perfectibility of man. This great truth, the new deists tirelessly explained, had been hidden from mankind by the sinister alliance of priests and kings, whose chief reliance had always been the absurd doctrine of original sin.

Indeed, had it not been that the clergy gained a complete ascendancy over the minds of men, the civil oppressions of the world would long since have tumbled into ruin.[15]

In our age, the great revolutions of America and France had broken this sinister hold on the minds of men, and the whole monstrous and unintelligible structure—sin, redemption, atonement, predestination, salvation through faith—was on the brink of oblivion. The new religion, teaching the goodness of man and God, would be as simple and understandable as it was benign. Its propagation, together with the universal spread of republican government, would bring about the universal reign of reason, peace, and justice. (At times the millennium of the deists could sound remarkably like that of some of their orthodox Christian contemporaries.) There were still struggles ahead, as the forces of evil and darkness conspired against the dawning order, but their outcome was certain. In the future, said the New York radical Tunis R. Wortman, fear and greed, propagated by monarchies and unnecessary in republics, would disappear. Then

> we can only expect to arrive at that ultimate state of perfection of which the human character is susceptible. . . . Persecution and superstition, vice, prejudice and cruelty will take their eternal departure from the earth. National animosities and distinctions will be buried in eternal oblivion.[16]

Along with these great changes, says Palmer, "must be included the total annihilation of the prejudices which have established between the sexes an inequality of rights, fatal even to the party which it favours."[17]

So attractive and noble are the aspirations contained in these prophecies, that one may be surprised at the failure of militant deism to survive as a religion. In the form devotedly preached by Palmer and his allies, it never spread beyond a half-dozen committed societies, which tried vainly to invent satisfying deist observances and rituals and left as their monument two or three short-lived and little-read journals. Part of the reason for this failure, no doubt, is that the new religion was tied too closely to the fate of the French Revolution. By 1800, after the Napoleonic seizure of power, we find even Palmer having to protest that he does not approve particular events in France, but rather of the general spirit and destiny of the Revolution.[18] Obviously, another major explanation for the failure of militant deism is the deep hold of Christian doctrine on most Americans, including many radical Americans. Still another reason, and in my opinion an important one, is that deists were divided among themselves, over both politics and religion.

Between the old aristocratic and skeptical deism and the new republican and millennial variety there were all sorts of shadings and compromises. It is worthwhile to look at a few of them. Two of the many discussion groups formed by earnest young men, both in upstate New York, were the Calliopean Society and the Schaghticoke Polemic Society. The Calliopean Society, moderately pro-French in its political resolutions of 1793-94, was moderately deistic as well. It resolved that the French were justified in beheading their king, but not in entering the territory of Holland. Hypocrisy, the Calliopeans sturdily resolved, was more dangerous to virtue than open infidelity. When it came to Paine's *Age of Reason*, the group believed (by a majority of 13 to 7) that it was likely to produce more good than evil in the world.[19]

The Schaghticoke Polemic Society was more closely divided. It split evenly on whether it would be good for the United States if property were more evenly divided. Even in 1798 a call for war with England and peace with France prevailed (7 to 2) over the opposite combination. But this group in the same year voted unanimously that it is "consistent with Deity to decree from all eternity, whatever comes to pass," and the casting vote of the president decided in the affirmative that God had "from all eternity elected part to salvation."[20]

The Friendly Society of New York City, perhaps the most brilliant of all the organizations of earnest and enlightened young men, illustrates best of all the paradoxes and complexities that hindered the development of the Revolutionary Enlightenment in America.[21] This group, which flourished from 1793 or 1794 to about 1798, was made up of well-placed, ambitious, and idealistic young intellectuals, many of them recent Yale graduates. Its leading spirit was the physician and aspiring author Elihu Hubbard Smith, whose early death in 1798 ended the club. Among the other members were William Dunlap, the indefatigable dramatist and theater manager; James Kent, the future Chancellor of New York, then first professor of law at Columbia College and Recorder of the city; Samuel Latham Mitchill, the Columbia scientist, later a Jeffersonian politician; Samuel Miller, a leading Presbyterian minister; and the novelist Charles Brockden Brown.

The Friendly Society, mildly convivial but nonetheless intellectually serious, read together in Condorcet, Volney, Mary Wollstonecraft, and Godwin, to whom Smith and a number of the others were devoted. Except for Miller and also Latham, who was a moderate Presbyterian, the members inclined toward deism. Of the deists, Kent was a typical representative of the old skeptical and pessimistic variety, an admirer of Voltaire and Hume. Most of the others, though their reading was eclectic, were captivated by the most general and abstract writers of the Revolutionary Enlightenment, especially Godwin. Smith in particular discusses at length in his diary his movement away from Christianity on moral and rational grounds, and urges his friends to share his admiration of Godwin's *Political Justice* with its prophecies of republican Utopia.

By the late 1790's, however, Smith had completely lost confidence in the actual French Republic, and he never had any in the American Republican Party. With the exception of Mitchill and, at this time, Miller, members of the club tended to be Federalist in politics. Revealingly, Smith distinguished between democracy in general (in its pure Godwinian form), and "the common idea of democracy which prevails in the United States (i.e., anarchy)."[22] This was the period when New York City, until now a bulwark of Federalism, was turning toward the Republican Party, and in the process politics were becoming rougher. It was a time of parades and demonstrations, when John Jay was burned in effigy and Alexander Hamilton stoned. Popular turbulence distressed Smith and doubtless most of his friends. These bright young men, idealistic but also ambitious, were living in the age of Hamilton and also Napoleon. Their Godwinian principles notwithstanding, they were eager to distinguish themselves from the ignorant and prejudiced masses, in politics as in religion. A great many Americans had admired Paine's political works but were shocked by his attack on Christianity. Exactly to the contrary, Elihu Smith disliked Paine's politics but found the *Age of Reason* "lively and humorous."[23]

This combination of conservative politics with radical religion, though not as common as its opposite, was often found among college undergraduates from the eighties until the end of the century. Piously brought up youths were sometimes, like Smith himself at Yale, suddenly exposed to a cheerful and convivial way of life and also to exciting new ideas, quite different from those of their teachers. Condorcet, Volney, Paine, Wollstonecraft, and especially Godwin attracted students by their iconoclasm, and also their idealism. Throughout the republic, college teachers and presidents were shortly to be horrified by an outbreak of student revolts which went beyond the usual standard in numbers and violence. Not surprisingly, conservatives blamed these excesses on subversive doctrines, and concluded that the students were both deists and Jacobins. It has recently been demonstrated that this conclusion was quite mistaken. In 1798 indeed, except at arch-Republican William and Mary, the collegians of the country rushed to attest their Federalist patriotism, offering Adams their allegiance and support in the quasi-war with the French Republic, and having to be calmed down by their elders. Turbulent, skeptical, and somewhat snobbish, the freest spirits of this college generation were the nearest American equivalent to a *jeunesse dorée*.[24]

Sometimes hostile to the colleges, and usually conscious of the shortcomings of the schools, many radical republicans hoped to reform society through the establishment of a new school system: free to all, soundly republican in all its teachings, secular, and practical. No cause got more attention from the Democratic Clubs. The whole educational program of the Revolutionary Enlightenment can be found, for instance, in the proposals of Robert Coram, a Delaware teacher, librarian, and active member of the Republican Party.[25]

Coram's pamphlet of 1791 admiringly quotes Raynal, Beccaria, and the *Encyclopédie* as well as Locke and Mrs. Macaulay. It is suffused with the spirit of Rousseau. Coram, like many adherents of the Revolutionary Enlightenment, was an advanced egalitarian, an environmentalist, and an admirer of primitive society. The Indians are free and happy, he insists at length, while civilized man is miserable. The evils of civilization arise from property, whose origin is appropriation. Coram, however, does not propose any radical redistribution. Society must right the wrongs it has done by establishing universal republicanism, just laws, and above all equal schools. These must be free, public, and uniform. They must teach "no modes of faith, systems of manners, or foreign or dead languages,"[26] and must refrain from encouraging invidious competition by awarding medals and prizes. Their principal aim must be to equip all to earn an honest and equal living.

Much of this program and the attitudes underlying it had a big future in American educational reform. It was much too sweeping to get far in practice in the America of the 1790's.

As the most ardent reformers were well aware, far the greatest steps toward free and equal education had been made in Federalist New England, under auspices far removed from those of the Revolutionary Enlightenment. Robert Coram himself repeatedly praises the New England system and its major spokesman, Noah Webster.[27] When the public school movement really got under way in America in the nineteenth century, it owed something to New England and something to the Enlightenment, but was probably closer to the pattern of Webster than to that of Condorcet.

In England, some of the millennial vision of the Revolutionary Enlightenment, often subtly combined with emotions and metaphors from the Christian millennial tradition, found its way into the work of the early Romantic poets.[28] Notoriously, the sympathy for the French Revolution felt at first by Wordsworth and his poetic contemporaries was short-lived. Yet it left, in the few specifically revolutionary poems of Blake and Shelley and in Wordsworth's recollections of his vanished youthful zeal, a great chapter in the history of revolutionary poetry and poetic revolution.

In America, very few people even tried to bring together the new feelings and the new style. The Romantic revolution in poetry was delayed until the second quarter of the nineteenth century, the day of Bryant and Poe. American resistance to Romantic taste is a puzzling fact. Perhaps provincials, having painfully learned the correct English taste of the mid-eighteenth century, were reluctant to abandon it. Many, no doubt, felt little need for a new religion with new mystical emotions, having an old one still in satisfactory repair. Most mystical feeling in America was still expressed in directly Biblical terms; most revolutionary feeling was expressed in sober prose.

Only one American of the 1790's came close to combining the new politics with something like a new poetry, and usually even Philip Freneau kept the two separate. During the American Revolution Freneau's ample and facile talent was mostly poured into anti-British propaganda. His verse and prose were well known to Thomas Jefferson and of course to Freneau's old Princeton friend James Madison. The two statesmen brought the poet to Philadelphia to occupy a bureaucratic sinecure and to found an anti-administration paper. During the brief life of the *National Gazette* (1791-93), Freneau did his job, counterattacking the vitriolic pro-Federalist *Gazette of the United States*, giving as good as he got in jibe and epithet, ceaselessly pillorying and parodying the aristocrats, British sycophants, and monarchists he found in the administration, earning Hamilton's hatred and causing Washington acute distress.

Like many others, Freneau was exalted to new heights of enthusiasm by the proclamation of the French Republic and the outbreak of its war with Britain. A few poems convey these feelings with some success. Freneau hails the fourteenth of July:

> BRIGHT DAY, that did to France restore
> What priests and kings had seiz'd away,
> That bade her generous sons disdain
> The fetters that their fathers wore . . .
> Bright Day! a partner in thy joy,
> COLUMBIA hails the rising sun,
> She feels her toils, her blood repaid . . .[29]

In religion, Freneau broke completely with the Christian orthodoxy he had learned at Princeton, condemning like many others the cruelty and irrationality of the Calvinist system, and failing like many others to find a satisfactory substitute religion.[30] In the *National Gazette* he reprinted Condorcet, Paine, and Barlow. Later, in New York, he helped Elihu Palmer get a room to speak in, published one of his orations, and carried advertisements for his lectures in the *Time-Piece*, one of his less successful editorial ventures.[31]

Usually in his public journalism he hung onto some faint connection with Christianity:

> When the human mind was immerged [*sic*] in ignorance, forms and ceremonies were thought essential to religion, and superstition usurped the empire of reason; but those shackles have been broken by truth, and the purity of the gospel has received additional strength from its present simplicity . . .[32]

In his poetry and occasional writings he sometimes moved farther in the direction of the new deism:

> Joy to the day, when all agree
> On such grand systems to proceed,

> From fraud, design, and error free,
> And which to truth and goodness lead:
> Then persecution will retreat
> And man's religion be complete.[33]

Barlow dabbled also in post-Newtonian mechanistic materialism and he at least once came close to proclaiming, after Pope, that whatever is must have been designed by deity, and is therefore right.

It is clear, however, that the affirmations of deism, millennial or mechanistic, failed to convince Freneau completely. In the same year in which he championed Palmer's right to speak, he addressed a poem "The Millennium" to "a Ranting Field Orator." Here he seems to reject not so much the Christian millennium as exactly Palmer's version of sudden secular dawn:

> With aspect wild, in ranting strain
> You bring the brilliant period near,
> When monarchy will close her reign
> And wars and warriors disappear . . .
> Ere discord can from man depart
> He must assume a different heart.

Some day, indeed, Freneau agrees, humanity may grow more reasonable,

> But you and I will not be here
> To see the lion shed his teeth
> Or kings forget the trade of death.[34]

Freneau, like Franklin, was too intelligent to be comfortable with the conclusion that God and nature were simple and beneficent, or that man's nature was essentially good. Unlike Franklin, he could not accept paradox with equanimity and adorn it with wit. Instead, Freneau repeatedly and sadly concludes, between assertions of optimism, that nature is unreliable and unpredictable, and that it and man are finally mysterious.

Long before Coleridge separated the workaday Understanding from the poetic and imaginative Reason, Freneau took for granted somewhat the same division, using an eighteenth-century vocabulary. For him, that is, Reason was the prosaic faculty, and Fancy the mysterious and more powerful one. As early as 1770 he declares his allegiance to the latter:

Wakeful, vagrant, restless thing,
Ever wandering on the wing,
Who thy wondrous source can find,
FANCY, regent of the mind . . .[35]

At the end of his most successful poem, "The Indian Burying Ground,"
Reason specifically surrenders:

By midnight moons, o'er moistening dews,
In habit for the chase arrayed,
The hunter still the deer pursues—
The hunter and the deer, a shade!
And long shall timorous fancy see
The painted chief, and pointed spear,
And Reason's self shall bow the knee
To shadows and delusions here.[36]

In his political emotions, and sometimes in his religious beliefs, Freneau was a part of the Revolutionary Enlightenment. Very occasionally,
often in his best work, his gifts and his feelings carried him around a
well-known corner from radical reason to radical imagination, from the
world of Godwin or Paine to that of Shelley or Wordsworth. For twenty
years, almost no American was to follow him.

America's other revolutionary poet of this period, Joel Barlow, was far
more of a revolutionary, and despite strenuous effort, far less of a poet.
Barlow, who moved spiritually as well as physically from Connecticut to
Paris in 1788, was the only native American who played, like Paine, a
major role in the international revolution at its height. This gives his
career much fascination, but it also limited his influence in his own
country. From 1778 until 1805, while the Revolutionary Enlightenment
rose and fell, Barlow shared its fortunes in its center, not its provinces.[37]

Arriving in Paris in 1778 as agent for a land company, Barlow like
many other revolutionary characters in Europe and America was always
occupied with the task of making a fortune, and unlike many he eventually succeeded. In France at the height of his influence he was a part
of the ardent, enthusiastic, expansionist, ambitious circle of Girondin intellectuals. In England, where he lived most of the time from 1790 to
1792, he was a friend of Richard Price among the older radicals, and a
full member of the newer circle that included Paine and Godwin. Mary
Wollstonecraft was the close friend of Barlow's wife. As "the prophet

Joel," Barlow was a major target for Burke's heavy artillery, and answered it as boldly if not as effectively as Paine. The height of his influence came when the British radical Society for Constitutional Information made him one of its two delegates to the French National Convention in 1792.

Barlow's political prose of this period is addressed to Europe, not America, and his main purpose is to persuade the French to move forward rapidly: abolish the monarchy, feudalism, the national Church, and (in 1792) the army. Without much discussion of his own country, he assumes that America provides Europe with a pattern: "In the United States of America, the science of liberty is universally understood, felt and practised, as much by the simple as the wise, the weak as the strong."[38]

Unlike Paine, Barlow believed that the full program of the Revolutionary Enlightenment should not be applied to America, and he explained why this was not necessary:

> The Americans cannot be said as yet to have formed a national character. The political part of their revolution, aside from the military, was not of that violent and convulsive nature that shakes the whole fabric of human opinions, and enables men to decide which are to be retained as congenial to their situation, and which should be rejected as the offspring of unnatural connections. Happily, the weight of oppression there had never been so great, nor of so long a duration, as to have distorted in any extravagant degree the moral features of man.[39]

As to Europe, however, Barlow was sure in 1792-93 that the French Republic had completed the conquest of liberty; other nations needed only to add to the superstructure. In his pamphlet which tried unsuccessfully to persuade the people of Savoy to join their liberators, he admits that the French Revolution has been marked with cruelty and murder. This, however, he blames entirely on the evils of expiring despotism, only to add (in 1794) a footnote regretting recent events.[40] In the Jacobin phase of the Revolution, when Barlow was in some danger and many of his friends were executed, Barlow bravely defended Paine, and continued both to make money and uphold the Revolution.

Qualms and doubts set in with the triumph of the Directorate, and Barlow began to think of going home. He began to give some attention to American politics, and from 1798 to 1800 attacked Federalist policies and urged reconciliation with France in a series of pamphlets. These were not as informed or as effective as his European works, and in any case by this time Barlow, like Paine, was under heavy attack both as a French apologist and an infidel. In 1792 Barlow urged the French to persuade each man "to sell his crucifix and buy a musquet,—and you have made him a good citizen."[41]

This sort of thing could, of course, be defended as anti-Catholicism or anti-clericalism rather than infidelity. Like Jefferson or Freneau, Barlow usually claimed in public that he opposed only the historical trappings of Christianity and not its true spirit. Like Freneau and Franklin, however, in private he went far beyond this stance, and also beyond even the fervent revolutionary deism of Volney and Paine. One can find much of this last in his works, but Barlow was either too much a New Englander or too experienced in Europe to find a resting place in the fervent secular hopes of an Elihu Palmer.

Barlow's rejection of the Secular Millennium did not take him, as it did Freneau, in the direction of romantic melancholy. Rather, he reverted increasingly to a position that had always attracted him: uncompromising naturalistic determinism. There is reason to think that Barlow got his atheistic tendencies from Holbach as much as from anybody.[42] And he was certainly influenced by the minor *philosophes* Nicholas-Antoine Boulanger and Charles Alexandre Dupuis. Both of these explained the origin of all religions in entirely naturalistic terms.

In 1792, at the height of his revolutionary fervor, Barlow argued that habit, not innate tendencies in man, was the source of both good and evil, and suggested that habits could be rearranged by new social institutions.[43] When the great republic seemed to him to falter, this hope became more difficult to sustain. In a letter of 1795, Barlow expressed fully his growing belief that all religion stood in the way of human progress.

> I rejoice at the progress of Good Sense over the damnable imposture of Christian mummery. I had no doubt of the effect of Paine's Age of Reason. . . . I am glad to see a Translation . . . of Boulanger's Christianisme Devoilé. . . . I wish Mr. Johnson would go on, and give us the next volume, the History of that famous Mountebank called St. Paul.[44]

Though Barlow specifically asked that this letter not be given to any newspaper, it eventually found its way to the press and caused him a lot of trouble. Some still more daring speculations remained private. In a notebook of 1796-97 he prophesies the disappearance of all religious illusions:

> Questions. If man in all ages & countries had understood astronomy & physics as well as they do now generally in Europe would the ideas of God & religion have ever come into their minds?
>
> Have not these ideas been greater sources of human calamity than all other moral causes? . . .
>
> If we admit that those ideas are wholly chimerical, having risen altogether from ignorance of natural causes is it not the duty of every person who sees this evil tendency to use his influence to banish them as much as possible from society. Is it not possible wholly to destroy their influence & reduce them to the rank of other ancient fables to be found only in the history of human errors? If the existence of Philosophy would have prevented their existence why shall it not destroy them.[45]

Here Barlow parts company not only with Freneau and Jefferson, but also with Paine and Robespierre, both of whom detested atheism and sought to replace Christianity with a new religion. In his ultimate phase, Barlow has more in common with the most skeptical savants of the old regime—Holbach or Helvétius or La Mettrie—than with the romantically inclined heralds of a new dawn. Significantly, he was never much influenced by Rousseau. In his atheism, his dabbling in behaviorism, and his hope for the human future—a combination hard to maintain but yet powerful—he resembles a great many radicals of much later periods.

In his day and in America these views could not be publicly expressed by a man who wanted both to make money and influence affairs. They are also an unpromising basis for poetry in a romantic age. From 1797 until 1807 Barlow labored on a new version of his epic poem of the American Revolution, now called the *Columbiad*. As many close students have pointed out, there are important differences between *The Vision of Columbus* of 1787 and the *Columbiad* of 1807. One is that Christian references have nearly gone: the angel prophesying to Columbus becomes a vaguely pagan Hesper, the evening star. Of course, the dedication to Louis XVI has gone, and French intervention in the American cause is now credited to "the Gallic sages" who see "the expanding dawn" in "the bright Occident." Hesper still shows Columbus a vision of the bright future of the world, including a federated universal republic as well as the founding of all the American colleges and even the poetry of Dwight and Trumbull. Much as in 1787, Columbus is warned that things must change slowly:

> Man is an infant still; and slow and late
> Must form and fix his adolescent state,
> Mature his manhood and at last behold
> His reason ripen and his force unfold.[46]

The mighty effort got a mixed reception. Some admired it, but Jefferson, who had promoted Barlow's prose works, admitted in a letter that he could not judge the *Columbiad* because his relish for poetry had long gone.[47] Needless to say, the Federalists found in its heavy couplets a rich mine for ridicule. In politics and religion, Barlow had been a cosmopolitan and a daring revolutionary. In poetic diction, he never left either Connecticut or the age of Alexander Pope.

In geographical terms, one could well see Philadelphia and New York City as one major center of the Revolutionary Enlightenment. The two cities, both cosmopolitan and deeply divided in religion and politics, had always had much in common. Both now had very active Democratic Clubs and struggling deist cults. Leading radical intellectuals like Elihu Palmer, Philip Freneau, and the young Charles Brockden Brown moved back and forth between the two.

When Philadelphia became capital of the United States in 1790, however, it also became capital both of the Revolutionary Enlightenment and the political opposition to that movement. In the early 1790's, as we have seen, the post-Revolutionary Philadelphia elite, circumspect and relatively tolerant, was still in charge. Underneath the decorous and Enlightened surface, however, were ancient antagonisms, going back to the radical *coup d'état* of 1776 and the conservative resistance to it, and beyond that to a long history of ethnic and religious controversy.

On May 2, 1793, the French warship *L'Embuscade* sailed up the Schuylkill, decorated with liberty caps and revolutionary slogans, towing a captured prize with the British flag flown upside down. In a city occupied by the British twenty years before, this was almost irresistible; the banks of the river were lined with rejoicing citizens. According to Jefferson, however, the jubilation was not universal; it came from the "yeomanry of the city (not the fashionable part or paper men)."[48]

For a while, especially after Citizen Genet arrived two weeks later and was welcomed with bells, cannon, and odes, the partisans of France had it all their own way. At one banquet a French ode was read by Du Ponceau and translated into verse by Freneau, while the red cap was passed from head to head. At another the British flag was burned, and the guests marched round and round an obelisk, singing the "Marseillaise" and staggering a little from the effects of revolutionary toasts.[49] Wealthy and Anglophile circles, always strong in Philadelphia, shuddered with distaste and also—remembering the past—with fear. One old gentleman recalled his impressions later: "What hugging and tugging! What addressing and caressing! What mountebanking and chanting! With liberty-caps, and other wretched trumpery of sans culotte foolery!"[50]

John Adams always believed that the Republic had been in danger of destruction, and suggested much later that Providence had saved it only by extreme measures:

> You certainly never felt the Terrorism, excited by Genet, in 1793, when ten thousand People in the Streets of Philadelphia, day after day, threatened to drag Washington out of his House, and effect a Revolution in the Government, or compell it to declare War in favour of the French Revolution, and against England. The coolest and the firmest Minds, even among the Quakers in Philadelphia, have given their Opinions to me, that nothing but the Yellow Fever, which removed Dr. Hutchinson and Jonathan Dickenson Sargent from this World, could have saved the United States from a total Revolution of Government.[51]

Whether or not either Providence or the yellow fever had anything to do with it, revolutionary enthusiasm in Philadelphia lost some—by no means all—of its strength with the fall of Genet and the new Jacobin order in France. From about 1793 to the end of the decade, radicals and conservatives contested the city fairly evenly and with passions rising high on both sides. Jefferson, always sensitive, felt so deeply the hatred of the Philadelphia social elite that he was glad to leave in 1794 and, despite the APS, somewhat reluctant to return in 1797. In the crisis of 1798-1800, as Volney fled, Priestley suffered, and Republican editors were indicted, polarization in the capital had its effect on polarization in the country.

There were many reasons for the revival of rancorous passions in the City of Brotherly Love. Philadelphia, as many political historians have pointed out, led the way in party organization. In the city's two Democratic Clubs, one of them German, old Constitutionalists of 1776 like Rittenhouse and Peale mingled with younger radicals like B. F. Bache, and the fiery Michael Leib. Party newspapers of both sides in the capital were more vitriolic and unscrupulous than anything that had been known since the sixties and seventies, and their contents were copied throughout the nation. French and still more British and Irish residents contributed their special feelings, from William Cobbett, the Jacobin-hunter, to William Duane, the scourge of the "aristocrats."[52]

Most of these causes of high feeling came from the fact that Philadelphia was the national capital, but one should not forget the history of the province and of the city itself. When the farmers of western Pennsylvania resisted the whiskey tax in the so-called Whiskey Rebellion of 1794, fears of the Scotch-Irish and radical West were aroused in the city that went at least back to the march of the Paxton boys twenty years earlier. Westerners and some city radicals resented in turn the federal show of force. In Philadelphia, the Federalists barely retained their ascendancy until almost the end of the decade. By that time, the French enthusiasm was waning, and moderates defeated radicals within the successful Republican camp.[53] Yet the bitterness of the conservatives lingered on and the special, carefully tended compromises of the Philadelphia Enlightenment were gone.

In South Carolina, hotly contested between Federalists and Republicans, the most radical Republicans were perhaps more extreme than anywhere else. The Charleston Democratic Club actually petitioned, humbly and successfully, to be officially adopted by the Jacobin Club of Paris. At one point it toasted the guillotine as the right fate for "all tyrants, plunderers and funding speculators."[54] This is the rhetoric of a beleaguered group, conscious of the power of the local Federalists and the state's strong economic and emotional ties to England.

In Virginia, as in all the South except hotly contested South Carolina and Maryland, Republican allegiance and pro-French views were the norm and deism common, especially among the top aristocracy. This does not mean, of course, that deism and republicanism always fused together to produce the hot amalgam of the Revolutionary Enlightenment. Yet sometimes this too occurred, and most often among the ardent youth of the planting class.

In 1793 John Randolph, extreme in everything, wrote his stepfather, St. George Tucker, suggesting that he give up the study of law for a nobler enterprise:

> I have a proposal to make to you, in which I can see very little solid objection; without preface, it is this:—
> That you permit me to go immediately to France, and to enter into the army of the Republic. . . . My wish is to *serve* the noblest cause in the world.

Young Randolph is sure that he can rise to an ensigncy, and wants no more:

> What life can be so glorious what death so honorable? how preferable to the pursuits of a miserable attorney who stoops to a thousand petty villainies in order to earn the sum of fifteen shillings. . . . I feel the most ardent enthusiasm for the cause. I dream of nothing else. I think of nothing else; what [word blotted] do you suppose, then, I should make of old Coke, when my thoughts are dwelling on the plains of Flanders?[55]

Tucker, despite his own pro-French sympathies, did not encourage this degree of devotion, and no Virginian foreign legion crossed the ocean.

William and Mary, fallen on hard times but still the college of the Virginian aristocracy, was the principal stronghold of the Revolutionary Enlightenment among American colleges.[56] The young men under Bishop Madison's benign and liberal care quite commonly, like Randolph, addressed each other in their letters as "Citizen" and used the Revolutionary calendar. Without conscious irony, they sometimes referred to their political opponents as "aristocrats," and feared lest the country under Federalist leadership would fall into "slavery."[57] In and out of class, the favorite authors of William and Mary students seem to have been Locke, Rousseau, Volney, Paine, and Godwin. These tastes, reported and exaggerated in the Federalist press, caused widespread and bitter attack on the College and especially its president. Yet in 1798, the peak year of anti-Jacobin panic, Joseph Cabell reports that among the graduating class, Enlightened radicalism still reigns. While learning, he says, is indeed declining at Williamsburg, and many are moving to Richmond, yet

> on Moral, Political, and Religious subjects, my fellow-Students continue to display the same freedom and liberality of opinion, the same independence of investigation the same defiance to old-fashioned precepts & doctrines they formerly did. There is not a man among us that would not enlist himself under the banners of a Paine or a Volney. There are some (of which number I have the honor to be one) who even border on the gloomy verge of Atheism, as it is called, & who would say to a Deist what think you of an *Uncreated* first cause. They say that there are a few *Rusty Cats* [Aristocrats] among the students. Of this I'm not certain. But the political principles of the greater part of the Students are purely Democratic. Rousseau seems to be the standard book on politics, & of consequence the government of the People the great desideratum with us. Democrats we have in abundance, some moderate, some warm, and some red hot. . . . On the subject of Morals there appears to be less of Godwin's opinions advanced than formerly, & more silence & moderation generally displayed.[58]

In 1801 another student writes that Rousseau, Locke, and Paine are

> the most celebrated, and, perhaps, the most excellent that have written upon the Science of Politicks. I suppose it will be considered an act of treason against truth, to utter a syllable to the prejudice of Rousseau.[59]

Well into the new century, as the attacks increased and the number of students continued to decline, those who remained at William and Mary stuck to their Enlightened authors and opinions.

Virginia planter society was transplanted more or less successfully to the bluegrass region of Kentucky. With it went a good deal of upper-class skepticism and some distorted echoes of pro-French radicalism. Here as elsewhere one must be wary of the torrent of pious autobiography, published after the revivals of 1800, which depict a state sunk in infidelity just before the amazing work of grace. Yet it is true that mixed with much frontier ignorance was considerable active religious radicalism. Among the books in demand in Lexington in 1795 were Hume's *Dialogues* and works by Paine, Wollstonecraft, and Volney. Paine especially was much discussed and quoted in the *Kentucky Gazette*.[60]

In 1793 a Democratic Club was formed in Lexington, devoted to the republican and French cause in general, and the natural right of navigating the Mississippi in particular. Its leaders were involved with the schemes of Genet and others to spread the Revolution to Spanish Louisiana. A manifesto addressed to the Committee of Public Safety in Paris by the "officers in the French Revolutionary Legions of the Mississippi" hints broadly of the possibility of French military help:

> Should France the dispensers of Liberty to the unfortunate sons of men, ever turn here yes to subjugated Louisiana and the Floridas; to her, Western America will look up for the use of the Mississippi. . . . May prosperity attend your arms, wherever they are carried, may plenty and tranquility pervade your extensive Empire; And may you never sheath your swords while there remains within your powerful Grasp, one of those curses of mankind called Kings.[61]

The leader of the Democratic Club was the most powerful citizen of the new state, John Breckinridge. Breckinridge, a western Virginian who had married into the aristocracy and a graduate of William and Mary, had crossed the mountains in 1793 with fifteen volumes of Rousseau, among other books, in his saddlebags.[62] Attorney-general and later representative and senator, Breckinridge is known to history chiefly as the mover of the Kentucky Resolutions against the Alien and Sedition acts of 1798, a protest which was really the work of his friend Thomas Jefferson. In his effort to reform the Kentucky laws, carried over from Virginia, and especially to reduce the number of capital crimes, Breckinridge could make free use of the rhetoric of the Revolutionary Enlightenment:

> It has been the unhappy lot of man, almost in all ages, to come under the iron sceptre of a tyrant of some kind. These, enemies of the Human race, knowing themselves to be usurpers of the rights of mankind, found it necessary to retain their power by sanguinary Laws & cruel punishments. . . .[63]

Breckinridge was the leader of the liberal faction among the trustees of Transylvania Seminary (after 1798 Transylvania University) in Lexington. At the urging of Jefferson, in 1794 Breckinridge and his friends managed to elect Harry Toulmin president of the institution. Toulmin was an English Unitarian, a rationalist and democrat, and a friend of Priestley (who had also been considered for the position). The balance at Transylvania between Presbyterians and liberals was close, and Toulmin was forced out in 1796. However, the battle did not end there. The

Breckinridge liberal faction retained a footing on the board of trustees and at least as late as 1798 a student could be found who admired Paine, Boulanger, Voltaire, and particularly Godwin.[64] The wars at Transylvania were not to end until 1827, when another Unitarian president was forced out by the triumphant forces of orthodoxy, now linked with egalitarianism.

Another storm center of Kentucky in the 1790's was the Constitution of 1792, which contained a liberal bill of rights, excluded the clergy from the legislature, and protected slavery. Here Breckinridge and his Jeffersonian allies were lined up against anti-slavery revivalists, led by the redoubtable Presbyterian missionary and educator, "Father" David Rice. In 1799, the year after his passionate defense of civil liberty against the Federalists, Breckinridge won this battle also, successfully defending the constitutional provisions for liberty, property, and slavery. In this struggle, interestingly enough, one of his anonymous pamphlets was signed "Algernon Sidney."[65]

The special case of Breckinridge, Francophile, Jeffersonian, libertarian, and defender of slavery, serves only to underline the general fragility of the Revolutionary Enlightenment in the South. Some Enlightened Southerners, especially Virginians, had long been trying to come to terms with the paradoxes of Enlightenment and slavery by planning the gradual abolition of the latter. In the radical younger generation, a few young Francophiles stretched the ideological tensions right up to the point of danger. One William and Mary student writing to another started from the premise that liberty was a perfect right:

> For this reason ought our Negroes to enjoy Freedom, and for this reason has it been said that they would be perfectly right in obtaining it by turning upon their masters. But have they a right to desolate the World, have they a Right to exterminate from the face of these States every Vestige of Virtue & Science, and to bring back an age of Barbarism & Darkness. Anger would prompt them to do it, all the foul passions which torment the human Breast would prompt them to do it, but can that philosophy which bids us to calculate the consequences of our Actions justify it? Every One must answer No.

Sadly, the young reasoner comes to a conclusion which reduces the Revolutionary Enlightenment to nonsense:

> . . . perfect Rights may sometimes be imperfect ones, & imperfect Rights, perfect . . .[66]

Somewhat haltingly, the French Republic turned its attention to the problem of slavery in its own West Indian empire, and especially in the fabulously rich sugar island of Santo Domingo. Under the gradualist influence of Brissot, Condorcet, Mirabeau, and the other members of the philosophic *Amis des Noirs*, the National Assembly in 1791 left alone the difficult question of the slave trade, and began by defending the rights of mulattoes, not Blacks, to political representation.[67] After long argument the National Convention, in the Jacobin period, finally abolished slavery in the French colonies in 1794. The result of French indecision, planter intransigence, and the spread of egalitarian principles was the outbreak of a bloody race war in Santo Domingo, fought with courage and cruelty on both sides. As the refugees streamed into Southern cities, many Southerners began rethinking the limitations of universal liberty.

The process of retreat was hastened by the abortive Gabriel conspiracy in Virginia in 1800. It was not lost upon Southern observers that this group of slaves, who had planned to achieve liberty by killing their masters, made use in their recruiting of revolutionary as well as religious rhetoric. One of them, under sentence of death, reported that it had been planned to spare Quakers, Methodists, and Frenchmen from the general massacre, because these were believed to be "friendly to liberty."[68] By 1800 the special Virginian variety of the Revolutionary Enlightenment, aristocratic, free-thinking, libertarian, and reluctantly slaveholding, was clearly on the way out. Within twenty years the Southern Enlightenment with all its varieties and paradoxes was to be almost gone, replaced by an equally paradoxical combination of Christian orthodoxy, pro-slavery rigidity, and white egalitarian rhetoric.[69]

Instead of sweeping all before it as its fervent partisans hoped, the Revolutionary Enlightenment in America in anything like its pure French or English form was confined to small groups and individuals: to some of the Democratic Clubs, to groups of bookish young men, to sprigs of the Virginia aristocracy. Radical politicians like the Pennsylvanians Bache, Leib, and Duane had strong class feelings and sympathized keenly with France, but had little program for fundamental change in America. Except in Philadelphia, New York, and to a lesser extent in other cities, most relatively radical republicanism in America was agrarian, and defensive rather than aggressive or centralizing. While much radical rhetoric used the words "slavery" in contrast to "liberty," the only actual slaves in America were debarred from political thought and action. Some of them, indeed, were owned by libertarians.

No ideology could triumph in America which broke sharply with Protestant Christianity, itself the source of much American radicalism of the recent past. The quasi-romantic, millennial, supremely optimistic dream of the universal republican future that stirred in different ways Condorcet and Volney, Danton and Robespierre, Paine, Godwin, and the early Wordsworth roused only occasional echoes in America. Like many kinds of American radicalism in the future, the Revolutionary Enlightenment failed to attain either ideological firmness or, especially, mass support.

Yet for all that it left very important legacies. The most obvious was the reaction against it. Yet it is also true that many Americans, without abandoning either constitutionalism or Protestant religion, believed to some degree in the progress of republicanism in the world. Later, many remembered with mixed feelings the emotions they had felt in 1789 or 1793 as well as 1776. Nobody who goes through any sort of emotional conversion, political or religious, is quite the same afterwards even if he fully or partly recants.

A millennial habit of thought, always strong in America, lasted through the period of the Secular Millennium in France. For most Americans, the millennium remained the period prophesied in the Bible, the return of Christ and his thousand-year reign. For many, increasingly, this tended to be vaguely identified with the success of American institutions. For some, however, in all later periods, the new morning meant some future overthrow of all injustice and tyranny on earth, and their replacement by universal brotherhood and peace.

Five   *Counterattack*

In the last five years of the eighteenth century many Americans moved from admiration of the French Republic to hate and fear. Some came also to associate Jacobinism with irreligion, and both with the Utopian theories of the Revolutionary Enlightenment. It was in this crisis that conservative opinion began to lump together Voltaire, Hume, Paine, Godwin, and Jefferson, and to see all these as heirs of a conspiracy of philosophers against all religious and social order.

One of the oddities about American anti-Jacobinism, the nub of the American counter-Enlightenment, was that it reached its peak only after 1795, when Robespierre had gone to the guillotine and the Jacobins were out of power in Paris. There are both rational and irrational explanations of this curious chronological fact. American fears in the next half-decade were brought to a climax by all sorts of real and exaggerated dangers, foreign and domestic, and they came to embody all the many insecurities of a new nation.

American anti-Jacobinism developed a few years later than English anti-Jacobinism and some Americans were much affected by British counter-revolutionary precedents. The contrast between French dictatorship and British parliamentary government became an important part of American conservative argument. This contrast, and also an eloquent condemnation of a literary cabal intended to destroy the Christian religion, Americans could find in Burke's great anti-revolutionary polemic. Yet Burke's attachment to ancient prescriptive institutions, and especially to monarchy and the established Church, made him difficult to adapt to American uses. The repression that started in Britain in 1793 was both anti-republican and anti-Dissenter, and many of its targets

252

were admired friends of the American Revolution like Joseph Priestley. Thus British anti-Jacobinism cut both ways, and some of its characteristic arguments could not be used until the panic at the end of the century, when Britain was seen by conservative Americans as the sole hope for the survival of freedom and religion, and even Burke was quoted and admired. Before American anti-Jacobinism could really become effective, it had to be built on a basis that was both impeccably republican and impeccably Protestant.

Part of the development of anti-Jacobinism in America is connected with the history of the Federalist Party, a history which embodies many kinds of local and economic interests and is not in itself a part of our story. Yet the history of Federalist ideology, and especially that articulated by the extreme wing of the party, the High Federalist moguls of eastern Massachusetts, is very much a part of the history of the American Enlightenment. Most of the High Federalists, and some other Federalists, were devoted to the classical republican political theory of checks and balances, and beneath this lay the traditional view of man as balanced precariously between reason and passion. In other words, the mainstay of much of the early opposition to the Revolutionary Enlightenment in America was the ideology of the Moderate Enlightenment. The High Federalists, like some of the Constitution-makers of 1787, drew from their reading of the classics and moderns the view that the passions of the mob must be countered by the reason of the educated few, and that the job of republican institutions was to safeguard this delicate balance. Like some of their most radical opponents, they clung to a gloomy view of human nature shaped partly by the Calvinist past. Like Commonwealth radicals, they believed that republics were fragile and liable to decline. While radicals found the main source of decline in corruption, High Federalist conservatives found it in the ignorance and emotionalism of the majority.

Some of the Federalists went so far in their gloomy assessment of human possibilities that they were closer to the views of the Skeptical Enlightenment than to those of the Moderate Enlightenment. This was especially true of Alexander Hamilton, who was much more deeply influenced by David Hume than most of his colleagues. In 1793, while still in power, he rejected any idea of political regeneration:

> The triumphs of vice are no new thing under the sun, and I fear, till the millennium comes, in spite of all our boasted light and purification,

hypocrisy and treachery will continue to be the most successful commodities in the political market.

Later, in time of defeat, he echoed Hume's conclusions still more directly:

> Nothing is more fallacious than to expect to produce any valuable or permanent results in political projects by relying merely on the reason of men. Men are rather reasoning than reasonable animals, for the most part governed by the impulse of passion.[1]

To different degrees, other High Federalists echoed Hamilton's pessimism. There was much in the history of the 1790's to make believers in moderation and order doubt the survival of delicate institutions, and particularly to make them question whether passionate democracy could be held at bay. That was the question for High Federalist ideologues in the Whiskey Rebellion, which they took much more seriously than its concrete dangers seemed to warrant. And above all, High Federalists were genuinely frightened by the founding of the Democratic Clubs. It was not alone the pernicious principles proclaimed by the clubs that were alarming. The worst thing about them was that they existed at all, disturbing the balance between the few and the many, bypassing elected authorities, and appealing to the people directly, "deceiving and inflaming the ignorant and weak."[2] A Philadelphia correspondent of Jedidiah Morse found it hard to understand how men could be so wicked:

> It is astonishing to see that they cannot see the impropriety of their meeting for the express purpose of influencing measures of government and forming themselves into *Societies*, with that view: notwithstanding they appear to be in the decline, they must be carefully watched & their machinations guarded against, or we shall yet see such scenes as have been acted in France.[3]

Obviously, it was the events in France, and the vogue of the French Revolution in America, that gave every event its most sinister meaning for High Federalists. It was not alone the violence and irreligion of the Terrible Republic that scared them. It was also the fact that the Jacobins justified their actions by an appeal to the General Will, and that they specifically opposed and detested any idea of balanced institutions or local autonomy. Worse still, some Americans, who should know better, admired the new French principles. George Cabot, the arch-Federalist senator from Massachusetts was characteristically gloomy in a letter to Secretary of State Timothy Pickering:

> . . . I cannot forbear to express to you my apprehensions, which are now greater than ever, that our country is destined to act over the same follies, to practise the same vices, and of consequence to suffer the same miseries which compose the history of revolutionary France. . . . I have fondly cherished the belief that our countrymen would give a fair chance to the experiment of a just government altogether elective by the people and perfectly free; but I am ready to say that, as I understand human nature, *such a system cannot long be supported by any people whatever.*[4]

Two American phenomena underlined, for balance-and-order conservatives, the danger of French principles prevailing in the United States. One was the decline of deference, a clear indication that it might prove impossible to balance the rights of the few against the power of the many. Another was the spread among the masses—greatly exaggerated by Federalist fears—of the doctrines of Utopian philosophers. Fisher Ames, the High Federalist congressman from Dedham, Massachusetts, condemned:

> . . . the dreams of all the philosophers who think the people angels, rulers devils; information will keep all right, quell riots and rebellions, and save the expense of armies; the people always mean right, and if the government do not oppress, the citizens will not resist; that man is a perfectible animal, and all governments are obstacles to his apotheosis. This nonsense is inhaled with every breath. It gives a bias to the opinions of those who are no philosophers, or who, at least do not imagine they are such. Errors so deep, so hostile to order, so far out of the reach of all cures, except the killing one of experience, are to be mitigated and palliated by truth, perhaps delayed from exploding for some years. But they will have vent, and then all will shake to the Alleghany [*sic*] ridge.[5]

As a more or less democratic two-party system slowly developed, the right tactics for a consciously anti-popular group of political leaders became a difficult problem. From time to time the High Federalist moguls assured each other that they must learn from their enemies how to appeal to the people, and from time to time they tried this tactic with varying success—in the fight against war with England in 1794, in the offensive against the Democratic Clubs, and in the climactic battle over ratification and implementation of the Jay treaty. Yet the Federalist leaders—even Ames, whose oratorical skill made some of his friends call him the American Burke, or even call Burke the English Ames[6]—knew that they were not very good at rallying the people, and some of them had real scruples about making the effort. Reverting to a tactic more in line with their political ideology, they tried to exalt the various checks which the Constitution placed on the popular will—to assert boldly the countervailing power of the executive, the Senate, the courts, and finally the electoral college. In the late 1790's, however, none of these tactics seemed sufficient, and the Federalist leaders resorted, in something like panic, to arousing some of the deepest fear of New England, and even to beating the drums of war. In doing this, they gravely damaged the ideology of balance, order, and moderation which had always held their allegiance.

To understand the fears of the Federalist leaders it is necessary to try to look at European and domestic events through their eyes. At home the heroic Washington gave place to the irascible and stuffy Adams, whom the High Federalists deeply mistrusted despite their efforts to work up enthusiasm, and the Vice-President was a Virginia "philosopher," already a term of abuse. Abroad the French were turning Italy into a string of subservient republics. Worse, they had subverted and re-modelled the ancient aristocratic and balanced republics of Venice, the Netherlands, and Switzerland, the principal mainstays of conservative republican historical theory. French landings in England seemed possible, and in Ireland, where revolt was in progress, probable. To some it seemed thoroughly possible that the ever-victorious Bonaparte, after his curious Egyptian venture, would next turn his attentions westward. In America he could recapture a strong base in the revolted French island in Santo Domingo, and then take over Louisiana from weak and subservient Spain. Calling on the disloyal inhabitants of the West like Genet a few years earlier, he could then establish first a Trans-Appalachian and then a Cis-Appalachian Republic on the Italian model. Moreover, he was sure to find plenty of Americans flocking to the banners of French liberation. Fuming, Federalists cited statements by Frenchmen, particularly the *philosophe* Volney, to the effect that the American people were more pro-French than their government.[7]

All this seems, and part of it was, exaggerated. Yet there is nothing intrinsically absurd in the prediction that Napoleon would turn westward, as indeed he strongly considered doing a few years later. In the Louisiana crisis of 1802-3, after all, Jefferson himself was to consider an American-British alliance and an attack on Louisiana. In 1798 some High Federalists believed that this program was the only safeguard against French invasion. (In the fall of 1799, when news came of the destruction of the French fleet at the battle of the Nile, such fears lost whatever plausibility they had had, but by that time the High Federalists had become addicted to the tactics of panic.)

By 1797 hopes of victory began to be mixed with Federalist fears. When the French Directorate insulted American envoys in the XYZ affair, some High Federalists were delighted. Even Alexander Hamilton, who seldom deluded himself, joined the other in suggesting that the public tone was at last improving: "The conduct of France has been a very powerful medicine for the political disease of our country. I think the community improves in soundness."[8]

Hamilton and his High Federalist friends, in cataloguing the wickednesses of the French Republic, sometimes charged it with propagating atheism. Yet the religious issue, before 1798, plays very little part in the correspondence of High Federalists with each other. Federalist leaders, like their opponents, had all sorts of religious views, from the fervent evangelical Christianity of John Jay and the millennial zeal of Elias Boudinot to the probable deism of Southern leaders like William Davie and Charles Cotesworth Pinckney. Among the New England Federalist moguls the norm was a calm, rationalist, liberal Christianity descended directly from the mid-eighteenth-century Enlightened views of Charles Chauncy and Jonathan Mayhew. All the New England High Federalists believed morality essential to republics, and some sort of religion essential to morality. Some, like Franklin and Voltaire, thought it especially necessary for the masses. Josiah Quincy, George Cabot, Ellery Sedgwick were all Unitarians. Timothy Pickering, much later in calmer times, was actually to admit that his beliefs were much like those of his archenemy, Thomas Jefferson.

As early as 1795, some of the High Federalists realized the potential usefulness of the clergy, a group they did not always find congenial but one that commanded public influence. In 1795 Washington, prompted by Hamilton, proclaimed a day of National Thanksgiving, but clerical responses were mixed. Many of the clergy still saw, in the French Revolution, the hand of God using unlikely instruments to work eventual good. Others were beginning to change their minds. David Osgood of

Medford delivered a polemic sermon that left nothing to be desired. According to a friend's reminiscences:

> From this period he was greatly admired and caressed by many of our leading politicians of the Federal school, and both in public and in private he stood forth the earnest and powerful advocate of their principles.

As Fisher Ames observed to Christopher Gore: "Tom Paine has kindly cured our clergy of their prejudices."[9]

Hamilton, always trying to dominate the Adams administration from behind the scenes, wrote both Pickering and James McHenry, his two friends in the cabinet, that it would be useful to have the President proclaim "a day of humiliation and prayer":

> In such a crisis this appears to me proper in itself, and it will be politically useful to impress our nation that there is a serious state of things—to strengthen religious ideas in a contest, which in its progress may require that our people may consider themselves as the defenders of their country against atheism, conquest, and anarchy.[10]

Acting as always for his own complex reasons, Adams in this one instance did what Hamilton had suggested. Following ancient New England precedents, on March 23, 1798, Adams proclaimed the next May 9 as a day of "solemn humiliation, fasting and prayer" and urged that citizens on that day gather in their churches to confess their sins, proclaim their repentance, and pray that their country might be delivered from its pressing dangers.[11] On the day appointed, the Reverend Jedidiah Morse of Charlestown, Massachusetts, a man who had very little in common with Fisher Ames or Alexander Hamilton, answered the President's call with a Fast Day sermon. This sermon, reflecting and concentrating the long developing fears of Morse's special constituency, provided the High Federalists with a whole new set of not very congenial allies.

Even in their gloomy moods, the High Federalists often counted on New England to remain firm in the old ways, resisting the tides of demagogy and license. Ames, for instance, believed that the wicked demagogues who were gaining control of the large towns everywhere could do no irreparable harm if only the "country folks keep firm and steady."[12] While there was a lot about rural and small-town New England that Ames and his friends did not understand, they were not altogether wrong about its conservative tendencies in the late 1790's. New Englanders of many kinds still believed in a special New England culture, centered on education and the village way of life, and buttressed by religion. The old ideology of virtuous and frugal republicanism had played a strongly radical role in the 1760's and 1770's, and still had a radical potential, but in the late nineties much of it was turning conservative. Of the host of evils which always beset New England, two were fast growing stronger. One of these was luxury and ostentation but the other, now seen as the more menacing, was turbulence. Turbulence, as always, included crime, vice, neglect of the Sabbath, lack of deference to the clergy, extreme religious sectarianism, and also deism and infidelity. Of these, the last especially seemed to be flourishing. It took courage to be a deist in New England, but New England had always produced courageous rebels. Some, like Franklin in his day and Elihu Palmer now, left New England, but quite enough stayed home to alarm the sincerely religious majority. Vermont, especially, was a notorious hotbed of every kind of religious dissent, from ultra-Calvinism to the most radical kind of clergy-baiting Paine-ite deism.[13]

A new variety of turbulence was seen by many New Englanders in the growth of the Republican Party. This represented in the first place the South, a region of luxurious and irreligious slave-owning nabobs, in the second, cosmopolitan cities like New York and Philadelphia, and in the third place all the malcontents in New England itself. Samuel Goodrich, a small-town minister's son, remembers in his old age how Democrats seemed in his boyhood to epitomize the breakdown of the old ways:

> We who are now familiar with democracy, can hardly comprehend the odium attached to it in the age to which I refer, especially in the minds of the sober people of our neighborhood. They not only regarded it as hostile to good government, but as associated with infidelity in religion, radicalism in government, and licentiousness in society . . . men of blemished reputation, tipplers, persons of irregular tempers, odd people, those who were constitutionally upsetters, destructives, comeouters, flocked spontaneously, as if by a kind of instinct, to the banner of democracy. . . .[14]

The growing conservatism of New England was represented much more accurately by three Connecticut intellectuals than by the High Federalist moguls of Boston or Essex County. By the late 1790's most of the Hartford Wits, once urbane, moderately Enlightened, and anti-clerical, had either given up writing or turned to routine Federalist polemics. Their silence left Connecticut's intellectual leadership to Timothy Dwight, Noah Webster, and Jedidiah Morse.

All three of these men were less snobbish, less Anglophile, and closer to the plain people of their region than were the Bostonians. Timothy Dwight, always more conservative in religion and morals than his former Hartford friends, was entrenched at Yale from 1795, devotedly strengthening the College and increasingly deploring the decline of piety in the nation. Noah Webster, always the most rebellious and republican of the Connecticut writers, by 1796-97 was turning against the French Republic which he had long defended. By 1800 he had even overcome his hostility to the New England aristocracy, and argued that New England owed its kind of liberty, the best kind in the world, to "the advantage and superior influence of particular men, derived from their property, their education, their age, their tried virtue and integrity, and their public services."[15] Perhaps a little ruefully, he joined with some slight qualification the attack on the thinkers of the Revolutionary Enlightenment:

> The theories of Helvétius, Rosseau, Condorcet, Turgot, Godwin and others, are founded on artificial reasoning, not on the nature of man; not on fact and experience. And hence the convulsions and miseries which have been occasioned by an attempt to carry them into practice, have every where exceeded the evils of the old tyrannies. Between these theories and the old corrupt establishments, there is a *mean*, which probably is the true point of freedom and national happiness.[16]

This statement, with its echo of eighteenth-century balance and its continuing suspicion of the old order, is closer to the real voice of New England than the ultra-Anglophile, quasi-Burkean laments of Ames or Cabot.

Jedidiah Morse, the third major member of the conservative Yale intelligentsia of this period, was a friend of both Webster and Dwight.[17] A Connecticut clergyman's son who had found Stiles's Yale lacking in piety (he did not blame Stiles personally), Morse was steeped in the moderate Calvinist orthodoxy of Connecticut. He was never at home either with Hopkinsian extremists nor Arminian liberals.

Since its first publication in 1784 Morse had been engaged in revising and rewriting his *Geography*. For this purpose he had established a nationwide and worldwide network of correspondents, who fed him information about their regions and helped him in his indefatigable campaign to promote his book. Among his fairly frequent correspondents were William Wilberforce, John Erskine, the leading Moderate in the Church of Scotland, and Professor Christoph Daniel Ebeling of Hamburg. His most frequent American correspondents in the Middle and Southern states were inevitably Presbyterian ministers, who were both learned and congenial.

In 1789 Morse had been called to the First Church of Charlestown, Massachusetts, where he found himself, uncomfortably, a part of the liberal intellectual ministerial society of Boston. Like Dwight, Morse was a man who combined sincere piety, immense energy, and a tendency to suspect the worst of his opponents. In his frequent letters to his aged father at Woodstock, Connecticut, Morse complains frequently of the secular and luxurious habits of the Boston area, coupling these with the usual ministerial complaints of neglect, irreligion, and division.

Like Webster and like most of the Calvinist clergy, Morse was until about 1795 a defender of the French Revolution on anti-papist and millennial grounds. He took for granted, however, an allegiance to the Federalist Party, and his fame as a geographer brought him into correspondence with such major Federalist politicians as John Jay and Oliver Wolcott. As early as 1794 Wolcott, the chief representative of Connecticut among the High Federalists, was suggesting to Morse the existence of a vaguely defined worldwide conspiracy:

> While a mental epidemic is spreading through the world, & threatening all Society with Destruction, it is a matter of consolation that the principles & habits of New England are best calculated to resist its contagion.[18]

At some point in the late 1790's, just while all Morse's friends were becoming more hostile to the French Revolution, Morse read John Robison's *Proofs of a Conspiracy*, a book which was recommended to him by John Erskine and probably by Dwight.[19]

Robison, who wrote with the prestige of an Edinburgh chair, discusses with great learning and little realism the history of a special secret branch of the Masonic Order, the Illuminati of Bavaria. Through their

machinations, he explains, the Illuminati have acquired immense influence in all countries, and especially in France. Their purpose is to de-
story first morality, then religion, and then government everywhere.
Though Robison nowhere makes them solely responsible for the Revolution in France, he credits them with a considerable part in it. In a post-
script, Robison praises another book, *Mémoires pour servir à l'histoire du
Jacobinisme* by the Abbé Barruel. Barruel adds to Robison's account of
the origin of the Revolution the crucial connection between the Freemasons and the "Philosophists." He shows, says Robison:

> that a formal and systematic conspiracy against Religion was formed
> and zealously prosecuted by Voltaire, d'Alembert, and Diderot, assisted
> by Frederic II, King of Prussia.[20]

This nefarious group, meeting at the Hôtel d'Holbach, devoted themselves to corrupting the public with anti-religious and pornographic
literature, controlling the schools, and eventually subverting the government.

The promulgation of this theory, linking the midcentury philosophers
to the Revolution, was a major event in popular historiography. Radicals
had already suggested the connection of Enlightenment and Revolution.
From this point on that link became an article of faith with many conservatives, whether or not they believed the whole Robison-Barruel theory of conspiracy. From both radicals and conservatives of the eighteenth
century, it passed into historical writing of the nineteenth century and
later. And in Charlestown, Massachusetts, the Illuminati theory in its
most literal form furnished Morse the principal substance of his Fast
Day sermon, preached on May 9, 1798, in answer to President Adams's
proclamation.[21]

In his sermon Morse extends and simplifies the theories of Robison
and Barruel, making the conspiracy of Illuminati and philosophers
clearly responsible for the French Revolution and its spread, the "Jacobin Clubs" in the United States, and the astounding effort to deni-
grate the American clergy. The attack was immediately taken up by
Dwight, whose still more famous Fourth of July sermon is almost an
echo of Morse's, implying that Voltaire himself was the head of the international conspiracy, and prophesying the most dire consequences
were the anti-religious party ever to come to power in the United States.
Our churches may then become temples of reason, "our Sabbath a dec-

ade, and our psalms of praise Marseillais hymns. Our children may then be turned against us by terror or wheedling, and we may finally see our wives and daughters the victims of legal prostitution." (Dwight does *not*, as is often alleged, connect these horrors specifically with Thomas Jefferson.)[22]

In assessing the results of this counter-revolutionary call to arms we must remember that Dwight and Morse were no mere isolated clergymen. Dwight was the able and admired head of a revered institution. Morse was the author of a best-seller. Moreover, he was a gifted organizer and propagandist who from this point on turned his energies to promoting the Illuminati theory in exactly the same way he had long been promoting his *Geography*. Among a large section of the clergy, in New England and throughout the country, Morse's message fell on fertile ground, giving them a plausible and learned explanation for much that they had gradually come to believe.

Until about 1795 the New England clergy of the Standing Order had been, like their allies and leaders among the Connecticut intellectuals, balanced between hopes and fears. On the one hand, nearly all of them were proud of their own major contribution to the American Revolution and had long taken for granted the intimate connection between Protestantism and progress. Most had, like Morse and Webster, welcomed the Revolution in France as the spread of American principles or at least a scourge to popery. On the other hand many, like Morse and Dwight, were deeply concerned about old and new evils: religious apathy, immorality, ignorance, and luxury. Many were challenged in their own towns by dissenters of various sorts; many found themselves not taken as seriously as they had once been. The first missionaries going forth to save the frontier for New England were sending back disquieting reports about ignorance and infidelity in Vermont and upstate New York.[23]

Among the New England clergy and their allies to the southward the publication of Paine's *Age of Reason* was a major event. The book's wide and rapid circulation, its appeal to the ignorant, and above all its coupling of political and religious radicalism seemed to many of the clergy to represent something new, far more alarming than the half-forgotten arguments of the English deists, long the staple of routine pulpit denunciation. The book produced a flood of replies, some tempered and some violent. Ebenezer Bradford of Rowley, one of the principal clerical defenders of the French Revolution, set a tone of shocked sadness. Fervently praising *Common Sense*, the *Crisis* papers, and *The Rights of Man*, Bradley lamented that Paine had turned from the defense of republican principles to:

> the most indefensible of all causes, I mean that of the Deists; by this means he has wounded the warm and tender feelings of more than a million of his real friends, and given an unnecessary triumph to as many of his inveterate enemies, both in America and Great Britain.[24]

A number of the early clerical replies to Paine tried seriously to refute rather than simply to denounce his arguments. It was never difficult to damage some of them. Ministers were on familiar ground in pointing out that his beneficent deist universe had no place in it for evil, no way even to explain the triumph of mistaken opinions down to the present time.[25]

Rational argument, however, seemed not to stop the spread of Paine's opinions, and these were echoed by even bolder deists. Astonished, the clergy heard the assertions of Elihu Palmer and others that the time had come to expose the frauds of Christianity once and for all, and almost more astonished, they found ministers listed as enemies to liberty. They noticed the publication in America of Holbach and Boulanger, and exaggerated the prevalence of deism both in the colleges and among republicans.

As many of the clergy learned for the first time to associate political radicalism and deism, the Federalist press increased its emphasis on the Jacobin menace to religion, and ministers were increasingly courted by Federalist statesmen. Not all the clergy swallowed such flattery whole, as David Tappan of Harvard makes clear in a letter to his brother:

> I have a poor opinion of those federalists & christians, however respectable on other accounts, who declaim against french *principles*, & yet resemble them in *practice*; who speak highly of religion & the clergy in charges to Juries, in Orations, Toasts, or Newspaper-paragraphs, & yet practically neglect or trample them under foot.[26]

Yet many of the clergy deeply admired Washington and Adams themselves, greatly exaggerating the Christian piety of both,[27] and believed
that the whole social-religious order of New England was dependent on
the continued rule of the party of order.

Before clergymen could completely oppose the cause of France, they
had to come to terms with their recent fear of Britain and the British establishment. For clerical opinion, a crucial event was the founding in
1795 of the London Missionary Society, drawing together evangelical
churchmen and Dissenters in an effort to convert the world, and especially France. The rising British evangelicals, particularly William Wilberforce, had far more to say to most American Protestants than political conservatives like Edmund Burke. For many decades, starting in the
1790's, England was to seem the great center of evangelical power, leading the assault not only against French infidelity but also against every
kind of heathenism, vice, and sin. Thus, as an acute student of Connecticut missionary circles points out, the feelings of 1763 were revived to
counteract those of 1776. Once more, the Anglo-Saxon Protestant world
seemed to come together with an immense mission to fight a powerful
foe, this time not Catholic but infidel, but again centered in Paris.[28]

Before the New England clergy on their close allies could wholly subscribe to the anti-Jacobin campaign of Morse and Dwight, they had to
revise their understanding of the millennial theory by which many of
them interpreted current history. During the period of the American
Revolution, many of the clergy had seen the great event as a confirma-
tion of their long-standing hope that the North American continent was
destined to be the theater of the triumphant return of Christ and his
thousand-year reign. Now the earthshaking events taking place in Europe had forced them to turn their eyes there.[29]

At first, as we have seen earlier, the French Revolution was accepted
cheerfully and even jubilantly as a major step in the overthrow of the
Antichrist, whose chief worldly representative was the Pope. The irreligion or bloodthirstiness of some revolutionaries was not in itself a reason
to change this view. Nothing was more certain than that God sometimes chose his agents very mysteriously. An anonymous tract on prophecy published in Baltimore in 1794 put this common theory very clearly:

> It is certain that the authors of the French revolution had nothing less
> in view than the accomplishment of prophecy; yet had this been their
> only design they could not have done it more effectually. It is the Lord's

usual method to effect his purposes by undesigning, and even refractory agents. . . .

> He may indeed permit unprincipled Infidels, to overturn the monstrous fabric of superstition, they are, perhaps, the fittest instruments to accomplish a work which would necessarily seem to require, the most violent exertions, an utter disregard to the feelings of humanity, and an unrestrained exercise of blind passion for a time.[30]

By the middle of the decade, however, several events made it more difficult to take a sanguine view. One was the advance of French arms and French principles into the two sacred homelands of the Reformation, Switzerland and the Netherlands. Still worse was the supposed power of French agents in America itself. Clearly, the divine plan involved more than the overthrow of French Catholicism. As always, God's ultimate purposes were difficult to penetrate even for the most devoted students of prophecy. Elias Boudinot, perhaps the most deeply religious of Federalist statesmen, was near despair over a combination of events including the yellow fever and the opposition to the Jay Treaty:

> In short, we do indeed live in a dying world. May we all stand on the Watch, with our Loins girt, and our lamps trimmed and brimming, waiting for the coming of the Bridegroom.[31]

Henry Channing, the relatively liberal Calvinist of New London, rejoiced over the narrow victory of the Federalists in the Jay's Treaty fight:

> For had Columbia made shipwreck of the republican faith, I am persuaded that the time would soon come, when the creed of Freeman would be expunged from the records of nations, and the hopes of a republican Millennium been blunted forever.[32]

Most New England clergymen, I believe, continued to think that the last days were not far off, and that the reign of peace and justice would be established on earth before the judgment.[33] But in the late 1790's they began to place more and more emphasis in their sermons on the upheavals and calamities that had to come about in the period right before the second coming, and among these calamities was the triumph in Europe of the French. Even in America, the Lord's plans might include severe tribulations. In its doctrine of the millennium, as in every way, Morse's Fast Day sermon exactly fitted the prevailing mood:

By these awful events—this tremendous shaking among the nations of the earth, God is doubtless accomplishing his promises, and fulfilling the prophecies. This wrath and violence of men against all government and religion, shall be made ultimately, in some way or other, to praise God. . . . But while we contemplate these awful events in this point of view, let us beware, in our expressions of approbation, of blending the *end* with the *means.* Because atheism and licentiousness are employed as *instruments,* by divine providence, to subvert and overthrow popery and despotism, it does not follow that atheism and licentiousness are in themselves good things, and worthy of our approbation.[34]

Some New England clergymen, like David Osgood, had been denouncing the French longer than Morse. What Morse and Dwight added to the anti-deist crusade was, however, crucial. In the first place, they gave circulation to the Illuminati theory, which they and their close allies defended against even the most convincing refutations. Second, even for those who did not accept this argument fully and specifically, they brought a new tone of apocalyptic urgency. Third, they brought Morse's untiring and talented organizing efforts, and Dwight's towering prestige. The result was an anti-French, anti-deist, and indeed anti-Enlightenment campaign which focused all the fears of conservative Americans.[35]

The anti-French sermons preached on the two Fast Days of 1798 and 1799, on thanksgivings and elections, and sometimes on no occasion at all make dull reading. Almost all connect Voltaire with the French Revolution and with Paine, and many bring in Hume, Godwin, Helvétius, and others. Especially in New England, some are surprisingly specific in their political partisanship, not only lamenting the death of Washington but praising Adams, damning his opponents (usually leaving out the name, well understood, of the chief American infidel), and defending the necessity of the Alien and Sedition Acts to curb the seditious press.

Taken as a whole, however, the crusade started by Morse has deep historical resonance. The anti-deist sermons can be seen as one episode in the long series of New England jeremiads, going back to the seventeenth century in their method and organization, calling New England or the nation to account, urging the faithful to remember their blessings, repent of their many sins, and redouble their efforts to resist decline and corruption. Very often such efforts are said to be particularly necessary because of the many signs of the approaching Last Day. Like earlier jeremiads, the jeremiads that began in 1798 were also an effort to rally and assert the power of the churches themselves. In tone and language they resemble closely clerical campaigns of the past, when the American Israel was rallied against quite different conspiracies: against the French papists in the 1750's, or against the machinations of mitre and sceptre in the 1760's.

Within New England, Dwight and Morse and their close collaborators in the Connecticut Valley and elsewhere were also trying to bring together on an anti-infidel platform the long-divided Congregational-Presbyterian establishment. In this they were at least temporarily successful. The crusade began among moderate Calvinists, like Dwight, Morse, and their close collaborators in Connecticut and Massachusetts. One of these, David Tappan, despite his Calvinism held the uneasy but prestigious position of Professor of Divinity at Arminian-leaning Harvard. Tappan, in his sermons of 1798 and 1799 completely abjured his recent defense of France and swallowed Morse and Robison whole.[36] Despite recent wounding disagreements, it was not hard for the moderate Calvinist leaders to enlist some of the New Divinity men. Nathanael Emmons, in his own way one of Edwards's most devoted followers, began in 1798 and 1799 to denounce the anarchistic and infidel French. He was soon to become one of the most extreme and persistent pulpit anti-Jeffersonians.[37]

Perhaps more surprisingly, the Morse crusade got wide support among the religious liberals of the Boston area, who were soon to break away from the Congregational Church into organized Unitarianism. Abiel Abbott of Haverhill, a liberal, asks Morse for more evidence to help him defend Robison, and asks where he can get a copy of Barruel. At Harvard, the stronghold of religious liberalism, each student was presented with a copy of Bishop Watson's reply to Paine in 1794, and in 1798 the anti-French excitement reached almost as high a pitch there as at Yale. Samuel Bentley of Salem, Morse's chief opponent, makes clear throughout his diary that he was ostracized by his liberal brethren for his Jeffersonian sympathies.[38]

Sometimes, though not always, the tone of the anti-French liberals was less violent than that of their orthodox brethren. Like their close friends among the High Federalists, some of them were reluctant to rouse the rabble for any purposes. Rather than emphasizing the coming millennial struggle, they laid stress on the dangers of Jacobinism to order and to rationality itself. Yet the Massachusetts establishment was still precariously intact, and the liberals were a part of it. They could fully agree with their Old Calvinist and Hopkinsian colleagues on something like the following chain of argument: morality is necessary to good government, religion is necessary to morality, and public support and respect is necessary to religion. And there was no doubt at all in most Boston Arminian minds which of the two political parties was more likely to give religion such support. Above all, Boston liberal clergymen, among the oldest and strongest adherents of the Moderate Enlightenment in its most moderate form, were eager to distinguish their own liberal or Unitarian views from modern and militant deism.

Beyond New England the chief strength of the anti-deist crusade lay in the Presbyterian Church, the best-organized and still probably the most powerful religious organization in the country. Here Morse was in a specially strategic position. A Connecticut Presbyterian by origin and sympathy, he was in close touch with Princeton, the capital of Scotch-Irish and Southern Presbyterianism. One of his close friends was Ashbel Green, the chaplain of Congress, later president of Princeton, and already perhaps the most powerful of Princeton Presbyterians. Morse's Presbyterian correspondents ranged through the leading ministers and professors of the Middle and Southern states. They included, for instance, such prominent Presbyterian intellectuals as the historian David Ramsay, who writes from Charleston in 1799 to praise Morse's Fast Day sermon, trusts "that it will have a good effect by opening the eyes of the Americans," and assures him that "The French have lost the friends they had among us. . . ."[39]

No group joined the Morse crusade more enthusiastically than the authorities of American colleges, then mostly Presbyterian. Perhaps the most extreme Francophobe in America was Charles Nisbet, president of Carlisle College. Nisbet, like Witherspoon a Scot imported largely through the efforts of Benjamin Rush, had been a supporter of the American cause during the Revolution. The low state of piety and learning at Carlisle—or one might say his own failure to adapt successfully to new circumstances—made him a violent opponent of republics in general, almost as pessimistic about America as about France.[40] Samuel E. McCorkle, the co-founder of the University of North Carolina, and the leader of its militant faction, is more typical. McCorkle, a powerful Presbyterian minister who carried on a tireless battle against Republicans and religious liberals in Chapel Hill, found a simple reason for the

strength of his enemies: "It is deism—deism—deism—detestable deism
. . . that has disadjusted and disorganized society."[41]

At Princeton, the great Presbyterian capital, the moderate enlightened
liberalism of Samuel Stanhope Smith became untenable. Smith, who
combined genial orthodoxy, Moderate Enlightenment, and monumental
urbanity, had hitherto been a full member of the Enlightened elite circle whose center was the American Philosophical Society. Now, as Philadelphia became the most politically polarized city in the country, the
APS was struggling to avoid a similar fate. Priestley was in danger of actual arrest or deportation, many of the French had left, and even Benjamin Rush, Smith's close friend, was being forced on the defensive by
the vitriolic attacks of William Cobbett. Rush himself, always a Calvinist, was being pulled by his religious concerns away from his Jeffersonian
sympathies.[42] The stance of the Moderate Enlightenment was becoming
difficult for any Presbyterian, and for a president of Princeton impossible.

Smith probably found the necessary rightward move easy enough to
make sincerely. His enlightened opinions, like those of many adherents
of the Moderate Enlightenment, found no place at all for democracy.
The French Revolution confirmed his belief in the irrationality of the
masses and heightened his sense of the danger of this fault. By 1799 he
fully approved Morse's crusade.[43] When student riots made Smith's life
miserable, he, like almost all the other college presidents, blamed student discontent (quite mistakenly) on a Jacobin conspiracy. By 1801 all
his urbanity was gone. Commenting to a Federalist senator on the do-
ings of the Jefferson administration Smith predicted that America was
probably destined to follow France all the way to anarchy and dictatorship:

> Good men will be obliged to retire from public affairs; blockheads &
> villains will soon hold the reign & the scourge over us. May the *patricians*
> yet be able to save the republic when the tribunes shall have urged it to
> the brink of ruin![44]

Yet no degree of reaction was enough to save Smith from suspicions occasioned by his earlier liberalism. Under steady attack for years, he was
finally forced out of the Princeton presidency in 1812 and replaced by
Ashbel Green.

Like the rest of the orthodox clergy, American college authorities were willing enough to blame their many troubles on a single source. According to a thorough study, no refutation of the Illuminati theory ever came from an American college, and most colleges were highly receptive to it.[45] Thus Morse's crusade played a part, among many other causes, in increasing the conservatism and provincial isolation which damaged American academic life for the next half-century.

Among the other churches, the Dutch and German Reformed naturally went along with the closely allied Presbyterians, furnishing such heavy guns to the anti-Jacobin crusade as William Linn of the Collegiate Dutch Church in New York. Somewhat less uniformly, the battered Episcopalians followed suit. In the Middle states, where the Church had come back strongly from the catastrophes of the Revolution, the anti-Jacobin cause provided a way for moderate Episcopalians like James Abercrombie of Philadelphia to play a patriotic and unifying role, to line up on the side of the British without disloyalty, and even to make some progress toward reconciliation with their ancient Puritan enemies.

Even the eccentric fringe which has always plagued the Episcopal Church found a place in the anti-Jacobin Front. Joseph Dennie, the talented and frivolous minor poet, a little later editor of the arch-Federalist *Port Folio*, yielded to nobody in his Anglophilia and his hatred of New England. In a letter to his parents of 1800 Dennie bewails the American Revolution, without which he would be a rich and successful man of letters, and blames it on:

> the Jewish and canting and cheating descendants of those men, who during the reign of a Stuart, *fled away* from the claim of the Creditor, from the tithes of the Church, from their allegiance to their Sovereign and from their duty to their God. . . .

In the same letter, he assures his mother that he has reached, with the soundest Anglican authority, a perfect conviction of the divine origin of the Scriptures, and sees their prophecies fulfilled in "the horrible convulsions of *subverted* France."[46]

In the South, the Episcopal Church was slowly groping its way back from the many troubles of its past, culminating in Jeffersonian disestablishment. In Maryland, where the Church was a bit stronger than in Virginia, the clergy were strongly Federalist. Some Maryland Episcopalians sounded exactly like their most conservative English counterparts. J. G. Bend assures a correspondent that:

I have been fully convinced for some time of the Jacobinic principles of the Methodists: nor is this fact wonderful. They are, for the most part, persons of the lower classes in life, & distinguished by that ignorance upon which the Jacobin chiefs work so successfully.[47]

Charles Pettigrew of North Carolina, sore beset to keep the Church alive in a region full of Baptist Belshazzars, was as violently anti-Jacobin as Morse, and so were his correspondents.[48]

In a society with any freedom of choice there are bound to be exceptions to all generalizations about political and religious opinions. Among Episcopalians, Bishop Madison stuck to his liberal and Republican guns. In New England the Episcopalians had long been part of the resistance movement against the Standing Order, and this put some of them strongly in the Republican camp. John Cosens Ogden, of St. John's Church in Portsmouth, New Hampshire, was one of the best-known opponents of Dwight and Morse, accusing them of being themselves the New England equivalent of the Illuminati and forming a conspiracy to control church and state.[49] In Pennsylvania, where many Presbyterians had long been radical democrats, some of them remained so.

Anti-Federalist resisters and come-outers are still more noticeable in the New England Congregational establishment itself, where stiff-necked dissent was as old a tradition as orthodoxy. Republican politicians at the time and some historians later make much of such conspicuous and fiery Jeffersonian Calvinists as David Austin, the somewhat eccentric millennial preacher; or Thomas Allen and John Bacon, both New Light Calvinist democrats and leaders of the Jeffersonian party in Berkshire County; or Stanley Griswold of New Milford. One can find a number of others among the publishing clergy, and doubtless there were still more who left no record, applying to the French Revolution the radical millennial interpretation that most of their colleagues had abandoned, fighting Morse and Dwight with the old Puritan hatred of establishments. But these exceptions really do prove the rule. Some, like Austin and Griswold, lost their pulpits. The writing of the pro-French New England clergy and reminiscences by those who knew them, testify to the isolation they felt, suffered from, and in the New England manner sometimes gloried in also.

There is no doubt that in New England and the nation the overwhelming majority of the settled, established clergy—those whose instincts and emotions were on the side of any kind of traditional order, those whose habitual allies were the leading citizens—were by 1798 lined up against the French republic, the Republican Party, and particularly Thomas Jefferson. Many of them, not all, expressed themselves with extreme partisan violence on political issues. This does not mean, however, that the Federalists had on their side American religion, or for that matter American Calvinism.[50]

The Morse crusade and the Federalist-orthodox lineup in general drove in the other direction those American Christians, whether Calvinist Baptists or Separates in New England or Arminian Methodists in Virginia, whose experience or theology made them deeply suspicious of alliance with the state. Most Methodists and Baptists were, of course, as strongly opposed to deism or any form of infidelity as Morse and Dwight. But they were also opposed to coercion, and particularly to coercion by Presbyterians or Episcopalians.

In the last two years of the century the High Federalists and the established orthodox clergy drew together. Each of these groups was actuated by quite genuine fears for deeply held values. Each greatly damaged these values by extreme and in some cases hypocritical tactics. The combined effort did not save America either from Jacobinism, which was unnecessary, or from increasingly democratic Republicanism, which was impossible. The counterattack did, however, have important effects on the history of American culture and religion, and on the fate of the Enlightenment in America.

Its immediate effect was to raise political partisanship to the point of hysteria. Robison and Barruel were both endlessly circulated in the press, as were other lurid tales of plot and atrocity. J. Mallet Du Pan, *History of the Destruction of the Helvetic Union* became a staple of sermon and pamphlet. The most popular of all anti-Jacobin works was Anthony Aufrère's *Cannibals' Progress*, a tale of rape and murder by the French armies in Germany, which ran to fourteen American editions between 1798 and 1790. Underlining the possibility of European horrors spreading to America, some Federalists discovered French conspiracies in the United States.[51]

Both the High Federalists and the high clergy indulged in xenophobia, attacking the French, the Irish, and other aliens in America. And despite the sincere anti-slavery feelings of many New England Federalists and clergymen, both could draw lurid pictures of armies of Santo Domingo blacks, led by Frenchmen in spreading servile war through the South.[52]

Both the clergy and the High Federalists made religion a staple of the coming campaign, turning the campaign against French deism specifically against the personal religion of Thomas Jefferson. At first, sermons did not usually name Jefferson specifically, rather pointing to the dreadful danger of the republic having as its first magistrate a man lacking in the piety of Washington and Adams. As the campaign went on and it became clear that the charge really hurt, Dwight, Morse, Linn, and many others accused Jefferson directly of being a deist (which he was) and an atheist (which he was not), and predicting that his election would lead to the complete destruction of Christianity in America.

The seriousness and power of such charges in America in 1800 are clearly demonstrated by Republican tactics in answering them. It is almost impossible to find any Republican, from Jefferson down, who defended or admitted the deist views of the Republican candidate. Three tactics were used instead to counter the orthodox campaign. Some simply denied the charges and insisted on Jefferson's actual piety. Others picked up the orthodox hand-grenades and threw them back over the barricades. The Republican press never got tired of pointing out that Hamilton was an adulterer, and Republican pamphleteers suggested, not without truth, that Charles Cotesworth Pinckney was a deist and Adams himself by no means an evangelical Christian. And finally, most successfully of all, Republicans neglected the substance of the charge but counterattacked the New England clergy and the Presbyterians everywhere, rousing against them the anti-establishment fears of the popular and voluntaristic sects. Adams himself believed that this anti-establishment tactic decided the election:

> With the Baptists, Quakers, Methodists, and Moravians, as well as the Dutch and German Lutherans and Calvinists, it had an immense effect, and turned them in such numbers as decided the election. They said, let us have an Atheist or Deist or any thing rather than an establishment of Presbyterianism.[53]

The political crisis of 1798-1800, including the quasi-war with France, the Alien and Sedition Acts, the plans of Hamilton and some of his friends for changing the nature of the republic in the course of foreign war, the dramatic frustrating of these plans by John Adams, and the complex and precarious struggle that ensued are one of the most familiar and dramatic episodes of American history. I think they amount also to one of its most dangerous crises. As men of the eighteenth century, whatever their politics, often realized, constitutional republics are fragile, especially when they are new. It is not impossible to imagine the outbreak of civil war, if an actual declaration of foreign war had given the High Federalists the opportunity of carrying further programs of militarism and suppression in which some of them seriously believed. There is I think no doubt about the strength or success of the resistance that would have ensued, and the republic would have been saved. It would not however have been the same. It might, like the French Republic from the Directorate on, have entered a history of successive coups left and right.

Since the American First Republic survived, our concern here is with the effects of this crisis on American thought, belief, and culture, and especially on the history of the Enlightenment. The crisis of 1798-1800 marked the real end in America of the three forms of Enlightenment we have so far discussed. Of course these political events did not affect this momentous cultural change by themselves; they were rather catalysts and symbols for broader and deeper forces, whose complexity will be suggested later in a brief look at the beginning of the new century.

Though the Republican press and such Enlightened stalwarts as Freneau and Barlow stuck to their guns and their side won, the Revolutionary Enlightenment was put permanently on the defensive by the Federalist-orthodox counterattack, and especially its religious element. How strong and deep were the roots of Protestant Christianity in America has I hope been suggested throughout this book. Hostility toward deism or infidelity was far-wider than the considerable group mobilized by Dwight, Morse, and their immediate allies. On the other hand, the convinced adherents of the Revolutionary Enlightenment in the United States were, as the last chapter attempted to demonstrate, a devoted and scattered few.

In defeating the Revolutionary Enlightenment, the Federalists also gravely damaged the Moderate Enlightenment in which many of them sincerely believed. Moderation, balance, order, compromise, respect for complexity, tolerance, and cosmopolitan breadth were the watchwords of the first Enlightenment. By the Federalist anti-Jacobin crusade, these ideals were distorted and associated with the interests of a perishing elite. Already, both in Europe and America, it had often proved hard to separate the Moderate Enlightenment from snobbery and exclusiveness. In 1789-1900, as the Federalists adopted demagogic tactics against those they regarded as dangerous demagogues, Enlightenment and elitism went down together.

Samuel Bentley, the lone Republican among the Arminians of eastern Massachusetts, sensed some of the meaning of the Federalist tactics. Though a staunch religious and political liberal, Bentley was no democrat, and for this reason deplored the bad manners of the upper classes:

> This day it was my service to open the Supreme Court with prayer. In the conversation I discovered such virulence of political prejudices as exceeded even the vulgarity of Jacobinism or what is stigmatized as vile democracy. When the higher orders have such unmanly prejudices, can a country be safe and well governed?[54]

Like the Enlightened High Federalists, the Federalist clergy by their conduct in this crisis seriously damaged themselves and their principles. This was especially true of Dwight, Morse, and the most politicized members of the New England establishment. Having ventured into the political arena, they became fair subjects for political attack. Morse, his integrity as well as his judgment questioned with regard to the Illuminati campaign, exhausted his energies in self-defense and scattered his shots among a host of enemies. Dwight, a man of far more intellect and ability, became the Connecticut pope, a byword for provincial bigotry.

In its articulate centers New England Calvinism, which had so long wavered between its revolutionary and reactionary elements, was moved a long way to the right. One aspect of this can be seen in the problem of its attitude toward Jacobin attacks on French Catholicism. For a long time the anti-Catholic feelings of New England had been associated with a progressive view of history: the American churches were on the side of the future against a monarchical and papal past. This vision had informed the view of nearly all ministers toward the French Revolution until the middle years of the decade. Now, in circulating the works of Catholic apologists like Barruel for instance, American Protestants seemed to move into uneasy alliance with their old arch-enemy. Dwight was intelligent enough to see this difficulty and try to writhe out of it, explaining that although the French Church had included many good and pious men, *both* the infidels and the Pope were enemies in the battle with Christ.[55]

Well beyond the sphere of Dwight and Morse and their immediate allies, the clergy of the Congregational, Presbyterian, and Episcopal churches lost heavily in prestige and damaged values in which the best of them deeply believed: solid intellectuality, doctrinal firmness, and ecclesiastical discipline. For better or for worse, the more conservative elements in American religion, which were also the more literate and the more organized, lost all chance they may have had of channeling or controlling the great and chaotic religious energies of American society. Tempted to try to restore their privileged position by one more jeremiad, they hastened its already inevitable decline. And partly because the Federalist and Presbyterian clergy controlled most of the colleges, American education and even American higher culture took on a fearful and defensive cast that was to persist well beyond the eighteenth century.

Six   *The End of the Eighteenth Century*

"There is nothing which I dread so much," said John
Adams in 1780, "as a division of the republic into two great parties, each
arranged under its leader, and concerting measures in opposition to each
other."[1] Twenty years later, just such a division had taken place, and
Adams was one of the two contending leaders. This is only the beginning
of the ironies of the campaign of 1800. In this campaign two dear
friends were temporarily ranged against each other and each was unmer-
cifully lampooned. Both candidates were major figures of the American
Enlightenment. One was at the time president of the American Philosophical Society, the other of its rival the American Academy of Arts
and Sciences—a coincidence very unlikely ever to be repeated in American politics.[2] Yet the campaign of 1800 was as unenlightened as any in
American political history, and the year marked the real end of the Enlightenment in America.

John Adams and Thomas Jefferson are perhaps the two most baffling
major figures in American history. The complexity is obvious in the case
of Adams, a mass of quirks and contradictions. Jefferson at first seems
clear and consistent, but those who have really tried to get beneath the
calm and ordered surface have found understanding ever more elusive.
I have argued in this book that in order to understand the Enlightenment it is helpful to divide it into categories. Of course such categories
are organizing devices imposed by the historian. They are valid only insofar as they help to understand the chaotic reality of history, and they will
do this only insofar as they are drawn from that reality. Such vigorous
and reflective men as Adams or Jefferson never fit neatly into any category. And yet I believe that the categories we have been using are of

278

some help in understanding these two men, their differences and similarities, their mutual hostility in 1800 and their earlier and later agreement. Adams was a man of the Moderate Enlightenment, with a considerable element of the Skeptical Enlightenment, and very little of the Revolutionary Enlightenment. Jefferson was brought up in the Moderate Enlightenment also, but was deeply and permanently affected by the early phase of the Revolutionary Enlightenment and had no trace of skepticism in his nature.[3]

In looking at Adams and Jefferson, we will for the moment abandon chronology. Each was shaped well before 1800. And both expressed their ideas most fully in the tranquility of old age, especially in their letters to each other. We will start at the beginning, and this is not in politics. Adams and Jefferson, like most great figures of the Enlightenment began their serious thinking with religion in the broadest sense, with assumptions and ideas about God, the universe, and the nature of man.

In 1820 the aged Adams responded to a query from the Reverend Samuel Miller about his attitude toward Calvinism:

> I must be a very unnatural son to entertain any prejudices against the Calvinists, or Calvinism, according to your confession of faith; for my father and mother, my uncles and aunts, and all my predecessors, from our common ancestor, who landed in this country two hundred years ago, wanting five months, were of that persuasion. Indeed, I have never known any better people than the Calvinists. Nevertheless, I must acknowledge that I cannot class myself under that denomination.[4]

He had indeed abandoned Calvinist doctrine from his early youth. In the 1740's, when Lemuel Briant preached against predestination on the grounds of morality he started a quarrel among his parishioners at Braintree and eventually lost his pulpit.[5] In this controversy young Adams was entirely on Briant's side. Having heard Whitefield, Tennent, and other preachers of the Great Awakening, he rejected them, and came to be very suspicious of all prophets, enthusiasts, and revivalists, in and out of the sphere of religion: "Awakenings and Revivals are not peculiar to Religion. Philosophy and Policy at times are capable of taking the Infection."[6]

In his youth Adams read deeply in the early English deists of the early part of the century and also in their latitudinarian and orthodox refuters. Repeatedly expressing his contempt for theological speculation, he was fascinated by it all his life. He could speak with standard Enlightened hostility not only of Catholicism—here his hatred was almost obsessive—but of Athanasius and Calvin, and of the most central doctrines of orthodox Christianity, including both the Trinity and the Incarnation:

> The Europeans . . . all believe that great principle, which has produced this boundless Universe, Newtons Universe, and Hershells universe, came down to this little Ball, to be spit-upon by Jews; and untill this awful blasphemy is got rid of, there never will be any liberal science in the world.[7]

Adams was, that is, an Arminian and a unitarian, theologically somewhat to the left of Chauncy, Mayhew, and his own High Federalist enemies like Pickering. But his abandonment of Pauline Christianity and original sin never carried him, as it carried some of his proper Bostonian contemporaries, into optimism about human nature or certainty about the nature of a liberal God. As deeply as any of his Calvinist ancestors, he believed in a God beyond human understanding:

> When we say God is Spirit, we know what we mean as well as we do when we say that the Pyramids of Egypt are Matter. Let us be content therefore to believe him to be a Spirit, that is, an Essence that we know nothing of, in which Originally and necessarily reside all energy, all Power, all Capacity, all Activity, all Wisdom, all Goodness.[8]

Adams considered himself a Christian and believed that revelation—pared and refined by the most strenuous criticism—was both valid and necessary. Working out this difficult and paradoxical faith all his life, he was often clearly tempted into the most complete Swiftian misanthropy. More typically, however, he managed to achieve a difficult combination of stoicism, skepticism, and hope. At times he sounded almost exactly like Franklin:

> It has been long, very long a settled opinion in my Mind that there is now, never will be, and never was but one being who can Understand

the Universe. And that it is not only vain but wicked for insects to pretend to comprehend it.[9]

Yet Adams's agnosticism was different from Franklin's, and different
also from that of Voltaire in *Candide*, less bland, richer, and more profound. Having abandoned the doctrines of the Calvinist, he retained
some of the Calvinist's paradoxical joy—at times expressing a love of
being in general as moving as that of Jonathan Edwards:

> The Love of God and his Creation; delight, Joy, Tryumph, Exultation
> in my own existence, tho but an Atom, a Molecule Organique, in the
> Universe; are my religion. Howl, Snarl, bite, Ye Calvinistick! Ye Atha-
> nasian Divines, if You will. Ye will say, I am no Christian: I say Ye are
> no Christians: and there the account is ballanced. Yet I believe all the
> honest men among you, are Christians in my Sense of the Word.[10]

Adams's mixture of doubt and confidence, joy and despair, were of
course related not only to his religious speculation but to his own psychological makeup, and doubtless this had many springs which went
deeper than religious or metaphysical theory.[11] Masochistic, suspicious,
constantly feeling that he was injured and that this made him somehow
superior to his enemies, he was as greedy for fame as his ancestors had
ever been for salvation, and as certain that it would be unjustly denied
him. Yet he was capable of great generosity, and seldom lost for long
that feeling for the incongruities of life that it seems trivial to call a
sense of humor—a quality Jefferson entirely lacked. Despite all his sufferings and resentments, one believes him when he says at the age of
seventy-seven

> . . . I am not weary of Living. Whatever a peevish Patriarch might say,
> I have never yet seen the day in which I could say I have had no Pleas-
> ure; or that I have had more Pain than Pleasure.[12]

Adams was through and through an Enlightened post-Calvinist skeptic—
in his daily life and politics, in his religion and philosophy, a man of
doubt and hope, of gusto and despair.

An agnostic Christian, Adams was a dogmatic political philosopher.
Always an omnivorous reader, he drew his political credo from the ancients, the writers of the Renaissance (especially Machiavelli), the seventeenth-century English controversialists and speculators (especially

Harrington), and those writers of his own time that agreed with him. His first article of belief was the mixed nature of man. He could quote with approval Pope's pithy couplets on this matter, but often sounded a little more gloomy than the standard spokesmen of complete balance. Post-Calvinist skepticism shows through frequently, for instance in his dismissal of democracy as a means of preventing tyranny:

> To expect self-denial from men, when they have a majority in their favor, and consequently power to gratify themselves, is to disbelieve all history and universal experience; it is to disbelieve Revelation and the Word of God, which informs us, the heart is deceitful above all things, and desperately wicked.

> My fundamental maxim of government is, never to trust the lamb to the custody of the wolf.[13]

His second political dictum was drawn from the first, and proved by citations from the standard classical and modern writers: that history must always be a cycle of rise and decline. The third item was the absolute necessity of virtue to republics. For this Montesquieu was the usual source, but Adams drew it also from the Commonwealth writers: Sidney, Trenchard and Gordon, Mrs. Macaulay, and Burgh, all of whom he greatly admired. Virtue was as fragile as it was essential, and luxury was its constant enemy. Finally, Adams like his contemporaries and predecessors in the Moderate Enlightenment deduced from all these beliefs his working principle: that the task of statecraft was to devise institutions which would check and balance man's greed and ambition, and delay if they could not prevent the inevitable decline. Adams assumed that because of a diversity in human talents there would always be rich and poor, though he was never an admirer of the wealthy. Thus balance involved the protection of each class against the other.

So sure was Adams of the importance and truth of this credo that he could sound rigid and dogmatic in its enunciation, and sometimes ignore, in its application, the skepticism and relativism he elsewhere admitted:

> I am so well satisfied of my own principles, that I think them as eternal and unchangeable as the earth and its inhabitants. I know mankind must finally adopt a balance between the executive and the legislative powers, and another balance between the poor and the rich in the legislature, and quarrel till they come to that conclusion.[14]

Almost always, Adams clung to these skeptical and balanced principles. He came nearest to abandoning them during the American Revolution, when he could sound exultant about the great opportunity for constructing sound institutions, and seem to forget, in his cheerful prophecies of the future, the inevitability of decline even here. America, after all, was in an early stage of the cycle, and clearly on the rise. The virtue of American society was such that decline might be long retarded. The wide distribution of property and education in America made proper a large element of democracy in the necessary mixture of forms of government. This was of course especially true in New England, the only society Adams deeply loved and understood. Yet in 1775 and 1776 and for a few years after, not only Adams's pessimism but his provincialism were shaken. To his surprise, he discovered some Virginians and Pennsylvanians of sound principles. In his most hopeful moments, however, Adams was never Utopian. He never really believed either in absolute equality or inevitable progress. In America as elsewhere, it was necessary to shun demagogues, foolish to abandon old institutions for those completely untried, and fatal to neglect mechanisms of balance. The unicameral, unbalanced Pennsylvania constitution of 1776 was a leading example of dangerous folly: Adams must have regretted, if he remembered, his own unintentional share in its adoption.[15]

In the 1780's, while Jefferson was absorbing with delight the ideas of the reformist *philosophes*, Adams was becoming prey to growing doubts and fears. Less adaptable than Franklin or even Jefferson, he was uncomfortable both in England and France, and all his beliefs in decline were confirmed by what he saw of luxury, poverty, and sexual immorality. Convinced that his own prospects for advancement were blocked and his diplomatic efforts unsupported, he became increasingly doubtful about the special virtues of America. Instead of revolutionary purity, he seemed to see increasing disaffection, class division, greed, luxury, and vice. The Constitution, though it was not quite correctly constructed, was basically sound in Adams's view, but he deplored an increasing tendency to bring forward new men, not tested in the austerities of revolutionary times.[16]

At the same time he became increasingly aware of the spread of new opinions, and the decline of belief in the solid principles of balance and order. Despite his own deep agnostic tendencies—or perhaps because of them—he detested and feared anti-religious skepticism. Though much impressed by Berkeley at an early age, he persisted always in venerating Locke, and regarded Hume as a cynical Tory. As for the French, Adams had always accepted the New England stereotypes of that backward, frivolous, luxurious nation. He read Voltaire with the usual mixture of admiration and disapproval. For the Encyclopedists and all dabblers in materialism he had a violent dislike. Some light remarks of d'Alembert about God's errors in making both the moral and material world drew one of Adams's most violent marginal outbursts:

> Thou Louse, Flea, Tick, Ant, Wasp, or whatever Vermin thou art, was this Stupendous Universe made and adjusted to give you Money, Sleep, or Digestion?[17]

At its best, the belief that all was unchanging matter in motion seemed to Adams old hat:

> All this, I think, is neither more nor less than the creed of Epicurus set to music by Lucretius.[18]

Rousseau Adams particularly disliked for his primitivism, his belief that property and distinction were artificial, and his unorthodox sexual views.

In politics Adams was disturbed by the French preference for centralization. Over this he was drawn into his celebrated argument with the centralizing reformers of the end of the *ancien régime*, Turgot, Rochefoucauld, and Condorcet. In his calmer moments he knew that these were all good men of excellent intentions. He was roused to polemical effort, however, when they presumed to criticize separation and division of powers in America, partly because this meant that they preferred the Pennsylvania Constitution, which they credited to Franklin, to Adams's own balanced Constitution of Massachusetts. Learned and honest as these authors were, Adams said, he would trust "the most ignorant of our honest town meeting orators to make a Constitution sooner than any or all of them."[19] Concentrating power in either a benevolent monarch or one assembly, would shortly produce tyranny and disaster.

Thus Adams was dubious about the promise of the French Revolution even before it happened. By 1790, he was writing to Richard Price about the same sermon that produced Burke's thunderous denunciation. In general, Adams said, he had devoted his life to the principles Price was enunciating.

The revolution in France could not therefore be indifferent to me; but I have learned by awful experience to rejoice with trembling. I know that encyclopedists and economists, Diderot and d'Alembert, Voltaire and Rousseau, have contributed to this great event more than Sidney, Locke, or Hoadley, perhaps more than the American revolution; and I own to you, I know not what to make of a republic of thirty million atheists.[20]

The centralized Constitution of 1791 confirmed his doubts, and from the time of the execution of the king until his own death, Adams became as implacable an enemy of the French Revolution as Morse and Dwight. He did not explain it as the result of a Masonic plot, like Dwight or Morse, and in his old age came to see it as the inevitable result of oppression. Most characteristically, however, he blamed the bloodshed of 1793 on the false doctrines of 1750:

Helvetius and Rousseau preached to the French Nation *Liberty*, till they made them the most mechanical Slaves; *equality* till they destroyed all Equity; *humanity* till they became Weasels, and African Panthers; and *Fraternity* till they cut one another's throats like Roman Gladiators.[21]

The English defenders of the Revolution, especially Mary Wollstonecraft, drew some of Adams's most detailed rebukes, but his real detestation was reserved for Paine, whom he had found superficial and misleading even in 1776. Always a sincere believer in reason, he deeply resented Paine's use of the word in the title of his own deist polemic:

Call it then the Age of Paine. He deserves it much more, than the Courtezan who was consecrated to represent the Goddess in the Temple at Paris, and whose name, Tom has given to the Age. The real intellectual faculty has nothing to do with the Age the Strumpet or Tom.[22]

Well before the crisis of 1798-90 Adams, who never ceased to believe in reason, free inquiry, and moderation, was pushed by changing times and his own perhaps archaic loyalties into a phase of reaction. His principal works, the *Defence of the Constitutions* and *Discourses on Davila*, belong to the period from 1787 to 1790, and show a steady movement toward the right.[23] Largely unreadable, in part accumulations of quotations, they contain much wit and sense in short bursts. Not only the doctrines of balance in general, but a particular set of balanced institutions is proclaimed as the indispensable for all times and places. The propertied classes, at first the special focus of Adams's fears, must be isolated in one house of the legislature, where they can exert their proper influence but will never be able to corrupt the commoners. One house must always be democratically elected. A strong executive, with long tenure and absolute veto, must arbitrate between the two. Courageously and unwisely, Adams made use of the words "monarch" and "aristocracy" in describing these institutions, and even suggested that eventually, and contrary to his hopes, increasing differences of wealth might make it necessary for America to make the executive or the upper house or both hereditary on the English model. Here Adams seems as out of touch with American realities of 1790 as Turgot or Condorcet had been with American realities—or he with French—a few years earlier. Inevitably, violent denunciation fell on Adams's head, a fate he took to be the penalty of wisdom in bad times. More accurately, it was the penalty of rigidity and literalness, and also of saying in public what others said only in private, in letters, or at little dinners in Boston or Philadelphia.

In 1796, with some misgivings, the Federalist chieftains adopted him as their champion. After a brief move toward rapprochement with Jefferson at the very beginning of his administration, President Adams was turned by French intransigence back toward an apparent alliance with the High Federalist and aristocratic element he had always deeply distrusted. In his answer to the fervent addresses from ardent young Federalists in 1798 he seemed to be taking on the role of a war president. He approved and selectively enforced the Alien and Sedition acts, apparently believing for the moment that French spies and partisans constituted a real danger.[24]

If Adams was close to jumping off the deep end, it was his own leap and not that for which the delighted High Federalists were preparing him. His independence, amounting to eccentricity and wrong-headedness, had got him into trouble when it had seemed that almost everybody else was bewitched by the Jacobins. Now the same qualities got him and the country out of great danger. His decision for peace with France may have been, as he thought, the greatest act of his life. Certainly it split and helped to doom his own party and led directly to the accession of his estranged friend. Quite rightly, some of the High Federalists believed that their former champion had always been hostile to

Great Britain, well disposed to revolution in general if not in particular, and above all soft on Jefferson.[25]

After their reconciliation, Adams assured Jefferson that nothing had really separated them but their different reactions to the French Revolution. For once, Adams was too simple here. The two men had much in common, including the saving grace of generosity that made the reconciliation possible. Yet there were also deep differences both of temperament and of principle between these two great specimens of the American Enlightenment, and these differences reflect the schisms and divisions in the Enlightenment itself.

On the surface, Thomas Jefferson seems all sunlight and clarity, the superb aristocrat who trusted the people, the American Condorcet, the perfect example of the early and non-violent period of the Revolutionary Enlightenment, transferred from Europe to America with new reasons for its boundless hopes. We know that Jefferson believed that in America, and later in Europe, an age was coming when government could be carried on by morality and not by force. We remember his confidence in progressive change, so strong that it once led him to say that all constitutions and other institutions should be changed every nineteen years, the approximate life of a dominant generation. Above all, we remember his ringing statements in favor of unalienable rights, especially the right of free speech. As he hoped they would be, the most familiar phrases are those of the Declaration and the Statute of Religious Freedom; we know that Jefferson declared his eternal hostility against every form of tyranny over the mind of man. The phrases are not hollow; the great libertarian is real. But those who have tried to get far beneath this glowing surface have found themselves in a difficult tangle of contradictions and complexities.[26]

Part of the difficulty in interpreting Jefferson has been created by his admirers in all periods. More important to the American secular religion than any other man but Lincoln, he has been moved out of the eighteenth century and forced into conformity with the needs of Jacksonian Democracy, Wilsonian progressivism, the New Deal—even those of popular-front Communism and anti-New Deal free enterprise. But the difficulty of interpretation comes not only from distortion, but also from the divided and extremely reticent nature of the man himself, and from the deep contradictions in his own mind and life.

The most obvious and familiar of the contradictions lie in Jefferson's political principles and are reflected in his political career. Like other spokesmen of the Revolutionary Enlightenment, he stood at once for unalienable natural rights and for progressive change. Devoted to science and the progress of the human mind, Jefferson never completely came to terms with the Commonwealth preference for the world of the simple Roman farmers or the sturdy Anglo-Saxons. His agrarianism could lead him to extreme statements, that cities are sores on the body politic, that the yellow fever may have its beneficent side insofar as it prevents urbanization.[27] America's workshops are to be kept in Europe, though this would seem to make permanent the power of Britain, a country Jefferson always deeply distrusted.

Most of all, Jefferson's view of democracy is difficult for a modern reader fully to understand. There is no question that he counted himself among those who trust the people, or that he believed the majority a safer reliance than the minority. Yet he seems to have been full of fear that the people might be at least temporarily misled by monocrats and aristocrats. Their government was to have as little power as possible to do evil. Moreover, Jefferson never doubted that the actual work of government should be carried on by the natural aristocrats, chosen freely by their fellows. His proposed educational system for Virginia demonstrates this most clearly. It is designed to make the people safe repositories of power by giving all an elementary education, but only the "best geniuses" are to be "raked from the rubbish" and given the liberal training needed by Enlightened leaders.[28]

Heartily, sometimes even violently in favor of revolutions in general, Jefferson took a moderate position in all but one of the particular revolutions in which he took part—and that one was itself a moderate revolution. By 1774 he had reached an advanced position in favor of American independence, and from this he never drew back. The story is different in the Virginia revolution. Jefferson was very proud of this systematic effort to make over his beloved "country" in the image of Enlightenment. Recently, historians have concluded that he changed little. Entail and primogeniture, the institutions designed to preserve landholding aristocracy, were abolished and religion made free. But for tactical reasons Jefferson abandoned his plan for a systematic revision of the laws. His educational system was never seriously attempted. And above all, he drew back from his program for ending slavery, concluding that the public mind was not ready for it.

In France, Jefferson played a remarkably cautious role as visiting expert on revolutions. When he left Europe in 1789 all seemed to be going exactly as he had hoped. Through the heroism of the Revolutionary leaders, the generosity of the aristocrats who had renounced their privileges, and the generosity of the best of princes, France had become a constitutional monarchy, a stage of political development that exactly suited the needs of her people. As the Revolution came under attack from British monarchists and—as he saw it—their partisans in America, Jefferson became far more radical in his view of European affairs. The French Republic was the hope of the world, and in defense of it the execution of the king and the Jacobin seizure of power were justified. At the beginning of 1793 he made his most radical statement, justifying the Terror:

> In the struggle which was necessary, many guilty persons fell without the forms of trial, and with them some innocent. These I deplore as much as any body, & shall deplore some of them to the day of my death. But I deplore them as I should have done had they fallen in battle. It was necessary to use the arm of the people, a machine not quite so blind as balls and bombs, but blind to a certain degree. . . . The liberty of the whole earth was depending on the outcome of the contest, and was ever such a prize won with so little innocent blood? My own affections have been deeply wounded by some of the martyrs to this cause, but rather than it should have failed, I would have seen half the earth desolated. Were there but an Adam & Eve left in every country, & left free, it would be better than as it now is.[29]

Despite these emotions, Jefferson as Secretary of State supported Washington's policy of neutrality as in the national interest and condemned the hot-headed actions of the French minister. While he never abandoned his support of the French Republic until the French Republic no longer existed, he began by the middle of 1793 to admit the importance of the errors that had been made. He seems like most of his countrymen to have welcomed the fall of Robespierre in 1795, and he cordially approved the policies of the Directorate.[30]

Most of all, Jefferson astonished both his friends and his enemies by the moderation of his own "Revolution of 1800," which left undisturbed institutions he had denounced and made most of its changes by cutting back governmental activity and allowing a beneficent nature to take its course.

Despite the moderation of his program, however, Jefferson proved to have both the will and the skill needed for the use of power. Few have more effectively used and expanded the subtle but limited powers of the presidency, that almost impossible office which changes all its incumbents. Few presidents, perhaps none until that other scholar and idealist Woodrow Wilson in his first term, have dealt more adroitly or more commandingly with Congress. And for the supreme necessities of national interest, including territorial expansion, nearly all Jeffersonian shibboleths could be put aside: states' rights, agrarianism, and the dislike of executive government. An acute recent student has strikingly characterized Jefferson's presidential style:

> However conventionally enlightened his political theory, . . . in his direct, tactical involvement with public affairs, he was an unconventional, as imaginative, resourceful, and tough as the best, or worst, of Old World politicians, and more adroit than most.[31]

One might add, far more adroit than John Adams. Jefferson himself, not long after taking office, explained to a philosophic friend: "What is practicable must often control what is pure theory; and the habits of the governed determine in a great degree what is practicable."[32]

Toughness and the stretching of presidential power have, at the moment I write, been discredited by a group of third-rate practitioners, and also, for many, by powerful reinterpretations of twentieth-century history. Yet few students of the past will altogether regret that Jefferson in power, confronting Pitt and Bonaparte and a bitter, irreconcilable domestic opposition, showed some of the toughness of—for instance— Franklin Roosevelt. Some critics on the left, at the time and later, have deplored his moderation in the use of his great political power. On the other hand his conservative opponents, once he showed his mettle, were forced to abandon their image of the impractical dreamer and try to substitute another, of a ruthless operator. Actually, one suspects that what they resented most was the combination of idealism and practicality that, in the first administration at least, seemed to work so well.

If one is to understand the man and his ideas, one must go beyond his toughness and practicality. In any close look at his career one is confronted by a trait that is both baffling and disturbing—a trait hard to describe, that lies somewhere between secretiveness and duplicity. It is surprising how consistently Jefferson tried to cover his tracks in important actions, especially political actions. Sometimes these efforts were successful, as in the case of the Kentucky Resolutions of 1798, whose authorship did not become known until 1821. In other cases, Jefferson got into bad trouble through his habit of making private statements that he could not defend in public. This is what happened in 1791, when in praising Paine's *Rights of Man* he attacked the "political heresies which have sprung up among us," and then denied that he had had his friend John Adams in mind. Much the same thing happened again in 1795 in the famous Mazzei letter, when he lamented the "apostates" who had gone over to British heresies, "men who were Samson in the field & Solomons in the council, but have had their heads shorn by the harlot England." In this case Jefferson denied that he had referred to Washington. The denials were full of embarrassment in both these cases, and they did not thoroughly convince either contemporaries or historians. It is not easy for the most devoted and painstaking biographer to explain the murky depths of Jefferson's relation with the worst of the journalistic prostitutes of the day, James Callender, who used Jefferson's secret money payments as the basis of something like attempted blackmail.[33] One cannot help being surprised to find the great spokesman of free speech suggesting in a very private letter, that the extremism of the Federalist press might be moderated by "a few prosecutions of the most prominent offenders. . . . Not a general prosecution, for that would look like persecution; but a selected one."[34]

What is disturbing is not that Jefferson like other great men had his faults and inconsistencies, but that it is so hard to square the particular faults he had with his greatest virtues: his love of freedom and his high sense of honor. Part of the explanation lies in his adherence to the glowing hopes of the Revolutionary Enlightenment. The great Revolution in France, involving the liberation of the whole world, for a time justified the bloodshed it brought about. Far more deeply and consistently, Jefferson believed in the revolutionary future of the New World. Ahead lay a great era of peace, justice, and freedom, in which almost all Americans outside Connecticut and Massachusetts would dwell together in fraternal harmony. In time, Europe would imitate the American example more successfully, and probably more slowly, than the mistakes of the French Revolution suggested. With this great ideal so close to realization, it was necessary to deal with saboteurs and obstructionists in ways that were sometimes distasteful. Jefferson, after all, went much less far in acting on this dangerous principle than most sincere believers in revolution. We can believe that he did what he thought the times required. We can wish that he had shown a little more charity toward some opponents, and a little more willingness to admit to himself and others what he was doing. Finally, we can easily believe that his dislike for the political arts he practiced so successfully was genuine, that in the Federal City he longed constantly for his books and his serene hilltop. This distaste in itself no doubt acted as a sort of restraint; it is not felt by most successful politicians.

All Jefferson's inconsistencies cannot be explained by his lofty hopes. Contradictions run through his ideas as well as his actions. This fact is particularly poignant in view of the utter distaste which Jefferson, like most men of the Enlightenment, felt for everything that smacked of mystery or paradox. In part, the contradictions in Jefferson's ideas can be explained by their origins in two contrasting environments. Most of them were formed either in the colonial Virginia of his youth or in the France of the *philosophes,* to be more exact in Paris at the very end of the *ancien régime.* He is very explicit about the authors he admired most, and his vast reading has been thoroughly explored.[35]

If we knew of Thomas Jefferson only from pre-Revolutionary sources, we would find him a highly intelligent and well-read young Virginian, not very different in his basic intellectual allegiances from others of his kind. He had of course been taught the classics, and unlike most of his Virginian contemporaries, was to read in them deeply if selectively all his life. He delighted in Homer, and was adept in the intricacies of Greek grammar. His principal admirations, however, were reserved for the sternly moralist Roman historians: Livy, Tacitus, and Sallust. Like most of his educated contemporaries, he admired Cicero and Seneca. In moral philosophy he followed the Stoics and, with more conviction, a very disciplined and somewhat ascetic version of the doctrines of Epicurus. One finds very little of the seductive, fleshly, and amoral side of the Roman poets, and none of their frivolity, in Jefferson's tastes. His reading was serious from the beginning.

Jefferson repeatedly declared his allegiance to an Enlightened trinity:

Bacon, Newton, and Locke. Of these the central figure was clearly Locke, from whom Jefferson derived not only some of his political theory but all the beginnings of his theory of knowledge. All his life he insisted that we must not travel far from the sensations or we get into the swamps of metaphysics. Rather earlier than most Americans, Jefferson complemented his sensationalism with the doctrine of the unfailing moral sense, implanted by their creator in ploughboy and professor alike, but capable of being developed by discipline or enfeebled by luxury. He learned this article of faith from Shaftesbury, Hutcheson, and especially Lord Kames, who was his lifelong guide in such diverse fields as law and aesthetics. Like almost all his Revolutionary contemporaries, Jefferson was strongly affected by the Commonwealth tradition of Sidney, Milton, and Trenchard and Gordon. Detesting Puritan theology, he accepted much of Puritan political theory. He believed very literally in the purity of Anglo-Saxon civilization, destroyed by the corrupt and tyrannical Normans.

While practicing the easygoing Anglicanism of the Virginia establishment and serving his turn on the vestry like others of his station, Jefferson read the deists and some of their Anglican critics and sided firmly with the former. Curiously, the deist he most intensely admired and most frequently copied in his commonplace book was that dissolute Tory and arch-aristocrat, Lord Bolingbroke. Two aspects of Bolingbroke appealed to the young Virginian: in politics his belief that the country gentleman was superior to the men of the city and the court, and in religion his insistence on subjecting revelation to the test of reason. Like Bolingbroke, Jefferson all his life detested Calvin and "Austin" (St. Augustine), Plato and all "Platonizers," but unlike Bolingbroke he was to take seriously the quest for the pure doctrines of Jesus that these theologians and mystics had obscured. Jefferson sometimes considered himself a unitarian rather than a deist, and admired first Richard Price and then Joseph Priestley, both of whom clung to far more of Christianity than he did.

This is a fairly unsurprising set of admirations for a liberal and bookish young American of the Revolutionary generation. With this intellectual baggage, Jefferson journeyed to France. There he was confronted with the brilliance, variety, and daring of the French Enlightenment, poised on the sharp edge between the old skepticism and the new Revolutionary enthusiasm. Dabbling only a little in the former, Jefferson unhesitatingly gave himself to the latter, making his own selections from both.

Never anything of a skeptic at bottom, Jefferson had little interest in Voltaire and roundly detested Hume as a Tory. He was not attracted by Rousseau. He devoted a great deal of energy to his arguments with Buffon and Raynal about the alleged inferiority of New World animals and man. He was excited by the experiments of Cabanis, who was trying to locate the various mental faculties in particular parts of the brain. Rejoicing in this behaviorist enterprise as a blow to his old enemies the "spiritualists," he yet preferred the strange theistic materialism drawn by Priestley from one of Locke's most beguiling *obiter dicta*, the suggestion that the deity could if he pleased endow matter with the power to think.

Jefferson's closest connections among the French thinkers, however, were with the idealistic radicals who looked forward to a new dawn of justice and equality. He maintained friendly relations with the two abbés, Mably and Morellet , though he did not adopt their sweeping proposals for social reform. He formed deeper and more lasting friendships with the most Utopian and aristocratic of the Enlightened radicals, the Marquis de Condorcet and Comte de Volney.

In Paris, Jefferson discovered two new thinkers who seemed to him to have solved the central problem of Enlightened philosophy, the problem of the reliability of the information given us by our senses and our mental faculties. Many years later he was to do his best to convince John Adams that Destutt de Tracy and Dugald Stewart were "the ablest metaphysicians living; by which I mean investigators of the thinking faculty of man."[36] Few have agreed with Jefferson here, but both men were competent and both were reassuring. Tracy tried to demonstrate the reliability of our ideas through a complex but entirely naturalistic system of classification and analysis, in which psychology is annexed to zoology. Stewart, a polished but not very original disciple of Thomas Reid, continued Reid's tactic of appealing to the common sense of mankind as the principal support for the truths most men accept.

Jefferson built his working religion and working philosophy on these complex foundations, of which the main pillars were Locke, Stewart, Tracy, and Priestley. These purposeful and practical thinkers come back again and again in his lifelong correspondence with philosophic friends;

a host of others come and go. A naturally reverent and even pious man, Jefferson studied religion and moral philosophy, as he studied everything else, for a purpose, and primarily a moral purpose. His precepts for individuals and his programs for society had the same basis, and for both a cosmos that made sense for man was utterly necessary. Yet Jefferson, a child of the Enlightenment if there ever was one, had to base his belief on some sort of rational proof. The very definition of belief was "the assent of the mind to an intelligible proposition."[37] The leap of faith, the resignation of the agnostic were not for him.

And yet Jefferson's universe was as purposeful as that of Timothy Dwight, and presupposed as completely the existence of a ruler and creator. The world was intelligently planned, benevolently intended, and understandable to man. Such a creed leaves no place for mystery, or even for mess. As a scientist Jefferson was in the habit of proving that things must be true because their contrary would reflect on the beneficence of the Creator. A belief in rewards and punishments after death was valid because it was salutary.

From an early age Jefferson rejected most of orthodox Christianity. He was, however, very conciliatory about this matter and also extremely reticent; in almost all his discussions of religion with his friends he asks for confidentiality. This was not alone a matter of prudence; he sincerely believed that religion should be a private matter. He was, therefore, deeply hurt and bitterly angry when the orthodox attacked him in 1800. When his assailants denied that Jefferson was a Christian, Jefferson insisted that he was; and it was this that launched him into his serious investigation of what Christianity meant.

What it meant, Jefferson like many of his Enlightened contemporaries concluded, was the pure and noble teachings of Jesus. One must strip away all the work of theologians and Platonizers beginning with Paul, and then one must isolate in the Gospels those portions which are clearly the work of Jesus himself. Jefferson had no doubt at all that this was an easy task: the words of Jesus show the marks of a superior, even a sublime mind; they stand out from later interpolations like "diamonds from dunghills."[38] Most of what survives in Jefferson's Jesus is his moral teachings, which went beyond the ancient philosophers in placing our duty to others alongside our duty to ourselves. Jesus' mission was to correct the distorted deism of the Jews; he made no claim to divinity. The sublimity of his teachings lies in their simplicity: they are within the comprehension of a child.[39] For the priests who, from Jesus' day to our own, had distorted these teachings of simple benevolence, Jefferson had as deep a hatred and contempt as Elihu Palmer or any other deist pamphleteer:

> They crucified their Savior, who preached that their kingdom was not of this world; and all who practice on that precept must expect the extreme of their wrath. The laws of the present day withhold their hands from blood; but lies and slander still remain to them.[40]

The faculty which enables us to tell truth from falsehood in the realm of morality is reliable because the creator made it so. In 1787 Jefferson explained this to his nephew:

> I think it is lost time to attend lectures on moral philosophy. He who made us would have been a pitiful bungler, if He had made the rules of our moral conduct a matter of science. For one man of science, there are thousands who are not. What would have become of them? . . . The moral sense, or conscience, is as much a part of man as his leg or arm. . . . This sense is submitted, indeed, in some degree, to the guidance of reason; but it is a small stock which is required for this; even a less one than what we call common sense. State a moral case to a plowman and a professor. The former will decide it as well and often better than the latter because he has not been led astray by artificial rules.

This view Jefferson never gave up, and indeed could not give up. In 1815 he states it more succinctly:

> The moral sense is as much a part of our constitution as that of feeling, seeing, or hearing; as a wise creator must have seen to be necessary in an animal destined to live in society; that every human mind feels pleasure in doing good to another.[41]

These articles of faith had to coexist with Jefferson's theistic materialism and also with his frequently stated relativism; his belief that principles change with times and manners. Moreover, he had no way of explaining any errors or contradictions in the work of the benevolent creator, no way of accounting for the evident failures of the human moral sense. For the problem of evil, cosmic or human, the Jeffersonian faith has no answers. It is for this reason, I believe, that Jefferson frequently and vehemently abjured metaphysical speculation. When he does this,

his agnostic conclusions have something in common with those of Franklin or Adams, but the tone in which they are expressed is very different.

By temperament Jefferson was a man of faith. He could not indulge either in Franklin's ironical resignation or Adams's intellectual playfulness. In 1801 he answered a friendly cleric who had asked his opinion about the destiny of the soul:

> When I was young I was fond of the speculations which seemed to promise some insight into that hidden country, but observing at length that they left me in the same ignorance in which they had found me, I have for very many years ceased to read or to think concerning them, and have reposed my head on that pillow of ignorance which a benevolent Creator has made so soft for us, knowing how much we should be forced to use it. I have thought it better, by nourishing the good passions & controlling the bad, to merit an inheritance in a state of being of which I can know so little, and to trust for the future to him who has been so good for the past.[42]

I doubt, however, that the pillow of ignorance—he uses this figure more than once—was always soft for Jefferson. In his old age, when Adams demonstrates, with obvious enjoyment, that it is difficult to prove the existence of either matter or spirit, Jefferson replies in a revealing manner: ". . . let me turn to your puzzling letter of May 12. On matter, spirit, motion, etc. It's croud of scepticisms kept me from sleep."[43] Jefferson ends this letter with the familiar assertion that all the senses, aided by reason, cannot be wrong. But one wonders whether his strenuous efforts to dispel all doubts were really successful.

At a deeper level than his somewhat bookish allegiances in religion and philosophy lie the contradictions of Jefferson's taste, embodied in his lifelong style of living. Nothing is more consistent than his disciplined and sometimes ascetic preference for that which is useful as against that which is only pleasant and ornamental. Yet this preference caused him many agonies. Far more than any other major figure of the American Enlightenment, Jefferson was a man of acute aesthetic sensibilities. According to his Virginian contemporary Peyton Randolph, in his youth Jefferson:

> panted after the fine arts, and discovered a taste in them, not easily satisfied with such scanty means, as existed in a colony, ...[44]

In the 1780's two visiting European noblemen, both cultivated in the arts and liberal in politics, recognized in Jefferson a completely kindred spirit. The Duc de Rochefoucauld-Liancourt thought Monticello—as yet far from satisfactory to Jefferson—equal to the most pleasant mansions in France and England. The Marquis de Chastellux felt a deep and instantaneous agreement of opinions, sympathies, and tastes with Jefferson, was astounded at the breadth of his knowledge, and thought he understood the reasons for Jefferson's retirement from the world:

> the minds of his countrymen are not yet in a condition either to bear the light or suffer contradiction.[45]

In 1785 Jefferson first encountered not only the ideas of the French Enlightenment but, quite as important, the glories of European art. His tastes, indeed, were not quite catholic. He never cared a great deal for belles-lettres, considering novels unwholesome and rhymed poetry a waste of time. His own poems were failures, and he regarded himself as deficient in imagination. On the other hand, he always delighted in music, and the musical life of Paris almost made him reluctant to go home. Americans, he once suggested, since they could hardly afford to employ full orchestras, might find Europeans trained in the various instruments who could double as gardeners, weavers, and other kinds of useful craftsmen.[46]

Exactly like any young English nobleman making the Grand Tour, Jefferson assiduously collected on the Continent the most approved French statues and Italian pictures to adorn his mansion at home. But his strongest passions were reserved for architecture, the art in which he was to become a most impressive practitioner. Jefferson did not, like later American pilgrims, have any interest at all in cathedrals—he abominated the Gothic style, and disliked the Baroque almost as much. For the Georgian buildings among which he had grown up in Virginia he had nothing but contempt. His tastes in all the arts were severely neoclassical. He loved the paintings of David, the statues of Houdon, and above all classical and the best neoclassical architecture. There are few passages in Jefferson's writing as emotional as his familiar description of his pilgrimage to the Maison Carrée, the excellently preserved Roman temple at Nîmes: "Here I am, Madam, gazing whole hours at the Maison Quarree, like a lover at his mistress."[47]

Yet this American traveler, as moved by the perfections of Europe as any later American aesthete or expatriate, finally and conclusively re-jected the seductions of Europe. No marvels of music or architecture, no perfection of wine or manners, could make up for immorality and misery: the aristocratic past must be rejected for the republican future:

> If all the sovereigns of Europe were to set themeslves to work to eman-cipate the minds of their subjects from their present ignorance and prejudices, and that as zealously as they now endeavor the contrary, a thousand years would not place them on that high ground on which our common people are now setting out. . . . If any body thinks that kings, nobles or priests are good conservators of the public happiness, send them here. It is the best school in the universe to cure them of that folly. They will see here with their own eyes that these descriptions of men are an abandoned confederacy against the happiness of the mass of people. The omnipotence of their effect cannot be better proved than in this country particularly, where not withstanding the finest soil upon earth, the finest climate under heaven, and a people of the most benevo-lent, the most gay, and amiable character of which the human form is susceptible, where such a people I say, surrounded by so many blessings from nature, are yet loaded with misery by kings, nobles, and priests, and by them alone.[48]

The vehemence of these repudiations of French *douceur de vivre* and European culture in general may suggest something of the emotional struggle out of which they came. Franklin in Paris was able to adapt him-self with immense skill and gusto; Adams reacted as a grumpy and disapproving Puritan; here as in everything Jefferson had to fight a severe battle with himself.

Nor did the battle end when Jefferson returned to the pure and frugal republic. For the rest of his life he was an ardent missionary for neo-classical architecture, building Palladian houses in Virginia, designing the University of Virginia as a museum of correct styles, and insisting that the public buildings of the republic be modeled only on the four or five most correct edifices in Paris.

What is most surprising is that Jefferson himself, for the rest of his life, made a strenuous and sometimes ruinous effort to live in America the life of an Enlightened European aristocrat. Eighty boxes of books and furniture were shipped from Le Havre in 1789. Jefferson's republi-can style of life as President—the famous waistcoat and carpet slippers, the insistent ignoring of the diplomatic conventions of precedence—all this is unimportant and somewhat didactic. What is more consistent and revealing is the great effort made to import and retain a French maître d'hôtel, the careful and very large orders for wines, the elaborate and excellent food. Above all, Jefferson sacrificed a great deal of the tranquility he prized in his effort to achieve perfection in his Palladian mansion at Monticello, constantly tearing down and rebuilding, constantly running hopelessly into debt, and even repeatedly mortgaging large numbers of slaves.[49]

This last fact brings us of course, to the hardest paradox of all. It says a lot about American iconography that until very recently historians almost ignored the fact that Jefferson's way of life depended completely on the labors of about two hundred slaves.[50] His Federalist opponents never forgot this basic fact, nor did Jefferson himself. Hating slavery and hoping, even sometimes planning, for its ultimate extinction, he had none of the cynical toughness of some of his contemporaries, nor did he make any effort in the newer nineteenth-century style to persuade himself that the institution was really benign. Tentatively and almost apologetically, he advanced in the *Notes on Virginia* the hypothesis that the Negro was different and in some ways inferior—an argument as yet uncommon among Virginian whites. With regard to this problem and this alone he admitted, very occasionally, not only the existence of tragic and unresolved paradoxes but even the possibility of divine judgment:

> What a stupendous, what an incomprehensible machine is man! Who can endure toil, famine, stripes, imprisonment or death itself in vindication of its own liberty, and the next moment be deaf to all those motives whose power supported him thro' his trial, and inflict on his fellow men a bondage, one hour of which is fraught with more misery than ages of that which he rose in rebellion to oppose.

> Indeed I tremble for my country when I reflect that God is just: That his justice cannot sleep for ever: that considering numbers, nature, and natural means only, a revolution of the wheel of fortune, an exchange of situation, is among possible events; that it may become probable by supernatural interference! The Almighty has no attribute which can take sides with us in such a contest.[51]

In his daily life, Jefferson does not seem to have been much affected by these dark forebodings. Like his fellows, he tried to run a plantation for profit (in his case without success). He was, as many Southern tombstones say of others, "a kind and affectionate master." He tried to keep families together, but both bought and sold slaves on occasion and could talk of breeding in terms of profit. He tried to catch runaways, respected insurrectionists but knew that severity was necessary, and worried about the spread of anti-slavery ideas among the blacks by immigrants from Santo Domingo. Like many of his contemporaries, he tended as he got older to forget his expectations of emancipation.

Recent writers have resurrected the story, long dismissed as a Federalist *canard*, of a liaison with the slave Sally Hemings.[52] The evidence is impossible to dismiss, yet certainty is impossible. There are only two possibilities. Either Jefferson, a serious and somewhat puritannical man with a deep distrust of passion carried on this relation through a long period, either concealing it from his daughters or allowing them to conceal it from themselves. Or else Sally's white-skinned children were the children of another member of the Monticello family, probably Jefferson's favorite nephew Peter Carr. Either of these hypotheses means that Jefferson lived in constant contact with practices he disapproved of to the depths of his being. Either gives resonance to his comment on the effect of slavery on the slaveowners: "The man must be a prodigy who can retain his manners and morals undepraved by such circumstances."[53]

It is clear that Jefferson, by temperament a deeply reserved and private man, led a far more controlled and ascetic sex life than most of his Virginian contemporaries. The most his recent biographers can bring to light outside his ten-year marriage is three brief affairs, only one of them clearly passionate. Nowhere does he even begin to indulge the usual eighteenth-century fashion for genial ribaldry in the manner of Franklin or even Adams; on sexual relations even more than on other subjects he is always severely reticent and moralistic.

Perhaps the most striking quality of his personal life is its devastating sadness. He was almost paralyzed by the loss of his wife. After this he deluged his two daughters with possessive and demanding affection, giving detailed advice on everything from their lessons to their marriages, and striving to keep them and their husbands physically close to him. In 1804 he lost the younger of them, once more suffering atrociously and only very rarely letting his sufferings appear.[54]

On the surface Jefferson's home life, particularly in the long years of retirement, was one of exemplary calm. He is the very pattern of an Enlightened gentleman, cultivating his garden, planting his fruit-trees by the hundred, reading the classics, playing the violin, and meditating about the universe. It is quite clear that this serenity was maintained only by constant and even heroic effort.

The same conclusion emerges from the study of Jefferson's ideas of religion and politics. A benign God, a purposeful universe, and a universal moral sense are absolutely necessary at all points to Jefferson's political system. If one assumes all these, revolutions are worthwhile yet need not go too far. Freed from the grip of aristocratic or monarchical conspiracies, the people will make the right choices and their enlightened leaders can guide them in complexities. Virtue and reason will eventually triumph even over the corruptions of cities, even, somehow, over the terrible paradoxes of race and slavery. To doubt this means to doubt the beneficence, even the consistency of the universe. Inconsistency, to men of the Revolutionary Enlightenment, was something like sin. Jefferson could not tolerate it for long, either in the universe or in himself.

The close and bitterly contested election of 1800 was not decided by ideology alone, but rather, like most American elections, by a complicated mixture of ideas, tactics, organizations, and local and regional interests—by election maneuvers in New York and Pennsylvania, changes of mind in South Carolina, and above all by divisions within the Federalist Party. Nevertheless, the campaign and its outcome were milestones in the history of the Enlightenment. The Revolutionary Enlightenment was almost driven underground by the Federalist and clerical crusade. The Moderate Enlightenment in turn was damaged by the defeat of the Federalists, by the narrowing of their base, and by the violence of their tactics. Moreover, both candidates were highly individual and neither quite belonged in any ideological or political camp. Adams had too much temperamental skepticism to be quite comfortable with doctrinaire Federalists, and Jefferson too much moderation and too many inner divisions to be comfortable with doctrinaire Republicans. Thus Adams repudiated his right wing by making peace with France, and Jefferson repudiated his left wing by the moderation of his program.

Much of the Revolutionary Enlightenment, often passionately espoused by Jefferson in private, was renounced in his extraordinarily conciliatory inaugural address. The French Revolution, on which so recently the liberty of the whole world had seemed to depend, was almost deplored. Appealing for an end to political intolerance, Jefferson blamed its rise on European contagion:

> During the throes and convulsions of the ancient world, during the agonizing spasms of infuriated man, seeking through blood and slaughter his long-lost liberty, it was not wonderful that the agitations of the billows should reach even this distant and peaceful shore; that this should be more felt and feared by some and less by others; that this should divide opinions as to measures of safety.

Election by the people was praised as a preventive of revolution, and the American government, not the French, was eloquently hailed as the world's best hope, partly because it was "Kindly separated by nature and a wide ocean from the exterminating havoc of one quarter of the globe."

Jefferson cut out of the draft of his address a wounding reference to "the whigs and tories of nature"[55] and assured his astonished audience that we were all both republicans and federalists. He went out of his way to praise the achievements of the nation under the former regime. Instead of being on the brink of tyranny, the republic had been blessed with a government "which has so far kept us free and firm," and was even "in the full tide of successful experiment." All Americans, said the new President, practiced a benign religion, though in different forms, and adored the same overruling Providence. All that was needed was a minimum program of wise and frugal government, which would leave people alone, provide for the payment of the public debt, and encourage both agriculture and "commerce as its handmaid."

Of course no conciliatory words from the great infidel could calm the fears of some of Jefferson's orthodox enemies. Jedidiah Morse in April 1800 wrote a letter to Charles Nisbet which followed exactly the ancient pattern of the jeremiad.[56] For our many sins, said Morse, God seemed to have abandoned us to the fate of Holland and Switzerland. No human means could prevent at least a temporary "Jacobin" rule. The leaders of the American Jacobins:

> appear to be deeply learned in the schools of France and are skilled in the practice of all their acts. By their flattery of the people their artful

lies insinuations, by blackening the characters of good men & misrepre-
senting the measures of Government they have infatuated many good
people & drawn them in to aid their detestable designs. These things in
connexion with the wonderful increase of licentious principles & conduct in many parts of our country have I confess almost extinguished
my hopes of better times. . . .

And yet in the manner of his forefathers Morse was sustained by faith
in the eventual justice and mercy of Providence. Sources of hope amid
many grounds of despair included the colleges which:

were never more flowering nor better taught & governed—& their influence is warmly in favor of the measures of administration & of the Christian religion. . . .

A "goodly number of the Clergy (in Connecticut nearly all)" were ad-
hering to the doctrines of Grace abandoned by so many, and most ministers were also friends of government. Moreover, Morse saw a new
ground for hope:

. . . remarkable revivals of religion have taken place in many parts of
our country, & the good work is increasing. . . .

The ways of Providence, or the ironies of history, were even stranger
than Morse knew. Not only did the election of Jefferson coincide with
the greatest evangelical outburst in American history, but the revival was
about to strike hardest in those parts of the country which had voted
most solidly for Jefferson's election—in the South and West and especially in Republican Kentucky. Both Jefferson and Adams understood
the reasons for this better than Morse. Jefferson, indeed, not only kept
his religious views quiet but consciously courted the approval of the
Baptists and Methodists, who detested quite as much as he did the heavy
hand of the New England establishment. Isaac Backus, the great leader
of New England Baptists, saw both Jefferson's election and the Great
Revival as harbingers of the millennium.[57]

Together, the very moderate Revolution of 1800 and the by no means
moderate Revival of 1800 did a great deal to differentiate America from
Europe and thus to cut off the country from the European Enlighten-
ment. The new era brought in neither Jacobin terror nor enlightened
Utopia, but something quite different from both: nineteenth-century
America.

IV

The Didactic Enlightenment,

1800-1815

One   *The Decline of the Enlightenment*

In the first fifteen years of the nineteenth century, Americans were conscious that they were living in a new period, but the nature of this period was not yet clear. All the forces of change which were to produce nineteenth-century culture were gathering strength, but their effects were as yet unmanifest.[1] The population was growing, perhaps even faster than before and after, largely from natural increase. Immigrants, held back by European war, were arriving in smaller numbers than before the Revolution. The movement westward was under way, with some migrants moving into western New York and Pennsylvania, and others venturing farther—over the mountains into flourishing Kentucky and Tennessee, or into the little towns scattered along the Ohio. Both New England and Virginia knew that they were losing people and power. Yet Indians, with the help of the British and Spanish, still prevented the westward trickle from becoming a torrent: in 1810 the new West had only 13.3 percent of the population.

At least nine-tenths of the people everywhere were farmers. The handsome little cities were growing only slowly. Manufacturing was still on a very small scale, though embargo and war were to give it a decisive push. The economy of the nation was still colonial. The prosperity of the period depended on burgeoning foreign trade, in which American raw materials were still traded for European manufactures. The prestigious merchants and ever-anxious planters still lived as nearly as they could in the style of the European upper classes. Ministers, doctors, and lawyers still expected a certain deference, and complained more frequently than ever that they did not get it.

Two great historians, both masters of irony, have relentlessly underlined the contrasts between promise and performance in matters of high culture.[2] Exuberant Jeffersonians constantly proclaimed the dawn of a new enlightened age, in which republican science, art, and literature would far outstrip the performance of the decadent and exhausted European world. Yet this was in Europe the day of Goethe and Shelley, of Beethoven and Kant, of Turner and Goya, of Cuvier and Lamarck.

In America, no Franklin or even Rittenhouse was anywhere in sight. Patrician support for science was failing, and no new sources of money and organization appeared. In Philadelphia, no longer the capital, the American Philosophical Society was becoming less cosmopolitan and less confident. Its kind of science was coming increasingly under attack as impractical, unphilosophical, and perhaps French. Some Federalist critics were insisting on the superior dignity and moral seriousness of Newtonian astronomy as against taxonomic natural history, and some Republicans questioned the Republic's need of either.[3]

In the arts the situation was if anything worse. Freneau and Brown were running out of steam, the Connecticut Wits had long been silent, Irving and Cooper had just barely begun to publish. What Americans seemed to do best was historical painting and highly traditional architecture.

European travelers were starting their endless hostile chorus about the failure of American society. Mildly impressed sometimes with the conventional proprieties of Boston or Philadelphia or New York, they gave a delightfully dismal picture of what they found a little way beyond these small outposts of Europe—a picture of impossible roads, dirty inns, and above all of whiskey-drinking, tobacco-spitting democrats lecturing their visitors on the superiority of republican manners. Only a few of the most perspicacious understood in 1810 what Henry Adams understood so well in 1890, that the high hopes and proud boasts were anything but ridiculous, that they were themselves part of the evidence that a really new society was painfully being born.

In the first years of the century important and obvious innovation was taking place mostly in two spheres, politics and religion, and in these what was new was method and organization rather than theory. Beyond these all-important realms, and also in the center of both, the real movement was taking place in the elusive realm of feeling. What was expressed in the crude assertions Europeans found so hard to take was an ardent and emotional insistence on social equality. Egalitarian feelings, in America, often ran far ahead of fact, but yet in the long run affected many kinds of reality. This was a kind of egalitarianism quite different from that proclaimed in Europe by the Revolutionary Enlightenment, arising less out of frustration and resentment and more out of confidence.

At the end of this period this odd society, so full of its problems of identity that its members longed and needed to be let alone, found itself caught up in European war. Naturally, at the end of this struggle, sufficiently successful if not glorious, interest in Europe went into a long lapse. Frontier expansion, mass immigration, the continental market, and even manufacturing were set free to create nineteenth-century America, with all its chaos, turbulence, unsolved problems, and gathering power. Eventually, these forces were to be expressed in fresh and appropriate cultural symbols.

Before 1815, however, new realities and new feelings had not found adequate expression. Familiar modes and ideas derived from the old European world, including most of those associated with Enlightenment, were obviously becoming less useful and appropriate in America. If they hung on for a while in attenuated form, it was because no substitutes were yet available.

For the first twenty-four years of the century Enlightened gentlemen, all with European experience, reigned in a new capital, laid out by a French architect with the closest collaboration of Thomas Jefferson. Yet the Federal City, as it was usually called, is not the happiest symbol of triumphant Enlightenment. For a long time L'Enfant's broad avenues, circles and squares existed only on paper. The reality was a draughty square mansion separated from an unfinished Capitol by an almost impassable swamp. Meantime Philadelphia, the center of the American Enlightenment for the past generation, was no longer the capital even of a state. With its decline America lost for a long time its chance of having a real national capital—a political, scientific, literary, social, and financial center on the model of London or Paris. Commercial leadership went to New York, literary pre-eminence to Boston, scientific prestige for a while to nowhere in particular, and Philadelphia became a provincial city, famous for the conservatism of its upper class.

To believers in Enlightenment, the election of Thomas Jefferson was a tremendous vindication. The fears of his persecuted friends like Joseph Priestley vanished, and some of them predicted a great era of enlightened progress. As always, however, Jefferson in power displayed a curious combination of astute moderation in practice and occasional, usually private, radical rhetoric. In his first administration he made one truly daring gesture. Thomas Paine, detested by conservatives not only for his religious views but also for his personal attacks on Washington, was offered a federal ship to bring him back to America. Jefferson received him in the White House cordially, if not as enthusiastically as Paine had hoped. This was a courageous gesture toward a man whose principles Jefferson admired, even if his manners were not entirely congenial. Jefferson must have expected the Federalist furor which ensued. Significantly, even the radical William Duane, editor of the *Aurora*, urged Jefferson to prevent Paine from making any further pronouncements on religion lest he injure the President's party.[4]

In his substantive acts and major policies Jefferson, always confident of the benign operations of nature once the right people were present to forestall interference, avoided unnecessary provocations. With great political skill he aimed at creating a solid majority of the center. All but extreme and clerical Federalists could be reconciled, he thought. On one issue after another he consistently sided with the moderates in his own party against the relatively radical. Of the issues between these two wings of the Republican Party and the American Enlightenment, the most important was that over the law and the courts.[5] The radicals among the republicans, the party of simplicity and equality, wanted the law stripped of complexities and technicalities. The English common law was to be eliminated as a relic of feudalism, judges were to be elected for short terms, and changes were to be made in the national and state constitutions to decrease the strength of the judiciary. To this program of simplification, the last drive of the Revolutionary Enlightenment in America, Jefferson gave only the most limited support. In the nation as a whole, and also in the states except for radical Kentucky, moderates and conservatives combined successfully to preserve intact—not without judicious compromise—the legal heritage of the moderate Enlightenment and the British past.

The battle was particularly acute and visible in Pennsylvania, where serious radicals like William Duane and Michael Leib had some political power and some memories of past radical triumphs. With the support of Paine, these men tried to bring back the radically democratic Constitution of 1776. In this battle one side used the rhetoric of revolutionary purity and simplicity, the other that of balance and order, of liberty against anarchy. Here as elsewhere, the moderates carried the day with the full support of the Jefferson administration.[6]

President of the American Philosophical Society as well as of the United States, and beyond question deeply devoted to inquiry into nature, Jefferson was expected by friends and enemies to devote the energies of the government to the support of science and education. He had observed, in pre-Revolutionary France, the kind of organization and leadership that a government could provide. During his presidency Napoleon was providing impressive stimulus and support for a great age of French science, and Jefferson himself in 1802 was made a member of the Institut de France, the only American to be so honored.[7]

As President, Jefferson did what he could for science, maintaining his own interest, giving quiet support to the work of others, and vigorously involving the government in those few activities which were most obviously useful and in his mind most clearly constitutional. The best instance of these is the loving and intelligent supervision he provided for the great exploratory expedition of Lewis and Clark. What Jefferson could do however was sharply limited both by his own scruples and public indifference or hostility. Much as he was interested in paleontology (bones in the White House were a staple of the most philistine Federalist ridicule), he refused to give national support to the museum, complete with mammoth skeleton, of his friend Charles Willson Peale. In 1802 another Enlightened friend, Joel Barlow, presented Jefferson with a complete scheme for a national institution on the French model, including a university, laboratories and libraries, support for research, and the provision of republican and Enlightened textbooks for the schools. Jefferson was deeply interested and cautiously presented the proposal to Congress, coupling it with more obviously practical suggestions that the treasury surplus be used for roads and canals after a Constitutional amendment. In 1806 he regretfully informed Barlow that the proposal had got nowhere, partly because of the threat of foreign war.

> There is a snail-paced gait for the advance of new ideas on the general mind, under which we must aquiesce. A 40. years' experience of popular assemblies has taught me, that you must give them time for every step you take. If too hard pushed, they baulk, & the machine retrogrades. . . . People generally have more feeling for canals & roads than edu-cation.[8]

Jefferson knew his constituents.

After Jefferson, the pattern of Enlightenment qualified by political caution continued. James Madison was the very symbol of the Moderate Enlightenment and moderation in general, though in his diplomatic leanings and also his literary tastes he was at least as Francophile as Jefferson. James Monroe had once been one of the chief American apol-ogists for the French Revolution, but he had several times had his fin-gers badly burned in efforts to implement Franco-American cooperation. Experience and also the advice of Jefferson had long toned down his radicalism before he became President, and he is remembered for the hesitations of his domestic policy as well as for the boldness of his mani-festo of republican foreign policy. Finally, in 1825 John Quincy Adams, the last of the Enlightened presidents, reached the White House. Inti-mate in his youth with Enlightened society in Paris and London, brought up under the immediate influence of Jefferson as well as of his father, John Adams's son set out to inaugurate, under moderately conservative auspices, an entire political program for an Enlightened republic, includ-ing the long-delayed project for a national university. Europe, he pointed out, had more than 130 astronomical observatories and America none. With the needs of New England navigators no doubt in his mind, he coined the term "lighthouses of the skies," for these useful products of science. Adams was defeated and his program rejected for many reasons, but it is significant for us that the program for the university and espe-cially the celestial lighthouses was pitilessly ridiculed in the election of 1828. In this election Adams's son and Jefferson's protégé was rejected for a man whom Jefferson, dead two years, had long considered a danger-ous military chieftain.[9]

During the long Jeffersonian hegemony the High Federalists and their immediate followers alternated between moods of fierce resistance and lapses into despair, with the latter the more common. In their view America had chosen to abandon the ideal of balanced government, throwing aside the precepts of all wise men of the past from Aristotle to Montesquieu. The golden age of Washington had been replaced by government of the worst, in which an ignorant crowd was manipulated by a sly ideologue. Uncontrolled democracy was bound to end, as it had in France, in the familiar cycle of anarchy and dictatorship. Fisher Ames put it succinctly: "Liberty is no longer the question; to mitigate the rigors of despotism is all that is left to us."[10]

Especially in New England, many Federalists read in Republican gains the doom of New England and the end of her special kind of society, based on frugality, religion, and education. The land of schools and churches would be dominated by the haughty and brutal South, in alliance with the barbarous West, disastrously doubled by the Louisiana Purchase. According to the *Port Folio*, arch-Federalist but also Philadelphian, "a jacobinical journal has the insolence to style New England the La Vendée of America."[11]

Apocalyptic lament was the language of many High Federalist leaders, while younger and more flexible Federalists were finding that they could work successfully with some Republicans, and that there was still some hope of hanging on to some bases of strength, especially if one played the political game by the new rules.

From the point of view of the High Federalists, and probably of most New England Federalists, the ultimate disaster was the imposition of Jefferson's embargo in 1807, and the drift to war in 1812. As they had always predicted, the Jeffersonians had led the country to war on the side of despotic and atheistic France against constitutional and Protestant England. In a mood of defiance, the High Federalists recovered some confidence as their party recovered New England. A few, rejoicing in allied victories, verged on treason. In the Hartford Convention (1814) the High Federalists made their last desperate effort, not as their opponents charged to break up the Union, but to change it, taking advantage of what seemed a desperate situation to end once and for all the Virginian hegemony.

With the end of the war, it became slowly evident to Federalists and others that the United States faced not disaster and disintegration, but an unparalleled historic opportunity for peace and expansion. This fact produced a major change in American political rhetoric. The fears for the safety of the republic, inherited from Commonwealth theories of inevitable corruption, could no longer be successfully invoked—not that is for a while, until new fears found a focus in Catholics or abolitionists or the slave conspiracy.

What had really happened in the politics of this transitional period was an adjustment of American political practice and—a little later—American political rhetoric to the realities of political democracy. Jefferson and Madison, like most men who had received a good education in the eighteenth century, stopped well short of a belief in complete political equality. In his administration, a recent study has shown, Jefferson like his predecessor tried hard to fill major offices with men of education and "respectability," which could mean only money and social position. He was limited in this effort by the fact that comparatively few "respectable characters" belonged to his party outside Virginia.[12] Yet Jefferson and Madison fully accepted the fact of broadening suffrage. Men, or at least small property-holders, could confidently be trusted to choose their governors. In actuality, in the period we have been discussing, American suffrage, already the widest in the world, rapidly widened further.[13] By 1815 white male suffrage existed in most states, qualified at most by low taxpaying or property qualifications. Such restrictions were often mere sops to theoretical prejudices, unenforced in practice. Where they existed, they were subjected to heavy ideological attack. The argument over suffrage was carried on in familiar terms, with Aristotle, Harrington, Locke, and Montesquieu invoked on one side and Sidney, Paine, and Rousseau on the other. In this major battle, unlike the equally important battle over the courts, the radicals won.

What came into existence was a nation radically democratic—by any existing standards—in suffrage—and moderately conservative in institutions. To this situation the rhetoric of American political discourse had to be adjusted. The rhetoric of classical political theory and of the Moderate Enlightenment, while it was still invoked in state constitutional conventions and employed as a matter of course by conservatives among themselves, was increasingly impossible to use in serious national politics. The theory that man's reason must be protected against his passions, the axiom that numbers must be balanced against property, still more the suggestion that wisdom was likely to lie with the smaller part, could not be used to appeal to a mass electorate. The argument for checks and balances had to be watered down, emphasizing the defense of *everybody's* liberty and property, or the prosperity achieved under existing institutions. Among radicals the old and passionate appeal for the clean sweep, the new start, the destruction of corrupt and tyrannical institutions became almost equally useless. Most nineteenth-century Americans continued to find their political institutions reasonably satisfactory, and many increasingly felt them to be a sacred heritage. The Secular Millennium gradually turned into Manifest Destiny.

The optimism of nineteenth-century America, which often had the effect of blinding Americans to their own failings, becomes understandable if not attractive when one considers the Jeffersonian period in contrast to the same period in Europe. One sees, as contemporaries saw, a developing constitutional democracy as against a plebiscite empire in France and a Tory oligarchy in England, a period of devastating war briefly interrupted by peace as against one of peace briefly interrupted by comparatively small-scale war. One sees also a period of cultural doldrums contrasted to one of brilliant creativity, but that is an aspect of the difference many Americans refused to admit and others considered unimportant. It is not surprising that there was less and less disposition to dwell on political doctrines, including the political doctrines of the Enlightenment, closely associated with the increasingly different European world.

Many though not all of the established clergy of New England, together with their Presbyterian allies to the South and some of the less cautious Episcopalians, continued their anti-Jeffersonian campaign during the Jeffersonian administrations. Some of them were at first inclined to turn away from politics, but were brought back by the Paine visit and especially by the drift toward war. By Jefferson's second administration some of them had reached a pitch of frenzy unequaled even in 1798. The Reverend J. G. Bend, a Maryland Episcopalian wrote to a friend that

> The more I see of democracy, the more I detest its principles, if its votaries act upon them. The reign of the Goths & Vandals was not more destructive, than the ascendancy of these men has been.[14]

Pulpit attacks on the President became ever more vindictive. Nathanael Emmons of Franklin, Massachusetts, a man of learning and grim humor, preached one of the most famous of these sermons, addressing himself to the career of Jeroboam, the wicked king of Israel. This monarch, he pointed out, had begun as a man of natural genius coupled with a base and ambitious spirit. He had spent too long in the land of Egypt, a place of moral darkness and false religion to which he remained attached. Returning to Israel, he was given high office by Solomon, whom he betrayed. Through his evil arts he secured the support of an unprincipled majority, and succeeded to the throne after two good and great kings. Once in power, he devoted himself to destroying religion and to corrupting the people through bad appointments and evil example.[15]

As they had for several generations, many ministers saw in every event the portent of the Last Days, and indeed they had much promising material to work on. The Reverend George Lampert summed it up:

> In my day America has been dismembered from the parent stock—Poland as a nation extinguished, the throne of France subverted and reestablished—Holland from an influx of trade and riches reduced almost to poverty—His holiness of Rome degraded to the very dust, and exalted again by the same power that overturned him—Switzerland despoiled of her boasted liberty—and Germany overrun and subdued in a manner, which probably in half a century will appear to posterity as a feigned romance. Where, or when these vicissitudes will end, we can in no wise conjecture: but undoubtedly they are all intended to introduce the rights of HIM, to whom all the kingdoms of this earth shall finally be given.[16]

If the anti-Jeffersonian clergy agreed on any one thing, it was that this great sequence of events would include the punishment of America, the favorite and apostate land, where true religion and decent manners were declining, wicked men were being elected to office, and an evil government moving toward an unjust war.

Jefferson, who had always put the New England clergy and their allies in the camp of unreconcilable enemies, was not surprised by their attacks. Quite wrongly, he thought them the enemies of education and science as well as Enlightenment—their defenders could answer with unpleasant comparisons of education in Massachusetts and Virginia. Madison, though always more circumspect, fully shared Jefferson's hostility to the New England "priesthood."[17]

When war came, the anti-Jeffersonian clergy were carried away by their passions. The circumstances seemed to provide an opportunity for one more campaign like those of the past, in which the Standing Order would recover its influence and overcome its many enemies, all in the service of right and truth.

Even more obviously than for the High Federalists, the end of the war seemed a disaster for the established clergy. They had misjudged their own power, which though it was by no means negligible had long been slipping. Within New England, and even within the established churches themselves, there was far more resistance to the antiwar campaign than there had been to anti-Jacobinism in 1798.[18] Still more important, the outcome of the war greatly increased the prestige and power of those churches which had supported it, and in general had cheerfully accepted the new social and political dispensation.

The two great rising churches, the Baptists and Methodists, together with a number of smaller sects, were even more solidly Jeffersonian than the New England Standing Order was Federalist.[19] Both Baptists and Methodists had longstanding reasons to detest England and her Church, and both, especially the Baptists, had suffered in the past at the hands of the established clergy of New England. Though these Dissenters had no love whatever for anything French, they could point out that it was Napoleon who had humbled the Pope and abolished the Spanish Inquisition. Baptists and Methodists moreover remembered with gratitude the services of Jefferson and especially Madison for religious freedom in Virginia, and tended to discount stories of their infidelity.

The New England clergy and their orthodox allies were bewildered and confused by the turn of events—by their own loss of power, by the turning of the people away from traditional leadership, and above all by God's seeming decision to reward instead of punish America for its recent actions. Then suddenly the meaning of recent events became clear: all was to be understood as preparation for an immense revival of religion in America. This event was so important that in its light even the political victories of Jacobins and atheists were only a temporary setback, even the tribulations of the clergy themselves only a necessary trial and preparation.

The revival of religion that began in the 1790's in certain towns of Connecticut and Massachusetts was, we know now, the beginning of a vast reshaping of American religion, and even of American culture.[20] At first, however, the New England phase of the Great Revival, sometimes called the Second Great Awakening, seemed a restoration rather than a revolution, a long-delayed answer to old hopes and prayers. As all reports emphasized, the revivals in Connecticut and Massachusetts, and also a little later in upstate New York and the Ohio valley, were under sound Calvinist—often Edwardsian—leadership; they were conducted by settled clergy and not by itinerants; and they seemed to be avoiding completely the emotional excesses that had marred the Awakening of the mid-eighteenth century. A correspondent of Jedidiah Morse assured him in 1799 that the revival in Hartford had begun "in a calm but very impressive manner" and continued to gather strength in the same way. "There does not appear to be any degree of enthusiasm," he noted approvingly.[21]

Even while many of the Federalist clergy were continuing and intensifying their anti-Jeffersonian polemic, some of their leaders, including both Morse and Dwight, were turning from jeremiad to organization, with impressive effects. Partly under Morse's skillful leadership, a treaty was worked out between the Calvinist factions left over from the first Great Awakening. Old Calvinists and New Divinity men together founded the missionary magazine *The Panoplist* in 1805 and Andover Seminary in 1808. Founded to fight Unitarian Harvard, Andover for the rest of the century was a center of moderate orthodoxy, training a long list of distinguished theologians, college presidents, and preachers; playing a major role in founding other seminaries and colleges throughout the East and Northwest. Under the auspices of reunited New England Calvinism, and in close imitation of the British evangelical model, a network of missionary societies came into being. At first the main goal was the conversion of the Indians. From 1810, with the foundation of the American Board of Commissioners for Foreign Missions, American Calvinists began to send young men to India and Africa. Increasingly, however, the major energies of the new organizations were directed toward the task which was at once the easiest and the most crucial: the reform of American religion, morals, and society.

The movement from anti-Jacobin crusade to missionary activity and thence to social reform was a gradual one. Fighting Jacobins meant a kind of missionary work, and missionaries tended to respond to the needs of their audiences. Training missionaries put demands on colleges and seminaries, and the pious organized to support the college education of pious youth, and incidentally to promote morals and religion in the colleges. From promoting morals and religion to defending the Sabbath and fighting vice, crime, and drink was a natural movement. Gradually the mood of 1798—of desperate defense of Protestant culture against infidelity and barbarism—gave place even among the New England clergy to one of restrained but fervent hope.[22]

By 1815 it was already possible for members of the moderately orthodox, moderately revivalist segment of New England Calvinism to feel that New England, long traduced and humiliated, had been vindicated. Unitarianism was contained in eastern Massachusetts, deism was almost wiped out, the manners and morals of the young were improving, and the West seemed on the point of being captured for the forces of order and piety. Only the political scene was still a cause for sadness.

In the process of successful evangelical reorganization, of course, Calvinism itself had changed. In its dominant New England form it was becoming less speculative and more practical; the harsh doctrines of election and reprobation were being endlessly restated, redefined, and softened. Yet the essentials, so far, remained: in 1812 Lyman Beecher, the rising figure in New England evangelical Calvinism, rejoiced that American religion was loyal to the central teaching of its past:

> Our fathers were not fools; they were as far from it as modern philosophers are from wisdom. Their fundamental maxim was that man is desperately wicked, and cannot be qualified for good membership in society without the influence of moral restraint.[23]

Of course New England Congregationalists, though they clung to the shreds of state support in Massachusetts and Connecticut, no longer expected to recover religious monopoly. Their attitude toward the continuing growth of the Baptist and Methodist minorities in New England, which shared the revivals and formed their own evangelical organizations, ranged from gingerly cooperation to downright hostility. In some sermons and many private letters, orthodox clergy lamented the gains being made by "sectaries," "ill-minded schismatics," and "careless illiterate itinerants."[24] Fortunately, New England Congregationalists were able to solidify their old alliance with the Presbyterians. In 1801 this was formalized in the Plan of Union, which provided for close cooperation in missionary work and led to actual union, often in fact Presbyterian absorption, in many frontier areas.

Whatever was lost for theological subtlety and diversity, much was obviously gained for the orthodox evangelical cause by the leadership of the Presbyterian church, the most powerful, learned, disciplined, and national of American churches. From 1799 the General Assembly and several local presbyteries contributed money and men to the missionary cause. In the Ohio valley men from New Jersey and Virginia cooperated with men from Connecticut in founding schools and churches. In the Southwest, however, the early revival was largely under Presbyterian auspices.[25]

Ever since the Great Awakening, Presbyterians had been strongly entrenched in the valley of Virginia, and now their missionaries poured over the mountains. In Virginia, Kentucky, Tennessee, and North Carolina the Presbyterian pattern was much the same, dominated by men like John H. Rice and Archibald Alexander of Hampden-Sydney, and David Rice of Lexington, Kentucky, men of solid learning achieved by great struggle, men of clear if somewhat rigid theological views. Under the guidance of such figures, the early phases of Southwestern revival seemed like the Northern ones to be proceeding along reasonably decorous lines. Reports from the revival front denied rumors of emotional excesses, and insisted on the sound Calvinism of the revivals. In 1802 a letter to Alexander from the president of Washington Academy described a remarkable change which seemed to have come over that hotbed of deism and dissipation, Kentucky:

> On my way to Kentucky I was told by settlers on the road, that the character of Kentucky travellers was entirely changed and that they were now as distinguished for sobriety as they had formerly been for disolluteness: and indeed I found Kentucky the most moral place I had ever been in, a profane expression was hardly heard; a religious awe seemed to pervade the country, and some Deistical characters had confessed that from whatever cause the revival might originate, it certainly made the people better.[26]

Until 1815 Presbyterians lamented that no major revival had taken place in Princeton, the great center of Presbyterian culture. In 1812, partly for this reason, Princeton Seminary was founded as a separate institution and became the stronghold of conservative Calvinist theology for the rest of the century. In 1815, however, Ashbel Green, president of the College, reported to a friend that his prayers and diligent efforts had at last been rewarded:

> It has indeed pleased a gracious and condescending God to visit our college, in a very remarkable manner. Nothing like it has been seen here for more than forty years. The house is literally a house of prayer, yet all is still & silent—No noise, no extravagance, no enthusiasm. . . . Instead of meetings for plots & conspiracies, we have now nothing but meetings for religious conferences, & fervent social prayer.[27]

Now there were two major allied headquarters for orthodox missionary revival effort. Yale could command the allegiance of the Northwest, while Princeton sent forth its pious graduates to man the schools and seminaries which in turn provided the learned clergy for the South and West. The revival could be both encouraged and kept in decent bounds; the nation could be reformed and uplifted. Indeed, Protestant America in close and friendly collaboration with Protestant England could reform the world, in gradual and orderly fashion.

The Congregational and Presbyterian clergy of this transitional period, especially those who ran the colleges, were seen by surviving followers of Jefferson and Paine as fanatics and bigots, and this image has been carried on by some recent historians. It is only fair to remember, however, that in their own eyes they were fighting a two-front war. Certainly concerned to extirpate infidelity, they were equally hostile to ignorant enthusiasm, and believed deeply that learning must go hand in hand with piety. Dwight at Yale was especially devoted to logic and mathematics; Green at Princeton tightened up the regulations enforcing the study of Latin and Greek. John H. Rice of Hampden-Sydney admired Swift and Addison, and read the classics for pleasure all his life. Old enemies of some forms of Enlightenment, they believed in rationality and despised both undue excitement and idle speculation. In other words, the college presidents of this period, and many of their colleagues among the orthodox and moderately revivalist clergy, were men of the eighteenth century. This is why they were unable to contain the energies of American religion, even though they dominated American high culture in their day.

In 1809 Samuel Miller, a highly intelligent Princeton Presbyterian, wrote to his friend Ashbel Green, that while he did not for a moment doubt the genuineness of the Southern revivals, he was disturbed about

certain circumstances attending the work, which, to those who have
been accustomed only to the still, small voice of the gospel, appear, to
say the least, very singular.[28]

More and more, men like Miller had to admit the presence not only of
such outlandish phenomena as the barking, jumping, running, and falling "exercises" but also of theological looseness and denominational warfare. In the immense revival at Cane Ridge, Kentucky, in the spring of
1801, Presbyterian, Methodist, and Baptist ministers worked together,
exhausted by the emotional needs of the tens of thousands of praying,
weeping people. As revivals of this general sort spread through the South
and West, however, Presbyterians rapidly lost not only their leadership
but many of their members. The two issues on which they fought their
long losing battles were first, the Westminster doctrines of election and
reprobation, and second, the necessity of a learned clergy. Both were
closely connected with another, the legitimacy of extreme emotional
methods.

Those who inherited were those willing to give free reign to the egalitarian and emotional religion of the heart, and those able to supply the
felt needs of the frontier with preachers chosen for their fervor rather
than their learning. The Methodists proved best adapted to the social
circumstances. Part of their strength lay in their hopeful theology of free
grace, and their teaching of the duty of seeking perfection. Part lay also
in their institutions, centering on a disciplined itinerant clergy, the
shock-troops of revival who could go wherever they were sent, fan the
flames of revival, and then move on, leaving behind them organized laymen who maintained their fervor through regular class-meetings. The
Methodists gained strength easily against the orthodox and conservative,
and they used some of this strength to fight the wilder vagaries of American, particularly Western and Southern revivalism, and also to crusade
against drink, dancing, cards, and carnality in general. Instead of intellectual control, that is, they stressed social and moral control, and this
choice seemed to fit the needs of many parts of American society.

The Baptists came second, and though they did not have the Methodist strength in organization and hierarchy, they made some of the
same choices. On the frontier volunteer preachers could be licensed first,
study when and if they could, and be ordained only when they were
called to a church. Sometimes their long hatred of upper-class establishments, Congregational or Episcopalian, led Baptists in this period to be

positively hostile to education. They learned to compromise their ancient theological battles with each other, but they did not compromise
with departures from strict and conventional morality.

New sects also grew and flourished, growing out of discontents with
the old, particularly the Presbyterians. Of these the most important was
the complex group who called themselves at first simply "Christians,"
and later Disciples of Christ, who grew from several secessions from
Baptist and Presbyterian churches. As their name implies, these people
sought to return to the unity and simplicity of the early church, ending
theological complexities and quarrels by strict adherence to the New
Testament.[29] All these groups and others, especially in the West and
South, shared methods and feelings that transcended their differences.
A letter from a Methodist convert conveys the atmosphere and power of
this popular pietism:

> . . . Religion flourishes as much among the Baptists presbytereans &
> peace & Harmony seems to abound pretty generally among the profes-
> sors except some of the old Presbytereans we were at Meeting to day &
> it was a day of the Outpouring of the Spirit & a day of Joy & gladness
> There was Eight gave in a Reasonable Hope & were receiv'd & will be
> Baptized tomorrow & over on the north Side of the River I am informed
> in Several Churches they Baptize 15 20 & 80 a day singing Preaching
> Praying & rejoicing from place to place both night & day several times
> in a week god is working wonders Here the meleneum is Certainly about
> to commence. . . .[30]

Faced with such an unbeatable challenge to what they regarded as
good order and sound doctrine the Presbyterian and Congregational orthodox faced a hard choice. Some, especially those influenced by
Dwight's Yale, moved slowly toward accommodation and compromise,
qualifying ever more drastically the doctrines of predestination, accepting
what they could of the "new measures" of revivalism, and devoting
themselves increasingly to moral and social reform. Others, especially
those centering in Princeton and its offshoots, drew back into an increasingly strict orthodoxy, opposing speculation, revivalism, theological compromise, and most kinds of social reform. Slowly, over decades, the two
wings moved once more, as they had in the time of the First Great
Awakening, toward outright schism, which was to take place in 1837.

By 1815 it was clear that what might be called the Presbyterian Age
in American religion was over, giving place to what has been called the

Methodist Age.[31] And yet in their coming time of relative decline the Presbyterians and Congregationalists were to play a crucial role, resisting or at least qualifying popular emotionalism, insisting on the necessity of sober self-criticism, defending the importance of literary culture and even—with many qualifications—some of the heritage of Enlightenment.

The immense consequences of the popular phase of revivalism can for our purposes be reduced to two. The first and greatest, nothing less than the reshaping of American religion and with it much of American culture, is largely beyond the scope of this book. Flexible, activist, moralistic, increasingly un-theological, American evangelical Protestantism in the nineteenth century was in its own terms the most successful form of nineteenth-century Christianity. Even more powerfully than British evangelicism, to which it was closely related, it permeated and changed its society.[32] The ultimate influence of popular evangelicism in the United States can be seen in almost every facet of American social history, from anti-slavery to xenophobia.

Second, and almost incidentally, it was the second and more popular phase of religious revival that largely finished off what remained of both the Skeptical and the Revolutionary phases of the Enlightenment in America. Southern and Western Baptists and Methodists did not join the crusade led by Dwight and Morse—indeed most of them were fervent Jeffersonians. Their preachers, listing the evils of the time, sometimes mentioned deism and Jacobinism, but they gave far more time to denouncing coldness, indifference, and formalism. They defeated the Skeptical and Radical Enlightenments not by head-on attack, but by providing what their opponents could not—the necessary minimum of social control needed by any society and, still more important, experiences of peace, love, and joy for individuals living in harsh and barren surroundings. For all these great benefits, the society paid heavily in cultural decline, isolation, social conformity, and liability to occasional hysteria. By 1815 many of the strengths and weaknesses of nineteenth-century American Christianity were becoming clear.

In these years of spreading social democracy and religious revival, all of the varieties of Enlightenment we have examined found themselves under heavy attack. This is partly because all were, to one degree or another, associated with an intellectual elite, and still worse, with Europe. There was little in the European scene in 1800 to 1815 which Americans could admire. In France, the Enlightenment was in its way cherished and promoted by Napoleon. It was also conscripted and directed through a centralized network of academic institutions, a system few Americans could appreciate. In Britain, only the evangelicals and the Scottish Common-Sense philosophers seemed to offer useful patterns for America. The government was in the hands of reaction and oligarchy, and the heritage of the Revolutionary Enlightenment was passing to Benthamite reformers, too agnostic in their opinions and also too centralized and bureaucratic in their methods to be much use for America.[33]

In some of the American hostility to Europe in this period one can find elements of isolation, patriotism, and anti-intellectualism that were to have a long future together. A well-informed Virginian, in a letter of 1805, contrasts European cultural pretensions to American freedom:

> Where is the boasted science of other countries, that they should dare in any one of them to spurn at American genius; when she alone is enjoying all the sweets and blessings of freedom while they are creeping in the dust, fawning on, and watching with trembling awe the smiles and frowns of a noble Idiot or a human monster. If these Philosophers and wise men as they may think themselves would only take a just view of the degraded situation of their devoted Countries, and the estimation in which their greatest of all rights, that of Worshipping God according to the dictates of our own conscience is held, they would then see of how little practical benefit their boasted sciences had been to their native Countries.[34]

As we have seen, even the Moderate Enlightenment principles of balance and order, had to be stated cautiously in the Republican ascendancy. Obviously, skepticism of the Voltairean or Humean variety, never strong in America, became impossible to defend in public. Had Gibbon lived to see it, he would certainly have found nineteenth-century America to be the supreme example of the triumph of barbarism and religion. Gibbonean or Voltairean scoffing, or Humean dissection of religious belief, had now to be carried on in private. Even the mild combination of political conservatism and religious liberalism that had been common in the colleges nearly disappeared. In 1806 James Kent, once a deist and a pillar of the New York Friendly Club, praised the ultra-evangelistic and Calvinist *Panoplist* in a letter to Jedidiah Morse.[35]

The decline of the Revolutionary Enlightenment was less sudden than legend made it: in its pure form it had never had much strength. It was only in orthodox fantasy that an infidel attack on American religion had almost triumphed, and had been defeated only by heroic missionary work. Actually the strength of this kind of Enlightenment had been on its periphery, not at its center; among those favorably inclined toward deism and French republicanism, rather than among the active, full-time propagandists of either.[36]

For a few years after 1800 the tiny groups and journals that supported Elihu Palmer and his friends maintained a brave existence, continually predicting that the nation was soon to be converted to their beliefs. Philip Freneau, still a deist, was apparently sinking into the complacency to which intellectual deism is likely to lead: since the deity and man are both benign, evil must be illusory:

> All, nature made, in reason's sight
> Is order all, and *all is right.*

This poem appeared in a collection published in 1815, whose lack of success was blamed by its author partly on orthodox hostility: "Had I written a Volume of psalms, hymns, and Spiritual Songs, I believe the success would have been infinitely greater."[37]

Joel Barlow, the other major literary spokesman of the Radical Enlightenment, was constantly attacked on both religious and political grounds. In a letter to a liberal French priest, he insisted somewhat lamely that he had never really abandoned Christianity.[38] Long since, Barlow had been deeply disillusioned by the Napoleonic triumph in the nation he had long admired. In 1811, despite Federalist attack, he was appointed ambassador to the Napoleonic empire, and died the next year in Poland, where he was trying to find the emperor during the retreat from Russia.

Almost vanished from sight by 1805, radical deism enjoyed a brief revival in the "Jacksonian" 1820's and 1830's.[39] Again small groups announced that Christianity, the religion of priests and kings, was about to give way to a more rational and democratic belief. Frances Wright, the eloquent English reformer, can perhaps be seen as the Paine of this period, and Abner Kneeland, the New England "Free Enquirer," as its Palmer. Once again, however, truly anti-Christian radicalism was confined to small circles. When similar sentiments seem to be expressed by major politicians, such as Vice-President Richard M. Johnson, they turn on close examination into mere anti-clericalism. Clerical activity in politics is denounced as injurious to true Christianity.

Both aristocratic skepticism and (in an odd form) radical deism had been strongest in Virginia and in the other states where the Virginia aristocratic pattern had some influence: North Carolina, Kentucky, and Tennessee. By 1815 all forms of religious questioning and political radicalism were on their way to extinction throughout the South. By 1830 one can see the outlines of the Solid South—fiercely Christian, united in defense of slavery, patriotic, and proud of its immunity to the cults and isms that were cropping up in the North. An example of the defensive nature of Southern religiosity is furnished by a clause in the North Carolina Constitution of 1832:

> No person who shall deny the being of God, or the truth of the Christian religion, or the divine authority of the Old or New Testament, *or who shall hold religious principles incompatible with the freedom or safety of the state,* shall be capable of holding any office or place of trust or profit in the civil department within this state.[40]

So sharp a change, with such fundamental importance in American history, needs some special attention here.

The center of the change was the nearly universal triumph of a special kind of evangelical religion, focused on personal conversion through divine grace, to be evidenced in strict personal morality rather than social reform. In the South of the early nineteenth century there were arguments between denominations about such matters as baptism through immersion, but little of the fundamental theological debate which never ceased in the North. Increasingly, conversions occurred among the formerly skeptical upper class. At first, these were often reported by evangelists as especially strong indications of divine favor, something like

changes of heart in notorious drunkards. Daniel Jones describes a special
kind of harvest gathered at Cane Ridge, Kentucky, in 1802:

> Here let it be remarked, as worthy of special notice, that the Governor
> of the State, a Lawyer, and a Physician were among the number; and
> that the two latter came to the ground under the influence of inveterate
> prejudice; the Doctor being an avowed Deist, and the Lawyer, in the
> plentitude of contempt, ascending his scorner's chair. To what probable
> cause shall we ascribe these things, unless it be the immediate agency
> of some invisible superior Being?[41]

Conversion to evangelical Protestantism can be seen as part of the
assimilation of the old Virginian aristocracy and its offshoots to the
bourgeois mores of the whole section. In this Virginia's relative loss of
economic and political power—a loss constantly lamented by Virginians—played some part, as did the necessities of democratic politics.
In the nineteenth-century South the classes were drawing together, and
drawing together partly in defense of the peculiar institution.

One cannot of course discuss any topic in Southern cultural history
without arriving at this one. It is common among historians to suggest
that the need to defend slavery led to religious uniformity, but the relation is more complex than this statement implies. Certainly it is true
that tightening tensions, centering around slavery, made every kind of
criticism or dissent suspect. The collapse of evangelical anti-slavery is
the most melancholy fact in American religious history. Some Presbyterians such as David Rice, and most Baptists and Methodists outside
South Carolina, had been militant opponents of slavery. They had
learned to attack the institution on moral and also on social grounds: it
was related in their eyes to aristocratic luxury, frivolity, and religious
looseness; it was often condemned in the same tone, though more
harshly, as card-playing, dancing, and horseracing. In a process familiar
throughout the history of religion, as Presbyterians, Baptists, and Methodists in turn became respectable and made converts among the upper
classes, their sectarian radicalism turned to churchly discretion. As evangelical fervor continued to grow, sincere home missionaries succumbed
to the plausible argument that it was their duty to put first things first.
What came first, in the individualist theology of the time and place, was
the saving of souls, black and white alike. It was increasingly difficult to
preach the gospel at all unless one made it quite clear that preaching
would not threaten the peculiar institution—that it would even safe-

guard it by producing pious and contented servants. So good men emphasized some New Testament texts more than others, and salved their consciences by trying—not without some success—to make the institution a little less inhumane as they made it stronger.[42]

As the tightening defense of slavery made for rigidity in religion, so also religious uniformity changed the character of the pro-slavery defense. In the eighteenth century some slaveowners hoped for the eventual disappearance of the institution, and others admitted among themselves both that it was bad and that they had no intention of giving it up. Now this sort of robust cynicism was impossible: pious masters had to convince themselves that slavery was a positive good for the slaves, that it helped to uplift the barbarous African, that it was made necessary by his moral deficiencies. This kind of moralistic racism had been rare in the years of Enlightenment. Thus the universal triumph of evangelical religion, which in the North provided most of the heat for abolitionism, in the South warmed up the pro-slavery defense.

Finally, in discussing the changes of heart in the Southern upper class, one cannot leave out the religious power of the new preaching and the religious weakness of deism. Slaveowners, like other people, had feelings that could not be satisfied by stoicism or cool rationalism. There is no reason to assume that their increasingly common conversions were emotionally shallow, or that their intentions of moral amendment were insincere. The most instructive example of an upper-class conversion is that of John Randolph of Roanoke, who had been brought up without religion and had been in his youth the most extreme example of a slaveholding pro-Jacobin deist. By 1813 he had long changed his mind about France, as John Adams caustically reports:

> John Randolph, tho he was 14 years ago, as wild an Enthusiast for Equality and Fraternity, as any of them; appears to be now a regenerated Proselite to Napoleons Opinion and mine, that it was all madness.[43]

In 1810 John H. Rice, a leading Presbyterian divine, writes Archibald Alexander about his surprising experience with Randolph and his sister Judith:

> You remember that in Virginia there was a class of persons who never went to church at all; they thought it beneath them. That class is diminishing in numbers pretty rapidly. . . . Mrs. Judith Randolph, of

Bizarre, lately made a profession of religion. I have been much in her company since, and I think her among the most truly pious in our country. John Randolph attended the sacrament when his sister joined with us, and seemed to be much impressed. . . . There were at the last Cumberland sacrament from eight to ten of the Randolph connections at the table of the Lord. . . . Upon the whole we are encouraged.[44]

Rice became a close friend and spiritual adviser of Judith Randolph, who had been involved in one of Virginia's most famous scandals. In 1815 we find John Randolph writing him at length about his own deep inner conflicts, not only about the doctrine of predestination but also about the stylistic deficiencies of divines he otherwise admires.[45] Several other letters of the same year movingly attest the sincerity and depth of his struggles. To James M. Garnett he admits in 1815 that "I cannot express what I feel upon this subject, & I can hardly think on any other." A little later he explains further:

Do not however mistake me for a disciple of John Calvin, or of John Wesley. I look for no revelations or extacies: at the same time, I trust that the grace of God will in due season work an entire change in my heart. I am (if I do not deceive myself) already sensible of some change in my rebellious and stubborn nature.[46]

To another friend, Henry Middleton Rutledge, Randolph associates his own feelings with a general movement:

A change has certainly been wrought in Virginia, the most ungodly country on the face of the earth, where the Gospel has ever been preached. I flatter myself that it is the case elsewhere in the U.S. . . . The last was a generation of free thinkers, disciples of Hume & Voltaire & Bolingbroke, & there are very few persons, my dear Rutledge, of our years who have not received their first impressions from the same die. . . . There are however some striking instances in this country, as well as in Europe, of men of the first abilities devoting themselves to the service of the only true God. That cold formality which pervaded our church and passed for religion has been exploded by Wilberforce & Miss Moore [sic]. . . . Let us hope that a mighty change is about to be wrought & let us leave nothing undone to effect it in ourselves.[47]

Three years later Randolph's hopes were fulfilled, as he announces in a jubilant letter to Francis Scott Key:

Congratulate me Frank—wish me joy you need not—give it you cannot—I am at last reconciled to my God and have assurance of his pardon through faith in Christ, against which the very gates of Hell cannot prevail. Fear hath been driven out by perfect love.[48]

During the rest of his life Randolph remained a convinced adherent of the evangelical branch of the Episcopal Church, maintaining cordial relations with a number of Presbyterians but a continuing hostility to cant and undue enthusiasm, especially when associated with New England.

Randolph's former guardian, St. George Tucker, whom Randolph bitterly blamed for his own lack of religious education, stuck to deism all his life. In 1806, however, we find him writing to John Page in horrified reaction to the famous murder of George Wythe, and connecting this event with atheism. Tucker agrees with Page, he says, in wishing that all men were Christian. Though he cannot himself accept Christianity as divine revelation, he believes (like Jefferson) that it offers the best moral code. We have suffered so much, says Tucker at this point, from "the words philosophy, philanthropy, & the rights of man" that we are approaching anarchy. He would, he concludes, be quite willing to support a state subsidy for teachers of religion regardless of sect.[49]

Tucker's prudential retreat from irreligion offers a contrast to Randolph's emotionally convincing conversion. Other examples of each are many, and the two are not always distinguishable. John Hartwell Cocke of Bremo, in his youth a typical member of his light-hearted William and Mary class, was converted to fervent though non-sectarian Protestantism at the death of his wife in 1817, and became the leading Virginian advocate of temperance, slave evangelization, and agricultural reform.[50] In 1817 Joseph Breckinridge of Kentucky, the son of the state's leading Jeffersonian and deist, writes to his younger brother at Princeton warning him against enthusiasm and pitiful, base fear of hell. In vain: in 1820 young John Breckinridge reports his complete and joyful conversion.[51]

Holdouts of course there were, but they found life in the South increasingly difficult, and most of them kept very quiet. John William Walker of Georgia was a cheerful young man whose letters to his friend Larkin Newby of North Carolina abound in frivolous gossip and amorous longings. He insists that he is not a deist, that he has never even read the deist writers, that he has no serious religious opinions:

". . . *Ease* is my deity—and him will I worship—dispute my philosophy who will." This attitude, not uncommon in Virginia in 1790, was absolutely unacceptable in Georgia in the first decade of the new century. Young Walker's lukewarmness gets around, and he finds himself denounced from the pulpit and rebuked by friends of his family. "Never oppose the stubborn wills of the ignorant, bigoted multitude," he warns his friend.[52]

In 1816 a friend of St. George Tucker writes him from Norfolk that even the Episcopal Church of Virginia, the last bastion of rational and gentlemanly religion, has finally fallen:

> There seems to be a race between some of the dissenting sectaries & I
> think our Mother Church is inclined to enter the Lists. The Contest is
> shocking to my mind. And I will never conspire at it in any way. I will
> not agree to become a Methodist at Home or abroad. We have Camp
> Meetings by the Week every Month or two—70 Proselytes were made
> in the last. The Baptists have taken the alarm & the Presbyterians hold
> meetings by double Tides. Our Church has service twice a week & Family
> meetings in the Evening. The Lord preserve & keep us safe from
> Folly & Hypocrisy.[53]

As in the North, the colleges in the South one by one became strongholds of orthodoxy and moderate revivalism. In the Republican South, religious orthodoxy and egalitarian suspicion of intellectuals were more often allied than in New England. Thus the colleges were sometimes denounced as aristocratic or Federalist as well as infidel. This happened, for instance, at the University of North Carolina, where the triumphant Republicans in the legislature cut off the University's endowment in 1800.[54]

The stoutest fortresses of Enlightenment in the South were the College of William and Mary and the University of Transylvania in Lexington, Kentucky. Ever since 1794, Transylvania had been the scene of a back-and-forth running fight between bluegrass Republican and aristocratic liberalism on the one hand and Presbyterian orthodoxy on the other. In 1818, the liberals seemed to have won the day with the appointment of Horace Holley, an elegant and able Boston Unitarian, whose views were a mixture of those of Jefferson and William Ellery Channing. Under relentless attack from the Presbyterians, Holley was finally forced out in 1829, partly because of the triumph in Kentucky politics of the agrarian "New Court" Party, whose members resented the Bostonian's style as well as his doctrines.[55]

As we have seen, William and Mary under Bishop James Madison stuck to its special sort of aristocratic radicalism well after the turn of the century. Paine and Volney continued to be read, discipline was loose, the classics were not required, and according to student memories, free and elegant manners continued to prevail. Ever more harshly, the bishop and his college were attacked in the national press on religious, political, and moral grounds. After a serious student riot in 1802 harsh measures were taken to restore order and St. George Tucker, a survivor of the free-and-easy past, resigned as Professor of Law. Shortly after Bishop Madison's death in 1812, his successor asked the Episcopal Church to re-establish the chair of theology which had been abolished after the Revolution. Fearing the contamination of Williamsburg liberalism, the Church refused.[56]

Long before this the College had been abandoned by its most famous alumnus and defender. The last years of Jefferson's life were given to his hopes of establishing a modern, secular university at Charlottesville. In architecture, student government, and curriculum the University of Virginia was expected to be the last great center of the Southern Enlightenment. Jefferson was determined that there was to be no theological department, and that liberal doctrines of government and philosophy were to be taught at Charlottesville even if the professors had to be imported from Europe. The crucial importance of this battleground was fully appreciated by Jefferson's Presbyterian opposition: as John H. Rice put it, the University had to be either "Deistical, Socinian or Christian," and if the "Monticello-men" had their way it would certainly not be the last of these.[57] The war came to a climax in 1820, when Jefferson fought to obtain an appointment for Thomas Cooper. Cooper was a somewhat cranky British Unitarian, a close friend and follower of Priestley, and a courageous, combative victim of the Alien and Sedition acts. By 1820 Cooper was rapidly growing more conservative in politics, but was still outspokenly liberal in religion.[58]

Jefferson and his friends, to Jefferson's bitter disappointment, were defeated in this struggle, and Cooper became instead president of the College of South Carolina. There he managed to hang on until 1833, partly because he had become a leading defender of slavery and states' rights and had the support of some of the state's powerful planters. Finally, however, even this devoted service could not save him, and the South's last major anti-clerical went down denouncing his Presbyterian enemies.

By this time, sectionalism and orthodoxy together ruled in all the Southern colleges, and indeed in the South as a whole. In 1836 Thomas R. Dew, Professor of Political Economy and a leader of the pro-slavery polemic, addressed the assembled students at William and Mary:

> Avowed infidelity is now considered by the enlightened portion of the world as a reflection both on the head and the heart. The Atheist has long since been overthrown by the light of nature, and the Deist by that of revelation. The Infidel and the Christian have fought the battle, and the latter has won the victory. The Humes and Voltaires have been vanquished from the field.[59]

For the American South, at least, Dew was right.

———————————

When John Adams and Thomas Jefferson renewed their friendship in 1812, they began a wide-ranging correspondence which went on until both died in 1826. Both realized during their long and contemplative retirement that the world of their youth was gone. Though their styles still differed—Jefferson's lapidary and stately, Adams's cranky and whimsical—they found that they agreed on almost every subject. Both now knew that the French Revolution had turned out badly. Both abominated Napoleon and welcomed his overthrow, but were dismayed by Metternichian reaction. Looking at the European scene in 1821, Jefferson was forced to ask a startling question: "Are we to surrender the pleasing hopes of seeing improvement in the moral and intellectual condition of man?"[60]

American politics, under the conduct of their immediate successors, seemed a great deal more cheering, though both were disturbed by the persistence and apparent strengthening of slavery, and deeply alarmed by the re-emergence of the slavery question in politics in 1820. Neither took much pleasure in current literature, both preferring the books of their youth. To both, American culture seemed distressingly shallow.

Struggling tenaciously for his idea of a university, Jefferson had little respect for current secondary education, especially in his own section. He deplored the multiplication of

> petty *academies*, as they call themselves, which are starting up in every neighborhood, and where one or two men, possessing Latin, and sometimes Greek, a knowledge of the globes, and the first six boooks of Euclid, imagine and communicate this as the sum of science.[61]

On no topic did the two men agree more cordially than on their detestation of religious revivals, missionaries, and Bible societies. The topic aroused Adams's old polemical gusto:

> We have now, it seems, a National Bible Society, to propagate King James' Bible, through all Nations. Would it not be better, to apply these pious Subscriptions, to purify Christendom from the Corruptions of Christianity; than to propagate these Corruptions in Europe, Asia, Africa and America!
>
> Suppose, We should project a Society to translate Dupuis into all Languages and offer a Reward in Medals and Diamonds to any Man or Body of Men who would produce the best answer to it.
>
> Enthusiasms, Crusades, French Revolutions are Epidemical or Endemial Distempers, to which Mankind are liable.[62]

Jefferson agreed, and commented in turn about the sending of Bibles and missionaries to China:

> These Incendiaries, finding that the days of fire and faggot are over in the Atlantic hemisphere, are now preparing to put the torch to the Asiatic regions. What would they say were the Pope to send annually to this country colonies of Jesuit priests with cargoes of their Missal and translations of their Vulgate, to be put gratis into the hands of every one who would accept them?[63]

Both men, thinking over the failures of some of their hopes and confronting the sorrows of old age, debated whether they would if they could live their lives over. Not without serious doubts, both decided that they would. Precariously, they clung to their hopes for the nation and, with more difficulty, for the world. As they approached extreme old age, however, both tended increasingly to leave alone the events and ideas of the present, and to revert to the Enlightened past. Nothing pleased them more than to recall the age of the American Revolution, when they had been together and issues had seemed clear. With increasing gusto and increasing detachment, they read and discussed the French philosophers of the eighteenth century, including many that both had disapproved of in their day. It was Adams who stated most succinctly the pride both felt in the Age of Enlightenment and the doubt about the future both felt it hard to avoid:

> . . . according to the few lights that remain to us, We may say that the Eighteenth Century, notwithstanding all its Errors and Vices has been, of all that are past, the most honourable to human Nature. Knowledge and Virtue were increased and diffused, Arts, Sciences useful to Men, ameliorating their condition, were improved, more than in any former equal Period.
>
> But what are We to say now? Is the Nineteenth Century to be a Contrast to the Eighteenth? Is it to extinguish all the Lights of its Predecessor?[64]

This correspondence, in which the two sages ask this question in one way or another and usually answer it with restrained hope, is the greatest document of the American Enlightenment, written after the American Enlightenment was clearly over. One of the greatest legacies of the Enlightenment was the two statesmen themselves, who were both by the time of their death revered by almost everybody. Perhaps fortunately, their confidential comments on the past and present were not fully available until two hundred years later. Thus the nation was able to admire them selectively, and make them over into acceptable nineteenth-century heroes.

Two   *The Enlightenment Assimilated*

In the period 1800-1815, America was changing fast, and the European Enlightenment of the eighteenth century, in almost all its major phases, had ceased to fit American needs insofar as it ever had done so. Yet this same Enlightenment, translated and adapted, was too deeply embodied in American institutions and habits of thought to be abandoned altogether. For conservatives, the precepts of the Moderate Enlightenment were forever embedded in the nearly sacred Constitution. For the party of hope and change, the early hopes of the Revolutionary Enlightenment—the belief in new institutions and in the progress of the mind—were exemplified by the American republic itself. Scientific progress, despite some dangers, was still connected with practical improvement. And for the sincerely religious who believed deeply in the rule of Providence, the movement of history was very difficult to condemn outright.

Thus the semi-official intellectual culture of early nineteenth-century America could not preach reactionary counter-enlightenment consistently or with a whole heart. Instead it was necessary, in looking at the intellectual achievements of the past century and a half, to make distinctions. Locke, Newton, Montesquieu; science, progress, intellectual freedom, republicanism were good; Voltaire, Hume, Rousseau, religious skepticism, frantic innovation, undisciplined emotions, the French Revolution were bad. Moreover, these distinctions had to be made through rational argument, and not just through appeals to Biblical or other authority.

This was the task undertaken by two kinds of moderate conservatives. One group consisted of the Presbyterian clergy, who ran most of the col-

337

leges and were on the defensive against the New Divinity, extreme revivalism, and egalitarian anti-intellectualism. The other group consisted
of the Unitarian clergy and laity of the Boston area, who were on the
defensive against all these and against Calvinism as well. Obviously, for
both these groups and particularly the second, the task was partly to
rescue the early, English Moderate Enlightenment from any association
with later skepticism, materialism, or revolution. Samuel Clarke, Addison, and the Pope of the *Essay on Man* were still greatly to be revered,
but the world had changed since their day. Rationality and moderation
had to be defended against new adversaries. Therefore new arguments
had to be developed and new allies invoked. The style of argument created by these moderate and rationalistic conservatives can be seen as a
final form taken by the Enlightenment in America, less impressive intellectually than the others but important for its American uses. We
will call it the Didactic Enlightenment, not forgetting that all the other
forms also had their didactic elements. Since this fourth kind of Enlightenment was really in part a counter-Enlightenment, and since its
main influence came in the first half of the nineteenth century, it will
be treated here only briefly.

The task of formulating the Didactic Enlightenment was begun by
the preaching of "century-sermons" on the last Sunday of the eighteenth
century. Many Congregational, Unitarian, and Presbyterian ministers
used these to distinguish between true and false progress in the age that
was coming to an end, and to balance the threat of infidelity against the
gains of revival. One century-sermon grew into the most systematic and
most praised review of the recent past, Samuel Miller's *Brief Retrospect
of the Eighteenth Century*.[1]

Miller, a prominent Presbyterian clergyman of New York City, was
well qualified for the making of distinctions, being both an evangelical
Calvinist and a strong Jeffersonian Republican. In both of these loyalties
he differed in his youth from his friends of the Friendly Club, who
tended to be deists and Federalists.[2] In 1793 Miller was chosen by the
Tammany Society to preach a sermon at their Independence Day meeting. In this performance Miller, like many other clergymen of all political views, looked at the French Revolution in millennial terms, finding
it despite its excesses a long-overdue blow against tyranny in church and
state.[3] He stated this view more unequivocally than most, and was to
hang onto it longer.

In the election of 1800 Miller was a supporter of Jefferson, and a private letter making a strong statement found its way into print:

> Because Mr. Jefferson is suspected of Deism, are we to raise a hue and cry against him, as if he ought to be instantly deprived of his rights of citizenship? If he be an infidel, I lament it for two reasons: from a concern for his own personal salvation, and that a religion, which is so much spoken against, does not receive his countenance and aid. But notwithstanding this, I think myself perfectly consistent in saying that I had much rather have Mr. Jefferson President of the United States than an aristocratic Christian.[4]

Later, Miller was to move to the right. He became one of the three leading spirits of Princeton Theological Seminary in 1813, and thus was associated with the most intelligent and vigorous American opposition to all forms of intellectual and religious innovation. Eventually he found it necessary specifically to recant his Jeffersonianism and to denounce the former President in extreme terms. He had not moved far on this path in 1803, when the *Retrospect* was published.[5]

The *Retrospect* is the first American intellectual history, and foreshadows much that has proved both good and bad in that genre. Miller organizes his survey of all knowledge capably, and makes a real effort at fairness except when his deepest emotions are involved. He pleads in his Preface for justice even to infidels:

> A man who is a bad Christian may be a very excellent mathematician, astronomer, or chemist; and one who denies and blasphemes the Saviour may write profoundly and instructively on some branches of science highly interesting to mankind. It is proper to commiserate the mistakes of such persons, to abhor their blasphemy, and to warn men against their fatal delusions; but it is surely difficult to see either the justice or utility of withholding from them that praise of genius or of learning to which they are fairly entitled.[6]

Miller's book is a useful compendium, and monumentally dull reading—partly because of the author's caution, and partly because he depends on summaries, correspondence with authorities in each field, and sometimes even hearsay. He is quite honest about this, as about everything.[7]

In the century just ending Miller finds and catalogues great improvements, unimaginable earlier, in almost all the physical sciences. He rejoices in increasing politeness. Less wholeheartedly, he praises the new

and far wider diffusion of learning, which sometimes results in superficiality and hasty discarding of past gains. Another characteristic of the
century is increasing intellectual freedom, which is much to be admired
despite its abuse by false philosophers. The next century, to which
Miller looks forward, can be expected to bring equal improvement.

In moral and mental science, Miller repeatedly insists, the eighteenth
century's progress has been far more equivocal than in natural science.
False and infidel philosophy has been rife, despite the fact that all serious inquiry upholds Christian revelation. Gibbon, Diderot, the *Encyclopédie*, Helvétius, and Godwin are roundly condemned on both intellectual and moral grounds. Toward Voltaire, Hume, Priestley, and especially
Rousseau, however, Miller assumes the usual tone of regret: all are men
of great talents and achievements, whose talents have been used partly
for bad purposes. His treatment of *Emile* is typical:

> This singular production undoubtedly contains some just reasoning,
> many excellent precepts, and not a few passages of unrivalled eloquence.
> But it seems to be now generally agreed by sober, reflecting judges, that
> his system is neither *moral* in its tendency, nor *practicable* in its applica-
> tion. If the author excelled most other men in genius, he certainly had
> little claim either to purity of character, or real wisdom.[8]

Miller draws a careful distinction between the increased recognition
of female talent and ability, which he strongly defends, and the licentious doctrines of Mary Wollstonecraft, which aim at obliterating natural differences and can lead only to promiscuity.[9] In education as in
everything, the great mistake of the age is the belief of some in the perfectibility of man (or woman). Much progress in science and learning
will continue to take place, but neither the human mind nor heart will
ever approach perfection. The belief, central to the Revolutionary Enlightenment, that improvement in knowledge leads necessarily to improvement in character is rejected by Miller, as it had been by many
more profound critics of the age including both Rousseau and John
Adams. The Secular Millennium of false philosophy is contrasted specifically in Miller's conclusion with the millennium promised by the Bible,
which will be brought on by "divine illumination and evangelical holi-
ness, already so effective" and not by "the progress of knowledge."[10]

Here Miller, despite his limitations, almost becomes a major figure in
American intellectual history. His two central distinctions, one between

scientific and moral progress, and one between progress and perfectibility, were to become one of the mainstays of American official culture for more than a century. These distinctions, and Miller's selective attitude toward the Enlightenment, were implied in the completion of the orthodox Protestant American version of history. In countless sermons and patriotic orations and eventually in such books as Philip Schaff's *America* (1855) the American eighteenth century was contrasted with the French. The providential founding of the colonies, the sober revolution for civil and religious liberty, were completed by the equally providential and almost equally important battle with French anarchy and infidelity. On the one side was sober progress, on the other the vain dream of human perfection.[11]

Those Americans of the beginning of the nineteenth century who dealt not with history, or even the history of philosophy, but with the all-important subject of moral philosophy itself, faced a harder job than Miller's. A reliable basis for moral judgments had been perhaps the central concern of eighteenth-century thought, and as Miller showed, many thinkers had come to dangerous conclusions. Contemporary Europe seemed to offer little help. French conservative thinkers, defenders of Catholicism and restored monarchy, were out of the question as allies. German philosophy was as yet incomprehensible to almost all Americans, and not only for reasons of language. Miller himself is characteristically honest and characteristically inadequate in his account of Kant. The philosopher of Königsberg, Miller dutifully reports, is much admired, but few can understand him. After a very unsuccessful effort at summary based on British sources, Miller concludes that

> the most impartial judges will probably assign him a place among those metaphysical empirics of modern times, whose theoretical jargon, instead of being calculated to advance science, or to forward human improvement, has rather a tendency to delude, to bewilder, and to shed a baneful influence on the true interests of man.[12]

Only to Britain, then, could the Didactic Enlightenment turn for real help. Even here, Burkean conservatives were *too* conservative for some

and Benthamite radicals far too radical for most. The evangelical movement was very influential in America, but even its most admired figures,
William Wilberforce and Hannah More, talked about the duties of
those in humble stations in a tone that could never be useful in America. England remained the home of the truest and greatest philosophers,
Newton and Locke. She had also produced the best of the last century's
apologists for Christianity, including Joseph Butler, still widely read,
and William Paley, now coming into increasing use in schools and colleges.[13] Yet Butler's *Analogy* was too difficult and too pessimistic for
nineteenth-century America, and Paley's careful demonstrations of the
prudential uses of Christianity were too utilitarian for American moral
taste. Americans wanted to believe at once in social and even scientific
progress and in unchanging moral principles. Thus the only completely
acceptable European teachers, for the early builders of nineteenth-
century American official culture, were the Common Sense philosophers
of Scotland.

Some of the Scottish thinkers were so successfully adapted for nineteenth-century defensive purposes that it has been hard for Americans
to see the Scottish Enlightenment as an important and vigorous part of
the European Enlightenment in general, which it certainly was.[14] Between the American and Scottish environments there were both similarities and differences. Like Philadelphia and Boston, Glasgow and Edinburgh were proud provincial cities in the eighteenth century, full of resentment against the English metropolis and yet tempted always to
copy English intellectual fashions. Unlike America, Scotland had a long
tradition of intellectual and even political ties with France. The Scottish
thinkers were, like the Americans, strongly influenced by Montesquieu.
They were probably more intrigued by Rousseau. As in America, so in
Scotland culture depended mainly on the upper middle class, with more
aristocratic patronage available. Ministers, lawyers, and doctors played
a large part in the genial and cultivated intellectual circles of the Scottish towns. Professors were more important than in America: the Scottish universities had an enviable reputation in the British Isles and on
the Continent.

Above all, the Scottish Enlightenment like the American flourished in
an environment shaped by Calvinism, and by a divided Calvinism. Most
of the key thinkers were members, and some were ministers, of the moderate wing of the established Presbyterian church, loyal to it on national

as well as religious grounds, opposed to the upper-class drift toward the Church of England, but above all hostile to the enthusiasm and ignorance of the popular, ultra-Calvinist faction. Thus they were in a position closely analogous to that of the conservative, literate, anti-enthusiastic portion of the American Presbyterian church. They tended, on the other hand, to be considerably more cosmopolitan and urbane. Moderate progressives in provincial politics as well as religion, they reacted against the French Revolution with rather less panic than their American analogues. Cautious by instinct, personally genial and not unworldly, they were always concerned to distinguish themselves from Jacobites and other extremists, from wild Highlanders, and from ignorant bigots. Within their many differences from each other, according to their closest student, they had a common purpose: to show that culture, science, and urbanity were compatible with morality, religion, and law. In this task most of them made use of example and argument rather than rhetoric; they were part of the discourse carried on by Enlightened Europe.

David Hume was at once the center of the group and the principal antagonist of many of its members, some of whom were also his lifelong friends. Like the rest Hume was much more at home in Edinburgh (or Paris) than in London, and like the rest he was at least polite to members of the moderate wing of the Church, who in turn could not afford to quarrel with him violently lest they fall into the arms of their obscurantist opponents.[15]

Since well before the Revolution, as we have seen earlier, a number of major Scottish thinkers had been well known to educated Americans. One of these was Adam Ferguson, one of the most skeptical and least cautious eighteenth-century students of the varieties of human society, an opponent of the prevailing facile assumptions about the state of nature. Another, more influential in America, was Henry Home, Lord Kames, David Hume's cousin. Kames's theories of jurisprudence, which helped form the early opinions of Thomas Jefferson, had a large element of historical relativism. No historians were more widely admired in America than Hume and William Robertson. Edinburgh was the capital of American medicine until well after the Revolution. Among moral philosophers, Francis Hutcheson and Adam Smith were influential before the Revolution, and before Smith published *The Wealth of Nations*. Neither Hutcheson nor Smith was strictly speaking a Common

Sense philosopher.[16] Thus when one speaks of the influence in America of the Scottish Enlightenment one is speaking of a rich and various body of thought, united by tone and origin rather than by doctrine. Not all of the Scots could be assimilated to the Didactic Enlightenment.

It remains true that before the Revolution, increasingly after it, and with growing volume through at least the first half of the nineteenth century, a specific *kind* of Scottish thought acquired a massive influence in America. This was the philosophy of common sense, whose central thinker was Thomas Reid. Reid, a Presbyterian clergyman of the Moderate faction who occupied the chairs of moral philosophy at Glasgow and Aberdeen successively, was one of the most genial and polished of controversialists. He had, like the men of the Moderate Enlightenment from Locke on, an ingrained preference for whatever was temperate as against all that was extreme or upsetting. According to his friend and biographer Dugald Stewart, Reid suffered from bad dreams in his early life. He disciplined himself to wake up by insisting, in his dreams, that these were unreal. Finally he arrived at the point of not dreaming at all.[17]

Reid started from the problem set by Bishop Berkeley and particularly David Hume, that it was impossible rationally to demonstrate any identity between the ideas in our minds and external reality. A friend of Hume, who respected his criticism, Reid granted the great skeptic a lot. Little indeed could be proved by reasoning, neither the existence of matter nor of our own or other minds. But are we, Reid asked

> to admit nothing but what can be proved by reasoning? Then we must be sceptics indeed, and believe nothing at all.[18]

Wittily enough, Reid begged leave to be more of a skeptic than Hume. Why, he asked, should we reject the beliefs common to mankind, and still accept the arguments framed by the minds of philosophers?

On such grounds as experience, consensus, and necessity Reid argues that we can assume what most people always have assumed: that our minds can know actual objects, and not mere images or ideas of them. On the same grounds we are justified in accepting the reality of causation and the possibility of prediction. Going further, and here arguing partly from analogy, he puts the dictates of the conscience into the same category of intuitions that are irresistible and therefore true.

His appeal is in its way democratic; he is arguing that philosophers should accept what all men know:

> It is a bold philosophy that rejects, without ceremony, principles which irresistibly govern the belief and the conduct of all mankind in the common concerns of life; and to which the philosopher himself must yield, after he imagines he hath confuted them.[19]

It is also in a way utilitarian: we have to make certain assumptions in order to think or act. Only occasionally does Reid ground his argument in a polite and moderate appeal to the divine benevolence. There is no reason to think God has deliberately fooled us:

> Indeed, if we believe that there is a wise and good Author of nature, we may see a good reason, why he should continue the same laws of nature, and the same connections of things, for a long time; because, if he did otherwise, we could learn nothing from what is past, and all our experience would be of no use to us.[20]

Here Reid's reasonable and predictable God is closer to the deity of Jefferson or Paine than to that of Edwards.

It has been argued that Hume cordially agreed that men had, in living, to act on many assumptions that they could not prove rationally, and that Reid was saying little more. However, Hume felt that this kind of action, relying on moral and sensory impressions rather than on reason, was merely a psychological necessity; Reid declared that it was rationally justifiable as well. Reid was, moreover, making this sort of intuitive certainty the center of his argument. If this argument hardly amounted to a systematic philosophy, it was not bad as a description of the way most people get along without such a system. It was an attitude with a big and various future, leading on the one hand to the wilder intuitionists of Romantic generations and on the other to the pragmatists and beyond, to all those philosophers who try to take seriously the needs of non-philosophers.

It was also, obviously, easily capable of extreme vulgarization. James Beattie, on the basis of Reid's principles, argued that what was obvious was far more likely to be true than what was difficult, and on the basis of Common Sense complacently restated all the tired axioms of natural religion. In denouncing Hume, Beattie's tone was moralistic and un-gentlemanly. He was lionized in England, but rather disapproved in the most polite circles of Edinburgh. With Reid and Beattie, the most pop-ular spokesman of Common Sense in America was Dugald Stewart, a student of Reid who, in a prestigious Edinburgh chair, refined and re-stated the ideas of his teacher from 1785 until his death in 1828. Among disciples and continuers and critics of the Common Sense school, all well known in the United States, one might in addition list James Os-wald, Thomas Brown, and Sir William Hamilton.

It is not hard to understand the conquest of academic America in the early nineteenth century by the philosophy of Common Sense. It was en-lightened, moderate, practical, and easy to teach. It could be used to sustain or validate any set of ideas, but was in fact associated with the Moderate Enlightenment and moderate Calvinism. It was never anti-scientific nor obscurantist, never cynical, and it opened no doors to in-tellectual or moral chaos.

Common Sense had begun its conquests just before and during the American Revolution. This should not be at all surprising; political revo-lutionaries are not usually very original or daring in their ideas about the nature of the mind or of morality. Those who are daring enough to pull down established institutions have to believe in what they are doing; they cannot afford to be skeptics. Jefferson had been nourished on Lord Kames. When he met Dugald Stewart in Paris in 1789 he was im-mensely impressed. For the rest of his life Jefferson believed that Stewart was one of the greatest of thinkers. He frequently affirmed the existence and reliability of the moral sense in terms very close to those used by both Stewart and Reid.[21] In their late correspondence Adams shares with Jeffer-son his admiration for Stewart, whom he calls a profound genius.[22] Madi-son, the great moderate, learned the Scottish principles from Wither-spoon at Princeton, and at the same time so did the radical Freneau. At Yale Timothy Dwight and Joel Barlow both studied Kames and Beattie.[23]

It was, however, in the 1790's and under moderately conservative aus-pices that the Scottish authors really moved into positions of great strength in America. Beattie, Kames, Reid, and a little later Stewart all appear on booksellers' lists in great numbers; all were repeatedly pub-lished in America in this period. Still more important, the Scots became the basis of the standard curriculum in American colleges.[24]

This was partly because the colleges were overwhelmingly under the control of moderate Calvinists, either Presbyterian or Congregationalist.[25] These found the Scottish arguments useful in their polemics not only against skeptics and deists but also against mystics and emotionalists in religion, and particularly the followers of Edwards, who made man's duty to love God too extreme and all-absorbing. John Witherspoon, as we have seen, had been associated with the ultra-Calvinist Popular party against the Edinburgh Moderates in Scotland. When he came to America, however, he moved quickly into alliance with moderate Calvinists against Edwardsian extremists, and it is in this camp that his successors, at Princeton and elsewhere, usually remained.

Thus this defensive philosophy became the center of the American curriculum at a time when American colleges, even more than is always the case, were at once charged with all-important tasks and subject to constant sniping. Colleges were expected as a matter of course to inculcate in their charges the ideals of a free, republican, and religious society; to maintain strict morality among the students; to provide lawyers, doctors, teachers, ministers, and statesmen for the republic; and to keep the road open for poor boys to rise in these positions. Considering the difficulty of these tasks, and considering that the colleges were underfinanced and understaffed, torn by student riots and harassed by egalitarian suspicions, one can hardly say that they performed too badly.

The universal method of assigning texts for close reading and recitation, while hardly stimulating, at least led to thorough reading of important books, not always the hallmark of American education. Not only Scottish authors were assigned: among moralists Richard Price, Paley, and Butler held their own, and sometimes less approved authors were read with due warning. At William and Mary, certainly more liberal than most, students at the opening of the century read Price, Paley, Butler; Reid, Stewart, and Blair; but also Locke, Montesquieu, and Rousseau.[26]

Following and developing the pattern set by Witherspoon, the colleges organized their curriculum with moral philosophy at its peak. Students dealt first with natural philosophy and natural history, studied of course in conjunction with Evidences of Christianity. Beyond this lay mental philosophy or psychology, consisting of an elaborate cataloguing and characterization of the faculties or powers of the mind, drawn from Locke's *Essay* and Locke's critics. Finally, the president of the college usually taught seniors moral philosophy, setting forth in orderly fashion the duties of man to God, his neighbors, and himself. Though Revelation was nowhere contradicted and always eventually sustained, it was a matter of honor to arrive at the correct conclusions only through methods of reasoning which would—or so the teachers insisted—carry conviction to any honest infidel.

At least until the Civil War, and in some places long after, the Common Sense philosophy reigned supreme in American colleges, driving out skepticism and Berkeleyan idealism, and delaying the advent of Kant. At first it was inculcated directly from Scottish books. Then, beginning in the twenties, these were replaced by American textbooks of moral philosophy that simplified the Scottish principles and used them explicitly to validate republican and Protestant institutions. In dealing with the faculties of the mind, American teachers either of mental or moral philosophy gave special emphasis to the moral sense. This, they made clear, was not a mere sentiment or feeling, but a rational faculty implanted by the creator, which made correct judgments in the field of ethics even more trustworthy than in any other.

The precise arguments of these books was far less important than their tone. One of the early ones, Asa Burton's (1824), stated the Scottish principles, without attribution, as self-evident beginning assumptions:

> . . . it will be taken for granted through these essays, that a material world does exist, distinct from the mind; and that all objects of which we obtain a knowledge through the medium of bodily sense, are real existences. It is objects as they are which we see, . . . and not images or representations of them.[27]

The greatest best-seller in the genre, Francis Wayland's *Elements* of 1835, correctly described its own style: "Being designed for the purposes of instruction, its aim is, to be simple, clear, and purely didactic."[28]

Obviously this manner of teaching, learned by all future teachers, spread downward through the schools of the republic. Nowhere were Common Sense principles taught with more enthusiasm than in Presbyterian seminaries, where they were used to reconcile natural religion and revelation in a manner reminiscent of the early eighteenth century, and to play down the moral paradoxes which have always troubled Christians. The study of law was also deeply affected. As early as 1790 James Wilson, a Scot who had studied at Edinburgh and St. Andrews, devoted considerable time in his famous lectures on the law to praising the principles of Reid, and contrasting them to those of Blackstone and even Locke.[29] In the republic, he insisted, the law must be grounded not in custom or tradition but in moral obligation, understood through the method of Common Sense.

Momentously, the principles of Common Sense were extended to the field of political economy, which was taught as a set of self-evident maxims about the laws of God and the duties of man in the material world. Here, perhaps more than anywhere else, a great Scottish thinker was crudely simplified. Adam Smith was a part of the Edinburgh Enlightenment, but not strictly of the Common Sense school. A friend of Hume, he grounded moral obligation in experience and especially in sympathy rather than in the dictates of a rational moral faculty. Well known as a moral philosopher by well-educated Americans before the Revolution, Smith published his great work in political economy in 1776, when most Americans were involved in other concerns. *The Wealth of Nations* was never prescribed in American colleges nearly as much as the works of Beattie, Reid, and Stewart. Instead, the doctrines of laissez-faire were taught in textbooks written by American clergymen, which simplified not only Smith's economics but also his morality. Instead of Smith's careful balance between justice and benevolence, the American texts taught the supreme virtue of competitive individualism as a part of the clear dictates of the conscience, implanted by the creator and apprehended through common sense.[30]

Yet the Common Sense philosophy was not always a force for maintenance of the status quo. On the one hand, it furnished authoritative backing for the harsh simplicities of didactic laissez-faire economists. On the other hand, it legitimated the moral imperatives of reformers. Moral simplicity, and a rapid easy movement from the precepts of individual morality to the duties of man in society, was characteristic of nineteenth-century American radicals as well as conservatives, and some part of this simplicity came from early exposures to the philosophy of Common Sense.

One more realm, as important as political economy or moral philosophy itself, was also deeply affected by the Scottish Enlightenment. This was the realm of aesthetic taste. Since taste in America usually dealt with literature, and since literature in early America usually was associated with Boston, it is necessary to look at the second main group of interpreters of the Didactic Enlightenment. These were the Unitarians of eastern Massachusetts.

The religious liberals of the Boston region were the last followers in nineteenth-century America of the Moderate English Enlightenment of the mid-eighteenth century. They had formed their ranks in the 1740's in their fight against the Great Awakening.[31] Lemuel Briant, Charles Chauncy, a little later Jonathan Mayhew, and others had struggled to maintain a moral, rational, and sober religion, constantly citing John Locke and Samuel Clarke.

In the long years since then this struggle against successive opponents had taken the Boston liberals, as it had earlier taken the English latitudinarians and Old Dissenters, a long way from the standard doctrines of Christianity. Original sin, the atonement, and the Trinity had been abandoned one by one as irrational; in fact many of the liberals had become Arians and a few Socinians by the end of the century. By interpreting rather than abandoning Scripture, they had come to believe in one rational and beneficent deity, who had sent Jesus, an intermediary being perhaps slightly more than man but less than God, to teach men the truth. The liberals had, however, remained inside the Congregational establishment, exchanging pulpits with neighboring Calvinists and claiming that they themselves were the true children of the Puritan founders.

An acute student of the liberals has suggested that the French Revolution and the anti-Jacobin crusade postponed for a decade the inevitable formal split between Congregationalists and Unitarians.[32] The liberals were quite as hostile to Jacobinism and popular deism as the Calvinists. In anti-deist sermons they revived most of the arguments used by British latitudinarians two generations earlier, once more proving the rightness of Christianity by the moral excellence of its doctrines and the reliability of its witnesses. To them, rational progress was even more acutely endangered by violence and demagogy than by Calvinist rigidity. Federalist with very few exceptions, the liberal clergy like the Calvinists feared that licentious democracy was weakening the whole social and moral heritage of New England. They were much concerned to distinguish their own views not only from those of deists, but also from those of the radical English Unitarians, particularly Joseph Priestley.

With the waning of the Jacobin panic and the growing exuberance of the orthodox in the early period of the Great Revival, an overt split between orthodox and liberal Congregationalists was bound to happen.[33] It came about in the famous quarrel over the appointment of a new Hollis Professor of Divinity at Harvard, an institution long sliding toward liberal control. Against the prospect of a Unitarian professor, Jedidiah Morse mobilized his new alliance of Calvinists, forged in the anti-Jacobin struggle. With the election of Henry Ware to the professorship, the orthodox were bitterly defeated, and the defeat rankled.

In 1815 a new opportunity for attack was offered by the publication of a book on American Unitarianism by Thomas Belsham, a British Unitarian who rejoiced that "rational Christianity" had conquered eastern Massachusetts. At once Morse seized the opportunity of demonstrating that the Boston liberals were really of the same stripe as Belsham, Theophilus Lindsey, Joseph Priestley, and other British Socinians except that the latter were more honest. He and his allies demanded that hypocritical pretenses of unity like pulpit exchanges come to an end. Hurt and shocked by this ungentlemanly attack, the liberals were forced to define their views and demonstrate that they and not their opponents were Christian and Biblical. Finally, in his dramatic Baltimore sermon of 1819, William Ellery Channing stated clearly and openly the Unitarian beliefs at which some of the liberals had arrived long before.

The importance of this long and bitter controversy, carried on in pamphlets and counter-pamphlets in the traditional New England manner, is that it resulted in a geographical and cultural definition of New England religious liberalism. Thomas Jefferson had believed that Unitarianism was shortly to become the religion of America: instead, it became the religion of the upper class of eastern Massachusetts. In the climate of revivalist and democratic America, Unitarianism—like deism—withered in the South where it had made promising beginnings, and in Philadelphia where Priestley had cherished high hopes for it.[34] Connecticut Calvinists not only defended their territory successfully, but sent evangelical Calvinists like Morse and later Lyman Beecher to invade the citadel of the enemy. Over and over, orthodox sermons bewailed the apostasy of Boston, once the great center of true religion.

Thus in their own eyes, liberal Bostonians in the early nineteenth century were, as their forerunners had been in the 1740's, the beleaguered defenders of rational culture against the hosts of popular bigotry.

In the long run, much of the theology of Unitarianism, without its Enlightened philosophical basis and with a sentimentalized rhetoric, was to spread into the middle-class and urban sections of some of the major Protestant churches. But it is important for our purposes that in the early nineteenth century, Boston Unitarianism, the most intact survival of the Moderate Enlightenment, was confined within a specific local culture.[35] The Boston Unitarian establishment was probably the most cohesive and influential local upper class in America. To a considerable extent it was the arbiter for the nation of literary taste. Yet it was also, and very consciously, a beleaguered minority, gradually losing hope that its views would ever prevail. In 1820 Edward Everett explained to a friend why he continued to fight the hopeless battle against the ignorant orthodox majority:

> Did Unitarianism, or any other issue, rest where it begins, in these critical, theological questions, they would have little of my aid, whether I tho't their cause just or not. But as the cause of Learning, Refinement, & Free inquiry is most intimately connected with it, & as the Ignorance, necessary to keep up Orthodoxy, is so gross as to darken everything else, I resist the Natural disdain I feel for the Narrow Controversial area. But I am almost sick of it & if things do not in a few Years take a different turn, I shall quit the field, and confine my efforts and studies to subjects where there is a reasonable Chance of a fair hearing; and whre Y'r adversary will not be listened to, in inverse ratio to his learning and sense.[36]

Unitarians admired the eighteenth century a little more wholeheartedly than moderate Presbyterians. Samuel Miller had contrasted the century's lack of progress in morality and religion with its achievement in the sciences. To Unitarians, religion also had changed for the better, though fundamental moral rules were eternally the same. A writer in the *Monthly Anthology*, the literary review of polite Boston, condemned the false philosophy of the infidels just as Miller had, and deplored the "horrible blot" of the French Revolution. Nonetheless, the century had "contributed more than the preceding to the development of general truth." Not only had "the condition of the human race improved, but it was tending as rapidly to a high degree of perfection, as the weakness and wickedness of man will allow," and this was especially true, for all its faults, of America.[37]

The Unitarians detested Voltaire and Gibbon and all moral skeptics. Despite some fascination and occasional youthful dabbling they disliked Rousseau almost equally, as they did anybody who deprecated culture. Worst of all were Godwin and Paine. *Their* eighteenth century began a bit early, with Newton, Locke, and their followers. Its luminaries included Bishop Butler, William Paley, Richard Price, Archbishop Tillotson, Samuel Clarke, and Philip Doddridge.[38] Unitarian intellectuals admired Reid and Stewart even more wholeheartedly than the Presbyterians had been able to do. For the latter, it was always necessary to overcome a contradiction between original sin and the universal moral sense. In ideas, tastes, and habits cultivated Boston resembled cultivated Edinburgh.

In their theology the Boston liberals were very similar to the English latitudinarians of a century earlier. Though they broke with most of the central doctrines of historic Christianity—atonement, Trinity, original sin—they insisted as against the deists that revelation was necessary to complement, and could never contradict, the book of nature. The Bible, properly understood, was always rational and moral. Indeed, the Bostonians shared the Enlightened horror of all paradox. They were, on the other hand, strong admirers of their own Puritan ancestors and more "puritannical" in private morals than their Calvinist contemporaries. Despite these loyalties to earlier centuries, however, they lived in the nineteenth, and along with sedate naturalism and rigid moralism gave a large place to religious sensibility and poetic emotion, duly controlled by reason. Among them there was considerable variation between the poles of Enlightened dryness and pre-Romantic sentimentality.

Timothy Pickering, the arch-Federalist statesman, represents as well as anybody the rationalist side of Unitarianism. Indeed Pickering, inveighing against Calvinism in private, could recapitulate the arguments of the British deists and even those of Paine.

> The absurdities of popery made infidels of reading men in Catholic countries, especially in France: and some of the same absurdities, with certain other doctrines called Calvinistic, have produced most of the infidelity among Protestants. All revealed doctrines are addressed to our *reason*, and to undervalue it, is an act of ingratitude towards Him who

by that faculty has placed us in an elevated rank in creation. It is only by our reason that we can judge of the evidence of whatever claims to be a revelation from Heaven; and we may rest assured, that such a revelation can present to our belief nothing incompatible with the most perfect wisdom, justice and benevolence.[39]

An example of the prudential and conventional side of Unitarian religion can be found in the letters of Robert Treat Paine, a Revolutionary statesman, lawyer, and descendant of Puritan ministers, to his scapegrace son Thomas, later renamed Robert. The younger Paine, who was to become a well-known minor poet, annoyed his father by his trifling way of life, his ephemeral literary career, his habit of consorting with people of no fixed occupation, and above all his neglect of public worship. In 1794 Paine is lecturing his son on this last topic. The worship of the deity is recommended, he points out, by the ancient Greeks and Romans, by revelation, and by the "Cultivated Sentiment of the present age of progress."[40] Ten years later this despairing father invokes family tradition:

> Can you possibly suppose that I can patiently see you, for so long a course of life, behaving as one unconnected with the religious part of Society, & bringing up your children in no better a manner than might be expected of the most dissolute part of the Community? . . . Your conduct is so totally different from the manner in which my Ancestors lived & educated their families, & which I have thought it my duty & happiness to Conform to (however remissly I may have done it) that I am shocked & distress'd that the behavior of any branch of my family, should constrain me to express myself in this manner: where would you have been if I had conducted in [sic] my affairs as you have done in yours?[41]

This represents liberal Boston looking back to the Puritan and enlightened past; the view forward to the romantic future is represented by Joseph Stevens Buckminster, the gifted, sickly, and immensely admired paragon of the Boston ministry. Buckminster, in addition to arguing logically that God could be seen in the design and organization of nature, felt religious emotion more directly in the presence of sunsets or Alpine scenery.[42]

Finally, the Enlightenment was gracefully laid to rest and fully assimilated to nineteenth-century piety and reforming morality in the complex life and works of William Ellery Channing. Channing pretty clearly belongs to another chapter of intellectual history than the one we are dealing with. It is worth pointing out, however, that in his arguments with orthodoxy he was carrying on, in a new environment, the defense of rational and moral religion begun in New England by Charles Chauncy and Lemuel Briant. In his old age Timothy Pickering, mellowing a little, thought enough of Channing's Baltimore sermon to send it to his arch-enemy Thomas Jefferson. Pickering hoped to persuade Jefferson to endorse the new variety of liberal Christianity and demonstrate once and for all that he was not really hostile to revelation. Jefferson, in his polite answer, characteristically refused to be drawn into religious controversy but implied that among varieties of Unitarianism he preferred that of Price and Priestley.[43]

There was much in the Boston style of life reminiscent of eighteenth-century London. Like London or colonial Philadelphia, Boston was clubby. Leading ministers mixed with professors, doctors, and lawyers in the meetings of the Wednesday Evening Club, the Massachusetts Historical Society, the Athenaeum, or the American Academy of Arts and Sciences. In conscious opposition to their Calvinist contemporaries, ministers insisted that there was no opposition whatever between the strictest and purest personal morality and an expert knowledge of good food, wine, and manners. On the other hand, correct principles in religion were inseparably linked to correct principles of politics.

The ancestral Federalism of the Unitarians was shown in their passionate love of English ways and institutions, their inveterate suspicion of France, and their strained relation to political democracy. The political economy taught at Harvard qualified its adherence to laissez-faire with contempt for greed and speculation and insistence on the obligation of public service. A surprising devotion to Burke lingered in Boston and Cambridge: society would always be based on tradition and hierarchy, not on contract.[44] The Unitarians passionately believed in free speech, and sought earnestly to define the function of gentlemen in a democracy. If aristocratic leadership in national politics was no longer possible, gentlemen could continue to lead the way through example, education, and support for rational and moderate movements of reform.

Above all, the special role of enlightened men of means was the support of a rational and uplifting literature.[45] A pure and refined taste could uplift democracy, and redeem it from vulgarity and greed.

According to the Scottish philosophers, men had, in addition to the rational moral sense which enabled them to make correct judgments, the ability to cultivate both moral and aesthetic taste, which enabled them to delight in the good and the beautiful. The critical principles of the Unitarian critics (and also of most other Americans concerned about literary values) were formed on the dictates of Kames, Reid, and Stewart, and their close followers Hugh Blair and Archibald Alison. Blair's *Lectures on Rhetoric* (1783) and Alison's *Essays on the Nature and Principles of Taste* (1790) were published and republished in America. Their principles were constantly repeated by American texts and invoked by American critics in the first quarter of the nineteenth century.[46]

The most important literary venture of the Unitarians was the *Monthly Anthology*, a literary review published from 1803 to 1811. Its principle movers were Joseph Buckminster and William Emerson, who organized the Anthology Club, a congenial group of clergymen, lawyers, doctors and philanthropic merchants, whose editorial meetings were assisted by fine wines and good cigars.

In the *Anthology* and its successor, the *North American Review*, the Unitarian critics hoped to promote a worthy national literature. It was their constant effort to defend rationality as well as morality. They were vigorous enemies of revolution, immorality, skepticism, and the undisciplined imagination, all of which they identified with the arch-enemy Jean-Jacques Rousseau. Until about 1820 they defended the canon of eighteenth-century taste: Pope remained the touchstone in poetry, Addison in prose.

Very cautiously and slowly, but yet earlier than most other Americans, they admitted some of the Romantics. Radicals like Godwin or Freneau were condemned along with the diabolical and fascinating Byron; Keats and Shelley were neglected, Coleridge not yet understood, and Scott warmly welcomed. Buckminster and William Ellery Channing, less bound by eighteenth-century standards than most, fought the crucial battle for Wordsworth.

For all its seeming impregnability, Unitarian literary taste, like the whole Didactic Enlightenment of which it was a part, was a fragile fortress. Though the faculties of the mind including literary taste were carefully catalogued and defined, the definitions rested on introspection, and introspection is difficult to control. Thus the Scottish criticism, called in as a guardian of eighteenth-century rationalism, gradually opened the gates to nineteenth-century emotion.[47]

Ralph Waldo Emerson, who as a senior at Harvard in 1821 got a prize for defending Reid and Stewart against the new German thinkers, later sweepingly condemned the period of Scottish domination in New England culture: "From 1790 to 1820 there was not a book, a speech, a conversation or a thought in the State."[48]

It is easy enough to condemn or to caricature the Unitarian critics and the principles they were trying to defend. Their criticism was rigid, their morality timid, and their religion often seemed an unattractive mixture of tamed Christianity and watered-down Enlightenment. It can be argued in their defense that *any* praise of literature had its uses in America in 1815. To many citizens of the republic, poetry and, still more, novels, seemed almost by definition immoral or frivolous, useless or undemocratic.

A quite different New England writer, with her roots in Calvinism and not Unitarianism, looked back with more sympathy than Emerson at the period after the Revolution—which she had not known directly. Harriet Beecher Stowe saw New England in that period, isolated and obscure, "burning like live coals under this obscurity with all the fervid activity of an intense, newly kindled, peculiar, and individual life."[49] At about the age of nine, at the excellent Litchfield School, Harriet Beecher had

> listened with eager ears . . . to recitations in such works as Paley's "Moral Philosophy," Blair's "Rhetoric," Alison's "On Taste," all full of most awakening suggestions to my thoughts.[50]

Apparently this childhood experience of the Didactic Enlightenment had not got in the way of her very acute romantic sensibilities.

Emerson thought that the new era of creation and poetry began with Channing. Channing, like Emerson himself and also Thoreau, studied the Scots at Harvard. Unitarian culture, like official New England culture since the beginning, nourished the rebels who were to overthrow it.

Three *The Enlightenment and America*

The Didactic Enlightenment, relying heavily on the Scots, was the principal mode in which the Enlightenment was assimilated by the American official culture of the nineteenth century. This official culture depended on a difficult credo with three articles: the essential reality and dependability of moral values, the certainty of progress, and the usefulness and importance of "culture" in the narrower sense, especially literature.[1] In the colleges of the early nineteenth century, in the republic's first literary reviews, in simplified version in the schools this credo was taught. Every article of it was supported by reference to the Scottish Enlightenment, but the official credo survived long after the Scottish thinkers had been superseded, in the form of the Genteel Tradition.

The Genteel Tradition, as George Santayana who named it memorably pointed out, was thin and unreal, detached from most of the sources of the nation's real vitality.[2] It is very easy to point out its faults. Its moral code, buttressed by the Scottish epistemology, was both rigid and unrealistic. At its worst American moralism could justify anything. The belief in progress could be used to put off the solution of hard problems. The literary culture promoted by the professional defenders of culture, often on the basis of Scottish arguments, was often trivial. Above all, the religion promoted by either the Unitarians or the increasingly compromising and compromised Calvinists was unsatisfying: it did not address the realities of human nature, it explained away everything that is profound and interesting in Christianity.

At least from the time of the anti-Jacobin panic, much of official American culture was based on fear: fear of France, fear of Europe, fear of the Negro, fear of popular passion. For some, beneath these fears lay

358

an ultimate metaphysical fear: fear of solipsism, of nothingness, of subject and object coming unstuck. This fear did not have to be taught by David Hume; Jonathan Edwards had been an adequate teacher. For others, the basic fear was probably passion itself, and beneath political passion, sexual passion. In other words, what the defenders of rational culture were finally most afraid of was themselves.

Now it is almost dead, we can perhaps look at the Genteel Tradition with some tolerance. Popular passion is a frightening reality when it is really aroused: not all the fears of the defenders of order were as unreal as Jedidiah Morse's conspiracy of the Illuminati. What is clear is that whatever its utility, the Scottish philosophy was not adequate to its task. Nor was the Genteel Tradition; in the long run American culture must come to some sort of satisfactory terms not only with democracy but with the material wealth that supports culture.

Already by 1815 or 1820 a revolt was under way against the compromises of the Didactic Enlightenment—one part of it was Jacksonian Democracy, another part romantic emotion, another the old enemy of enlightenment: popular religious revival. And the revolt of the 1830's was only one of many to come. The Didactic Enlightenment, the fourth and last form of Enlightenment directly to affect America, was an important fact in the history of high culture in America, but it was not the only way in which the Enlightenment of the eighteenth century affected the United States. Let us look briefly at the others we have discussed in this book.

The first Enlightenment, the Moderate Enlightenment, the defense of balance and order in all things, was deeply imbedded in the institutions of the republic and has never been dislodged. One of the most curious facts in the whole history of American culture is the deep hold on popular emotions of the very eighteenth-century, anti-majoritarian institution of judicial review. This institution, developed out of the theory of liberty and property, of checks and balances, has shown a strange durability. It has defended itself successfully not only against strong reforming emotions in the nineteenth century, not only against right-wing demagogy in the twentieth, but against direct attacks by the most popular and skillful leaders of the people: against Andrew Jackson and Franklin Roosevelt. Such other eighteenth-century survivals as the allotment of two senators per state, the presidential veto, the separate jurisdictions of state and federal government are impossible to explain except in terms of their eighteenth-century origins, and their modern defenders make use of eighteenth-century arguments. Yet we are often told that America is a country of extremes, of wild swings of opinion, of sudden sweeping movements in religion, politics, and intellectual fashion. Perhaps the political institutions of the Moderate Enlightenment have survived better than the spirit of balance and compromise which they originally embodied.

The second Enlightenment, the Skeptical Enlightenment, the Enlightenment of Voltaire and Hume, has influenced America least. Skepticism about religious dogma has led a vigorous minority existence from Abner Kneeland to Clarence Darrow. Yet those Americans of the village atheist tradition who enjoy baiting the clergy are usually anything but skeptics about moral values, and their morality is often not very different from that of the clergy they are baiting. They are very unlikely to be skeptical about democracy. And at least until recently, very few Americans have gone beyond political, religious and moral skepticism in the direction of Hume, to distrust the operations of their own minds and the validity of all general principles. It may be that when real skepticism of this sort becomes widespread, society becomes inoperable as it did in the France of Louis XVI.

The third Enlightenment, the Revolutionary Enlightenment, was easily turned back in 1798 in its pro-Jacobin or deist form. Yet its vitality and importance in America have been very considerable. It has been strongest in its comparatively moderate form, derived in part from the radicals of the American Revolution and the hopeful early prophets of the French. Like Condorcet and Volney, many Americans have believed that men in the future would be morally better and politically freer than in the past or present. Like Jefferson and Paine, most have usually thought that this improvement would be especially marked in America. Unlike Jefferson, however, many have believed that technological progress would be closely related to moral improvement. Paradoxically, the opposite, primitivist form of the Revolutionary Enlightenment has been almost equally powerful: the superiority of the wilderness or the frontier or the farm has been deeply lodged in American emotions.

Even the extreme forms of the Revolutionary Enlightenment, the belief in the clean sweep and the new start, the Godwinian principle of human nature so improved that institutions would be unnecessary, has had some influence in America. One can catch echoes of it in recurrent proclamations of the New Society, the New Politics, the New Morality, the New Woman, or the New School. Finally, the fiery millennium in which the past is destroyed to make way for the future has captured the imagination of a number of groups in America. After 1798 the location was no longer in France; it has only rarely and for a few people been any foreign country. Usually, it is in a purged and purified America. Whether this kind of millennialism has been religious or secular, of the extreme right or the extreme left, has hardly made much difference in its power or in its vocabulary.

We have been talking, just now, about the long-run assimilation of the Enlightenment, not about its direct survival. In its European form, as an actual historical entity, the Enlightenment was the culmination of many centuries of classical and aristocratic civilization. Condorcet, Voltaire, even Rousseau were products of their societies and could not be moved intact into the American nineteenth-century world. Nowhere in Europe, for that matter, did the Enlightenment in any pure form survive either the French or the Industrial Revolution. On the other hand, it spread nowhere among an agrarian population. The Enlightenment began in eighteenth-century towns. Paris, London, and Edinburgh could not dictate to nineteenth-century America—nor could Philadelphia and Boston.

What was usable was assimilated, and perhaps some essence of Enlightenment, difficult to define concretely, was more important than any direct heritage of books or ideas. George Washington, an untheoretical man, rejoiced at the end of the Revolution that "the foundation of our empire was not laid in the gloomy age of ignorance and superstition, but at an epoch when the rights of mankind were better understood and more clearly defined than at any former period."[3] We can agree; partly because the United States came into existence at the end of the eighteenth century, many Americans have continued somehow to believe that the republic *ought* to be more progressive than other countries, that equality and the pursuit of happiness are at least the proper objective, even that rational arguments ought to be rationally answered.

Whatever has survived has had to be accommodated to the other and older source of American culture: Christianity in its myriad and shifting American forms. And perhaps even more difficult: in America the Enlightenment has had to be combined with democracy.

It comes as a shock to Americans, who tend vaguely to identify Enlightenment with democracy, to find that almost none of the eighteenth-century philosophers had a program with a real place in it for most people. This is true of those who looked forward to democracy and believed in it theoretically, as well as of those who did not: of Rousseau and Jefferson as well as of Voltaire and Hume. Democracy in practice, from Jefferson's presidency on, has not been much like the dreams of any of the eighteenth-century thinkers.

American intellectuals have usually been partisans of some kind of Enlightenment. Often the Enlightenment, as promulgated by intellectuals, has been rejected by the people, or by large sections of the people. This fact has been very hard for American scholars to think about, or even to admit. To think about it seriously means to take account of the deficiencies of the Enlightenment as well as its virtues, and to try to understand the ideas and feelings of those who have sided against it in various periods: religious revivalists, Jacksonian democrats and their populistic successors, Transcendentalists and the long succession of cultural rebels who have sought to go beyond the goals of rationality and progress.

To understand both the Enlightenment and its opponents is a difficult and painful task for American intellectuals. It is also a necessary task. Neither the Enlightenment nor any other set of ideas has much of a future unless it can find its place in mass society, among human beings as they are. From the point of view of Enlightenment this may well be a tragic fact: there are hints that both Jefferson and Adams sometimes thought so. Yet Adams at least usually concluded that it is precisely this desperate and unpredictable struggle, this friction between principle and reality that gives life—and therefore history—most of its interest.

Notes

PART I

Notes for Chapter 1

1. David Hume, *Essays and Treatises on Several Subjects* (2 v., London, 1772), I, 509. This collection, first published in 1742, was read in the colonies, as were all British authors cited or discussed at length in this chapter.
2. J. H. Plumb, *The Origins of Political Stability: England, 1675-1725* (Boston, 1967), 2.
3. John C. Greene, *The Death of Adam* (Ames, Iowa, 1959), 12.
4. John Locke, *An Essay concerning Human Understanding* (1690), ed. Alexander Campbell-Fraser (2 v., New York, 1959), I, 26.
5. *Ibid.*, II, 186, 228-29.
6. *Ibid.*, II, 192-93.
7. *Ibid.*, I, 345.
8. Clarke's two sets of Boyle Lectures, *A Demonstration of the Being and Attributes of God* (London, 1705) and *A Discourse Concerning the Unchangeable Obligations of Natural Religion, and the Truth and Certainty of the Christian Revelation* (London, 1706), are republished in facsimile in one volume, separately numbered (Stuttgart, 1964).
9. *Natural Religion*, 202-3. This snobbish tone is extremely common both in the Christian apologists and deists of the day.
10. *Unchangeable Obligations*, 16; *Natural Religion*, 343.
11. *Unchangeable Obligations*, 236-37.
12. Statements about the relative popularity of European books in America rest in part on a study made in collaboration with David Lundberg of Enlightenment books found in American libraries and booksellers' lists. This study is briefly summarized in May and Lundberg, "The Enlightened Reader in America," to be published in *The American Quarterly* in May 1976. As this article points out, data of this sort, while helpful, need to be supplemented by other kinds of evidence.
13. Tillotson, "The Precepts of Christianity not Grievous," in *Works* (10 v., London, 1820), I, 468-69.
14. Anonymous preface in Wollaston, *Religion of Nature Delineated* (London, 1737), xiv.
15. Aaron Burr says to Philip Doddridge, New York, April 1, 1748, "I have often blest the God of all Grace for the Benefit I have received from your Works," and after much more praise describes the troubles of the College of New Jersey,

hoping for both advice and financial help from English Dissenters. Burr Papers, Princeton University Library.

16. Anthony Collins, *An Essay Concerning the Use of Reason in Propositions the Evidence whereof Depends upon Human Testimony* (London, 1707), 69, 171.

17. Matthew Tindal, *Christianity as Old as the Creation* (2nd ed., London, 1732), 44.

18. John Toland, *Christianity not Mysterious* (2nd ed., London, 1696), xxi-xxii.

19. Thomas Chubb, *Posthumous Works* (2 v., London, 1748), II, 77-78. Hazard attributes this argument to Voltaire, who, characteristically enough, must have copied it from Chubb without acknowledgment. Paul Hazard, *European Thought in the Eighteenth Century* (Paris, 1946), tr. J. Lewis May (paperback, Cleveland, 1963), 413.

20. Burke, *Reflections on the Revolution in France* (London, 1790), 135. One possible answer to this rhetorical question was unknown to Burke: Bolingbroke was read with devotion by both Thomas Jefferson and John Adams.

21. Quoted by Mark Pattison, "Tendencies of Religious Thought in England, 1688-1750," in *Essays* (2 v., Oxford, 1889), I, 49. The chief specimen of the Old Bailey theology was Bishop Sherlock's immensely popular *Trial of the Witnesses*, which applied English legal procedure to the evidence for the Resurrection.

22. Pattison, "Tendencies," 46.

23. Quoted in Stuart C. Henry, *George Whitefield, Wayfaring Witness* (New York and Nashville, 1957), 157.

Notes for Chapter 2

1. A valuable introduction to the new colonial social history with a good bibliography up to the date of its publication is furnished by Gary B. Nash, *Class and Society in Early America* (New York, 1970). James A. Henretta's, *The Evolution of American Society, 1700-1815* (Lexington, Mass., 1973) is an excellent interpretation of much of the work of the new historians, with a good deal of original material included. An article which I have found helpful both for this chapter and for Chapter 5 below is Joyce Appleby, "Liberalism and the American Revolution," which is soon to appear in the *New England Quarterly*. Recent historians of very different kinds whose work has influenced this chapter include Stewart Bruchey, Charles S. Grant, Philip Greven, Kenneth Lockridge, Jackson T. Main, and John M. Murrin. The *William and Mary Quarterly* and various sessions of the Organization of American Historians have proved most helpful to an outsider trying to understand recent developments in social history. Of the older kind of social history I have profited especially from Carl Bridenbaugh's *Cities in Revolt* (New York, 1955), which suggests a division within the late-colonial upper class which seems to me to be borne out by both social and intellectual history. It is one of my hopes that these two fields, as each is further developed, may come back together.

2. William Livingston *et al.*, *The Independent Reflector*, ed. Milton M. Klein (Cambridge, Mass., 1963), 359.

3. "Extracts from Capt. Francis Goelet's Journal . . . 1746-1750," *New England Historical and Genealogical Register and Antiquarian Journal*, XXIV (1870), 57.

4. Clifford Dowdey, *The Virginia Dynasties* (Boston, 1969), 127-28.
5. Carl Bridenbaugh, ed., *Gentleman's Progress: The Itinerarium of Dr. Alexander Hamilton, 1744* (Chapel Hill, 1948), 185-86.
6. William Smith, *A History of the Late Province of New York* (2 v., New York, 1830), II, 344-45.
7. Jonathan Boucher, *Reminiscences of an American Loyalist, 1738-1789*, ed. Jonathan Boucher (Boston, 1925), 98-99.
8. A helpful introduction to early American demographic history is J. Potter, "The Growth of Population in America, 1700-1860," in D. V. Glass and D. E. C. Eversley, *Population in History* (London, 1965), 631-68.
9. Henretta, *Evolution*, 15.
10. My ideas about early American education, in this chapter and later in this book, have been influenced by Bernard Bailyn, *Education in the Forming of American Society* (Chapel Hill, 1960).
11. At Yale the Puritan standbys, William Ames and John Wollebius, coexisted in the curriculum with Locke, Newton, and William Wollaston as late as 1777. Louis Franklin Snow, *The College Curriculum in the United States* (New York, 1907), 36.
12. The poem is quoted in Mercy Warren to Mrs. Hannah Winthrop, February, n.d., 1773, in Mercy Otis Warren Papers, Massachusetts Historical Society. Scientific developments, especially in Philadelphia, are treated at more length below in Part III, Chapter 3.
13. This change is brilliantly summarized by Ian Watt, *The Rise of the Novel* (Berkeley and Los Angeles, 1957).
14. This is the conclusion reached, on the basis of complex evidence, by Kenneth A. Lockridge, *Literacy in Colonial New England* (New York, 1974).
15. Bridenbaugh, ed., *Gentleman's Progress*, 112.
16. Joseph Addison, Richard Steele, *et al.*, *The Spectator* (8 v., London, 1767), no. 187, III, 74.
17. The influence of Radical Whig writers is discussed below in Chapter 5, and again in Part III, Chapter 1.
18. Benjamin Franklin, *Proposal Relating to the Education of Youth in Pennsylvania* (reprinted Ann Arbor, 1927), 15.

Notes for Chapter 3

1. James Henretta, in a brief discussion of the Great Awakening, suggests a whole series of economic and social antecedents, including a major epidemic of diphtheria, which had just killed 20,000 people, mostly children; an economic slump and the consequent closing of opportunities; war; and tensions arising from changing sexual mores. These plausible and interesting suggestions are part of a continuing discussion of the causes of the Great Awakening which has gone on for several generations and is beyond the scope of this book. Henretta, *Evolution of American Society*, 129-32.
2. A brilliant article by Norman S. Fiering demonstrates that the argument over the Great Awakening in New England grew out of a long and very complex seventeenth-century debate over the relation between will and intellect. This was itself part of an argument over the relative importance of head and heart which

had gone on since the beginning of Christianity. Fiering, "Will and Intellect in the New England Mind," *William and Mary Quarterly*, XXIX (1972), 515-58.

3. See Robert Middlekauff's discussion of Cotton Mather's ambivalent attitude toward science. Middlekauff, *The Mathers* (New York, 1971), 279-319.

4. The status of the New England ministers in the first half of the eighteenth century is interestingly described in J. W. T. Young, "God's Messengers" (unpublished dissertation, Berkeley, 1970).

5. Edwards, *Treatise on the Religious Affections* (1746), quoted in Joseph Haroutunian, *Piety versus Moralism* (New York, 1932), 44. I am inclined to agree with Vincent Tomas and others that Perry Miller, in his brilliant *Jonathan Edwards* (New York, 1949), forced Edwards into a modern mould. Tomas, "The Modernity of Jonathan Edwards," *New England Quarterly*, XXV (1952), 70-84.

6. Alan Heimert, *Religion and the American Mind* (Cambridge, Mass., 1966). I have been influenced in my treatment of the Great Awakening and many other subjects by this provocative book. I think Heimert's basic thesis, that the Awakening forced people to choose one of two sides, is correct, although there were important further divisions within each of these groupings. He seems to me right also in saying that the most crucial difference was between an emotional and a rational style and that this difference can be traced through the whole history of American culture. He is mistaken, however, I think, in suggesting that the same people took the same religious and political sides in a long series of crises down to the time of Jackson; in later chapters I try to suggest some of the shifts in these positions. In my opinion this book has been underrated by some of its reviewers, who have concentrated on its exaggerations to the neglect of its valuable insights.

7. The description is by Dr. Alexander Hamilton, at second hand, in Bridenbaugh, ed., *Gentleman's Progress*, 161; the general outlines of the incident are well known. It occurs to me that this might be the origin of the bonfire in which books and gewgaws are also burned in Nathaniel Hawthorne's parable "Earth's Holocaust."

8. Edwards, unpublished sermon reprinted in Perry Miller, "Jonathan Edwards' Sociology of the Great Awakening," *New England Quarterly*, XXI (1948), 70-71.

9. Killingly Convention of Strict Congregational Churches, 1781, quoted in C. C. Goen, *Revivalism and Separatism in New England, 1740-1800* (New Haven, 1962; reprinted Hamden, Conn., 1966), 183.

10. There are examples of Antinomian sexual doctrine and behavior in Martin E. Lodge, "The Great Awakening in the Middle Colonies" (unpublished dissertation, Berkeley, 1964), 259-60; in William McLoughlin, *Isaac Backus and the American Pietistic Tradition* (paperback, Boston, 1967), 17-18; and in Goen, *Revivalism*, 201-2, where a case of murder is also mentioned.

11. In this statement I am following Conrad Wright's *The Beginnings of Unitarianism in America* (Boston, 1955), one of the most satisfying monographs in the whole range of my inquiry.

12. Briant, "The Absurdity," etc. (pamphlet, Boston, 1749).

13. Chauncy, *The Benevolence of the Deity* (Boston, 1784), 135-36.

14. Mayhew, *Seven Sermons* (Boston, 1749), 5.

15. Eliot, "A Discourse on Natural Religion" (Dudleian lecture, Boston, 1771), xii

(pamphlet). Eliot, like Briant, can be considered either a very liberal Old Light Calvinist or a moderate Arminian.

16. Clifford K. Shipton, *Sibley's Harvard Graduates*, sketch of Jonathan Mayhew, XI (11 v., Boston, 1960), xi, 449.

17. Briant, "The Absurdity," 23.

18. Bellamy, "The Millennium," in *Works* (2 v., Boston, 1850), I, 457. I have been much influenced in my brief treatment of the New Divinity by the fresh insights contained in the unpublished dissertation on that subject of Charles Constantin (Berkeley, 1972).

19. Richard D. Birdsall, "Ezra Stiles versus the New Divinity Men," *American Quarterly*, XVII (1960), 256.

20. Samuel J. Moody, "An Attempt To Point Out the Fatal and Pernicious Consequences of the Rev. Mr. Joseph Bellamy's Doctrines Respecting Moral Evil" (pamphlet, Boston, 1759).

21. cf. William James: "The securest way to the rapturous sorts of happiness of which the twice born make report has as an historic matter of fact been through a radical pessimism." *The Varieties of Religious Experience* (New York, 1902; paperback, 1961), 126.

22. The figures are those of Edwards Amasa Park, citing Samuel Hopkins and Ezra Stiles, "New England Theology," *Bibliotheca Sacra*, IX (1852), 175. Despite these figures, Edmund S. Morgan's modest estimate of New Divinity success in his life of Ezra Stiles (New Haven, 1962) seems to me more plausible than the very high estimate made by Heimert in *Religion and the American Mind*. Morgan's view is, however, effectively criticized by Richard Birdsall, in the article cited above.

23. Rush to Witherspoon, Edinburgh, March 25, 1767, copy in John Witherspoon Papers, Princeton University Library.

24. V. L. Collins, *President Witherspoon* (2 v., Princeton, 1925), I, 137.

25. Samuel Stanhope Smith to William Woodward (a publisher), August 1, 1810. Samuel Stanhope Smith Papers, Princeton University Library. I have examined the text of these lectures as reproduced in notes by various students in 1772, 1774, 1782, and 1795 in the Princeton University Library, and compared these with the published versions of 1800, 1810, and 1822. Variations, even in authors cited as the most up-to-date, are minor. I have cited below the version contained in the notes of J. Edward Calhoun, of 1774, which are legible and complete, in a notebook with numbered pages.

26. Lectures, Calhoun notes, 232, 56.

27. *Ibid.*, 20.

28. *Ibid.*, 57.

Notes for Chapter 4

1. *The Spectator* (8 v., London, 1767), VI, no. 459, 247.

2. Thomas Cradock, sermon of 16 October 1753, in "Synodalia" (Records of the Meetings of the Clergy of the Province of Maryland, 1693-1772. Collected and Transcribed by the Reverend Ethan Allen of Baltimore, 1864. MS, Maryland Diocesan Library, Baltimore), 184. This sermon has been published by David L.

Skaggs in the *William and Mary Quarterly*, XXVII (1970), 630-53. The quotation is from "Synodalia," 184.

3. Thomas Barton to the Secretary [of the Society for the Propagation of the Gospel], Lancaster, Pennsylvania, 17 December 1770, in William Stevens Perry, ed., *Historical Collections Relating to the American Colonial Church* (5 v. in 4, Hartford, 1870-78), II, 448.

4. See Bruce E. Steiner, "New England Anglicanism: A Genteel Faith?" *William and Mary Quarterly*, XXVII (1970), 122-35.

5. As a superb example of this point of view, see Jack P. Greene, ed., *The Diary of Colonel Landon Carter of Sabine Hall, 1752-1778* (2 v., Charlottesville, 1965), esp. introduction and I, 25-26.

6. Unsigned letter from Pedee River, South Carolina, 1790, in John Rippon, *The Baptist Annual Register for 1790, 1791, 1792, and part of 1793* (London, 1793?), 106.

7. "Synodalia," 183.

8. Chandler to the Bishop of London, Elizabethtown, 21 October 1767, in Perry, *Historical Collections*, II, 334-35.

9. Boucher, *Reminiscences of an American Loyalist* (Boston, 1925), 35.

10. My generalizations about Southern sermons are drawn mainly from manuscript sermons in the University of Virginia Library and the Maryland Diocesan Library, Baltimore.

11. Quoted in Oswald Tilghman, *History of Talbot County, Maryland 1661-1861* (2 v., Baltimore, 1945), 429.

12. In 1724 the Commissary's questions to the Virginia clergy included the question: "Are there any Infidels, bond or free within your Parish; and what means are used for their conversion?" A typical answer is: "No Indians live in my Parish; there may be 6 free Negroes, there are many negro Slaves, and but very few baptiz'd, nor any means used for their Conversion, the owners Generaly not approving thereof, being led away by the notion of their being and becoming worse slaves when Christians." Perry, *Historical Collections*, I, 550. The answers to the same questions are somewhat more optimistic in Maryland. *Ibid.*, IV, 190-230.

13. The letter is in L. Tyerman, *The Life of the Rev. George Whitefield* (2 v., London, 1876), I, 353-54.

14. G. M. Brydon, *Virginia's Mother Church* (2 v., Richmond, 1952), II, 550.

15. Bacon to Secretary, 4 August 1750, in Perry, *Historical Collections*, IV, 325.

16. For example, James Nourse of Fauquier County, who wrote General Gates on October 18, 1776, "I burn to kick out the Athanasian Creed, to which we owe the existence of so many deists and atheists; and that in public worship we rationally adore the one only self-existent God through Christ Jesus." Quoted in Brydon, *Mother Church*, II, 368.

17. *Ibid.*, 38.

18. Paul F. Boller, Jr., *George Washington and Religion* (Dallas, 1963), 31 and *passim*.

19. David Ramsay, *The History of South Carolina* (2 v., Charleston, 1809), II, 46.

20. Quoted in Frederick Dalcho, *A Historical Account of the Episcopal Church in South Carolina* (Charleston, 1820), 110.

21. C. F. Pascoe, *Two Hundred Years of the S.P.G.* (2 v., London, 1901), I, 15.

22. See Frederick P. Bowes, *The Culture of Early Charleston* (Chapel Hill, 1942), 29-30.
23. "Letter of the Reverend John Joachim Zubly of Savannah, Georgia," Massachusetts Historical Society, *Collections*, 1st ser., VIII (1866), 214-19.
24. Penuel Bowen to William Henry Hill, Savannah, 7 August 1786, in Nathaniel Bowen Papers, South Carolina Historical Society.
25. Bowen to Col. Joseph Ward, Savannah, October 1876, Nathaniel Bowen Papers.
26. Robert M. Weir, " 'The Harmony we were Famous For'; An Interpretation of Pre-Revolutionary South Carolina Politics," *William and Mary Quarterly*, XXVI (1969), 473-80.
27. See Part II, Chapter 2, below.
28. This suggestion was made, for instance, by Alexander Murry of Reading and Thomas Barton of Lancaster, both in letters of 1764. Perry, *Historical Collections*, II, 356, 369.
29. A superb example of this hope is the letter of Deane [*sic*, n.b.] Swift to William Smith, 16 July 1764, in the William Smith Papers, in the Church Historical Society, Episcopal Theological Seminary of the Southwest, Austin, Texas. Here an *English* Episcopalian prophesies that America, under Anglican auspices, will "in four or five hundred years more be as renowned for wisdom and politeness as any part of Europe is now, or perhaps ever was in the political and philosophical days whether of the Greeks or the Romans."
30. Pascoe, *Two Hundred Years*, I, 79.
31. John Devotion to Ezra Stiles, Saybrook, 16 March 1768, in F. B. Dexter, ed., *Extracts from the Itineraries and other Miscellanies of Ezra Stiles*, etc. (New Haven, 1916), 472. Alison to Stiles, Philadelphia, 27 May 1759, *ibid.*, 424; Chauncy to Stiles, Boston, 14 June 1771, *ibid.*, 451. Bruce E. Steiner, "Anglican Officeholding in Pre-Revolutionary Connecticut, etc.," *William and Mary Quarterly*, XXXI (1974), 369-406, reports that Anglicans in Connecticut often held town offices in numbers disproportionate to their total strength. This was partly because of their money and social position, but also because of divisions among the Calvinist majority.
32. H. W. and C. Schneider, eds., *Samuel Johnson, His Career and Writings* (4 v., New York, 1929), I, 148-50, 295-96, 349.
33. Dietmar Rothermund, *The Layman's Progress* (Philadelphia, 1961), 15. In the interest of brevity, I have reluctantly decided not to treat the Quakers in this book. Their relation to the Enlightenment is excellently discussed in the works of Frederick Tolles.
34. Smith, "A General Idea of the College of Mirania," reprinted in *Discourses on Public Occasions in America* (2nd ed., London, 1762), 43.
35. Adams, in *Works*, ed. C. F. Adams (10 v., Boston, 1850-56), II, 358-59.
36. Quoted in E. P. Cheyney, *History of the University of Pennsylvania 1740-1940* (Philadelphia, 1940), 35.
37. Smith to Rev. Dr. Dearcroft, 1 November 1756, in H. W. Smith, *Life and Correspondence of the Rev. William Smith, D.D.* (2 v., Philadelphia, 1880), I, 143. Document undated, in Smith's hand, called "State of the Church in the College of Philadelphia," in the William Smith Papers, Church Historical Society, Austin.
38. William Smith, *Discourses*, contains a complete table of the curriculum, 116-17.

39. Jacob Duché, *Observations on a Variety of Subjects* (Philadelphia, 1774), 63-64, 150.
40. Smith, "An Oration Delivered, January 22, 1773, before . . . the American Philosophical Society, held at Philadelphia, for promoting Useful Knowledge" (pamphlet, Philadelphia, 1773), 6-9, 12.
41. A later and still more important stage in the development of the Genteel Tradition is discussed below in Part IV, Chapter 2.
42. See correspondence printed in appendix to A. L. Cross, *The Anglican Episcopate and the American Colonies* (New York, 1902), 320-32. I think Carl Bridenbaugh, in his interesting *Mitre and Sceptre* (New York, 1962), somewhat overstates the actual danger of episcopacy, though not the colonial feelings about the issue.

Notes for Chapter 5

1. This is much more fully discussed in Part III, Chapter 1.
2. Allan Nevins, *The American States During and After the Revolution, 1775-1789* (New York, 1927), 19.
3. Dickinson, *Letters from a Farmer* (Philadelphia, 1768; reprinted in *Memoirs of the Historical Society of Pennsylvania*, XIV, Philadelphia, 1895), 324.
4. The point about lack of opportunities for success is modestly presented, on the basis of very complex research, by Kenneth Lockridge in "Social Change and the American Revolution," *Journal of Social History*, 6 (Summer 1973), 403-39. A lot of research leading to this conclusion is very ably summarized in Joyce Appleby, "Liberalism and the American Revolution," MS article to be published in the *New England Quarterly*. Carl Bridenbaugh, in his *Cities in Revolt* (New York, 1955), 348-50, suggested a split in the colonial upper class in a way pointing toward a similar conclusion. A picture of a temperamentally conservative man with genuine attachment to Whig principles pushed by events in a Tory direction is convincingly drawn by Bernard Bailyn, *The Ordeal of Thomas Hutchinson* (Cambridge, 1974).
5. The Duché correspondence for this period is available in the Redwood Transcripts, Maryland Historical Society.
6. Alan Heimert, *Religion and the American Mind* (Cambridge, Mass., 1966), esp. 239-93.
7. *Ibid.*, esp. 159-236.
8. John Hubbard to Stiles, January 2, 1776, in Stiles, *Extracts from the Itineraries*, etc., 509-10.
9. For a useful interpretation of both Mayhew and Eliot, see Bernard Bailyn, "Religion and Revolution: Three Biographical Studies," *Perspectives in American History*, IV (1970), 87-124.
10. Alison to Stiles, August 1, 1769, in Stiles, *Itineraries*, 434-35.
11. The similarity is pointed out by Julian Boyd, *Anglo-American Union: Joseph Galloway's Plans to Preserve the British Empire 1774-1788* (Philadelphia, 1941), 18.
12. See Part III, Chapter 1.
13. S. M. Lipset, *The First New Nation* (New York, 1964), *passim*.
14. This is the judgment of Jackson T. Main, "Social Origins of a Political Elite:

The Upper House in the Revolutionary Era," *Huntington Library Quarterly*, XXVII (1964), 151.

15. On this subject, and indeed on the whole subject-matter of the American Revolution and Constitution, I have been influenced by Gordon S. Wood's *The Creation of the American Republic, 1776-1787* (Chapel Hill, 1969) more than by any other book that I have read. For Wood's brief but penetrating remarks on the debate over Charles Beard's interpretation of the Constitution, see esp. 626-27.

16. W. W. Sweet lists the religions of members of the Convention as follows: Episcopalian, 19, Congregationalist; 8, Presbyterian, 7; Roman Catholic, 2; Quaker, 2; Methodist, 1; Dutch Reformed, 1; deist, 1. (The overt deist counted here is Edmund Randolph; one could find others, starting with Franklin, who were tacit deists.) Sweet, *Religion in the Development of American Culture* (New York, 1942), 85. For the Methodist Bassett, see the character sketch by William Pierce of Georgia in Max Farrand, ed., *The Records of the Federal Convention of 1787* (3 v., New Haven, 1911), App. A, III, 93.

17. For an extremely valuable analysis of Madison's religion, see Ralph L. Ketcham, "James Madison and Religion—a New Hypothesis," *Journal of the Presbyterian Historical Society*, XXVIII (1960), 65-70. See also the same author's "James Madison and the Nature of Man," *Journal of the History of Ideas*, XXX (1958), 62-76; Edmund M. Cahn, "Madison and the Pursuit of Happiness," *N.Y.U. Law Review*, XXV (1952); James H. Smylie, "Madison and Witherspoon: Theological Roots of American Political Thought," *Princeton University Library Chronicle*, XVII (1961), 118-32.

18. Madison's personality as a whole seems to me best illuminated by Ketcham, *James Madison* (New York, 1971). The political influence of Hume is well demonstrated by several articles of Douglass Adair, all reprinted in *Fame and the Founding Fathers* (New York, 1974). For the 1783 booklist, see Irving Brant, *The Books of James Madison* (Charlottesville, 1965). This pamphlet also lists the books recommended by Madison to Jefferson for the study of theology in the University of Virginia in 1820. These include some of the Catholic fathers, a wide selection of Anglican theologians, and liberals like Price and Wollaston, but not Luther or Calvin.

19. Farrand, *Records*, I, 450-52.

20. Luther Martin, who left the Convention and later opposed the Constitution, reports that though the clause forbidding religious tests was adopted by a great majority and with little debate, yet "there were some members so unfashionable as to think, that a belief of the existence of a Deity, and of a state of future rewards and .punishments would be some security for the good conduct of our rulers, and that, in a Christian country, it would be at least decent to hold out some distinction between the professors of Christianity and downright infidelity or paganism." Farrand, *Records*, III, 227. "Agrippa," probably James Winthrop of Massachusetts, criticizes the Constitution severely for lack of a bill of rights and also for the absence of a religious test for the presidency. Cecelia M. Kenyon, ed., *The Antifederalists* (Indianapolis, 1966), 152-60.

21. Farrand, *Records*, II, 237.

22. *Ibid.*, I, 82, 135, 421.

23. *Ibid.*, I, 153; see also 159.

24. *Ibid.*, I, 186 (Paterson); I, 379 (Butler).

25. *Ibid.*, I, 87. Adams is discussed in Part III, Chapter 6, below.
26. *Ibid.*, I, 605.
27. *Ibid.*, I, 132; George Mason to George Mason, Jr., Philadelphia, 1787; *ibid.*, App. A, III, 32.
28. *Ibid.*, II, 196-202.
29. This was first pointed out in Cecelia Kenyon's well-known article, "Men of Little Faith," *William and Mary Quarterly*, XII (1955), 3-45. For a coupling of democracy and checks and balances, see Patrick Henry's speech in the Virginia ratifying convention in Kenyon, *The Antifederalists*, 238-65.
30. Mason to Jefferson, May 26, 1788, in Farrand, *Records*, I, 305.
31. *Ibid.*, I, 135.
32. *Ibid.*, III, 325.
33. Hopkins to Levi Hart, January 29, 1788, in Samuel Hopkins Papers, The New-York Historical Society.

PART II

Notes for Chapter 1

1. Jefferson's *Notes on Virginia* exaggerated the relative decline of England: "Her philosophy has crossed the channel, her freedom the Atlantic, . . ." *Notes*, ed. William Peden (Chapel Hill, 1954), 65.
2. Official suppression of Protestantism is interestingly discussed by David D. Bien, "Religious Persecution in the French Enlightenment," *Church History*, XXX (1961), 325-33. A fascinating account of the literary underground is presented by Robert Darnton, "France: A Case Study in the Sociology of Literature," *Daedalus*, C (1971), 214-56.
3. According to Alvin M. Weinberg, "The Axiology of Science," *American Scientist*, LVIII (1970), 612-17, the shift to a preference for pure science did not occur until about 1850. I am indebted for this reference to Jack C. Murchio.
4. This tendency in the thought of the Enlightenment is one of the chief insights of Ernst Cassirer's classic *The Philosophy of the Enlightenment* (Tubingen, 1932; Princeton, 1951).
5. This division of materialism into two main varieties is derived from Aram Vartanian's introduction to his edition of La Mettrie's *L'Homme machine* (Princeton, 1960).
6. Hume to Gibbon, March 18, 1776, in Edward Gibbon, *Autobiography* (1794) (critical edition, paperback, ed. D. A. Saunders, New York, 1961), 176.
7. Hume, "My Own Life," in *Philosophical Works*, T. H. Green and T. H. Grose, eds. (4 v., London, 1874-75), III, 6-7. There is a fine account of Hume's triumph in Paris in E. C. Mossner, *The Life of David Hume* (Austin, 1954), 423-506. Other biographical data used here are also from Mossner.
8. "Of the Coalition of Parties," *Philosophical Works*, III, 469.
9. "Of Passive Obedience," *Philosophical Works*, III, 461-62.
10. "The Natural History of Religion," *Philosophical Works*, IV, 363.
11. "My Own Life," III, 4.
12. *Autobiography*, 175.

13. *Ibid.,* 144.
14. *Ibid.,* 145.
15. John Morley, "Burke," in *Encyclopaedia Britannica* (11th ed., London, 1911), IV, 831.
16. Becker's illuminating essay, "The Dilemma of Diderot," is in his *Everyman His Own Historian* (paperback, New York, 1935), 264-83.

Notes for Chapter 2

1. St. George Tucker to Frances Tucker, September 5, 1781. Coleman-Tucker Papers, Library of the College of William and Mary in Virginia.
2. Ethel Armes, ed., *Nancy Shippen Her Journal Book* (Philadelphia, 1935), 125.
3. For example, George Duffield, "The Declaration of Peace," sermon of December 11, 1783, in Frank Moore, ed., *The Patriot Preachers of the American Revolution* (New York, 1862), 356.
4. Abbé Fernando Galiani, quoted in *Correspondance littéraire, philosophique et critique de Grimm et de Diderot* (15 v., Paris, 1830), IX, 226-27. Translation mine. The attitude of the *philosophes* toward America was complex. The kind of idealization I am quoting here was common. So was the belief of Buffon and others that animals and men deteriorated in the New World.
5. See Roland G. Paulston, "French Influence in American Institutions of Higher Learning, 1784-1825," *History of Education Quarterly*, VIII (1968), 229-45.
6. Gibbon's dislike of the rebellious colonists was a consequence of his belief in the necessity of order for high culture and his suspicion of popular passion. As a member of Parliament he swallowed his prejudices and voted for conciliation only because of his fear of French victory. See Solomon Lutnick, "Edward Gibbon and the Decline of the First British Empire: The Historian as Politician," *Studies in Burke and his Time*, X (1968-69), 1097-1112.
7. This letter, written somewhat earlier, was published in the *Independent Chronicle and Advertiser*, January 15, 1781. Clipping in Mercy Otis Warren Papers, Massachusetts Historical Society.
8. Adrienne Koch, *The Philosophy of Thomas Jefferson* (New York, 1943), 126. There is an excellent analysis of Hume's *History* in Duncan Forbes's introduction to the paperback edition published in London, 1970.
9. Stowe, *Oldtown Folks* (1869), ed. H. F. May (Cambridge, Mass., 1966), 394.
10. See the definitive "History of the Editions" (of the *Essays*) in *Philosophical Works*, III, esp. 72. May and Lundberg, "The Enlightened Reader in America" seems to indicate that the *Dialogues* were as often found in American libraries before 1790 as the *Essays*, but the latter are far more often referred to. After 1790, with a larger sample of libraries, the *Essays* are found far more often, though still not nearly as often as the *History*.
11. See especially *Philosophical Works*, III, 469 (overthrowing government); 444-46 (social contract), and 299-309 (culture and liberty).
12. Douglass Adair, "The Intellectual Origins of Jeffersonian Democracy; Republicanism, etc." (unpublished dissertation, Yale, 1943), 248-60; "That Politics May Be Reduced to a Science," in *Fame and the Founding Fathers* (New York, 1974), 3-26. Adair's demonstration of Madison's indebtedness to Hume is brilli-

ant, but I believe he associates Hume too closely with the other Scottish philosophers, and exaggerates in saying that Princeton was a carbon copy of Edinburgh ("That Politics," 96 fn.).

13. See E. C. Mossner, *The Life of David Hume* (Austin, 1954), 336ff.

14. Plumer's opinions are set forth in letters to his friends copied into his Letterbook of 1781 to 1804, in the Plumer Papers in the Library of Congress. The phrase quoted is from Letter 3, to John Hale, March 25, 1782. His changes of opinions are described in two biographies, by William Plumer (Boston, 1857), and Lynn W. Turner (2 v., Chapel Hill, 1962).

15. Allen, *Reason the Only Oracle of Man* (Bennington, 1784, repr. in facsimile with introduction by John Pell, New York, 1940), introduction, n.p.

16. Scholarly work on Allen's book is summarized in two articles: G. P. Anderson, "Who Wrote 'Ethan Allen's Bible'?" *New England Quarterly*, X (1934), 685-96; and Darline Shapiro, "Ethan Allen: Philosopher-Theologian to a Generation of American Revolutionaries," *William and Mary Quarterly*, XX (1964), 236-55.

17. John Fitch, unpublished autobiography, quoted in Thompson Westcott, *The Life of John Fitch* (Philadelphia, 1857), 45.

18. See J. T. Horton, *James Kent: A Study in Conservatism 1763-1847* (New York, 1939), 115, and Daniel Walther, *Gouverneur Morris* (New York, 1934), *passim*. Kent and deism in general are discussed further in Part III, Chapter 4.

19. The fullest information I have found on the elusive topic of Burr's early development is in Matthew L. Davis, ed., *Memoirs of Aaron Burr* (2 v., New York, 1837). The letter from Hopkins is in Edwards Amasa Park, "Memoirs of Samuel Hopkins," Hopkins, *Works* (3 v., Boston, 1852), I, 257-58.

20. I have been greatly assisted in dealing with this topic by A. O. Aldridge's excellent survey of Franklin's religious career, *Benjamin Franklin and Nature's God* (Durham, 1967).

21. Franklin to his parents, April 13, 1738, in Leonard W. Labaree, ed., *The Papers of Benjamin Franklin* (18 v., New Haven, 1960-1974), II, 204. This edition is henceforth cited as *Papers*.

22. To Jane Mecom, September 16, 1758, *Papers*, VIII, 154-55.

23. To Sarah Franklin, November 8, 1764, *Papers*, XI, 449-50.

24. Aldridge, *Franklin and Nature's God*, 175.

25. Franklin, "A Dissertation on Liberty and Necessity, Pleasure and Pain" (pamphlet, London, 1725; repr. New York, 1930), 29.

26. *Autobiography* (paperback ed., Dixon Wecter and Larzer Ziff, eds., New York, 1964), 57. Italics mine.

27. To Ezra Stiles, March 9, 1790, in *The Complete Works of Benjamin Franklin*, ed. John Bigelow (10 v., New York, 1887-88), X, 194-95.

28. To unknown correspondent, probably dated December 13, 1757, in *Papers*, VII, 294-95.

29. Franklin, "Opinions and Conjectures Concerning the Properties and Effects of Electrical Matter, 1750," in *Papers*, IV, 9-34.

30. Franklin to Priestley, June 7, 1782, repr. in Adrienne Koch, ed., *The American Enlightenment* (New York, 1965), 94.

31. See Mossner, *Life of David Hume* 314-15, 372-73.

32. The best treatment I have seen of this episode is A. O. Aldridge, *Franklin and His French Contemporaries* (New York, 1957), 9-13.

Notes for Chapter 3

1. I am not able to support this statement by citing contents of libraries, since the number of Southern libraries whose contents have been listed is too small. I am convinced that the statement is accurate by other sorts of evidence mentioned in the text, and especially by a considerable number of letters, cited and uncited, which take skeptical and deistic opinions for granted, as common in upper-class circles.
2. Edmund Randolph, *History of Virginia*, ed. Arthur H. Shaffer (Charlottesville, 1970), 253.
3. Elisha P. Douglass, *Rebels and Democrats* (Chapel Hill, 1955), 299. The persistence of unequal landholdings is documented in Jackson Turner Main, "Distribution of Property in Post-Revolutionary Virginia," *Mississippi Valley Historical Review*, XLI (1954-55), 241-58.
4. Winthrop D. Jordan, *White over Black* (Chapel Hill, 1968), 372-74. Jordan gives Virginia antislavery of this period credit both for sincerity and considerable accomplishment.
5. Thomas D. Clark, ed., *Travels in the Old South, A Bibliography* (3 v., Norman, Okla., 1956), editor's note, II, 73-74.
6. Robert Hunter, Jr., *Quebec to Carolina in 1785-1786*, Louis B. Wright and Marion Tinling, eds. (San Marino, Calif., 1943), 213-14, 218, 245. It should be pointed out that giving electric shocks to servants was a common pastime of European cognoscenti. For this information I am indebted to my colleague John Heilbron.
7. Good examples include James W. Alexander, *The Life of Archibald Alexander, D.D.* (New York, 1854); William Maxwell, *A Memoir of the Rev. John H. Rice, D.D.* (Philadelphia, 1835); R. H. Bishop, *An Apology for Calvinism* (Lexington, Ky., 1804); Devereux Jarratt, *The Life of the Reverend Devereux Jarratt* (Baltimore, 1806). Many such accounts are cited by John Boles, *The Great Revival, 1787-1805* (Louisville, 1972).
8. John Davis, *Travels of Four Years and a Half in the United States of America during 1798, 1799, 1800, 1801, and 1802* (New York, 1909), 250.
9. Jefferson's relative Edmund Randolph believes that he was "adept . . . in the ensnaring subtleties of deism and gave it, among the rising generation, a philosophical patronage, which repudiates as falsehoods things unsusceptible of strict demonstration." Randolph, *History of Virginia*, 277. One must remember that this was written after Randolph's own conversion to evangelical Christianity and also after his bitter political downfall, made no easier to forgive by Jefferson's great generosity to him.
10. Jarratt, 178.
11. Duke de la Rochefoucauld Liancourt, *Travels through the United States of North America, etc.* (2 v., London, 1799), I, 114; Isaac Weld, *Travels through the States of North America, etc.* (2 v., London, 1799), I, 167.
12. Jedidiah Morse, *The American Universal Geography* (2nd ed., Boston, 1793).
13. "Judge St. George Tucker's Pamphlet in Relation to Williamsburg, etc.," repr. in *William and Mary College Quarterly Historical Papers*, Vol. II, No. 3 (January 1894), 195 fn., 192.

14. Madison to Tucker, February 27, 1788, in [Bishop] Madison Papers, College Archives, The College of William and Mary in Virginia.
15. Madison to Tucker, January 22, 1779, in same collection.
16. Scott, *Memoirs of Lieut.-General Scott, LL.D.* (2 v., New York, 1864), I, 10. I am indebted for this reference to Professor Grady McWhinney.
17. Hunter, *Quebec to Carolina*, 271.
18. Theodorick Bland to Sophia Bland, Jonesborough, Tennessee, September 7, 1800, in Bland Papers, MS 134, Maryland Historical Society. Bland's letters provide an excellent example of the feelings of a young Virginian who is alternately gay and depressed, occasionally ribald, deistic but not dogmatic in religion.
19. Bernard C. Steiner, *The Life and Correspondence of James McHenry* (Cleveland, 1907), 146-47, 149.
20. William Meade, *Old Churches, Ministers and Families of Virginia* (2 v., Philadelphia, 1910), I, 29.
21. *Ibid.*, I, 50.
22. Randolph to Tucker, copy of letter, perhaps unsent, dated February 28, 1817, in Bryan Family Papers, University of Virginia Library.
23. Randolph to Tudor Tucker, December 13, 1813, quoted by William Cabell Bruce, *John Randolph of Roanoke* (2 v., New York, 1922), I, 75. According to another account by Randolph, Hume's *Treatise* was the first book Edmund Randolph put into his hands. Moncure Daniel Conway, *Edmund Randolph* (New York, 1888). Whether or not this is remembered correctly, Edmund Randolph, according to his biographer, *was* a deist in his early life and like John Randolph and many Virginians was later converted to a fervent belief in Christianity.
24. Randolph to St. George Tucker, Philadelphia, November 17, 1790, in Randolph Papers, Library of Congress.
25. Robert Innes to St. George Tucker, March 20, 1779, in Coleman-Tucker Papers, The College of William and Mary in Virginia. This magnificent collection of papers, full of interest of many kinds, should be published complete.
26. The letters mentioned here are all in the Coleman-Tucker Papers except the last one. This is to John Page, July 18, 1806, from Page Papers, Duke University Library.
27. According to Henry Adams's magnificent impressionistic sketch of American society in 1800, "the society of South Carolina, more than that of any other portion of the Union, seemed to bristle with contradictions." *History of the United States* (9 v., New York, 1890-91), I, 154.
28. Rutledge to Sarah Rutledge, October 12, 1794, in Rutledge Papers, Southern Historical Collection, University of North Carolina Library, Chapel Hill.
29. Kinloch to Müller, May 16, 1777. Kinloch-Müller letters, microfilm in American Philosophical Society; original in Stadtbibliothek, Schaffhausen, Switzerland. This correspondence, and other letters of Kinloch, is discussed and briefly quoted by Felix Gilbert, ed., "Letters of Francis Kinloch to Thomas Boone 1783-1788," *Journal of Southern History*, VIII (1942), 87-93. Gilbert indicates that he hopes to publish the Kinloch-Müller letters. There is some additional information about Kinloch in George C. Rogers, Jr., *Evolution of a Federalist* (Columbia, 1962). This is a biography of Kinloch's acquaintance William Livingston Smith.
30. Kinloch to Müller, May 16, 1777.
31. Kinloch to Müller, May 30, 1777.

32. Kinloch to Müller, August 17 and 30, 1777.
33. Kinloch to Müller, August 14, 1777.
34. Kinloch to Müller, April 24, 1778.
35. Kinloch to Müller, May 28, 1785.
36. Kinloch to Müller, March 25, 1802.
37. There are later Kinloch letters in the Rutledge Papers, University of North Carolina Library, and in the Cleveland Kinloch Papers, and also the Langdon Cheves Papers, South Carolina Historical Society. For Kinloch's participation in Episcopalian affairs, see Rogers, *Evolution*, 389-91.
38. Thomas Tudor Tucker to St. George Tucker, April 21, 1773. Coleman-Tucker Papers.
39. Same to same, November 27, 1773.
40. Same to same, April 27, 1774.
41. Same to same, April 17, 1788.
42. Same to same, February 2, 1788.
43. Same to same, November 21, 1787. Cf. Cecilia M. Kenyon, "Men of Little Faith," *William and Mary Quarterly*, XII (1955), 3-43.

PART III

Notes for Chapter 1

1. Cf. Michael Walzer, "Puritanism as a Revolutionary Ideology," *History and Theory*, III (1963), 55-90; J. L. Talmon, *The Origins of Totalitarian Democracy* (London, 1952; paperback, London, 1970), esp. 8-11, 263.
2. Norman Cohn, *The Pursuit of the Millennium* (New York, 1957; revised ed. paperback, 1970) is a brilliant survey of the socially revolutionary current in medieval revolution which compares this to modern revolutionary thought.
3. The importance of Commonwealth radicalism for the American revolution was decisively established by Caroline Robbins (*The Eighteenth-Century Commonwealthman*, Cambridge, Mass., 1954), and is further illuminated by Bernard Bailyn's persuasive introduction to the first volume of his *Pamphlets of the American Revolution 1750-1756* (Cambridge, Mass., 1965). The Commonwealth version of history is analyzed by H. Trevor Coulbourn, *The Lamp of Experience* (Chapel Hill, 1965). Zera S. Fink, *The Classical Republicans* (Evanston, 1945) and J. G. A. Pocock, *The Machiavellian Moment* (Princeton, 1975) emphasize the connections of British seventeenth- and eighteenth-century republican traditions with Renaissance and thus with classical antecedents. Pocock's rich and complex book reached me after I had completed my own. In it, and also in an earlier article, he suggests plausibly that something of this ancient heritage stretches forward into the history of the United States in the prevalent antithesis between the party of virtue and the party of economic development. Pocock, "Virtue and Commerce in the Eighteenth Century" (review article), *Journal of Interdisciplinary History*, III (1972), 119-34. I have emphasized here the "Commonwealth" tradition in British opposition thought rather than the "Country" tradition emphasized by Pocock and others for two

reasons. First, the Commonwealth tradition had more influence in America. The "Country" tradition of the disinterested landowner who lives in the simple manner of his fathers and opposes the decadence and corruption of the Court was especially powerful in South Carolina. One of its principal figures, Bolingbroke, was an important early influence on Thomas Jefferson. Yet the Commonwealth tradition, with its republican and often Puritan overtones had a far wider appeal. Second, the Commonwealth tradition is closer in spirit to the Revolutionary Enlightenment, the subject of this chapter.

4. John Tyler to Secretary, May 5, 1772, in F. L. Hawks and W. S. Perry, eds., *Documentary History of the Protestant Episcopal Church in . . . Connecticut* (2 v., New York, 1863-64), II, 183-84.

5. The best account of this episode is in a neglected book which I have found extremely helpful: Anthony Lincoln, *Some Political and Social Ideas of English Dissent 1763-1800* (Cambridge, Eng., 1938).

6. Quoted in Anne Holt, A *Life of Joseph Priestley* (London, 1931), 94.

7. Price, *Observations on the Nature of Civil Liberty* (London, 1776).

8. Carl B. Cone, *Torchbearer of Freedom* (Lexington, Ky., 1952), 158.

9. In libraries and booksellers' lists the older Commonwealth writer seem to retain their already wide popularity rather than to score spectacular gains after 1776. Of the later Radical Whigs Price, Priestley, Burgh, and Catharine Macaulay all make a considerable impact. Price especially is much reprinted. See May and Lundberg, "The Enlightened Reader in America."

10. Franco Venturi, in *Utopia and Reform in the Enlightenment* (Cambridge, Mass., 1971), emphasizes the connection of deism with republicanism in English radicalism, giving especial emphasis to John Toland. This juxtaposition was not common in American popular radicalism, though there were certainly American radicals who were deists, notably Thomas Jefferson. Toland was not read a great deal in America and was much more common on lists of dangerous deists than on lists of admirable republicans. Those English Radical Whigs who were important in America were usually either Dissenters—including rationalist Dissenters like Priestley—or reform-minded Anglicans like Hoadley or Trenchard and Gordon. Most American radicals were Puritan in their view of the past and many, like Samuel Adams, were Calvinist in allegiance and vocabulary.

11. Cf. Alan Heimert, *Religion and the American Mind*, esp. 500-509. In my opinion Heimert gives a most valuable picture of the Calvinist revolutionaries while somewhat exaggerating the political differences between them and their Arminian contemporaries.

12. Philip Freneau, *Poems*, ed. F. L. Pattee (3 v., Princeton, 1902), I, 80-81.

13. Hannah Winthrop to Mercy Warren, January 9, 1778, Mercy Otis Warren Papers, Massachusetts Historical Society.

14. For helpful suggestions concerning American millennialism in this period, until recently a neglected subject, see Perry Miller, "From the Covenant to the Revival," in J. W. Smith and A. Leland Jamison, eds., *The Shaping of American Religion* (Princeton, 1961), 322-68; Ernest Lee Tuveson, *Redeemer Nation* (Chicago, 1968); Stow Persons, "The Cyclical Theory of History in Eighteenth Century America," *American Quarterly*, VI (1954), 147-68; and Robert Middlekauff, "The Ritualization of the American Revolution," in Stanley Coben and Lorman Ratner, eds., *The Development of an American Culture* (New York, 1970), 31-43. I have also profited greatly from the unpublished thesis of Charles

Constantin on the New Divinity (Berkeley, 1972) and the seminar paper of Ruth Bloch on "Millennial Thought in the American Revolutionary Movement" (Berkeley, 1973).

15. Staughton Lynd, *Intellectual Origins of American Radicalism* (New York, 1968), 25.

16. "Thoughts on a Defensive War," *Pennsylvania Magazine* (July 1775), in Paine, *Complete Writings*, ed. Philip S. Foner (2 v., New York, 1945), II, 54-55.

17. Paine, "Common Sense," in *Complete Writings*, I, 4, 29, 45, 3.

18. Jefferson to Henry Lee, May 8, 1925, in *Writings*, ed. C. W. Ford. (10 v., New York, 1892-99), X, 342-43.

19. This point is made well by Otto Vossler, "Jefferson and the American Revolutionary Ideal," originally published as Supplement 17 of the *Historische Zeitschrift*. I have used this in the manuscript translation, soon to be published, by Bernard Wishy who drew it to my attention at a late stage in my work. Vossler's interpretation of the difference between the American and French revolutions has reinforced, and in some places supplemented, my own. See also Joyce Appleby, "America as a Model for the Radical French Reformers of 1789," *William and Mary Quarterly*, XXVIII (1971), 267-86; and R. R. Palmer, *The Age of the Democratic Revolution, I, The Challenge* (Princeton, 1959), 239-82.

20. Thomas Rodney to Thomas Jefferson, September 1790 (apparently unsent), in Jefferson, *Papers*, ed. Julian Boyd (19 v., Princeton, 1950-1974), XVII, 548.

21. Daniel Mornet's great *Origines intellectuelles de la révolution française* (Paris, 1933) has been criticized by many recent French investigators of the spread of the Enlightenment. And according to an acute recent writer this may never have penetrated far below "the elite." For the literate, and sophisticated, still a small part of the whole French population, Mornet's picture of gradually increasing permeation stands. See Robert Darnton, "In Search of the Enlightenment: Recent Attempts to Create a Social History of Ideas," *Journal of Modern History*, XLIII (1971), 113-32.

22. For a fascinating account of these vagaries, see Auguste Viatte, *Les Sources occultes du romantisme, I, Le Préromantisme* (Paris, 1928), and on mesmerism in particular, Robert Darnton, *Mesmerism and the End of the Enlightenment in France* (Cambridge, Mass., 1968). According to both authors, illuminism in many forms survived from the pre-Revolutionary ferment to the post-Revolutionary mystical reaction.

23. See Carl Becker, "The Dilemma of Diderot," in Becker, *Everyman His Own Historian* (paperback, New York, 1966), 262-83.

24. Rousseau, *Discours sur les sciences et les arts*, ed. G. H. Havens (New York, 1946), 197 (translation mine).

25. *Ibid.*, 125.

26. Rousseau, "Discours sur l'inégalité," in C. E. Vaughan, ed., *The Political Writings of Jean Jacques Rousseau* (2 v., Oxford, 1962), I, 142. Karl Barth persuasively describes Rousseau's religion as "a splendid, radiant and at the same time profound Pelagianism." Barth, *Protestant Thought from Rousseau to Ritschl* (New York, 1959), 115.

27. Rousseau, *The Social Contract*, in *Political Writings*, trans. and ed. Frederick Watkins (Edinburgh, 1953), 19.

28. The obvious debt to Rousseau of contemporary American radicalism is discussed in Marshall Berman, *The Politics of Authenticity* (New York, 1970).

29. The eulogy can be found in Condorcet, *Œuvres*, ed. O'Connor and Agaro (12 v., Paris, 1847-49), II, 372-423.
30. This is the final characterization of his best biographer in English. J. M. Thompson, *Robespierre* (2 v., Oxford, 1935), II, 275.
31. See C. C. Gillispie, "The *Encyclopédie* and the Jacobin Philosophy of Science: A Study in Ideas and Consequences," in Marshall Claggett, ed., *Critical Problems in the History of Science* (Madison, 1959), 255-89, and L. Pearce Williams, "The Politics of Science in the French Revolution," *ibid.*, 255-320; also Darnton, *Mesmerism*; and Roger Hahn, *The Anatomy of a Scientific Institution: The Paris Academy of Sciences, 1666-1803*. It is true at least that some people *believed* that there was a Jacobin science. It is probably more doubtful whether Newtonianism and conservatism, organicism and radicalism, went together with much uniformity. Here I am indebted to Roger Hahn and André Mayer.
32. Maximilian Robespierre, "Sur les rapports des idées réligieuses et morales avec les principes républicains, et sur les fêtes nationales," speech of May 7, 1794, in *Œuvres* (10 v., Paris, 1967), X, 444 (translation mine).
33. R. R. Palmer, *Age of the Democratic Revolution*, II, *The Struggle* (Princeton, 1964), 129-31 and *passim*.
34. Mrs. Barbauld, "Address to the Opposers of the Repeal of the Corporation and Test Acts, 1790," in Alfred Cobban, *The Debate on the French Revolution 1789-1800* (London, 1950), 421.
35. Benjamin Vaughan to Samuel Vaughan, Jr., September 2, 1789, in Benjamin Vaughan Papers, American Philosophical Society. This was also the judgment of Mrs. Macaulay, who visited America in 1785 and was disappointed by American propensities to luxury, commerce, and checks and balances. Lucy Martin Donnelly, "The Celebrated Mrs. Macaulay," *William and Mary Quarterly*, VI (1949), 194-98.
36. Richard Price, "A Discourse on the Love of Our Country" (pamphlet, Boston, 1790), 4.
37. W. Kegan Paul, *William Godwin: His Friends and Contemporaries* (2 v., Boston, 1876), I, 61.
38. *Political Justice* (facsimile), ed. F. E. L. Priestley (3 v., Toronto, 1946), II, 477.
39. *The Age of Reason* (2 v., Centennial ed., Boston, 1908), I, 101.
40. *Ibid.*, I, 132.
41. *Ibid.*, I, 69.
42. *Ibid.*, I, 268.
43. *Ibid.*, I, 68.
44. *Ibid.*, I, 44; see also 54.
45. *Ibid.*, I, 213.

Notes for Chapter 2

1. Alexander DeConde, "Williams Vans Murray's Political Sketches: A Defense of the American Experiment," *Mississippi Valley Historical Review*, LXI (1954-55), 624-40. Statements about relative popularity are based on data in May and Lundberg, "The Enlightened Reader in America."

2. Ezra Stiles, *Literary Diary*, ed. F. B. Dexter (3 v., New York, 1901), III, 161.

3. Among the more helpful of the many recent discussions of this problem are Frederick Tolles, "The American Revolution Considered as a Social Movement: A Re-evaluation," *American Historical Review*, LX (1954), 1-12; Elisha P. Douglass, *Rebels and Democrats* (Chapel Hill, 1955); the concluding essay in Richard B. Morris, *The American Revolution Reconsidered* (New York, 1967); and various books and articles by Jackson Turner Main.

4. R. R. Palmer, *The Age of the Democratic Revolution*, I, *The Challenge*, 188.

5. Benjamin Rush, *Essays, Literary, Moral and Philosophical* (Philadelphia, 1806), 10, 12.

6. Jedidiah Morse, *The American Universal Geography* (3 v., Charlestown, 1819, first published 1789), I, 213.

7. Richard D. Birdsall, "The Second Great Awakening and the New England Social Order," *Church History*, XXIX (1970), 345-50. There is a large literature on the New England social order in this period. I have found the following especially helpful: A. E. Morse, *The Federalist Party in Massachusetts to the Year 1800* (Princeton, 1909); Oscar and Mary Handlin, *Commonwealth* (New York, 1947); Allan Kulikoff, "The Progress of Inequality in Revolutionary Boston," *William and Mary Quarterly*, XXVIII (1971), 375-412; and the first parts of James M. Banner, Jr., *To the Hartford Convention* (New York, 1946) and Paul Goodman, *The Democratic-Republicans of Massachusetts* (Cambridge, Mass., 1964).

8. All these quotations are from Emmons's sermon, "The Dignity of Man," in his *Works*, ed. E. A. Park (5 v., Boston, 1863), I, 22. Emmons was later one of the fiercest anti-Jacobin and anti-Jefferson preachers.

9. William Bentley, *The Diary of William Bentley, D.D.* (4 v., Salem, 1905-14), I, 363. The best treatment of the Baptist struggle for freedom is William G. McLoughlin, *New England Dissent, 1630-1833* (2 v., Cambridge, Mass., 1971).

10. Simeon E. Baldwin, *Life and Letters of Simeon Baldwin* (New Haven, n.d.), 61-62.

11. Stiles, *Literary Diary*, III, 114, gives the following figures for 1783: Yale, 251 undergraduates; Harvard, 150; William and Mary, 100; Dartmouth, 70; Princeton, 40; Philadelphia, 30; Washington College, Maryland, 20; Rhode Island College, 8; King's College, New York, o (not listed in this order).

12. I have depended here on Edmund Morgan's excellent and affectionate *The Gentle Puritan* (New Haven, 1962), as well as Stiles's *Literary Diary*, vol. III. For his praise of democracy, Morgan, 453-54; for Franklin, Washington, and Revelation, *Literary Diary*, III, 395, 397; for his reading of Mary Wollstonecraft, *Literary Diary*, III, 502-3.

13. *Ibid.*, III, 101.

14. The principal source of the picture of deism and infidelity running rampant through Yale is the much quoted, lively, and unreliable autobiography of Lyman Beecher. For a challenge to this legend, see Edmund Morgan, "Ezra Stiles and Timothy Dwight," *Massachusetts Historical Society, Proceedings*, LXXIII (1957-60), 101-17.

15. *Literary Diary*, III, 147, 148, 257.

16. The most thorough book on this group is Leon Howard, *The Connecticut Wits* (Chicago, 1943), but V. L. Parrington's introduction to his anthology of the same title (New York, 1926) has some sharp insights.

17. David Humphreys, "The Happiness of America," in *Miscellaneous Works,* ed. William K. Bottorf (Gainesville, Fla., 1968), 37.
18. John Trumbull, quoted in Howard, *Connecticut Wits,* 47. Alexander Cowie's *John Trumbull, Connecticut Wit* (Chapel Hill, 1936) is a helpful biography of this representative Wit.
19. Hopkins, "The Hypocrite's Hope," in Parrington, *Connecticut Wits,* 419.
20. Trumbull, "The Progress of Dulness," in *The Satiric Poems of John Trumbull,* ed. Edwin T. Bowden (Austin, 1962), 60-62.
21. Humphreys, "On the Industry of the United States of America," in *Miscellaneous Works,* 107.
22. For this phrase see "Greenfield Hill," facsimile reprinted in *The Major Poems of Timothy Dwight,* eds. William J. McTaggart and William K. Bottorf (Gainesville, Fla., 1969), 514. Kenneth Silverman's study of Dwight (New York, 1969) is more penetrating than the fuller biography by Charles E. Cunningham (New York, 1942). Dwight's doctrine of the millennium is carefully analyzed in Ernest Lee Tuveson, *Redeemer Nation* (Chicago, 1968), 112.
23. "Greenfield Hill," in *Major Poems,* 521.
24. Barlow, "The Prospect of Peace" (1785), in *The Works of Joel Barlow,* eds. William K. Bottorf and Arthur L. Ford (2 v., Gainesville, Fla., 1970), II, 11-12.
25. Barlow, "Dissertation," in Joel Barlow Papers. Houghton Library, Harvard University.
26. Barlow, "An Oration . . . at the Meeting of the Connecticut Society of the Cincinnati, July 4th, 1787," in *Works,* I, 19.
27. *Works,* II, 103.
28. *Ibid.,* II, 311.
29. *Ibid.,* II, 342.
30. See Harry R. Warfel, *Noah Webster, Schoolmaster to America* (New York, 1936), 203. This is a very useful, though uncritical, biography.
31. It is interesting that New England education in general, and Webster in particular, are praised by Robert Coram in a pamphlet of 1791 expressing a point of view ardently Rousseauist and (for America) radically Enlightened. Coram, *Political Inquiries, etc.* (Wilmington, Del., 1791), reprinted in Frederick Rudolph, *Essays on Education in the Early Republic* (Cambridge, Mass., 1965), 79-145, esp. 82, 125.
32. Warfel, *Webster,* 174.
33. Quoted *ibid.,* 59-60.
34. C. D. Hazen, *Contemporary American Opinion of the French Revolution* (Baltimore, 1897; reprinted Gloucester, Mass., 1964), 166-71, describes such a celebration in Boston and mentions others in a number of New England towns.
35. Otis to Henry Warren, April 12, 1794, Warren Papers, Massachusetts Historical Society.
36. For earlier New England predictions of such upheavals, see Robert Middlekauff, *The Mathers* (New York, 1971), 27. A summary of New England millennial tradition which corrects earlier treatments of that subject is James W. Davidson, "Searching for the Millennium: Problems for the 1790's and the 1970's," *New England Quarterly,* XLV (1972), 241-61.
37. Tappan, "A Sermon Delivered to the First Congregation in Cambridge, etc.," April 11, 1793 (pamphlet, Boston, 1793), 27-28.
38. The date 1794-95 for the anti-Revolutionary turn in New England clerical

opinion was first convincingly argued by Gary B. Nash, "The American Clergy and the French Revolution," *William and Mary Quarterly*, XX (1965), 392-412.

39. Morse to Ebeling, Charlestown, May 27, 1794, in Morse Family Papers, Yale University Library.

40. Channing to Morse, New London, April 8, 1795, in the same collection. Henry Channing was the uncle of the famous liberal, William Ellery Channing.

41. Stillman, "Thoughts on the French Revolution, a Sermon Delivered November 20, 1794" (Boston, 1795), 12-13, 16.

42. Webster, "Revolution in France," in *A Collection of Papers on Political, Literary and Moral Subjects* (New York, 1843), 1-41.

Notes for Chapter 3

1. Much the best summary of New York history in this period, and one of the best studies of post-Revolutionary politics, is Alfred F. Young, *The Democratic Republicans of New York* (Chapel Hill, 1967). The New York Enlightenment, which might well be the subject of a separate study, resembles the Philadelphia one in some ways but was less important, partly because New York ceased to be the federal capital in the crucial decade of the 1790's.

2. Quoted in J. Paul Selsam, *The Pennsylvania Constitution of 1776* (Philadelphia, 1936), 113. The fullest account of the political struggles of the period is R. L. Brunhouse, *The Counter-Revolution in Pennsylvania, 1776-1790*. The text of the 1776 Constitution can be found in S. E. Morison, *The American Revolution, 1764-1788, Sources and Documents* (Oxford, 1923), 162-76.

3. Selsam, *Pennsylvania Constitution*, 139-40.

4. David Hawke, *In the Midst of a Revolution* (Philadelphia, 1961), 190.

5. Quoted in E. P. Oberholtzer, *The Literary History of Philadelphia* (Philadelphia, 1906), 98.

6. J. Thomas Scharf and Thompson Westcott, *History of Philadelphia* (3 v., numbered consecutively, 1884), 1273, 1395, 1423.

7. The best account of the post-Revolutionary proscriptions, and of the violence culminating in the attack on Wilson's house, is in Charles Page Smith's very useful biography *James Wilson* (Chapel Hill, 1956), 117-23, 129-39. A recent article emphasizes the many grievances of the radicals and points out that it is impossible to tell who fired the first shot in this affair. John K. Alexander, "The Fort Wilson Incident of 1779: A Case Study of the Revolutionary Crowd," *William and Mary Quarterly*, XXXI (October 1974), 489-612.

8. Smith, *Wilson*, 295.

9. The familiar travel accounts are supplemented by the accounts and estimates of the qualities of French visitors contained in Samuel Breck's "Recollections of my acquaintance and association with deceased members of the American Philosophical Society" (MS, 1862, in American Philosophical Society Library).

10. Du Ponceau's lively and charming though repetitive "Autobiography" (James Whitehead, ed.) is to be found in the *Pennsylvania Magazine of History and Biography*, LXIII (1939), 189-227, 432-61; and LXIV (1940), 97-120, 243-69. J. B. McMaster's informative but unimaginative *Life and Times of Stephen Girard* (Philadelphia, 1918) is supplemented by E. C. Kirkland's brief and lively

"Stephen Girard—Suggestions for a Biography," American Philosophical Society, *Proceedings*, CX, 10 (December 16, 1966), 387-91.

11. E. E. Rasmusson, "Capital on the Delaware: The Philadelphia Upper Class in Transition" (unpublished doctoral dissertation, Brown University, 1962), 69. This valuable thesis makes an intelligent distinction between the new, lavish "National Society" of the 1790's and the traditional "Provincial Society" which dominated Philadelphia before and after that decade. Du Ponceau, "Autobiography" remembers with disapproval the increasing luxury of the 1790's (434 ff.). There is a great deal of material on Philadelphia luxury and prices scattered through the first chapter of Volume II of Scharf and Westcott's *History*.

12. Smith, *Wilson*, 342.

13. Breck, "Recollections," 24-25; Scharf and Westcott, *History*, 911.

14. David Hollinger, "The Religious Enlightenment and the Intellectual Elite," seminar paper, Berkeley, 1966, examines the religious views of Ewing and of all other members of the faculty of the College and University of Pennsylvania in this period concerning whom information is available. He finds one person generally thought to be an infidel, almost all the rest somewhat short of deism in the "natural religion camp," with variations between Episcopalian rational piety and Old-School Presbyterian theological rationalism.

15. The Philadelphia Episcopal Church in this period is examined by Steven J. Novak, "The Narrowed Vision," seminar paper, Berkeley, 1970.

16. This story is told in W. S. Perry, *The History of the American Episcopal Church* (2 v., Boston, 1885), II, 101-28, and in other standard histories of the Church.

17. According to Samuel Eliot Morison "The federal government at the time was composed largely of gentlemen; in the Federal party . . . no man not a gentleman by birth or education was eligible to office. Eliminating certain Democratic members of Congress, the federal government resembled a large club of well-bred men from all parts of the country." Morison, *The Life and Letters of Harrison Gray Otis* (2 v., Boston, 1913), I, 126. With differing emotions, egalitarians and aristocrats of the period support Morison's generalization.

18. Scharf and Westcott, *History*, 1507 ff.

19. Quoted in Smith, *Wilson*, 277.

20. Wilson, *Works*, ed. James Dewitt Andrews (2 v., Chicago, 1896), I, 245-46.

21. See Part IV, Chapter 2.

22. See Whitfield J. Bell, Jr., "Philadelphia Medical Students in Europe, 1750-1800," *Pennsylvania Magazine of History and Biography*, LXVII (1943), 1-29.

23. See Richard H. Shryock, "Empiricism versus Rationalism in American Medicine 1650-1950," American Antiquarian Society, *Proceedings*, LXXIX (1969), esp. 104-18.

24. Rush, "The Progress of Medicine" (lecture), in Dagobert D. Runes, *The Selected Writings of Benjamin Rush* (New York, 1947), 236. Few men have been more misrepresented than Rush in general accounts of the period. Far the best treatment of his ideas is Donald J. d'Elia, *Benjamin Rush, Philosopher of the American Revolution* (pamphlet), American Philosophical Society, *Transactions*, New Series, LXVI, Part 5 (1974). This reached me after I had written the present brief treatment of Rush. It goes far beyond my treatment, but seems to me to confirm my general conclusions. I had read and greatly profited from d'Elia's earlier articles on Rush. D'Elia, unlike most other writers on Rush, em-

phasizes his central and consistent Christianity and especially his millennial views. D. F. Hawke's *Benjamin Rush, Revolutionary Gadfly* (Indianapolis, 1971) is a good account of his career, mainly political, up to 1790.

25. Rush, *The Autobiography of Benjamin Rush*, ed. G. W. Corner (Princeton, 1948), 31.

26. Rush to Elizabeth Graeme Ferguson, January 18, 1793, in *Letters of Benjamin Rush*, ed. L. H. Butterfield (2 v., numbered consecutively, Princeton, 1951), 628. This is a superbly edited collection.

27. These views are eloquently expressed in many letters. See, for example, his letter to Richard Price, June 2, 1787 (*Letters*, 419), in which he discusses universal salvation and insists that his belief in this doctrine is entirely Calvinist. For his combination of religious and secular millennialism see his letter to Jeremy Belknap, June 6, 1791 (*Letters*, 584).

28. Rush to James Kidd, May 13, 1794 (*Letters*, 748).

29. Quoted in D. J. d'Elia, "The Republican Theology of Benjamin Rush," *Pennsylvania Magazine of History*, XXXIII (1966), 187-203.

30. Rush, "The Influence of Physical Causes upon the Moral Faculty," *Selected Writings*, 181-211.

31. This is very thoroughly demonstrated in d'Elia, *Benjamin Rush, Philosopher*, 37 ff.

32. To Anthony Wayne, June 18, 1777; to Charles Lee, October 24, 1779 (*Letters*, 244).

33. See his letter "To the Ministers of the Gospel of All Denominations: An Address upon Subjects Interesting to Morals," June 21, 1788 (*Letters*, 461-67).

34. On "republican machines," see his essay "Of the Mode of Education Proper in a Republic," *Selected Writings*, 92; on the training of officeholders, "Plan of a Federal University," *Selected Writings*, 101-5; on division among sects, "To the Citizens of Philadelphia: A Plan for Free Schools," March 28, 1787 (*Letters*, 414).

35. The best treatment of this episode is J. H. Powell, *Bring Out Your Dead* (Philadelphia, 1949).

36. For various estimates of American scientific production, none exultant, see Brooke Hindle, *The Pursuit of Science in Revolutionary America 1735-1789* (Chapel Hill, 1956), *passim*; John Greene, "American Science Comes of Age, 1780-1820," *Journal of American History*, LV (1968), 22-41; and George H. Daniels, *Science in American Society* (New York, 1971). For lack of support, see Greene, "Science and the Public in the Age of Jefferson," *Isis*, XXXIX (1958), 13-26, and A. Hunter Dupree, *Science in the Federal Government* (Cambridge, Mass., 1957).

37. The best accounts of this organization are Brooke Hindle's two excellent books, *The Pursuit of Science* (Chapel Hill, 1956) and *David Rittenhouse* (Princeton, 1964). I have differed with Hindle in dealing with the Society's political history only by giving more emphasis to conciliatory elements in its political swings. The major sources, of course, are the Society's *Transactions* and its *Early Proceedings* (Philadelphia, 1884), compiled from manuscript minutes for the years 1744 to 1838. Letters, biographies, and individual writings by members are also helpful. I have also profited by the articles on the subject by Daniel Bell and John C. Greene.

38. Timothy Matlack, "An Oration, Delivered March 16, 1780, before the . . .

American Philosophical Society" (Philadelphia, 1780); Owen Biddle, "An Oration, Delivered the Second of March 1781, at the request of the American Philosophical Society, etc." (Philadelphia, 1781).

39. H. W. Smith, *Life and Correspondence of the Reverend William Smith, D.D.* (2 v., 1880), II, 360, quoted by H. E. Starr in his sketch of Smith in the *Dictionary of American Biography*, IX, 356.

40. The rule against taking positions is printed in *Transactions*, IV (1799), 2. It is not clear how long it had been in effect. The petition is in *Early Proceedings*, 292.

41. See Thompson Westcott, *The Life of John Fitch* (Philadelphia, 1857), 262. According to Westcott, Fitch failed to obtain backing for his invention partly because of his appearance, his lack of formal education, and his opposition to the United States Constitution.

42. The Vaughan Papers, in the American Philosophical Society Library, are extensive and fascinating. Most consist of brilliant political letters from Benjamin Vaughan in his Maine retirement, but one can learn a good deal from them of John Vaughan as well. John Vaughan is discussed briefly in Elizabeth Geffen, *Philadelphia Unitarianism 1796-1861* (Philadelphia, 1961).

43. Vaughan to Adet, May 21, 1800, Vaughan Papers.

44. Both anecdotes are in the excellent sketch of Smith by S. H. Monk in Willard Thorp, ed., *The Lives of Eighteen from Princeton* (Princeton, 1946), 86-111 (anecdotes on pp. 100-101). Another highly perceptive essay is Winthrop Jordan's introduction to Smith, *An Essay on the Causes of the Variety of Complexion and Figure in the Human Species* (Cambridge, Mass., 1965). There is also interesting material on Smith in John Maclean, *History of the College of New Jersey* (2 v., Philadelphia, 1877), II, 5-146.

45. Smith to Rush, February 19, 1790, photostat in Samuel Stanhope Smith Papers, Princeton. In this correspondence and in Monk, cited above, there is ample information on Smith's secretive liberalism in this period.

46. Smith on creation, *Essay on Causes*, 95. For Rush and Barton on remedies, see Daniel Boorstin, *The Lost World of Thomas Jefferson* (New York, 1948), 51-52. Boorstin's whole treatment of the APS seems to me full of insights though I do not always agree with it. It does not seem to me correct to identify the organization with the Jeffersonian circle. Jefferson did not take much part in the Society before 1793 when its policies were already firmly set, and he did not come close to dominating it until he became its president in 1797. The society was not entirely Jeffersonian in politics at any point, and Jefferson differed on religion from Rush, Samuel Smith, and others more than Boorstin suggests. I think it is a mistake to consider Paine at any time a part of the Jeffersonian circle, though Jefferson later supported Paine under attack. Yet Boorstin's book is one of the most interesting attempts to define a section of the American Enlightenment, and it has influenced both this chapter and my later treatment of Jefferson.

47. Barton, "A Memoir concerning the Fascinating Faculty which has been ascribed to the Rattle-Snake, and other American Serpents," American Philosophical Society, *Transactions*, IV (1799), 74-113. Quotations are from pp. 80, 113, 107, 108. Barton's general secularity, as well as his learning and cosmopolitanism, are fully documented by his extensive scientific correspondence, in the American Philosophical Society archives.

48. Smith to Rush, May 18, 1786, photostat in Smith Papers, Princeton.

49. Peale, *Introduction to a Course of Lectures on Natural History* (Philadelphia, 1800), 9.
50. For stimulation of research in paleontology and archaeology, see circular, *Transactions*, IV (1799), xxxvii-lx; for prizes offered 1796, *ibid.*, iv-vi.
51. Nicholas Collin, "An Essay on those inquiries in Natural Philosophy, which at present are most beneficial to the United States of North America," Introduction, *Transactions*, III (1793), iv-xxvii.
52. Peale, *Introduction*, 12.
53. Matlack, "An Oration . . . 1780," 32, 34. The comparison of Russia and America as rising nations was not uncommon.
54. Boorstin, *Lost World*, 111.
55. Frances Sergeant Childs, *French Refugee Life in the United States, 1790-1800*, is a very helpful account of this immigration. Constantin Volney, *View of the Climate and Soil of the United States of America* (Philadelphia, 1804), and M. L. E. Moreau de St. Méry, *Moreau de St. Méry's American Journey*, K. and A. Roberts, trans. and ed. (Garden City, 1947), are both revealing.
56. One of the better accounts of Priestley's American sojourn is in Geffen, *Philadelphia Unitarianism*. Edgar F. Smith's *Priestley in America* (Philadelphia, 1920), is brief and inadequate. Caroline Robbins, "Honest Heretic: Joseph Priestley in America, 1794-1804," in American Philosophical Society, *Proceedings*, CVI (1962), 60-76, is very useful. I have also used collections of Priestley letters, published and unpublished, in a number of libraries. The best of these is the series of letters to his friend Jonathan Lindsey in the Priestley-Lindsey Papers, Dr. Williams's Library, London.
57. Priestley to Lindsey, June 15, 1794, Priestley-Lindsey Papers.
58. Reprinted in Smith, *Priestley in America*, 48-51.
59. Priestley to Benjamin Vaughan, July 30, 1794, photostat in Priestley-Wilkinson Papers, American Philosophical Society Library.
60. [William Cobbett], *Observations on the Emigration of Dr. Joseph Priestley* (Philadelphia, 1794), 18.
61. *Ibid.*, 13.

Notes for Chapter 4

1. Donald H. Stewart, *The Opposition Press of the Federalist Period* (Albany, 1969), 15. I am much indebted for a detailed study of a section of the press to E. Wayne Carp's seminar paper (Berkeley, 1974) "The Southern Press and the French Revolution." The reaction in the United States to the successive events in France needs further study. C. D. Hazen's *Contemporary American Opinion of the French Revolution* (Baltimore, 1897; reprinted Gloucester, Mass., 1964) is still the most useful summary.
2. Even William Duane, the fiery radical editor of the *Aurora*, blamed "all that was evil in the Revolution" on Robespierre, and praised the Constitution of the Directorate as "the most perfect form of republican government yet devised." Kim Tousley Phillips, "William Duane, Revolutionary Editor" (unpublished dissertation, Berkeley, 1968), 48.
3. Theodorick Bland to Sophia Bland, November 16, 1799, Bland Papers, MS 134, Maryland Historical Society.

4. William Boyd, *Woman: a Poem, delivered at a Public Exhibition, April 19, at Harvard University, in the College Chapel* (pamphlet, Boston, 1796), 12-14.

5. Channing to William S. Shaw, undated; in W. H. Channing, *The Life of William Ellery Channing, D.D.* (Boston, 1880), 56-57.

6. Dumas Malone, *Jefferson and the Rights of Man* (Boston, 1951), 354-70.

7. William Wells to Morse, June 16, 1792; same to same March 12, 1799, Morse Family Papers, Yale University Library.

8. John R. Howe, Jr., "Republican Thought and the Political Violence of the 1790s," *American Quarterly*, XIX (1947), 165. A number of historians have recently advanced this Commonwealth, Country, or classical Republican interpretation of the politics of this period, carrying it forward from the interpretation of the ideas of the American Revolution made familiar by Caroline Robbins, Bernard Bailyn, and others. See especially J. G. A. Pocock's review article dealing partly with the work of Gordon Wood and Gerald Stourzh, but going beyond both: "Virtue and Commerce in the Eighteenth Century," *The Journal of Interdisciplinary History*, III (1972), 119-34.

9. This point, implied by much recent work, is brilliantly made explicit by Lance Banning, "Republican Ideology and the Triumph of the Constitution, 1789 to 1793," *William and Mary Quarterly*, XXXI (1974), 167-88.

10. E. P. Link's *Democratic-Republican Societies, 1790-1800* (New York, 1942) remains the most satisfactory account. Hazen, *Contemporary American Opinion*, usefully reprints a large selection of the manifestoes of the clubs.

11. Quoted by Hazen, 189-90.

12. Link, *Democratic-Republican Societies*, 119-21.

13. The two accounts of this kind of deism, both informative though uncritical, are G. A. Koch, *Republican Religion* (New York, 1933) and Herbert M. Morais, *Deism in Eighteenth Century America* (New York, 1934).

14. John Fellows, Memoir of Elihu Palmer, in Palmer, *Posthumous Pieces* (London, 1824), 6-7.

15. Elihu Palmer, "Extract from an Oration Delivered . . . on the Fourth of July 1793, etc.," in *Political Miscellany* (pamphlet, various authors, New York, 1793), 23.

16. Tunis R. Wortman, *An Oration on the Influence of Social Institutions upon Human Morals and Happiness* (New York, 1796), 24-25.

17. Elihu Palmer, *An Inquiry relating to the Moral and Political Improvement of the Human Species* (New York, 1797), 32.

18. Elihu Palmer, *The Political Happiness of Nations, etc.* (New York, 1800), 13.

19. "Proceedings of the Calliopean Society Founded for the Express Purpose of Improving Education" (manuscript minutes; 2 v., 1788-95), New-York Historical Society, *passim*.

20. Schaghticoke Polemic Society, manuscript records, New-York Historical Society. All 1797-c.1807. All resolutions quoted are from 1798.

21. In my treatment of this group I depend heavily on a seminar paper by Robert McBain, Berkeley, 1974. The chief source is the immensely valuable *Diary* of Elihu Hubbard Smith, published by the American Philosophical Society (James E. Cronin, ed., Philadelphia, 1973). This can be supplemented by biographies of leading members, including Dunlap, Mitchill, Miller, Kent, and Brown.

22. Smith, *Diary*, 262.

23. *Ibid.*, 156.

24. Both the Federalist and the deist tendencies of college undergraduates in this period are amply documented by Steven J. Novak's unpublished dissertation, "The Crisis of the Old Time College. The Birth of American Student Revolt 1798-1815," esp. 55-66, 127-33. I follow Novak at a number of points below.
25. Robert Coram, *Political Inquiries, etc.* (pamphlet, Wilmington, 1791). This is reprinted by Frederick Rudolph in *Essays on Education in the Early Republic* (Cambridge, Mass., 1965), 79-145. Several of the other essays in this volume are also of interest in the present context, especially the less doctrinaire, but also reformist and French-influenced, program of Samuel Harrison Smith, which was awarded a prize by the American Philosophical Society in 1798. *Ibid.*, 169-223.
26. *Ibid.*, 141.
27. *Ibid.*, 82, 125, 135.
28. See M. H. Abrams, *Natural Supernaturalism* (New York, 1971).
29. *Poems of Freneau*, ed. Harry Hayden Clark (New York, 1929), 112.
30. I am greatly indebted here to Nelson F. Adkins, *Philip Freneau and the Cosmic Enigma* (New York, 1949). This is a more searching examination of a man's religious and philosophical attitudes than exists for most of the major figures of the Enlightenment in America.
31. Lewis Leary, *That Rascal Freneau* (New Brunswick, 1941), 281.
32. *The Prose of Philip Freneau*, ed. Philip M. Marsh (New Brunswick, 1955), 300.
33. *Poems*, 425.
34. *Ibid.*, 147-48.
35. *Ibid.*, 207.
36. *Ibid.*, 356.
37. Among general treatments of Barlow, the relevant parts of Leon Howard's *The Connecticut Wits* (Chicago, 1943) are more penetrating than the fuller account by James Woodress, *A Yankee's Odyssey* (Philadelphia, 1958). Barlow's European political career is excellently summarized by Robert E. Durden, "Joel Barlow in the French Revolution," *William and Mary Quarterly*, VIII (1951), 327-54. Like Durden, M. Ray Adams helps to place Barlow in the international revolutionary context: *Studies in the Literary Backgrounds of English Radicalism* (Lancaster, 1947), 23-82.
38. Barlow, "Advice to the Priveleged Orders," in *Works*, eds. William K. Bottorff and Arthur L. Ford (2 v., Gainesville, Fla., 1970), I, 115.
39. *Ibid.*, 284.
40. "A Letter Addressed to the People of Piedmont, etc." in *Works*, I, 284.
41. "Advice," in *Works*, I, 120.
42. This point is helpfully discussed by Howard, *Wits*, 279-80, 299. Barlow admired *Le Christianisme devoilé*, attributed to Boulanger but really by Holbach, as well as works actually written by Boulanger.
43. "Advice," in *Works*, I, 275.
44. Barlow to John Fellows, Hamburg, May 23, 1795, in Barlow Papers, Houghton Library, Harvard University. This letter is quoted briefly by Woodress and others. Johnson is the translator (New York, 1795) of *Le Christianisme devoilé*.
45. Barlow, MS. notebook (c. 1796-97), Barlow Papers.
46. "Columbiad," in *Works*, II, 311.
47. Jefferson to John P. Burke, June 21, 1800, in *Works* (Ford ed.), IX, 267.
48. Jefferson to Thomas Mann Randolph, May 6, 1793, quoted in Dumas Malone, *Jefferson and the Ordeal of Liberty* (Boston, 1962), 81.

49. One of the best accounts of these celebrations remains J. B. McMaster, *A History of the People of the United States* (8 v., New York, 1883-1913), II, 89 ff. For Freneau, see Leary, *Freneau*, 232; for the flag-burning episode, C. C. Sellers, *Charles Willson Peale, Later Life* (Philadelphia, 1947), 63.
50. Alexander Graydon, *Memoirs* (Philadelphia, 1846), 370.
51. Adams to Jefferson, June 30, 1813, in Lester J. Cappon, *The Adams-Jefferson Letters* (2 v., Chapel Hill, 1959), II, 346-47.
52. Duane was born in New York, but brought up in Ireland.
53. The Pennsylvania politics of this period is surveyed more or less adequately by H. M. Tinkcom, *The Republicans and Federalists in Pennsylvania 1790-1801* (Harrisburg, 1950), and further cleared up by Raymond Walters, Jr., *Alexander James Dallas* (Philadelphia, 1943). Important insights are added by Phillips, "Duane," and especially by Richard D. Ellis's excellent monograph, *The Jeffersonian Crisis* (New York, 1971; paperback ed., 1974), 157-72.
54. For the petitioning, Hazen, *Contemporary American Opinion*, 195-96. The toast is quoted by Thomas P. Abernethy, *The South in the New Nation, 1789-1812* (Baton Rouge, 1961), 119.
55. Randolph to Tucker, May 25, 1793, copy in Randolph Papers, Library of Congress.
56. Among *Southern* colleges, the University of North Carolina was racked by charges of teaching deism and Jacobinism, and also was accused in its Republican state of being under deist auspices. See Novak, "Crisis," 150-61; Kemp Battle, *History of the University of North Carolina* (2 v., Raleigh, 1907); and the Caldwell Papers at the University of North Carolina Library. Transylvania University, briefly discussed below, was always hotly contested by liberals and orthodox Presbyterians. Despite all the controversy, no Northern college was anything like the hotbed of Jacobinism that many were widely believed to be.
57. For instance, W. Brockenbrough to J. C. Cabell, November 1, 1798, laments the Alien and Sedition Acts: "Oh America! How fast art thou retrograding! Too soon wilt thou reach the very Pinnacle of Despotism! I think, Cabell, that nothing but a change of our Constitution, or at least an Amelioration of it, can possibly preserve us from Slavery. To change or Amend our constitution, nothing can be effectual but a Re-inspiration of the Principle of Democracy." Cabell Papers, University of Virginia Library. (Consulted through the courtesy of Miss Lila Somerville.)
58. Joseph C. Cabell to David Watson, March 4, 1798, in Garrett Minor and David Watson Papers, Library of Congress.
59. Joseph Shelton Watson to David Watson, January 17, 1801, in "Letters from William and Mary College, 1798-1801," *The Virginia Magazine of History and Biography*, XXIX (1929), 159-60. There are many similar statements quoted in this article, 129-79, and in "Letters to David Watson," in the same volume of the same periodical, 257-86, and many others in student letters in various collections at the University of Virginia Library and elsewhere.
60. The best account of Kentucky liberalism is Niels H. Sonne, *Liberal Kentucky 1780-1828* (New York, 1939; paperback ed., Lexington, 1968). T. P. Abernethy, *Three Virginia Frontiers* (Baton Rouge, 1940), illuminates its social matrix. For data on books, see Sonne, *Liberal Kentucky*, 25.
61. Manifesto dated October 1794, in Breckinridge Family Papers, Library of Congress.

62. Lowell H. Harrison, *John Breckinridge: Jeffersonian Republican* (Louisville, 1969), 33.

63. Draft of a speech dated January 17, 1798, probably delivered in the Kentucky legislature, in Breckinridge Family Papers, Library of Congress.

64. Sonne, *Liberal Kentucky*, 69-70.

65. Asa Earl Martin, *The Anti-Slavery Movement in Kentucky* (Louisville, 1918), 26. The constitutional struggle and related issues in Kentucky are illuminated by Ellis, *Jeffersonian Crisis*, 123-56.

66. W. Brockenbrough to Joseph C. Cabell, April 29, 1798, in Cabell Papers, University of Virginia Library. Frank discussion of the rights of slaves was not uncommon at just this period in the letters of young upper-class Virginians.

67. See Thomas O. Ott, *The Haitian Revolution 1789-1804* (Knoxville, 1973) for a lucid account of this upheaval. Though most historians of slavery and the South in this period mention the effects of the West Indian Revolution in America, this topic could stand further investigation.

68. There is a thoughtful account of this episode in Gerald W. Mullin's excellent *Flight and Rebellion* (New York, 1972), 140-63.

69. For an illuminating account of both the achievements and limitations of Southern antislavery, both Enlightened and Christian, see Winthrop D. Jordan, *White over Black* (Chapel Hill, 1968), 342-402. David Brion Davis, *The Problem of Slavery in the Age of Revolution, 1770-1823* (Ithaca, 1975) reached me too late for detailed use here.

Notes for Chapter 5

1. Alexander Hamilton to Richard Harrison, January 5, 1793; to James A. Bayard, April 1802; in Henry Cabot Lodge, ed., *The Works of Alexander Hamilton* (12 v., New York, 1904), X, 31, 433.

2. Thomas Fitzsimmons, a Federalist Congressman from Philadelphia, quoted in Richard Buel, Jr., *Securing the Revolution: Ideology in American Politics, 1789-1815* (Ithaca, 1972). Of the many books dealing with Federalist ideas and tactics, Buel's has most influenced my treatment.

3. Eben Hazard to Jedidiah Morse, April 20, 1795, in Morse Family Papers, Yale University.

4. Cabot to Pickering, November 7, 1798, from *Life and Letters of George Cabot*, ed. Henry Cabot Lodge (Boston, 1878), 181.

5. Ames to Timothy Pickering, November 5, 1799, in Seth Ames, *Works of Fisher Ames* (2 v., Boston, 1854), I, 263.

6. The *Columbian Centinel*, July 23, 1814, quoted in James M. Banner, Jr., *To the Hartford Convention* (New York, 1970), 3.

7. For indignation over Volney, see Rufus King to Timothy Pickering, April 6, 1798; same to same, August 1, 1798; William Bingham to Rufus King, December 8, 1798; all in Charles R. King, *The Life and Correspondence of Rufus King* (6 v., New York, 1894-1900), II, 305, 380, 483.

8. Hamilton to Rufus King, April 8, 1797, in Lodge, ed., *Works of Hamilton*, X, 255.

9. On Osgood, reminiscence by John Pierce, in William B. Sprague, *Annals of the*

American Pulpit, II, *Trinitarian Congregationalists* (New York, 1857), 76. For Ames's comment, Ames to Gore, February 24, 1795, in Ames, *Works*, I, 168. This early and partial rapprochement between Federalist leaders and the clergy is discussed in Buel, *Securing the Revolution*, 168-69.

10. Hamilton to Pickering, March 22, 1797, in Lodge, ed., *Works*, X, 244. His slightly later letter to McHenry, almost exactly similar in tone, can be found in B. C. Steiner, *Life and Correspondence of James McHenry* (Cleveland, 1907), 295. I am entirely persuaded by Douglass Adair and Marvin Harvey that Hamilton, who had strong skeptical inclinations and used religion opportunistically during the height of his career, underwent a serious religious conversion at its end. Douglass Adair and Marvin Harvey, "Was Alexander Hamilton a Christian Statesman?" *William and Mary Quarterly*, XII (1955), 308-29. For Hamilton's draft of Washington's Thanksgiving Proclamation in 1795, replete with conventional religiosity, see Harold C. Syrett, ed., *The Papers of Alexander Hamilton* (22 v. to date, 1961-75), XVIII, 2-3. For his famous trial balloon urging the formation of a Christian Constitutional Society (because men are moved by their passions not their reason) his letter to James A Bayard, April, 1802 (Lodge, ed., *Works*, X, 432-37. For his very moving last letters, the same volume, 475-76.

11. For Adams's proclamation, see James D. Richardson, ed., *Messages and Papers of the President, 1789-1897* (9 v., Washington, D.C., 1899), I, 268-70.

12. Ames to Thomas Dwight, September 27, 1795, in Ames, *Works*, I, 174.

13. An interesting account can be found in the first chapter of D. L. Ludlum, *Social Ferment in Vermont, 1791-1850* (New York, 1939).

14. S. G. Goodrich, *Recollections of a Lifetime* (2 v., New York, 1867), I, 117, 119-20.

15. Webster, *Ten Letters to Dr. Joseph Priestley* (New Haven, 1800), 28.

16. *Ibid.*, 21.

17. James King Morse's *Jedidiah Morse* (New York, 1939) is of some use but needs revising. Vernon Stauffer's *New England and the Bavarian Illuminati* (New York, 1918) is full of helpful insights despite its age. By far the best source for Morse, however, and also a very rich one for clerical opinion in general, is his vast correspondence. The Morse Family Papers in Yale University Library are supplemented by the Morse papers in the Gratz Collection at the Historical Society of Pennsylvania, at the New York Public Library, and in the New-York Historical Society.

18. Wolcott to Morse, Philadelphia, June 22, 1794. Copy in Morse Papers, New York Public Library.

19. On Erskine, Morse, *Morse*, 54-55. Dwight knew about the book by 1797 and was in close touch with Morse. It is clear that Morse and other Americans knew of both Robison and Barruel before either was published in America.

20. John Robison, *Proofs of a Conspiracy* (1798), (paperback ed., Boston, 1967), 297. This edition, published under the auspices of the John Birch Society, is proof of the enduring power of Robison's ideas. The publishers in an introduction to the 1967 edition make it clear that they believe that the Conspiracy of the Illuminati has lasted until the present, and includes both Communism and the movement toward World Government. Among historians, the theory of a direct, conspiratorial link between the Bavarian Illuminati and the French Revolution has generally been dismissed. Auguste Viatte, *Les Sources occultes du romantisme*, etc. (2 v., Paris, 1938) makes clear that there were both conserva-

tive and radical illuminists and masons of many varieties. Daniel Mornet, *Les Origines intellectuelles de la Révolution française* (Paris, 1933), allows freemasonry some general importance in the development of feelings of benevolence and bourgeois equality that contributed to the questioning of the old order and suggests that the masonic order was probably used by some revolutionists as one of the few available national networks—by improvisation, not planning. Eric Hobsbawm, *Primitive Rebels* (2nd ed., New York, 1963), emphasizes the development of radical freemasonry *after* the French Revolution. Viatte, I, 310 ff., Mornet, 357-87; Hobsbawm, 161-64. A recent article on Barruel and his predecessors in France shows that, ironically enough, French ultra-conservatives often linked masonry with Protestantism—even, specifically Presbyterianism—as causes of the Revolution. J. M. Roberts, "The Origins of a Mythology: Freemasons, Protestantism and the French Revolution," *Bulletin of the Institute of Historical Research*, XLIV (1971), 78-97.

21. Morse, A Sermon, Delivered . . . May 9, 1798, etc. (Boston, 1798).
22. Dwight, The Duty of Americans in the Present Crisis, etc. (New Haven, 1798).
23. Ruth Bloch, seminar paper, "The Emergence of the New England Evangelical Mind" (unpublished, Berkeley, 1974), 9 ff.
24. Ebenezer Bradford, "Mr. Thomas Paine's Trial, etc." (Boston, 1795), 12-13.
25. This is pointed out by an intelligent account of a number of Virginia anti-Paine tracts, most of them by Presbyterians, and most or all of them invoking standard eighteenth-century defenses of rational Christianity. James H. Smylie, "Clerical Perspective on Deism," *Eighteenth-Century Studies*, VI (1972-73), 203-20.
26. David Tappan to Benjamin Tappan, July 21, 1797, in Gratz Collection, Historical Society of Pennsylvania.
27. Bradford, dedicating to Washington the pamphlet on Paine quoted above (see note 24), gives as one of his reasons for the dedication "that you have exhibited the most unequivocal demonstrations of a firm and constant faith in Revelation." "This is the more extraordinary," Bradford goes on, "because, many characters, with whom your important station has called you to form an intimacy, have been open and acknowledged Deists."
28. This is pointed out with great acuteness by Ruth Bloch, in the seminar paper cited in note 23 above, 24 ff.
29. This change of emphasis is pointed out by the same paper, 17 ff.
30. *Prophetic Conjectures on the French Revolution* (anon., Baltimore, 1794), 78, 80.
31. Boudinot to Samuel Bayard, October 17, 1795, in Bradford Papers, Princeton University Library.
32. Channing to Morse, June 3, 1796, in Morse Papers, New-York Historical Society.
33. The view that most clergymen stopped short of a shift to premillennialism, a view which seems to me correct, was put forth in a very helpful discussion of millennialism in this period by Glenn T. Miller and James W. Davison at a meeting of early American and church historians at Williamsburg in 1973.
34. Morse, A Sermon . . . Delivered May 9th, 1798, etc., 25.
35. The most complete discussion of this campaign is still in Stauffer, *Bavarian Illuminati*. Among modern accounts, I have found especially rewarding those in Buel, *Securing the Revolution*, 167 ff. and (though he deals mainly with a slightly later period), James M. Banner, *To the Hartford Convention* (New York, 1970), 152 ff. Barbara Gray, "Politics and the Pulpit," an unpublished seminar

paper (Berkeley, 1971), examines a large number of sermons with much discrimination.

36. David Tappan, *A Discourse Delivered in the Chapel of Harvard College, June 19, 1798, etc.* (Boston, 1798).

37. Emmons, "Prayer for the Defeat of those who Attempt to Subvert Good Government," and "Obedience to Civil Magistrates" (his Fast-Day sermons of 1798 and 1799 respectively), in his *Works*, ed. E. A. Park, (5 v., 1862), V, 85-104, 125-55.

38. Abiel Abbott to Morse, December 9, 1798, Morse Papers, New York Public Library. On Harvard, Morais, *American Deism*, 161, as well as many memoirs. In finding the Boston liberals lined up with the Calvinists at this point I agree with Conrad Wright, *The Beginnings of Unitarianism in America* (Boston, 1955), 241-51, and on the political conservatism of these religious liberals with Alan Heimert, *Religion and the American Mind*. For the best evidence on this matter, and a most penetrating account of the political opinions of the liberals, I am grateful to Rebecca Allison, "Massachusetts Liberals in an Age of Revolution" (unpublished seminar paper, Berkeley, 1971). I disagree here slightly with Banner, who thinks the liberals less committed to Federalism than the orthodox—*To the Hartford Convention*, 203. I would say that they were even more uniformly and closely attached to Federalism, with Bentley almost the only exception, though their rhetoric was different.

39. Ramsay to Morse, April 9, 1799, copy in Morse Family Papers, Yale University Library.

40. There are many of Nisbet's letters, including some to Morse, in the Gratz Collection, Historical Society of Pennsylvania. See also Samuel Miller, *Memoir of the Reverend Charles Nisbet, D.D.* (New York, 1840).

41. McCorkle, *The Work of God for the French Revolution*, etc. (Salisbury, N.C., 1798), 27, quoted in Novak, "Crisis of the Old Time College," 152.

42. This is made clear by his letters. L. H. Butterfield, ed., (2 v., Princeton, 1951). See esp. II, 812, 935, 1806, 1007-9, 1174. Rush came to dislike Paine and detest Godwin, and was neutral in the election of 1800, but he never gave up his friendship with Jefferson and thus was able later to bring Jefferson and Adams back together.

43. Smith to Morse, February 24, 1799, Samuel Stanhope Smith Papers, Princeton University Library.

44. Smith to Jonathan Dayton, December 22, 1801, Smith Papers. See also the treatment in Novak, "Crisis," 164-72. Not surprisingly, Smith's anti-radical feelings became still more extreme when Nassau Hall was burned down in the midst of student disturbances in 1802.

45. Novak, "Crisis," 96.

46. Dennie to his parents, May 20, 1800, reprinted in H. M. Ellis, *Joseph Dennie and His Circle* (Bulletin of the University of Texas, No. 40, 1915), 116, 117.

47. J. G. Bend to the Reverend William Duke (?), November 3, 1798, Maryland Diocesan Library, Baltimore. The very learned curator of this collection assures me that he does not know of a single Maryland Episcopal priest who was a Republican.

48. See Sarah M. Lemmon, ed., *The Pettigrew Papers*, I, 1685-1818 (Raleigh, 1971). "Belshazzar" is Charles Pettigrew's own term for one of his chief Baptist enemies.

49. Ogden's best-known attack on the Federalist clergy is *A View of the New England Illuminati* (Philadelphia, 1799).
50. On this point I agree with other writers on this subject and disagree with Alan Heimert, whose opinions on the Revolutionary period I more nearly accept. Heimert believes that the Calvinists (or he sometimes says "Evangelicals") who had supported the American Revolution also supported the Jeffersonian cause—*Religion and the American Mind*, 510-52. Here I think he is wrong, as are those who find "Calvinists" lined up against Jefferson—an opinion Jefferson sometimes seems to express himself. The political line was not, I think, between Calvinists or Evangelicals on one side and religious liberals on the other. Neither will denominational lines quite hold up. Not only are there Republican Congregationalists but also ardently Federalist and anti-French Baptists, like Samuel Stillman of Boston, a collaborator with Morse. The real distinction is between those of whatever theology or denomination who had some feeling for social control under church auspices and those who were completely voluntarist. In *general*, this puts Presbyterians and Episcopalians on one side, Baptists and Methodists on the other. The distinction corresponds fairly closely with that between church and sect in the Troeltsch sense.
51. Robison had two American editions; Barruel, which had already been published once in 1794, had four, and Du Pan two. The main impact of all these came through press abridgments.
52. Morse connects the Illuminati with the United Irishmen in his Thanksgiving sermon of 1798. See Stauffer, *Illuminati*, 271. Federalist xenophobia, of which examples are legion, is summarized by David Hackett Fischer, *The Revolution of American Conservatism* (New York, 1965), 165 ff. Morse's Fast Day sermon predicted the Black army of insurrection, pp. 12-14. For examples of High Federalists expressing the same fears, see Pickering to King, March 12, 1799, in King, *Life and Correspondence*, 557; or Otis, quoted in Samuel Eliot Morison, *Harrison Gray Otis* (Boston, 1969), 65. Such fears were the principal reasons for the Federalist support of the independence of Santo Domingo under Toussaint L'Ouverture.
53. Adams to Mercy Warren, August 8, 1807, reprinted in *Collections of the Massachusetts Historical Society*, (4 v., 5th series, 1878), III, 436.
54. William Bentley, *Diary* (4 v., Salem, 1905-14), II, 245.
55. Dwight, *A Discourse on Some Events of the Last Century* (New Haven, 1801), 54-56.

Notes for Chapter 6

1. Adams to Jonathan Jackson, October 2, 1789, in *The Works of John Adams*, ed., C. F. Adams (10 v., Boston, 1850-56), IX, 511.
2. This sometimes overlooked fact was pointed out to me by André Mayer.
3. Both men were also influenced to some degree by the fourth variety of Enlightenment discussed in this book. See Part IV, Chapter 2, below.
4. Adams to Miller, July 7, 1800, in *Works*, X, 389. The most complete examination of Adams's religion in print is H. O. Fielding's mislabeled "John Adams: Puritan, Deist, Humanist," *Journal of Religion*, XX (1940) 33-46. A more penetrating study, as yet unpublished, is Walter E. Beardslee, "The Religious

Ideas and Attitudes of John Adams." This essay, to which I am indebted, was started in my seminar at Harvard, summer session, 1963, and continued at Northwestern Michigan College.

5. Briant is briefly discussed in Part I, Chapter 3.
6. Adams to Benjamin Waterhouse, October 29, 1805, in *Statesman and Friend: Correspondence of John Adams with Benjamin Waterhouse, 1784-1822*, W. C. Ford, ed. (Boston, 1927), 30.
7. Adams to Jefferson, January 22, 1825, in Lester J. Cappon, ed., *The Adams-Jefferson Letters* (2 v., numbered consecutively, Chapel Hill, 1959), 607.
8. To Jefferson, January 20, 1820, *ibid.*, 560.
9. To Jefferson, September 14, 1813, *ibid.*, 375.
10. To Jefferson, same letter, *ibid.*, 374.
11. For Adams's personality, I have profited most from the essays of Bernard Bailyn and Edmund Morgan. Bailyn, "Butterfield's Adams: Notes for a Sketch," *William and Mary Quarterly*, XIX (1962), 238-56; Morgan, "John Adams and the Puritan Tradition," *New England Quarterly*, XXIV (1961), 418-529.
12. To Jefferson, February 3, 1812, *Adams-Jefferson Letters*, 295.
13. A *Defence of the Constitutions of the United States* (1787-88), in *Works*, VI, 61. To Thomas Brand-Hollis, June 1, 1790, in *Works*, IX, 571. The most helpful works on Adams's political thought are John R. Howe, Jr., *The Changing Political Thought of John Adams* (Princeton, 1966), and Edward Handler, *America and Europe in the Political Thought of John Adams* (Cambridge, Mass., 1964). There is much information about Adams's political career in Page Smith, *John Adams* (Garden City, 1962). For his reading, see Zoltan Haraszti's fascinating and learned collection of his marginalia, *John Adams and the Prophets of Progress* (Cambridge, Mass., 1964).
14. Adams to Alexander Jardine, June 1, 1790, *Works*, IX, 568.
15. See above, Part III, Chapter 3, and David Hawke, *In the Midst of a Revolution* (Philadelphia, 1961), 178.
16. There is an illuminating treatment of this period in Howe, *Changing Political Thought*, 130-45.
17. Quoted in Haraszti, *John Adams*, 111.
18. To F. A. Vanderkemp, March 3, 1804, in *Works*, IX, 588.
19. To Samuel Perley, June 19, 1809, in *Works*, IX, 624.
20. To Richard Price, April 19, 1790, in *Works*, IX, 563-64. This difference in their response to Price's sermon demonstrates that Adams should not be identified too closely with Burke. His dislike of the French Revolution was as consistent as Burke's and his doubts arose even earlier. There is, however, none of the pre-Romantic in Adams; he admires properly balanced institutions rather than ancient traditions as such. See R. S. Ripley, "Adams, Burke, and Eighteenth-Century Conservatism," *Political Science Quarterly*, LXXX (1965), 216-35.
21. To Waterhouse, May 21, 1821, in Ford, *Statesman and Friend*, 155.
22. To Waterhouse, October 29, 1805, *ibid.*, 31.
23. Howe sees a sharp change in 1787, between the writing of the first two volumes of the *Defence* and the third, *Changing Political Thought*, 170. It is striking that the first volume was praised by Barlow as well as by Jefferson and Rush.
24. This genuinely painful subject is adequately covered in J. M. Smith, *Freedom's Fetters* (Ithaca, 1956). Adams's role in the crisis is also thoroughly dealt with in

Manning J. Dauer, *The Adams Federalists* (Baltimore, 1953) and Stephen G. Kurtz, *The Presidency of John Adams* (Philadelphia, 1957).

25. This is made clear in a number of letters to Rufus King in London from George Cabot and Fisher Ames. See *King, Life and Correspondence*, xix-xxii, *passim*.

26. Among the writers on Jefferson who seem to me to have made the most success-full efforts to penetrate the complexities of the subject are Albert Jay Nock, Gilbert Chinard, and in brief essays Richard Hofstadter and Bernard Bailyn. The magnificently researched biography by Dumas Malone is invaluable, and scrupulous in its presentation of fact. For my tastes, it tries too hard to apologize for the least creditable episodes in Jefferson's career. I have been greatly aided in my effort to understand Jefferson by the work of several students in graduate and undergraduate courses, especially Joseph Morganti, Gary Esarey, John Zvesper, and Michael Squibb. The history of the successive interpretations and misinterpretations of Jefferson is helpfully summarized in Merrill D. Peterson, *The Jefferson Image in the American Mind* (New York, 1960).

27. To Rush, September 23, 1800, in P. L. Ford, ed., *The Writings of Thomas Jefferson* (10 v., New York, 1892-99, hereafter "Ford"), VI, 153-54.

28. *Notes on Virginia*, in Ford, IV, 61.

29. To William Short, January 3, 1793, in Ford, VI, 153-54.

30. On the Directorate, to Démeunier, April 29, 1795, Ford, VII, 13. On June 1 he exclaims to Tench Coxe: "What a tremendous obstacle to the future attempts at Liberty will be the atrocities of Robespierre!," *ibid.*, 22.

31. Bernard Bailyn, "Boyd's Jefferson: Notes for a Sketch," *New England Quarterly*, XXX (1930), 393-94.

32. Jefferson to Du Pont de Nemours, January 18, 1802, in Ford, VIII, 127 fn.

33. All these episodes are fully dealt with, to his great credit, by Dumas Malone. See for the Paine introduction, his second volume, *Jefferson and the Rights of Man* (Boston, 1951), 357-70; for the Mazzei letter his third volume, *Jefferson and the Ordeal of Liberty* (Boston, 1962), 267-72; and on Jefferson's relations with Callender, *Ordeal*, 332-33, 466-72, and also Malone's fourth volume, *Jefferson the President*, 206-18. One can hardly help noticing the pain which this devoted biographer seems to feel in dealing with these and a good many similar episodes. He comes close to admitting this discomfort in his introduction to *Ordeal*, xix-xx.

34. Jefferson to Thomas McKean, February 19, 1803, in Ford, VIII, 218. Jefferson leads up to this statement by insisting on entire confidentiality, and explaining the dangers that he sees in the "licentiousness" of the "Tory Press." The statement is quoted and its context explained in Leonard Levy, *Jefferson & Civil Liberties, The Darker Side* (Cambridge, Mass., 1963). This book, a conscious effort to redress the balance against Jefferson, is almost necessarily less than profound. The facts it presents, however, should be taken into account more than they have been.

35. The sources of Jefferson's thought have been dealt with by many writers, among whom the most helpful are in my opinion Adrienne Koch, Gilbert Chinard, and Douglass Adair in his oddly unpublished dissertation, "The Intellectual Origins of Jeffersonian Democracy, etc." (Yale, 1943). Trevor Coulborn helpfully examines Jefferson's view of history and also Adams's in *The Lamp of Experience* (Chapel Hill, 1965), 83-106, 158-84.

36. To John Adams, January 11, 1817, quoted in Adrienne Koch, *The Philosophy of Thomas Jefferson* (New York, 1943), 55. Koch examines Tracy's system at some length here.

37. To Adams, August 22, 1813, in Cappon, ed., *The Adams-Jefferson Letters*, 368.

38. To Adams, January 24, 1814, *ibid.*, 421.

39. To Adams, July 5, 1814, *ibid.*, 433.

40. To Levi Lincoln, August 26, 1801, quoted in Fred C. Luebke, "The Origins of Thomas Jefferson's Anti-Clericalism," *Church History*, XXXII (1963), 352.

41. To Peter Carr, August 10, 1787; to Adams, October 14, 1815. Both of these letters are quoted in Koch, *Philosophy*, 18, 20.

42. To the Reverend Isaac Story, December 5, 1801, in Ford, IX, 318.

43. To Adams, August 15, 1820, in *Adams-Jefferson Letters*, 567.

44. "Edmund Randolph's Essay on the Revolutionary History of Virginia," in *The Virginia Magazine of History and Biography*, XLIII (1935), 122. There are other shrewd remarks about Jefferson here, by an intelligent and hostile critic.

45. Quoted by Eleanor D. Berman, *Thomas Jefferson Among the Arts* (New York, 1947), 152. Re Liancourt, *ibid.*, 153. Much of my information on Jefferson's artistic tastes comes from this helpful monograph.

46. *Ibid.*, 175-76.

47. To Madame de Tessé, March 20, 1787, in Julian P. Boyd, ed., *The Papers of Thomas Jefferson*, XI (1955), 226.

48. To George Wythe, August 13, 1786, Boyd, *Papers*, X (1954), 244-45.

49. On the eighty boxes, the maître d'hotel, etc., Malone, *Rights of Man*, 322-23. On mortgaging slaves to rebuild, Malone, *Ordeal*, 179, 239.

50. The problem of Jefferson and slavery was effectively restated in the context of white attitudes toward Black people by Winthrop Jordan, *White over Black* (Chapel Hill, 1969), 429-81. It has been further discussed since, especially by William Cohen, "Thomas Jefferson and the Problem of Slavery," *Journal of American History*, XVI (1969-70), 503-26; and Fawn Brodie, *Thomas Jefferson* (New York, 1974); and David Brion Davis, *The Problem of Slavery in the Age of Revolution 1770-1823* (Ithaca, 1975), 169-84. The more intensively this problem is examined, the deeper the contradictions become.

51. To Jean Nicholas Démeunier, June 26, 1786, in Boyd, X, 63; *Notes on Virginia*, in Ford, IV, 83 84; both quoted by Brodie, *Jefferson*, 184, 161.

52. For analysis of the Hemings story, see Jordan, Brodie, and also Douglass Adair's long-unpublished essay, "The Jefferson Scandals," now available in his collected essays, *Fame and the Founding Fathers*, Trevor Colbourn, ed. (New York, 1974), 160-91.

53. *Notes on Virginia*, in Ford, IV, 83.

54. See Malone, *Jefferson the President*, esp. 418.

55. See Ford, VI, 1. Ford gives Jefferson's draft here. I have quoted the address in its more familiar form, available in countless anthologies.

56. Morse to Nisbet, April 4, 1800, in Morse Family Papers, Yale University Library.

57. For an example of Jefferson's courting the Baptists, see his letter to Levi Lincoln, January 1, 1802, enclosing his famous address to the Danbury Baptists on the separation of church and state. Jefferson tells Lincoln that he knows this "will give great offence to the New England clergy; but the advocate of religious freedom is to expect neither peace nor forgiveness from them." Ford, VIII, 129. For

Backus's opinion, see William G. McLoughlin, *Isaac Backus and the American Pietistic Tradition* (Boston, 1967), 229.

PART IV

Notes for Chapter 1

1. The fact that we are getting to the end of this book is only one reason for the brevity of my discussion of social history. Here it is the *present* that is the age of transition. The old social history does not tell us enough of what we want to know, and the new social history, while interesting, is still fragmentary. Where the sources, especially statistical sources for this period, are so weak and the experts so divided, the outsider must be very cautious. The most helpful authorities I have found are Douglas C. North, *The Economic Growth of the United States, 1790-1860* (New York, 1966); Stuart Bruchey, *The Roots of American Economic Growth, 1607 1861* (New York, 1965); and J. Potter, "The Growth of Population in America, 1700-1860," in D. V. Glass and D. E. C. Eversley, eds., *Population in History* (London, 1965), 631-88. I have also been influenced by the periodization of American history suggested in Rowland Berthoff's brilliant article, "The American Social Order: A Conservative Hypothesis," *American Historical Review*, LCV (1960), 495-514. Berthoff's conclusions are amplified in his *An Unsettled People* (New York, 1971). David H. Fischer, in his provocative paper, delivered at the annual meeting of the Organization of American Historians in 1974, argues that according to a great many indices of social change the decisive period was the first quarter of the century rather than later. It is too early to come to grips with his arguments, though many historians seem to be in agreement that social changes *before* the period of Jacksonian democracy were more important than those after it. In any case, what is crucial for me here is not the precise moment of "take-off" in any field, it is rather that in 1800-1815 change was under way, and that people did not yet understand either the extent or the direction of this change.

2. Henry Adams, *History of the United States* (8 v., New York, 1889-91); Perry Miller, *The Life of the Mind in America* (New York, 1965).

3. Miller, *Life of the Mind*, 321-26; G. H. Daniels, *Science in American Society* (New York, 1971); John C. Greene, "Science and the Public in the Age of Jefferson," *Isis*, XLIX (1958), 3-25. The conflict between scientific ideologies is cautiously and intelligently discussed by Linda Kerber, in *Federalists in Dissent* (Ithaca, 1970). Instances of this division certainly existed; the question whether they formed regular patterns can be answered only by further research in both European and American sources.

4. Malone, *Jefferson the President*, 199. This visit is interestingly discussed by David Freeman Hawke, *Paine* (New York, 1974), 353-64.

5. This point is most compellingly made by Richard E. Ellis in *The Jeffersonian Crisis: Courts and Politics in the Young Republic* (New York, 1971). Much light is also cast on the struggle over the nature of American law, and on the relation of this struggle to the Enlightenment, in Perry Miller, *Life of the Mind*, 99-265.

6. Ellis, *Jeffersonian Crisis*, 157-83; Raymond Walters, Jr., *Alexander James Dallas*

(Philadelphia, 1943); Sanford Higginbotham, *The Keystone in the Democratic Arch: Pennsylvania Politics, 1800-1816* (Harrisburg, 1952); Phillips, "Duane," *passim.*

7. Malone, *Jefferson the President,* 178-79.

8. Jefferson to Barlow, December 10, 1807, in Ford, X, 530. See also James Woodress, *A Yankee's Odyssey: The Life of Joel Barlow* (Philadelphia, 1958), 241-43. An excellent brief account of Jefferson's scientific activities as President can be found in A. Hunter Dupree, *Science in the Federal Government* (Cambridge, Mass., 1957), 20 ff.

9. Writing to Adams about the campaign of 1824 in which John Quincy Adams was running against Jackson among others, Jefferson suggests that the question "whether we are at last to end our days under a civil or a military government" is involved. January 8, 1825, in Cappon, *Adams-Jefferson Letters,* 605. In a touching letter to Jefferson of January 22, 1825, Adams refers to the President-elect as "our John, because when you was at Cul de Sac at Paris, he appeared to me to be almost as much your boy as mine." *Ibid.,* 606-7.

10. Ames to unknown correspondent, February 6, 1804, quoted in James M. Banner, Jr., *To the Hartford Convention* (New York, 1970), 40.

11. *Port Folio,* July 25, 1801, 238. Helpful books on the Federalists in this period include Kerber, *Federalists in Dissent;* Banner, *Hartford Convention;* Buel, *Saving the Revolution;* and D. H. Fischer, *The Revolution of American Conservatism* (New York, 1965).

12. For Jefferson's appointment ideology, and also for the degree of democratization achieved by his actual appointments, see Sidney H. Aronson, *Status and Kinship in the Higher Civil Service* (Cambridge, Mass., 1964).

13. For the actual broadening of suffrage and also the ideological battles over this matter, see Chilton Williamson's valuable study *American Suffrage from Property to Democracy, 1760-1860* (Princeton, 1960).

14. Bend to William Duke, January 27, 1806. Maryland Diocesan Library. Useful accounts of the anti-Jeffersonian clergy are found in Banner, *Hartford Convention.* Manuscript and printed sources are legion.

15. Nathanael Emmons, "Jeroboam" (Fast Day sermon, April 9, 1801), in *Works,* E. A. Park ed. (5 v., 1802), V, 187-207.

16. George Lampert to Samuel Miller, June 7, 1806, in Samuel Miller Papers, Princeton University Library.

17. Hostile references to the New England clergy in Jefferson's letters are frequent. His attitude is ably summed up by Fred G. Luebke, "The Origins of Thomas Jefferson's Anti-Clericalism," *Church History,* XXXII (1963), 344-54. Henry Adams points out Jefferson's misconceptions about New England and her ministers, *History,* I, 310 ff. For Madison's attitude, see Ralph Ketcham, *James Madison* (New York, 1971), 593.

18. The rising resistance to the established clergy on the war and other issues is discussed in Banner, *Hartford Convention,* 155 ff., and in Richard J. Purcell, *Connecticut in Transition, 1775-1818* (Washington, D.C., 1918), *passim.* There is much excellent material on this in the Ephraim Kirby Papers at Duke University Library and in the Morse Family Papers at Yale. Morse himself ran into serious trouble in his Charlestown church.

19. This point is thoroughly canvassed in William Gribbin, *The Churches Militant: The War of 1812 and American Religion* (New Haven, 1973), 61-103. This

book, which bears out but goes beyond my own researches on the matter, has influenced my treatment of both pro- and anti-war churches and of the effect of the outcome of the war.

20. The Great Revival and its consequences have been the subject of an immense number of studies, many of them excellent. Among the most useful of the older works are Catharine C. Cleveland, *The Great Revival in the West, 1797-1805* (Chicago, 1916); E. W. Ellsbree, *The Rise of the Missionary Spirit in America* (Williamsport, Pennsylvania, 1923); Evarts B. Greene, "A Puritan Counter-Reformation in America," *Proceedings* of the American Antiquarian Society, XLI (1931), 17-46; D. R. Fox, "The Protestant Counter-Reformation in America," *New York History*, XVI (1935), 19-35; and C. R. Keller, *The Second Great Awakening in Connecticut* (New Haven, 1942). The subject has been a central one for the post-World War II school of historians of American religion, among whom the most illuminating is Sidney Mead. Perry Miller brought his special talents to bear upon it, first in his essay "From the Covenant to the Revival," in J. W. Smith and A. L. Jamison, eds., *The Shaping of American Religion* (Religion in American Life, I, Princeton, 1961), 322-68, and then in his *Life of the Mind in America*, cited earlier in this chapter. Regional aspects of great importance have been treated by T. Scott Miyakawa, *Protestants and Pioneers* (Chicago, 1964) and by John Boles's splendidly researched *The Great Revival in the South, 1787-1805* (Lexington, Ky., 1972). Important recent articles include D. G. Mathews, "The Second Great Awakening as an Organizing Process, 1780-1830: An Hypothesis," *American Quarterly*, XXII (Spring 1969), 23-43; Richard D. Birdsall, "The Second Great Awakening and the New England Social Order," *Church History*, XXXIX (1970), 345-65; and W. David Lewis, "The Reformer as Conservative: Protestant Counter-Subversion in the Early Republic," Stanley Coben and Norman Ratner, eds., *The Development of an American Culture* (Englewood Cliffs, N.J., 1970), 64-92.

21. Nathan Strong to Morse, February 21, 1799, in Morse Family Papers at Yale.

22. Of course there were secular elements as well as many kinds of religious sources, Calvinist and other, in the reform movements of the second quarter of the nineteenth century. It seems to me that despite the very large literature on these movements further discrimination among quite different ideological origins and purposes is still needed. Among those writers who deal with the early New England and Calvinist origins of reform most convincingly are Ellsbree and W. D. Lewis, both cited above; John R. Bodo, The *Protestant Clergy and Public Issues 1812-1848* (Princeton, 1954); and Lois Banner, "The Protestant Crusade: Religious Missions, Benevolence, and Reform in the United States, 1790-1840" (unpublished dissertation, Columbia, 1970). I have been much assisted in understanding this matter by the seminar paper of Ruth Bloch, cited above, and also by that of John Rollefson on the crucial and neglected American Education Society (Berkeley, 1974).

23. Beecher, A *Reformation of Morals Practical and Indispensable* (1812), quoted in Bodo, *Protestant Clergy*, 153.

24. All these expressions are used in a resolution unanimously adopted by a Presbyterian ministerial association in Hampshire County, July 29, 1799, found in the Morse Family Papers at Yale.

25. William Speer's *The Great Revival of 1800* (Philadelphia, 1872) is an almost official Presbyterian account. The Presbyterian phase of the revival is covered in

most of the books cited above. The revival in Westfield, New Jersey, largely Presbyterian, Calvinist, and decorous, is examined in interesting detail by Martha Blauvelt, "The Second Great Awakening in New Jersey" (unpublished dissertation, Princeton, 1974). The special character of Southern Presbyterianism in this period is best illuminated by Boles, *Great Revival,* and by a number of biographies, especially James W. Alexander, *The Life of Archibald Alexander* (New York, 1854); and William Maxwell, A *Memoir of the Reverend John H. Rice, D.D.* (Philadelphia, 1835).

26. G. Baxter to Archibald Alexander, January 1, 1802, reprinted in William W. Woodward, *Surprising Accounts of the Revival of Religion in the United States of America,* etc. (Philadelphia, 1802), 106. This collection, Baptist in origin but catholic in content, is one of the liveliest sources on all phases of the Great Revival.

27. Green to John A. Clark, February 2, 1815, Ashbel Green Papers, Princeton University Library. The revivals at Yale, Princeton, and elsewhere are discussed in Novak, "Crisis," 181-224.

28. Miller to Green, March 8, 1802, Miller Papers, Princeton University Library.

29. At times the effort to simplify Christianity made by men like Barton Stone or particularly Thomas and Alexander Campbell, by returning to the words of Christ as their sole authority, can sound somewhat like Enlightenment attempts (for instance Jefferson's) to separate the teachings of Jesus from the distortions of the priests. This similarity is pointed out by Sidney Mead, who has argued powerfully that pietism and rationalism have much in common. See especially his important essay, "American Protestantism During the Revolutionary Epoch," in *The Lively Experiment* (New York, 1963), 38-54. Mead, of course, is not unaware of the differences between these two movements, especially in their epistemology. From my present perspective the differences are more important than the similarities: people whose ultimate authority is either scripture or faith do not belong in the Enlightenment. The Campbellites made the New Testament their authority, and did not approach it selectively as Jefferson did. Their Jesus is a divine figure and not, like Jefferson's, a secular moralist.

30. Thomas Owen to John Owen, from Mercer, Tennessee, November 8, 1800, Campbell Papers, William R. Perkins Library, Duke University.

31. The term "The Methodist Age" is used by a number of American church historians, including Sidney Mead. The term is defined in detail by Winthrop S. Hudson, in "The Methodist Age in America," *Methodist History,* XII (1974), 2-15.

32. The similarities, differences, and reciprocal influence of British and American evangelistic movements need further analysis, though several historians have made an excellent beginning. See especially Charles I. Foster, *An Errand of Mercy* (Chapel Hill, 1960). Various acute suggestions have been made by Reginald Ward in his important studies of comparative religious responses to the French Revolution.

33. The failure of Bentham to achieve wide influence in America is intelligently discussed by Paul A. Palmer, "Benthamism in England and America," *The American Political Science Review,* XXXV (1941), 855-71. Palmer emphasizes the American attachment to the doctrine of natural rights.

34. David Campbell to Johnson Taylor, January 5, 1805, Campbell Papers. The

letter is the more significant in that Campbell was a Republican and religious liberal.

35. Kent to Morse, February 1, 1806, in Morse Papers, New York Public Library.

36. Booksellers' lists show less decline in frequency of the authors of the Revolutionary Enlightenment than one might have expected. To me this suggests that both in the 1790's and in the first decade of the new century interest in these authors was more likely to represent curiosity than conversion. See May and Lundberg, "Enlightened Reader."

37. Both Freneau quotations come from Lewis Leary, *That Rascal Freneau* (New Brunswick, 1941), 339.

38. Barlow to Abbé [Henri] Grégoire, reprinted in full but without precise date in C. B. Todd, *Life and Letters of Joel Barlow, LL.D.* (New York, 1886), 221-33.

39. See Albert Post, *Popular Freethought in America, 1825-1850* (New York, 1943).

40. Clement Eaton, *The Freedom-of-Thought Struggle in the Old South* (Durham, 1940; revised paperback edition, New York, 1964), fn. 310. There is a great deal of valuable information on this whole subject in this book.

41. Daniel Jones to editor, January 6, 1802, in Woodward, *Surprising Accounts*, 231.

42. The best recent account of this phenomenon that I have read is Donald G. Mathews, *Slavery and Methodism: A Chapter in American Morality, 1780-1845* (Princeton, 1965).

43. Adams to Jefferson, July 13, 1813, in Cappon, *Adams-Jefferson Letters*, 355.

44. Rice to Alexander, October 17, 1810, in William Maxwell, *A Memoir of the Reverend John H. Rice, D.D.* (Philadelphia, 1835), 55-56.

45. *Ibid.*, 115-16.

46. Randolph to Garnett, May 20, July 3, 1815; in James Mercer Garnett Letterbooks, University of Virginia Library.

47. Randolph to Rutledge, July 24, 1815, Randolph Family Papers, University of Virginia Library.

48. Randolph to Key, September 7, 1818, in W. C. Bruce, *John Randolph of Roanoke, 1773-1833* (2 v., New York, 1870), II, 655. There is much useful information about Randolph's conversion in this biography.

49. Tucker to Page, July 18, 1806, in Page Papers, Duke University.

50. The Cocke Family Papers at the University of Virginia contain an enormous amount of information about many aspects of Southern life in this period and later, but are not yet available for quotation. See also Martin Boyd Coyner, Jr., "John Hartwell Cocke of Bremo: Agriculture and Society in the Ante-Bellum South" (unpublished dissertation, University of Virginia, 1961).

51. This episode is fully documented in the Breckinridge Family Papers, Library of Congress.

52. Walker to Newby, May 9, 1805; September 2, 1803. Larkin Newby Papers, Duke University Library. Like most frivolous young Southerners of his type, Walker became a pillar of society in his maturity, when he was a prominent Alabama politician.

53. T. Barraud to St. George Tucker, September 3, 1816, in Coleman-Tucker Papers, College of William and Mary in Virginia. Bishop Madison, one of the last survivors in America of gentlemanly latitudinarianism, died in 1812, leaving the Virginian Church in a state close to breakdown. It was revived under his

successor, Bishop Richard Moore, who turned it distinctly in an evangelical direction.

54. See Novak, "Crisis," 150-61; also Kemp Battle, *History of the University of North Carolina* (2 v., Raleigh, 1907). There is much further information about this complicated and interesting struggle in the Caldwell Papers at the University of North Carolina and in other papers there.

55. This episode is described in the later chapters of an excellent monograph, Niels H. Sonne, *Liberal Kentucky 1780-1828* (New York, 1939; paperback ed., Lexington, 1968).

56. Novak, "Crisis," 149.

57. Maxwell, *Rice*, 151, 154.

58. For Cooper, see Dumas Malone, *The Public Life of Thomas Cooper, 1763-1839* (New Haven, 1926); for the controversy over the University of Virginia, the early chapters of P. A. Bruce, *History of the University of Virginia* (3 v., 1920-22) and Jefferson's correspondence.

59. Quoted in Boles, *Great Revival*, 190.

60. Jefferson to Adams, September 12, 1821, in Cappon, *Adams-Jefferson Letters*, 574.

61. Jefferson to Adams, July 5, 1814, *ibid.*, 434.

62. Adams to Jefferson, November 4, 1816, *ibid.*, 493-94.

63. Jefferson to Adams, November 25, 1816, *ibid.*, 496.

64. Adams to Jefferson, November 13, 1815, *ibid.*, 456.

Notes for Chapter 2

1. Miller, *Retrospect* (2 v., New York, 1803). This book is discussed intelligently by Gilbert Chinard. "Progress and Perfectibility in Samuel Miller's Intellectual History," in George Boas *et al.*, *Studies in Intellectual History* (Baltimore, 1953), 94-122. Harold S. Jantz, "The Samuel Miller Papers at Princeton," *Princeton University Library Chronicle*, IV (1943), 68-75, explains Miller's methods through reference to his letters. The only biography is by his son: Samuel Miller, *The Life of Samuel Miller, D.D., LL.D.* (Philadelphia, 1869). Much light is cast on Miller himself in his biography of his teacher, Charles Nisbet (New York, 1840).

2. See Chapter 4, Part 3., above. Charles Brockden Brown contributed to the *Retrospect*.

3. Miller, *A Sermon, Preached in New York, July 4th, 1793 . . . at the Request of the Tammany Society or Columbian Order* (New York, 1793).

4. Miller to the Reverend Mr. Gemmil, of New Haven, December 7, 1800, quoted in Miller, *Miller*, 131.

5. In the *Retrospect*, Miller treats Jefferson as a scientist, briefly and with strict objectivity. He corresponds with Jefferson in friendly fashion well after that date. By 1830, however, he has concluded that Jefferson was "a selfish, insidious, hollow hearted infidel" and a hypocritical demagogue. Quoted in Miller, *Miller*, 132.

6. *Retrospect*, I, Preface, xii-xiii.

7. "It will not be supposed that the author has attentively read all the works concerning which he delivers opinions. Some of them he never saw, and has ven-

tured to give their character entirely on the authority of those whom he considers better judges than himself. Many he has seen and consulted, with more or less attention, as his avocations allowed. It is only a small part which he can claim the honour of having read and studied with care. It is probable, however, that he might have spared himself the trouble of making this confession; symptoms of superficial reading, or of striking unacquaintance with many works of which he speaks, will, no doubt, be often discovered." *Retrospect,* Preface, xi. Nobody who writes a history of all branches of human knowledge covering a century can honestly claim a great deal more, but few of Miller's successors have been as humble.

8. *Retrospect,* II, 271.
9. *Ibid.,* II, 85.
10. *Ibid.,* II, 300.
11. See Perry Miller, "From the Covenant to the Revival," in J. W. Smith and A. Leland Jamison, *The Shaping of American Religion* (Princeton, 1961), esp. 351-52; Henry F. May, *Protestant Churches and Industrial America* (New York, 1949), 5-12.
12. *Retrospect,* II, 27.
13. For rising importance of Paley, see Wendell Glick, "Bishop [*sic*] Paley in America," *New England Quarterly,* XXVII (1954), 347-54; and Wilson Smith, *Professors & Public Ethics* (Ithaca, 1956), 44-73. For Paley's unsatisfactoriness in America, see Smith and also Donald H. Meyer, *The Instructed Conscience* (Philadelphia, 1972), 8-9. According to the May and Lundberg data from booksellers' lists and American editors (which are less satisfactory for this period than for the 1790's), Doddridge, More, and Paley are constantly reprinted and these and Wilberforce are present in libraries in large numbers. Of the authors associated with the Moderate Enlightenment, Locke continues to be very popular (probably because the *Essay* was still assigned in colleges, together with works by its Scottish critics); Clarke, Addison, and Pope hold their own. Voltaire and Gibbon continue to be much read. The authors of the Revolutionary Enlightenment decline less than one might have expected, but are overshadowed in popularity by Scottish moralists and Christian apologists.
14. For the Scottish Enlightenment in its own setting, I have found the following the most useful of the many relevant works: E. C. Mossner, *The Life of David Hume* (Austin, 1954); N. T. Phillipson and Rosalind Mitchison, eds., *Scotland in the Age of Improvement* (Edinburgh, 1970; especially the essays by Phillipson, Peter Stein, and John Clive); other essays published and unpublished by N. T. Phillipson; and D. Young, A. J. Youngson, G. E. Davie, *et al., Edinburgh in the Age of Reason* (Edinburgh, 1967). The comparison of Scotland and America was impressively suggested by John Clive and Bernard Bailyn, "England's Cultural Provinces: Scotland and America," *William and Mary Quarterly,* XI (1954), 200-213. During a recent year in Britain I had the good fortune to spend a few hours asking questions from Duncan Forbes of Clare College, Cambridge. Mr. Forbes's opinions, based on a lifetime of close study, have strongly influenced these few pages, whether or not I was able completely to understand his complex analysis.
15. This relation is illuminated by Mossner, *Hume.*
16. Whereas Reid and his followers grounded moral judgments on the Common Sense of mankind, essentially a rational faculty, Hutcheson and Smith both be-

longed to the more radically intuitionist school stemming from Lord Shaftesbury. Hutcheson based moral judgments on instantaneous feeling, Smith on human sympathy. Both were obviously less useful than Reid for the purposes of people like the American Presbyterians and Unitarians, who were on the defensive against popular emotions, including religious emotions.

17. Dugald Stewart, *Account of the Life and Writings of Thomas Reid, D.D., FRS.* (Edinburgh, 1802), 145 ff.
18. Reid, *An Inquiry into the Human Mind, on the Principles of Common Sense* (Edinburgh, 1765), 109.
19. *Ibid.*, 19.
20. *Ibid.*, 342-43.
21. See above, 296.
22. Adams to Jefferson, May 12, 1820, in Cappon, *Adams-Jefferson Letters*, II, 563.
23. See Howard, *Connecticut Wits*, 28-29, 108-9, 150.
24. For the Common Sense influence in American colleges, the best analysis is Donald H. Meyer, *The Instructed Conscience* (Philadelphia, 1972). Other helpful books include Wilson Smith, *Professors and Public Ethics* (Ithaca, 1956); Douglas Sloan, *The Scottish Enlightenment and the American College Ideal* (New York, 1971); and Jay Wharton Fay, *American Psychology before William James* (New Brunswick, 1939). Relevant parts of I. Woodbridge Riley, *American Philosophy: The Early Schools* (New York, 1907) are still very useful. There is an excellent brief review of the curriculum as it was organized under the rule of "Protestant Scholasticism" in Stow Persons, *American Minds* (New York, 1958), 189-94.
25. According to the *Christian Advocate and Journal*, quoted in Foster, *Errand of Mercy*, 89, of the presidents of 54 of the oldest colleges in the United States in 1829, 51 were clergymen and of these 40 were Presbyterians or Congregationalists.
26. Miller, *Retrospect*, II, 503.
27. Asa Burton, *Essays on Some of the First Principles of Metaphysicks, Ethicks, and Theology* (Portland, 1824), 22.
28. Wayland, *The Elements of Moral Science* (London, 1835), vi.
29. See above, Part III, Chapter 3.
30. See Joseph Dorfman, *The Economic Mind in American Civilization, 1606-1865* (2 v., New York, 1949), II, 512-835; Michael J. L. O'Connor, *Origins of Academic Economics in the United States* (New York, 1944). For an understanding of the relation of Smith's moral philosophy to his economics, and of the liberal principles of both, Glenn R. Morrow's *The Ethical and Economic Theories of Adam Smith* (New York, 1923) is very helpful.
31. See above, Part I, Chapter 3.
32. Conrad Wright, *The Beginnings of Unitarianism in America* (Boston, 1955), 251.
33. There are good accounts of the Unitarian controversy in standard histories of Unitarianism and in Joseph Haroutunian, *Piety versus Moralism* (New York, 1932); F. H. Foster, *A Genetic History of New England Theology* (New York, 1907); and H. Shelton Smith, *Changing Conceptions of Original Sin* (New York, 1955).
34. See Elizabeth M. Geffen, *Philadelphia Unitarianism 1796-1861* (Philadelphia, 1961); Clarence Gohdes, "Some Notes on the Unitarian Church in the Ante-

Bellum South," in David K. Johnson, ed., *American Studies in Honor of William Kenneth Boyd* (Durham, 1940), 327-66.

35. Boston Unitarian culture is excellently described in Daniel Howe, *The Unitarian Conscience* (Cambridge, Mass., 1970). There are many relevant and revealing biographies and autobiographies.

36. Everett to Mrs. Nathan Hale, February 5, 1820, in Everett Papers, Massachusetts Historical Society.

37. Anonymous review of Adams's Discourses on Davila, *Monthly Anthology*, II (1805), 199-206.

38. An undergraduate notebook of 1836-37 lists the assignments in Henry Ware's course in Natural and Revealed Religion. These include the following eighteenth-century authors: François Fénelon, William Derham, William Wollaston, Joseph Butler, Philip Doddridge, Abraham Tucker, Joseph Priestley, and William Paley. Howe, *Unitarian Conscience*, 335.

39. Pickering to Mrs. Hannah Reed, March 21, 1801; in Timothy Pickering Papers, Massachusetts Historical Society.

40. Robert Treat Paine to Thomas Paine, August 18, 1794, in Robert Treat Paine Papers, Massachusetts Historical Society.

41. Robert Treat Paine to Robert Treat Paine, Jr., February 24, 1810, in the same collection.

42. There is an excellent analysis of the sentimental and pre-Romantic side of Buckminster in the unpublished seminar paper of Daniel Howe, "Joseph Stevens Buckminster and the Unitarian View of Nature," Berkeley, 1963.

43. This exchange is available in Octavius Pickering and Charles W. Upham, *Life of Timothy Pickering* (4 v., Boston, 1867-73), IV, 324-28.

44. See Howe, *Conscience*, esp. 123-25.

45. Unitarian attitudes toward literature are illuminated by Howe, *Conscience*, 174-204; and in various works of Lewis P. Simpson, especially his useful anthology of selections from the *Monthly Anthology*, *The Federalist Literary Mind* (Baton Rouge, 1962).

46. The domination of American criticism by Scottish philosophy is very fully and helpfully discussed in two monographs: William Charvat, *The Origins of American Critical Thought 1810-1835* (Philadelphia, 1936) and Terence Mártin, *The Instructed Vision* (Bloomington, 1961). Neal F. Doubleday, "Channing on the Nature of Man," *Journal of Religion*, XXIII (1943), 244-55, is especially helpful on Channing's literary tastes.

47. The double nature of the relation between Common-Sense philosophy and Romanticism is suggested by Howe and also illuminated by Walter Jackson Bate, *From Classic to Romantic* (Cambridge, Mass., 1946), especially with regard to Lord Kames and Dugald Stewart. The persistence of eighteenth-century literary principles and tastes in America has been much discussed. According to Ruth Miller Elson, *Guardians of Tradition* (Lincoln, 1964), most of the literary excerpts in American readers and spellers were taken from "Franklin, Pope, Sterne, Dryden, and Swift, and from various religious tracts" until some time in the 1820's when the Romantic writers "became dominant," 227.

48. *Journals of Ralph Waldo Emerson*, ed. Edward Waldo Emerson (10 v., Boston, 1909-14), VIII, 339. For Emerson's Harvard Prize, Ralph L. Rusk, *The Life of Ralph Waldo Emerson* (New York, 1929), 83.

49. Stowe, *Oldtown Folks* (New York, 1869), 3.

50. Stowe, "Early Remembrances," in *The Autobiography of Lyman Beecher*, Barbara M. Cross, ed. (2 v., Cambridge, Mass., 1961), I, 398.

Notes for Chapter 3

1. See my *The End of American Innocence* (New York, 1959).
2. George Santayana, "The Genteel Tradition in American Philosophy," in *Winds of Doctrine* (New York, 1913).
3. Washington, "Circular to the States, June 8, 1783," *Writings*, ed. John C. Fitzpatrick (39 v., Washington, D.C., 1931-44), XXVI, 485.

Index